Dr Peter Truscott was a member of the European Parliament between 1994 and 1999, during which time he served as Labour's Foreign Affairs and Defence Spokesman, a member of the Foreign Affairs Committee, Vice-President of the Security Committee and a member of the delegation for relations with the Russian Federation. An Associate Research Fellow at the Institute for Public Policy Research, he is an independent policy analyst and broadcaster specialising in Russian, defence and security matters. He is the author of *Russia First: Breaking With the West* (1997), *European Defence: Meeting the Strategic Challenge* (2000) and *Kursk: Russia's Lost Pride* (2002). Following his doctorate from Oxford University, he has written extensively on foreign and security policy.

In June 2004 Dr Truscott was created Lord Truscott, Baron Truscott of St James's in the City of Westminster.

Further praise for Putin's Progress:

'The altered perception [of Putin] cannot be attributed to Putin himself, as Peter Truscott demonstrates in this book . . . For it is not that the man has changed, but rather that his Western admirers fell, once again, into the trap of thinking that a Russian statesman who appeared "Western" on the surface actually shared their values' Anne Applebaum, *Daily Telegraph*

'The key to Putin's Russia lies in the past of the man himself. This is why a political biography is so timely . . . The facts are fascinating . . . Truscott's psychological analysis is at times astute, his reflections are apposite and his objectivity and political balance exemplary' Michael Binyon, *New Humanist*

'Admirable . . . Truscott reports worrying conversations with Kremlin aides who, even before Putin has won his second term, are floating the idea of changing the constitution to allow the president to stand more than twice. Truscott is convinced Putin, still only fifty-two, aims to go on and on. We have been warned' Victor Sebestyen, *Spectator*

'Truscott offers a deft biographical portrait . . . Factually sound and written with verve' Robert Service, *Guardian*

'Well-informed . . . [Truscott] suggests rightly that the president's clash with the oligarchs and his re-centralisation of power may lead to a more normal, less chaotic Russia' Charlotte Hobson, *Sunday Times*

'[Truscott] remains worth reading on all things Russian, he clearly has an inside track to high levels' *Tribune*

'Anyone who tells you that it is perfectly clear where Russia is heading will be obliged to nuance their opinion after reading [this] excellent book . . . Elucidates the ambiguities surrounding [Putin], so that we emerge with a much clearer idea of his possible evolution . . . Truscott is especially persuasive on the significance of Putin's precocious attraction to the KGB' George Walden, *Sunday Telegraph*

'Carefully depicts the context in which the Russian president grew to maturity . . . Truscott's lively biography explains why Putin remains popular in Russia and increasingly distrusted by the West' Tim Luckhurst, *Glasgow Herald*

PUTIN'S PROGRESS

A biography of Russia's
enigmatic President,
Vladimir Putin

Peter Truscott

POCKET
BOOKS

LONDON • SYDNEY • NEW YORK • TORONTO

First published in Great Britain by Simon & Schuster UK Ltd, 2004
This edition first published by Pocket Books, 2005
An imprint of Simon & Schuster UK Ltd
A Viacom Company

PICTURE CREDITS
pp. 4, 5, 6, 27, 21: PA Photos; pp. 7, 15, 20: Sovfoto; p. 22:
EPA; pp. 1, 2, 8, 9, 10, 12, 13, 14, 23:
Novosti; pp. 3, 11, 16, 18, 19: Camera Press

1 3 5 7 9 10 8 6 4 2

Simon & Schuster UK Ltd
Africa House
64–78 Kingsway
London WC2B 6AH

www.simonsays.co.uk

Simon & Schuster Australia
Sydney

A CIP catalogue record for this book is available
from the British Library.

ISBN 0-7434-9607-8

Typeset by M Rules
Printed and bound in Great Britain by
Cox & Wyman Ltd, Reading, Berks

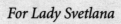

For Lady Svetlana

I cannot forecast to you the action of Russia. It is a riddle wrapped in a mystery inside an enigma.

WINSTON CHURCHILL, RADIO BROADCAST, 1 OCTOBER 1939

Contents

Preface

This book follows on naturally from my previous works, *Kursk: Russia's Lost Pride*, and *Russia First: Breaking with the West*. It is the third in a trilogy on modern Russia, and is the culmination of over twelve years of following events in the Russian Federation. Over the last decade I have visited Russia nineteen times, three times this last year alone, spending anything up to six months in the country at a time. As politician, writer and political analyst, I have met many hundreds of Russian politicians, academics, business people, bureaucrats, military and security officers. My work as a former Member of the European Parliament, member of the delegation for relations with the Russian Federation and author also put me in contact with many distinguished people in the former Soviet Union, and beyond. In my source notes, I list those who had a formative influence on the ideas behind *Putin's Progress*, not only on Russia and the former Soviet Union, but other linked issues like security, NATO, the European Union, international relations, the global economy and human rights. Such lists have a habit of being highly subjective and iniquitous, so I apologize in advance for any glaring omissions.

I decided not to use footnotes or endnotes in *Putin's Progress*, which I find maddeningly distracting in most books I read these days. In my view, footnotes should be restricted to only the most academic of tomes. However, for those who want to pursue further research, I have listed a number of references in my source notes at the end of the book, chapter by chapter. Most of my interviews were conducted on a non-attributable basis, and therefore cannot in any case be included in the notes. Some people interviewed did not want to be identified at all, which perhaps says something about the subject matter. The views expressed in the book are all my own, and any errors or omissions remain my sole responsibility.

In particular, I would like to thank a number of people who helped steer me in the right direction. I have been lucky and privileged to meet the UK's last three ambassadors to Moscow. Sir Brian Fall, Sir Andrew Wood and Sir Roderic Lyne were all generous with their time. Sir Andrew was patient and kind enough to answer my queries on several occasions, and I'm grateful for his ever-charming forbearance. Sir David Manning, Prime Minister Tony Blair's former chief foreign policy adviser and current ambassador to the United States, gave me a fascinating insight into British–Russian relations. In the British Foreign Office, Russian experts Janet Gunn, Nigel Gould-Davies and Duncan Allan provided an excellent background briefing. Duncan Allan directed me to some incisive articles on Russian domestic policy. Kate Horner at the Cabinet Office was also kind enough to share her extensive expertise with me. Dr Jonathan Aves, from the UK's Moscow Embassy, also provided me with superb background material. For the US view, among others, I am grateful to Alexander Vershbow, a Soviet expert and Washington's ambassador in Moscow. Thomas Leary of the US State Department and also based in Moscow, was most helpful. In St Petersburg, Consul-General Ulrich Schoning gave me the German view, and British Consul-General Barbara Hay gave me the benefit of her long service in Putin's home town. Dr Alexander Oslon, one of President Putin's polling and campaign advisers and a member of Yeltsin's 'family', was most generous with his time in Moscow. Apart from the many Russians listed in the source notes, I would like to thank Russia's last two ambassadors to the UK, Yury Fokine and Grigory Karasin, who were both extremely cooperative. Over the years I have met a number of people from the defence and intelligence communities from several countries, none of whom would wish to be identified. I was, however, present at an official briefing from the FSB security service in Moscow's Foreign Ministry, along with several parliamentary colleagues from the European Parliament. In Moscow I would like to single-out Alexei Ilyichev, a senior editor in the Foreign Relations Department of the RIA-Novosti state news agency, and effectively my Kremlin minder. Although the promised meeting with Vladimir Putin never materialized, Alexei Ilyichev liaised on my behalf with the Presidential Administration in the Kremlin, and provided me with some useful information. Frankly, I was not surprised I was not granted a presidential audience. My last book, *Kursk: Russia's Lost Pride*, was very critical of Putin's handling of the submarine disaster, and in an election year, the Kremlin was extremely protective of the president's image. Unlike Putin's Russian biographer, Oleg Blotsky, I am not a member of the Russian secret services, nor am I interested in writing a hagiography of St Vladimir of St Petersburg. What I hope I have produced here is a balanced, independent biography of President Putin, warts and all. I have studied Vladimir Putin and his close colleagues over the last decade in enough detail to claim this book portrays an accurate and comprehensive picture of Russia's leader.

In Britain, Simon and Schuster UK and their staff showed their usual devotion to their profession, and perhaps a little courage, in publishing my second consecutive book. For that I must thank Andrew Gordon, my tireless editor, who commissioned the book, and Martin Bryant, my second co-editor, who worked frenetically to meet our very tight production schedule. Edwina Barstow helped enormously with her invaluable picture research, and Hannah Corbett was brave enough to once more take on the task of publicizing one of my books. I would also like to thank my agent, Bill Hamilton, who has been very supportive of the project throughout.

It remains for me to thank my Russian relatives, who all helped with my enterprise. Uncle Pasha and Aunt Toma generously put us up in their lovely Moscow flat several times. Yevdokiya Ivanovna Kuznetsova, my wife's grandmother, provided me with her insight into banking and sausages. Yevdokiya Ivanovna and her late husband were evacuated from Moscow to Omsk in Siberia during the war, and like thousands of Russians, has stayed there ever since. Nikolai Chernikov told me the story about his friend and the rabid dog, and his mother and my mother-in-law, Svetlana Ivanovna, kindly sought out a deal of published Russian material on my behalf. As usual, my final word goes to my wife, Svetlana, a native of St Petersburg whose alma mater was Leningrad University, just like Vladimir Putin. Svetlana has joined me in many meetings over the years, and continued to display unremitting support as we both worked on much of this book's Russian research material. With true Russian stoicism, Svetlana was patience personified as we worked together right through our usual summer and winter vacations. As a small token of my love and appreciation, I dedicate this book to her, her second and my fourth.

Peter Truscott
House of Lords, London
February 2005

PUTIN'S
PROGRESS

1

THE 900 DAYS

Wartime Leningrad. A young girl asked: 'Mama what's ham?' After her mother explained, her daughter replied, 'And did anyone ever taste it?'

Across the curving grey Neva river in today's St Petersburg, nestling in the city's north-eastern Kalinsky District, lies the green swathe of the Piskarevsky Park. Carved out of its luscious woods and meadows is the Piskarevsky Memorial Cemetery. Outside the cemetery Russian flags fly perpetually at half-mast, and beyond the museums on either side of the entrance, past the eternal flame, the memorial park stretches to the left and right as far as the eye can see. The huge oblong grassy mounds that fill the park are well cared for, and beside each one is a simple stone slab, with a date, 1941, 1942, up to 1945. It is a quiet, dignified place. And it soon dawns on the visitor that these mounds are mass graves, containing almost one million Leningraders who died mainly through starvation, or as other casualties of the Nazi siege during the Second World War. It was slaughter on a huge scale, and behind the monolithic statue of Mother Russia that lies at the heart of the Piskaresvky cemetery, the words of the Soviet poet Olga Bergolts are engraved: 'Here Lies Leningrad'. For the former city of three million, reduced by the end of the siege to one-sixth of its former size by famine, death and belated evacuation, it was a simple statement of fact. Leningrad, more than any other Soviet city (including Stalingrad), bore the brunt of Hitler's wrath. In one of the museums by the entrance to the memorial park, an eleven-year-old girl records the effect of the siege on her family. A few lines are scribbled in blue crayon in a notebook, in a matter-of-fact way, with each entry listed under the Russian Cyrillic alphabet on a different page: 'Z – Zhenya died 28 December, 12.30 in the morning, 1941. B – Babushka [grand-mother] died 25 January, 3 o'clock, 1942. L – Leka died 17 March, 5 o'clock in the morning, 1942. D – Dyadya [uncle] Vasya died 13 April, 2 o'clock at night, 1942. D – Dyadya Lyosha, 10 May, 4 o'clock in the afternoon, 1942. M – Mama, 13 May, 7.30 a.m., 1942. S – Savichevs died. All died. Only Tanya remains.' Tanya herself died in a children's home in the Gorky area in 1943. Suffering from chronic dysentery, she had been evacuated from the besieged city too late to save her life.

Both Vladimir Putin's parents miraculously survived the Leningrad siege, known as the 'blockade' in the city, and the starvation and vicious fighting which accompanied it. For the future president's parents, the siege of Leningrad and the Great Patriotic War was the most harrowing experience of their lives. No one who lived through the blockade in Leningrad, or the war, could ever forget it. It was burned into their souls, as it was for every Russian who survived the Second World War. Twenty-six million people, including more than a million from Leningrad, had not survived, and those enormous but bland statistics included Vladimir Putin's elder brother.

Vladimir Putin's family were from humble stock. Before the 1917 Bolshevik Revolution, his family on both sides were rural peas-ants, and before the abolition of serfdom in the second half of the nineteenth century, they had been slaves to the Russian aristocracy. His paternal grandfather though had come into contact with some of Russia's elite. Born on 19 December 1879 in Pominovo, a village in the Tver region north-west of Moscow, Spiridon Ivanovich Putin had left home at fifteen to become a chef in the capital. Through sheer hard work, conscientiousness and attention to detail, Spiridon became one of St Petersburg's top chefs. He worked in the Astoria, St Petersburg's luxury five-star hotel on St Isaac's Square, opposite the golden-domed cathedral, and once cooked for the infamous monk Grigory Rasputin, who gave him a rouble tip. Rasputin, Spiridon recalled, was as ugly as sin, with a long beard, pointed nose and swarthy complexion. By that time, Rasputin, whose background was that of a Siberian peasant, was a legendary figure in St Petersburg circles and one of the country's most influential people. Close to the Tsar's family, especially the Tsarina Alexandra Fyodorovna, he had gained favour by easing the suffering of the young heir to the throne, a haemophiliac, and had reputedly slept with half of the women in the city's high society. The granddaughter of Queen Victoria, Alexandra Fyodorovna inherited the genes carrying haemophilia and passed them on to her son, which in turn had resulted from the widespread in-breeding prevalent in the royal houses of Europe.

Grandfather Putin earned 100 roubles a month in gold as a chef at the Astoria, which was a lot of money for those days. He was married to Olga Ivanovna; they had three boys (Alexei, Mikhail and Vladimir) and one girl, Anna, who were all born in the city between 1907 and 1915. After the Bolshevik Revolution and the outbreak of the civil war, famine struck St Petersburg as the Reds fought the Whites across the vast Russian Empire. Food shortages in the city drove prosperous Russians to barter fur coats and expensive jewellery for bread and potatoes in surrounding country villages. Stony-faced peasants made a killing as city folk desperately searched for enough food to survive the coming winter. Spiridon and his family left their rented flat near the Astoria on Gorokhovaya Street and moved back to Pominovo, where a number of Putin's relatives still live. People were starving to death in Petrograd (as St Petersburg had been called since the outbreak of the First World War) and the family moved back to the country to survive the horrors now engulfing the city. If the Whites took the city, they threatened to hang a Bolshevik from every lamppost. Four years later, on Lenin's death in 1924, Petrograd was renamed Leningrad in honour of the Bolshevik revolutionary leader. Fearful of the city's vulnerability to attack from Finland, the Communists 'temporarily' shifted the capital to Moscow. Leningrad was never to regain its status as the country's capital. Stalin despised and distrusted the city as a hotbed of radicals and intellectuals, and he avoided returning to the city of his Bolshevik youth and the birthplace of the Revolution.

In Pominovo, Spiridon and Olga had another child, Alexander, followed by Lyudmila in 1926, when they moved near to Moscow. Spiridon's culinary skills again landed him an enviable job, this time cooking for the Revolution's elite in Gorky, just outside Moscow. He found himself cooking for Nadezhda Krupskaya, Lenin's widow, at a compound reserved for the highest echelons of the Communist Party. He was also chef to Lenin's sister, Maria Ilinichna, working for both women until their deaths. Joseph Stalin used to drop by on occasions to see Nadezhda (or more likely to keep an eye on her), and Spiridon sometimes cooked for the great dictator. Years later, Vladimir Putin recalled his grandfather's life and work with evident pride. Stalin, a typical Georgian from the Caucasus, loved his food and drink. The president remains particularly proud of the fact that his grandfather survived his close encounter with Uncle Joe. 'Few of those who were with Stalin all the time survived intact. But my grandfather did,' he boasted.

From 1940 Spiridon worked as head chef at the Moscow City Communist Party sanatorium at Ilichovsky, where he had a small two-bed flat and where his young grandson, Volodya, used to visit him. Putin can still remember visiting his grandfather at the party's sanatorium outside Moscow, and the small allotment his grandparents had nearby. It was here, by a river, that his grandmother used to grow potatoes, strawberries and wild flowers. Gaunt and austere, Spiridon didn't drink, smoked a lot and liked reading and fishing. He worked until he was almost eighty, retiring finally in the late 1950s, dying at eighty-six. He and his wife, Olga, who lived until she was ninety, remained mentally alert until the end. Of their six children, two of their four sons died in the Second World War. Like millions of Russians, they never discovered the whereabouts of their graves. No one seemed to know where they had died. They were just another couple of victims of the Great Patriotic War. Two sons, including Vladimir Putin's father, survived the war. The two daughters also survived, Anna (Putin's aunt) and her infant son coming back alive from a German concentration camp in the Baltic States. Luckily for them, they had been forced to work on a farm as labourers. Prolonged internment in a concentration camp would have led to almost certain death, either through starvation, illness or mistreatment.

Some family members wondered whether the grandfather could have put in a word to get Putin's mother (his daughter-in-law) and brother out of Leningrad during the siege as the Nazi noose tightened around the city. It was probably a long-shot, he was, after all, only a cook. In any event, with Stalin sending his own son to the front (he was later captured by the Germans), he was unlikely to have found a sympathetic ear. Even worse, such unpatriotic special pleading could have got him shot. People around Stalin could be shot for a lot less. Instead, Putin's grandfather comfortably survived Stalin, and is buried in Ilinskoye cemetery, near where he used to work as a chef to the party hierarchy.

Vladimir Putin's father, Vladimir Spiridonovich (the second name is always a patronymic in Russia), was born in St Petersburg in 1911, before the family's hasty departure for Pominovo and safety in the countryside. It was in this village that Putin's father met Maria Ivanovna Shelomova, marrying at the age of seventeen. Vladimir senior had an eye for the village girls, and scandalized the other locals by his openly professed atheism. He had piercing eyes, swept-back short hair and a high forehead. His new wife was a comfortable-looking country girl, homely rather than outstandingly pretty. Maria's family were regarded as fairly well-to-do peasants, but weren't quite prosperous enough to be regarded as *kulaks*, wealthy peasants who had their property seized and who were 'liquidated' by the Bolsheviks. Before the birth of their first son the couple moved to Moscow for a while, then on to Leningrad in 1932. Maria's brother Ivan, a captain first rank in the navy, helped them with the move to Leningrad. Ivan would later save Maria's life during the blockade, when all around her people were starving to death.

At first Putin's parents shared a house in Petrodvorets, the small town south-west of Leningrad where Peter the Great built his magnificent summer palace, also known as Petrodvorets or Peterhof. With its majestic cascades and terraces leading down to the Gulf of Finland, Peterhof is rivalled in beauty only by Versailles, which lacks the sea views. During the war, the Nazis took the town and gutted the palace, stealing many of the artworks and statues in the process. The war, however, was still a few years away. Vladimir senior started work as a security guard, then as a factory worker. Maria worked as a carer in a kindergarten, then as a street sweeper. Then Vladimir was called up into the Soviet navy's 'Silent Service', its submarine fleet, to do his national service, and his wife went to work in a factory. To this day, Putin recalls his father's service as a submariner with pride. Within a year of Vladimir senior returning from the navy, the Putins had two sons. Vitaly died a few months after birth; Alik died of diphtheria during the 900-day German blockade of Leningrad.

After Adolf Hitler launched Operation Barbarossa in the early hours of 22 June 1941 against the Soviet Union, Vladimir Spiridonovich was assigned to the People's Commissariat of Internal Affairs (NKVD), the secret police and the precursor to the KGB. But Vladimir wasn't strictly speaking a NKVD man, which was both a feared and privileged career in the USSR. During the siege of Leningrad, the NKVD never went hungry, and unlike other parts of the city, never had their electricity cut off. Vladimir found himself assigned to the NKVD almost by accident. Shortly after the outbreak of the war, the Leningrad Communist Party authorities decided to establish 300 partisan groups of between 35–50 people (mainly men), 14,000 in all. The role of the partisans was to go

behind enemy lines to collect intelligence on German troop movements and supplies, and where possible conduct sabotage
operations. Comprised of ordinary people, usually workers without
any formal military experience, these units were hastily thrown
together and sent into action with only the most rudimentary training and equipment. They were under the direct control of the
NKVD, the same body which ran the secret police and maintained
internal security. For most Leningraders, being assigned to the partisans in those early days was a death sentence. They were joined by
ten divisions of the 'People's Militia', composed of hundreds of thousands of ordinary Leningraders, who with their hunting rifles,
knives, grenades and Molotov cocktails, marched out of the city to
stop the Panzers of Field Marshal von Leeb's Army Group North.
Initially, the Soviet Union's forces were poorly led and no match for
the overwhelming might of the Wehrmacht. Thousands were
slaughtered in the last-ditch defence of Leningrad.

In September, before the first winter of the war, Vladimir
senior volunteered for service and was sent with a partisan group to
cross the lines near Kingissepp, close to the Estonian border. The
area was less than three hours by train from Leningrad. Within a few
days, the besieged city of Leningrad would have its last rail link to
the outside world, already called the 'mainland', cut. From then on,
supplies would have to come over the frozen Lake Ladoga or by air.
As Vladimir's partisan group moved into Estonia, still nominally
part of the USSR but occupied by the Germans, their situation
quickly became desperate. They managed to blow up a munitions
dump, but soon ran out of food. Local Estonians, who had no love
lost for the Soviet Union or the Red Army, betrayed their presence to
the Germans after initially giving the partisans some provisions.
Thousands of Estonians joined the Waffen SS, and saw Hitler as a
liberator from Soviet occupation. Even today Estonian SS units hold
reunions in Tallinn, the country's picturesque capital. But for
Vladimir and his compatriots, time had quickly run out as they
were surrounded by German troops. Of the twenty-eight men in his

group, only four made it back to Soviet lines. The partisans decided to split up, trying to make their own way back to the front line. Vladimir avoided capture and probable death (partisans were usually shot on the spot) by hiding in a marshy pool and breathing through a hollow reed, as German troops scoured the surrounding countryside. Breathing in short bursts through the reed, Vladimir could almost feel the weight of the Germans' jackboots as they passed close to the edge of the pool, with their sniffer dogs trailing behind.

On reaching his own lines, Vladimir was detained by the NKVD's Special Department, who closely interrogated him. This was routine practice. If anyone escaped from encirclement or imprisonment, the first thing the NKVD wanted to know was how someone got away, and whether they were a spy or had been turned by the enemy. Vladimir was lucky; he was cleared and sent to fight at the front. Others were not so fortunate. Thousands of Russians who returned from German concentration or prisoner-of-war camps after the war were sent straight to the Gulag. Stalin and his regime assumed that such people were traitors (how had they allowed themselves to be captured?), or even worse, had been 'contaminated' by contact with the capitalist West. Alexander Solzhenitsyn, the Nobel Prize-winning author, was one such victim. His mistake was to have been captured during the war. Other offences could also send war veterans to the Gulag. My Russian wife's uncle, Fyodor, who had fought all the way through the war from the Eastern Front to Berlin and had been recommended for the medal 'Hero of the Soviet Union' (the USSR's highest medal), also ended up in the gulag. Going shopping in Berlin, he had inadvertently forgotten to leave his tank behind. He spent years in the gulag in the far north, and was confined to living in Archangel, in the Arctic Circle, for the remainder of his days.

Vladimir Spiridonovich's war wasn't over yet. The Germans were advancing closer to the city boundaries. In a valiant and determined attempt to throw them back, sixty-year-old Marshal

Voroshilov personally led a brigade of marines in a counter-attack near Krasnoye Selo, about 12 miles south of the city. It was the first time in living memory that a field marshal had led a ground attack from the front. The last field marshal in British history to lead an attack personally was arguably Richard the Lionheart. Marshal Georgi Zhukov was put in command of Leningrad's crumbling defences, and Vladimir senior was sent into one of the hottest fighting zones, across the Neva at Nevskaya Dubrovka, later nicknamed the 'Neva Nickel' (Nevsky Pyatachok). The Neva Nickel was so-called because it was a small triangle of land, 2 kilometres wide and 900 metres deep. Zhukov, the future hero of the defence of Moscow and Stalingrad, had been sent by Stalin to prevent the fall of Leningrad. Stalin calculated that if Leningrad fell, the Germans would concentrate all their forces on an encircling attack on Moscow. If Moscow were captured, then little would prevent the final disintegration of the Soviet Union, and Stalin's rule. Stalin ordered that all bridges, railroads, factories and institutions in and around Leningrad were to be mined and blown up. The Baltic Fleet would be scuttled. Churchill promised that Britain would replace some of the lost warships. Characteristically, Stalin replied that if he lost the Baltic Fleet he would pass the bill on to the Germans after the war. Hitler, busy preparing a victory parade through Leningrad, would instead inherit a pile of rubble.

A few days later the Germans pushed into the southern suburb of Ligovo, and some light tanks and motorcyclists even made it to the gates of the Kirov tank factory on Stachek Prospect, within the city boundaries. The Germans were quickly wiped out. Russian heavy 60-tonne KV tanks rolled off the production line and went straight into battle; Workers' Battalions left their assembly lines at the Kirov plant and took a streetcar seven stops to the front line. At one point, a thousand lightly armed workers of the giant Izhorsk steel and munitions factory, dug-in on the small Izhora river (less than 10 miles to the south-east), were all that stood between Leningrad and the mighty German 39th Army Corps. Armed with rifles, hand grenades and pistols, the Izhorsk workers were supported by a few home-made armoured trucks. Most had received just a day or two of training. Facing them were the 12th Panzer Division and the 121st, 96th and 122nd Infantry Divisions. But in the face of stubborn and dogged resistance, the line held. It was in these desperate circumstances that Zhukov ordered an attack across the left bank of the Neva river, south-east of the city. The orders from Zhukov to his commanders were 'Attack! Attack! Attack!' Not one step backward. Any commander who retreated would be shot. Generals and their staff were ordered out of their command bunkers to personally lead their troops in counter-attacks.

On the night of 19 and 20 September, in an effort to break the blockade, Zhukov sent two divisions and a brigade of marines to the Neva Nickel. After fierce fighting, the Red Army managed to secure a foothold on the left bank of the Neva, but failed to break the Nazi siege. Further reinforcements were sent in over the next few weeks, including elements of the 20th Division, where Vladimir Spiridonovich was now serving. German bombardment of the Neva Nickel was constant, and the area became soaked in blood. Hand-to-hand fighting was intense, frequent and vicious. After the war, they dug up one cubic metre of the Neva Nickel at random, and found it contained 10 kilogrammes of shrapnel, shells, mines and 38 bullets. The Red Army held the Nickel for seven months before withdrawing across the Neva river. It had been a brave, but ultimately futile attempt to break the Nazi blockade. Nevertheless, Zhukov's aggressive tactics and the massive sacrifice of the Workers' Battalions and People's Militia ultimately stopped the Germans. They came to a halt two and a half miles south of Leningrad. The enemy was at the gates, but it became the first city on continental Europe that Hitler had failed to conquer.

One night, while fighting in the Neva Nickel, Vladimir was ordered to capture a German *yazik*, or tongue, a German soldier who could give useful intelligence on dispositions and field operations. It was now early 1942, and the north Russian winter was bitterly cold. The temperature could fall to below minus 20 C, and the cold would freeze in your nostrils, giving a burning sensation if you breathed in too hard. A scarf and fur hat protected Vladimir's head, with only a slit left for his eyes, and he wore traditional Russian *valenky* felt boots to keep his feet warm. Leaving the Soviet trenches with another soldier, Vladimir crawled on his belly in the general direction of the enemy's lines. They came up to a foxhole and lay down, waiting for an opportunity to grab an enemy soldier. But a German trooper suddenly came out of the foxhole, and before they had time to react, threw a grenade and nonchalantly moved away. The grenade exploded at Vladimir's feet, wounding him in the leg, and leaving him with a permanent limp. No doubt the German soldier thought he had killed the two Russians. But a few hours later, Vladimir's colleagues crept up to the foxhole and dragged him back to their dugout. Vladimir was in excruciating pain, as both his legs were shot through with shrapnel. He had lost a lot of blood, and left where he was, he would probably have died of his wounds. No one was keen to make the hazardous river crossing, which would be necessary to get Vladimir to a hospital, and no officer felt his evacuation from the Nickel was a military priority. In one of those important quirks of fate, an old neighbour recognized Vladimir, and simply picked him up and carried him across the frozen Neva river on his back, and then all the way to a hospital in Leningrad. Putin's father spent several months in hospital, and was eventually discharged from the forces as an invalid. Maria came to visit her husband every day, and he, seeing how she was wasting away with hunger, gave her the best part of his hospital rations. Noticing that Vladimir was starting to faint with hunger, the doctors put a stop to the practice.

While Vladimir undoubtedly suffered from the shrapnel embedded in his leg, his own personal memento from the Great Patriotic War, he was luckier than his wife. Maria had been left behind in the city with their five-year-old son, Alik, at the height of the siege, when Leningraders were dying from starvation at a rate of

5,000 per day. Her brother Ivan, the naval captain, had earlier rescued her and her young boy when the Germans had started to advance on Petrodvorets, across the Gulf of Finland and just south of Leningrad. Although reluctant to leave Petrodvorets, staying behind would have meant coming under Nazi occupation. As the shelling and bombing started, and with her very survival at stake, Maria and her little boy left their home with Ivan and joined some of the last evacuees leaving for besieged Leningrad. Thanks again to Ivan, she was able to camp with relatives near the Obvodny Canal. The area, to the south of the city centre, bordered a number of industrial areas and railway stations, and was heavily bombed.

The winter of 1941 to 1942 was one of the coldest on record in Leningrad, with average temperatures reaching minus 20 C or below. The harsh winter temperatures were combined with the problem of dwindling food supplies in the city as the Germans closed the circle around the three million inhabitants. Leningrad was almost wholly unprepared for war, and even less prepared for a siege. Stalin had thought reports of the impending German invasion a 'provocation' by the West, especially Britain. So convinced was he that the Nazi–Soviet Non-Aggression Pact would hold, that he refused to allow Soviet troops to fight back in the first hours of the war, as the German Blitzkrieg powered across the USSR's borders. As war broke out, Andrei Zhdanov, Leningrad's party boss and close Stalin confidant, was on holiday in Sochi on the Black Sea. Despite repeated warnings from Soviet agents and Western governments that a German attack was imminent, Stalin and the Politburo were in a state of denial. They believed Bismarck's maxim that Germany could not and should not fight a war on two fronts. Once the attack had begun, no one in the Kremlin expected the Germans to reach Leningrad, let alone the outskirts of Moscow, so indoctrinated were the party elite by their own propaganda about Soviet military 'invincibility'. Party propaganda insisted that any invasion of the USSR would be immediately repulsed, and the south-western approach to the city had been left almost undefended.

The result of such complacency, fatal for many in Leningrad, was a haphazard and slow evacuation of civilians, as the Nazi war machine rumbled ever nearer to the city on the Neva. Less than half a million Leningraders, less than a sixth of the population, managed to get out of the city. A million women and children, who should have been evacuated, were trapped in Leningrad as the net closed. Emergency stocks, especially of food, were not high. Most of the city's factories, which made essential war material for the Soviet Union, remained in situ. Leningrad's factories formed part of one of the USSR's largest centres for the production of munitions. Only a few were dismantled and re-located beyond the distant Urals. Even worse, the Badayev Warehouses, which contained the city's flour supplies, went up in smoke after a Nazi incendiary bombing raid. The decision to concentrate the city's essential food supplies in one location was a catastrophic mistake. Later, people would sneak into the warehouses and dig out the frozen earth from the cellars to sell on the black market. Tons of molten sugar had saturated the earth, and after it was sold the sugary earth was mixed with flour to make a type of edible custard or jelly. The top three feet of Badayev soil sold for 100 roubles a glass, deeper and the price was 50 roubles.

The combination of siege, Soviet myopia and bad planning made starvation in Leningrad inevitable. Although rationing had been introduced a month after the outbreak of war, the situation only became critical by the beginning of winter. Initially, there had been little attempt to conserve food stocks. By October, people were entitled to receive one-third of a loaf daily, one pound of meat a month, just over a pound of cereals and macaroni, less than a pound of sunflower oil or butter and three pounds of poor quality pastry or confectionery. Excluding bread, that meant people had to survive on five and a quarter pounds of food a month. In practice, bread soon became the only food distributed to the hungry citizens of Leningrad.

In late November 1941, the bread ration was cut to 250 grams for factory workers, 125 grams, slightly more than a quarter pound or two thin slices, for everyone else. Troops at the front got 500 grams, those at the rear, 300. Dependants, the old, children, non-factory workers (including academics and intellectuals), were condemned to death. No one could survive on 125 grams of bread a day, and even that bread was adulterated. It contained 25 per cent 'edible cellulose' and often sawdust; its nutritional value was practically nil. A month on, as stocks dwindled, the bread consisted almost entirely of edible cellulose, sawdust and flour sweepings. The death toll for December alone was 53,000 people. Most had starved to death; some froze in the snow and ice. Ice began forming on the insides of apartment windows. Factories started to close down, the electricity was cut off, there was no water supply, no heating, and the trams and buses stopped running. People collected water from holes drilled in the frozen Neva river, carrying it in pails. Those who had small metal stoves (*burzhuikas*) tried to keep warm using scraps of wood, often from broken-up furniture. People, too exhausted to take another step, collapsed in the street. Some sat down for a rest on their weary way. They froze to death where they sat, head cupped in their hands. A constant sight were the small children's sledges, taking bodies wrapped in sheets to the rapidly filling graveyards, as sappers used dynamite to create mass graves at the Piskarevsky, Volkov, Bolshaya Okhta, Serafimov, Bogoslovsky and Tatar cemeteries.

Loss of the monthly ration cards meant certain death, and there were many cases of theft. One teenager stole someone's bread ration from them in a queue of people, and wolfed it down despite the blows raining down on his head. Organized gangs roamed the streets, robbing the weak, and stealing ration cards. Those stopped on the streets by military patrols with unaccounted-for ration cards or food supplies were shot on the spot. Phantom families would collect their rations despite having starved to death, as their neighbours quietly continued claiming the vital bread rations on their behalf for the remainder of the month. Dogs and cats disappeared in the city, as their reluctant owners ate them or traded them for bread or other food. Cannibalism stalked the streets. Bodies left in the streets where they fell were discovered with parts of the thighs and arms cut off. Similar discoveries were made in the thousands of bodies lined up for burial outside the city's cemeteries. Several cannibalistic gangs were broken up and summarily executed. Parents kept their young children indoors, as rumours of suspicious disappearances spread. No one questioned the provenance of the 'meat patties' sold by the dodgy black marketeers in the market at Sennaya Square (the Haymarket). Around 2,000 people were arrested for cannibalism during the blockade. Most of the accused were young unemployed women from outside the city, who therefore didn't have ration cards and had no way of feeding their young families. They had mainly entered the city with the flood of refugees before the encirclement.

Eating grass, wood bark and boiling leather goods for food was commonplace. Glue paste was a luxury, boiled and made into a stew. Staff at the Hermitage Museum were lucky in that respect, they had a good supply of linseed oil and wall paste. Some 2,000 staff members slowly starved in the Hermitage's vaults and cellars beneath the Winter Palace. Many of the most precious works of art had been sent out of the city by train before the ring closed around the city, mainly thanks to the foresight of its Armenian director, Joseph Orbeli. He had succeeded in taking action while the city authorities, the party and the Soviet Supreme Command (*Stavka*), sat on its hands. Meanwhile, the black market thrived as the city starved. Everything could be bought on the black market, but few could afford the prices. There were about half a dozen markets where people could buy bread at extortionate prices (up to 600 roubles a kilo), or barter cigarettes, bread, sour cabbage, alcohol, clothing, jewellery or art works. Bread as a currency had more value than roubles, vodka came second as the preferred medium of exchange. Even to bury the dead, gravediggers would demand a few slices of bread. Somebody would be lucky to exchange their fur coat for an adulterated crust of black bread. Horsemeat, cat and dog, even rat was for sale, although those who bought meat on the black market could never be sure what they were buying. Those who relied on just their food rations became increasingly desperate. Admiral Panteleyev, a top naval commander in the city, was visited by the wife of a friend, whose family were starving. He regretfully said he could do nothing to help. As she was leaving, she surprised him by asking for his worn leather briefcase. He agreed, and a few days later he received his bag's nickel fittings and a dish of meat jelly. The jelly had been made from his briefcase.

The city's population started to receive vital food supplies via the *doroga zhizni*, the 'road of life' route over the frozen Lake Ladoga to the east of the city. Soviet trucks braved the ice to supply the beleaguered city under the ever-present bombardment from the encircling Germans, who called the road the 'road of death' because for them it became a duck shoot. Many trucks sank below the lake's icy surface, either because they were too heavily laden, or because they were hit by enemy fire. British merchant convoys struggled, with huge losses, through the Arctic seas to Murmansk and Archangel to help supply Leningraders, a sacrifice Russia and the city never forgot. In the summer of 1942, the British Artic convoy PQ17 lost 24 of its 35 ships, after repeated attacks from German aircraft, U-boats and surface raiders. The PQ17 merchant losses were the worst recorded by the Royal Navy in any convoy during the course of the Second World War.

By this time the Germans had taken the strategic Pulkovo heights, overlooking the city. Their artillery spotters could see the gold dome of St Isaac's Cathedral, even though it had been painted over a dirty grey to disguise it from the air. The Russians went to great lengths to deceive German air force reconnaissance. On being told the Marinsky Theatre's mock-up tanks were fooling the Luftwaffe, Marshal Zhukov immediately ordered another 100 to be made and put into the line the next day. Faced with protests that it couldn't be done in time, Zhukov told his subordinates to do it or face court martial and the firing squad, adding ominously, 'I'll check on you tomorrow myself.' Artillery bombardment now joined the regular bombing raids as a daily hazard for the starving Leningraders.

On 22 September 1941 an infamous directive was issued by German naval headquarters outlining 'the future of the city of St Petersburg', or rather the lack of it. It stated that the Führer 'has decided to raze the City of Petersburg from the face of the earth. After the defeat of Soviet Russia there will be not the slightest reason for the future existence of this large city.' It was proposed to blockade the city and completely destroy it by ceaseless air and artillery bombardment. Random shelling of civilian targets was instigated. All calls for surrender would be ignored. If civilians tried to escape the besieged city, they were to be shot. On 8 November 1941 Hitler spoke at a Munich rally: 'Leningrad's hands are in the air. It falls sooner or later. No one can free it. No one can break the ring. Leningrad is doomed to die of famine.' Hitler had already decided to raze Leningrad to the ground, and to refuse to accept the city's surrender even if it was offered. During the blockade 16,000 civilians were killed by bombing and shelling. As Hitler turned his attention to the battle for Moscow, he and the German High Command were satisfied that the city's fate, and that of all its inhabitants, was sealed. The city would be destroyed by famine, bombardment, cold and terror.

Putin's mother only survived the horrific siege because her brother Ivan was keeping her alive with his superior navy rations. He was based at the fleet's headquarters in Smolny, the former Institute for Noble Young Ladies commandeered by Lenin to serve as his revolutionary headquarters, and today the city's administrative HQ. During the war it was heavily camouflaged by netting in a vain attempt to hide it from the air. Located right next to a distinctive curve in the river, the Smolny complex and its adjacent blue-and-white eighteenth-century cathedral would be a hard target for a bomber's navigator to miss. There were definite advantages in working from Smolny, as the wartime newsreels of plump Soviet commanders based there testify. President Putin recalled how his uncle yet again saved his mother's life. 'He fed her his rations,' he remarked. 'Then the brother was ordered away somewhere and she was on the brink of death. That's no exaggeration. Mama passed out from hunger. They thought she was dead and they even put her with the deceased. She was lucky she came to just in time and groaned. It was a miracle she stayed alive.' Many of the soldiers shared their better rations with their families during the blockade. It was the only way their families could survive.

Maria placed her son, Alik, in a *statsionar*, a convalescent feeding centre, which the Communist Party had established to try to help some of the most desperate cases, especially the children. There they received slightly better rations and some nursing care. The nurses themselves were often so weak that they could hardly stand. Children and the elderly had started dying first, followed by the men. Men have less body fat, and their cardiovascular systems are not as strong as women's. But Maria's five-year-old son didn't make it, he was too weak from hunger. He developed diphtheria and died. The experience of the blockade was traumatic for Putin's parents. His father had faced the daily threat of death at the front, and had been severely wounded. His mother had teetered on the edge of starvation, and had to watch her son die while the city reverberated to the sounds of German aircraft and artillery. The strain must have been almost unbearable, the sense of personal loss devastating. Nevertheless, both of them made it through the siege alive. Many did not. Whole families were wiped out by the fighting, starvation and the freezing cold. Some had been victims of the NKVD, which weeded out those with German or Finnish ancestry, former Whites or others deemed a threat to the Revolution and national security.

In many ways women like Maria became the backbone of the defence of Leningrad. They tried to keep the family together and alive, queuing endlessly for the pitiable rations, cooking when they could and trying to provide some heat at home. They had replaced the men in the factories as they went to the front, often joining front-line units themselves. Some became partisans behind enemy lines, and they expected no mercy if the Germans caught them. Hundreds of thousands of women had dug the trenches around and in front of Leningrad; they had manned the anti-aircraft units in the Field of Mars and grew vegetables in front of St Isaac's Cathedral. Women ran the transport system (when it was running), driving trams, trains and trucks, staffed the hospitals, and dominated air raid defence. Leningrad during the blockade was overwhelmingly a city of women, and the *blokadnitsy* later wore their medals 'For the Defence of Leningrad' with pride.

After discharge from hospital in early 1942, Vladimir Spiridonovich was demobilized from the army as an invalid. He went to work at the Yegorov railway carriage factory in the city's southern Moscow district, another favourite target for the Luftwaffe. During the war the factory started producing weapons and munitions, and groups of workers would visit the front to repair damaged or broken-down tanks. Vladimir was employed as a skilled worker, and later became a foreman. Like many factories in Leningrad, the Yegorov plant frequently lacked electricity or running water, and workers worked by candle light or dimly lit oil lamps in freezing conditions. Water was hauled in buckets from the Neva river. Working eleven-hour shifts, some workers were so exhausted they slept on the shop floor. There was no public transport at the height of the blitz, and many were simply too weak to make the trip home on foot. Nothing, not even the constant bombing raids, would stop the assembly line rolling. By 1943, electricity supplies were being gradually restored to the city. At home, the Putins were allowed to put on one light bulb between 7 p.m. and midnight, every day. American aid in the form of canned butter, sugar, powdered milk and eggs started to arrive. In 1944, things finally started looking up for Vladimir Spiridonovich and Maria. The blockade was broken and Vladimir's factory allocated him a room in a communal flat in Baskov Lane, central Leningrad. It was where the Putin family was to stay for a number of years.

The citizens of Leningrad had been determined, deadly determined, not to yield to the Germans the city of Peter the Great and Lenin, Dostoyevsky and Pushkin, the Hermitage and St Isaac's Square. The Fascists would have to roll over their dead bodies first. As a symbol of civic pride and defiance, the city authorities had refused to cut down any of the trees in Leningrad's public parks. Instead, they demolished a number of wooden-built buildings in the city, but they wouldn't touch the trees, even as people froze. It may seem a strange set of values for some, yet it was this fierce determination to protect the city and its heritage at all costs, that in the end saved Leningrad. Another famous event gives a strong flavour of the spirit of the times. Dmitri Shostakovich worked in the city as a fireman during the blitz, while completing his Seventh Symphony dedicated to Leningrad. He finally obeyed an order to leave the city for his own safety in October 1941, after refusing to leave several times, and the following August his symphony was performed in his home town. Conducted by Karl Eliasberg at the Philharmonic Hall just off the Nevsky, his orchestra comprised weak and emaciated musicians, some specially brought in from the front. The concert was broadcast throughout the USSR, and by short-wave radio to Europe and North America. Years later, a group of Germans met Eliasberg at the Astoria Hotel and told him they had wept when they heard his concert on the radio. They had been listening in their trenches just outside the city, and realized then and there that they would never overcome the Leningraders' indomitable spirit. Just who were they bombing?

After the siege was lifted, in January 1944, the city started to rebuild its shattered streets, as the surviving inhabitants tried to rebuild their shattered lives. The 900-day blockade had left an indelible mark on its citizens and the city itself. Even to this day, as you walk down Nevsky Prospect, the city's main thoroughfare, blue and white signs warn: 'Citizens: In case of shelling this side of the street is the most dangerous.'

As I write this sitting in my wife's family dacha an hour's drive from modern St Petersburg, there are first-hand reminders of those far-off days of the Leningrad blockade. The Germans occupied our village, and upstairs a German army doctor would play his violin from the balcony. He left in such a hurry when the Russians broke through in 1944 that he left behind some clothes hangers, and a nineteenth-century German edition of Goethe poetry. The book sits beside me now. In recent years, elderly local women still pointed their fingers accusingly at neighbours who slept with the enemy. Incidentally, if there is a retired German doctor somewhere in Bavaria who has mislaid his Goethe, perhaps he could contact me?

2

VLADIMIR JUNIOR

Old KGB joke: How do you find a lion in the desert?
You find a cat and beat it until it says it's a lion.

So it was that Vladimir Vladimirovich Putin was born into a relatively poor working-class family living in central Leningrad's Baskov Lane, house number 12, on 7 October 1952. The war had been over seven years, but memories were still fresh. Putin was a late child, but all the more welcome for that. His parents doted on him, especially his mother. Both just over forty, they thought they would never have any more children. 'I was surrounded by my parents' love. They loved me and I knew it, I felt it,' Putin would tell Russian TV years later. After the blockade it had seemed his parents were fated to die childless. Vladimir junior was born in the local Snegeryov maternity hospital, and shortly after he was born his mother quietly went with a neighbour and christened him at the nearby classical yellow and white Russian Orthodox Cathedral of the Transfiguration. Christian baptism was frowned on by the Communist authorities, and Vladimir senior (a lifelong party member) didn't believe in God, so Maria had to be circumspect. Leningrad, the former glorious St Petersburg, was a shadow of its imperial self, and the young Putin came into the world in the dying months of Stalin's dictatorship.

Leningrad had been the last great Soviet city to be restored after the ravages of the war, and the scars still showed. Stalin's enmity and vindictiveness knew no bounds, and as Moscow, Minsk, Kiev and Stalingrad were rebuilt, Leningrad's beauty faded. Stalin had also launched a purge against the city's party hierarchy in the late 1940s, the so-called 'Leningrad Affair'. All those associated with city boss Andrei Zhdanov (who died mysteriously in 1948) were arrested, shot or sent to the gulag, including Mayor Pyotr Popkov. Ludicrously, they were charged with treachery and planning to blow up the city and hand it over to the Germans. The conspirators were further charged with seeking to seize power, and of wishing to transfer the capital back from Moscow to Leningrad. Even Marshal Zhukov was sent off to a minor command post in Odessa, and intended oblivion. Leningrad's intellectuals were also targeted, such as the city's most famous modern poet Anna Akhmatova, who was deprived of a living and expelled from the Leningrad Union of Writers. Thousands were purged. Many minor party functionaries and other citizens who survived the siege became victims of Stalin's new wave of oppression. The Museum of Leningrad's Defence was closed, its archives seized and its director sent to Siberia. Official records of the blockade were closed. The people of Leningrad had shown too much self-will, independent organization and determination to save their city. Stalin was himself determined to wipe out any possible source of opposition to his rule. Those most closely linked to the defence of Leningrad, and the history of the people's heroic defence of their city (which owed precious little to Stalin and his totalitarian regime) would be expurgated. History would be rewritten, with Comrade Stalin appearing on every page.

Joseph Stalin deliberately let Peter the Great's capital fall into decay. Tsar Peter had built the city as a 'Window on the West', and the warm-water port on the Baltic Sea had the advantage of remaining ice-free throughout the year. During its eighteenth-century heyday, when Italian architects and Scottish engineers helped design and build the city, it became known as the 'Venice of the North'.

Thousands died building the city on a mosquito-infested swamp, but its canals, rivers and architecture rivalled the greatest of Europe's imperial cities. Peter's iron will and determination created the city, using the best foreign talent and the backs of the Russian peasantry. In 1714 he had issued a decree forbidding the construction of stone or brick buildings anywhere in Russia except St Petersburg. All stonemasons had to report for work in the new capital, carrying three stones of five pounds each if arriving by cart, and at least ten stones of ten pounds if arriving by water. The home to the Romanov Tsars and the Winter Palace, the city had the dubious distinction of being the cradle of the Bolshevik Revolution, prompted by the guns of the cruiser *Aurora* on the Neva in October 1917. But St Petersburg's 3,000 palaces started to rot slowly as Uncle Joe focused his attention on transforming Moscow into a showpiece workers' capital, with its emblematic triple-tower blocks and shining marble Metro stations, resplendent with chandeliers. Over seventy years after the Bolshevik Revolution, and three hundred years after the city was founded, St Petersburg is just starting to recover from decades of Communist neglect.

For Vladimir Putin, known as Vovka as a child and Volodya by his close friends and family, life in Leningrad meant living in a fifth-floor communal flat with several other families, with no running hot water and no bathroom. The family would wash from hot water in a bucket, which they had to boil. Every week they went to the public *banya*, or sauna, to wash. The apartment block had an inner airshaft for a courtyard. There was no lift, the stairs had gaps in them and the communal toilet stank. The kitchen was a square, dank, airless hall-way without windows and equipped with a single gas-burning oven and sink. Behind the kitchen lived a family of three, an elderly Jewish couple and their spinster daughter. The spinster's father was a tailor, and seemed to work constantly. A middle-aged couple lived next door. The Putin family used to live, sleep and wash in their one room, twenty metres square. The St Petersburg of old only existed in the crumbling palaces of the Tsarist aristocracy and the Hermitage Museum. The Putins counted themselves lucky. A dozen people can often find themselves sharing one bathroom and one toilet in a communal flat, even in today's St Petersburg. Twenty metres square was a good size. Communal flats had existed since the Revolution, when the proletariat had moved into some of the best properties in Leningrad, parcelled them out, and remained ever since. The centre of the city, including many of the old homes of the nobility and well-to-do, had been largely turned over to communal living. The Putins' rather shabby nineteenth-century block in Baskov Lane had originally been built as large separate apartments. The location, in the city's Central District, not too far from the Nevsky Prospect or the Moscow Railway Station, was pretty good by Leningrad standards. Nevertheless, a room in a communal flat was a comedown from Vladimir's parents' pre-war accommodation in Petrodvorets. In those now seemingly far-off days in another world, they had lived in a semi-detached house. It would be over thirty years before the Putins moved out of their communal flat, and into a flat of their own. The future president would spend half his entire life living in his parents' cramped communal accommodation.

The young Volodya still remembers chasing rats on the staircase. He learned what the expression 'a cornered rat' meant at first hand: 'My friends and I used to chase them around with sticks. Once I spotted a huge rat and pushed it down the hall until I drove it into a corner. It had nowhere to run. Suddenly it lashed around and threw itself at me. I was surprised and frightened. Now the rat was chasing me. It jumped across the landing and down the stairs. Luckily, I was a little faster and I managed to slam the door shut in its nose.'

When Putin was born, Maria decided not to send him to kindergarten after her two months maternity leave was up. Instead, feeling understandably protective towards her one surviving son, forty-one-year-old Maria took a number of part-time jobs near home to spend more time with Volodya. She worked in a bakery unloading trays of bread; as a nightwatchman in a shop; and took a succession of cleaning jobs, including working as a laboratory cleaner. Maria only had a limited education and hadn't finished school, which was quite common for the time, especially given the interruption of the war. Meanwhile, Putin's father continued working at the Yegorov plant, getting up at 5 a.m. every day to go to work. Money was tight, and the family counted every kopek. Vladimir senior had gone back to evening classes to finish his schooling, and ended up editing the factory newspaper. An active Communist Party member, he became a long-serving Party secretary of his department in the factory, and had a four-year stint as an elected member of the party committee for the whole plant in the 1950s. But that was about as far as Vladimir Spiridonovich's involvement with the party went.

As Vladimir junior was a late child, his mother had feared that he might be weak or disabled. Maria was relieved the birth was a normal one, but Volodya was small for his age. He was never to grow tall, perhaps partly influenced by postwar deprivations, and henceforth was politely described as 'diminutive'. The family suppressed any discussion of Putin's two dead brothers. Any emotions were simply bottled-up and contained. Psychologically, Putin's family never recovered from the loss of their two boys, but decided to deal with the hurt by never alluding to it. The emotional repression seemed to permeate the family, leaving its mark on young Volodya. When confronted with trauma in future years, he sometimes seemed unable to express his emotions. His outward expression of calm could give him the appearance of being cold and calculating, of almost being devoid of human feeling. As he matured, his emotions became periodically more visible, and he even on occasions publicly flashed with anger. But now, the single surviving son, Putin was the focus of his parent's attention. 'His parents were very protective of him,' said Alexander Nicolaev, one of his early school friends. Putin's father, however, was not the demonstrative type. 'No hugs and kisses; there was no sentimentality in their house,' said Vera Dmitrievna Gurevich, one of the young Putin's schoolteachers. His father was, in Putin's words, 'a silent man'. If he behaved badly, Putin could expect the belt. His father was a strict disciplinarian, and would sometimes walk around at home with an angry scowl on his face. The example of his father, and the lack of open emotional interaction with him, influenced the young Putin. Volodya could also appear emotionally aloof and introverted like his father.

From the first to the eighth grade, Volodya attended school number 193, in the same road as his apartment block and a brisk seven-minute walk from home. Interestingly, before the Revolution the school had been a former private girls' school, attended by Lenin's future wife, Nadezhda Krupskaya. And as mentioned before, Krupskaya went on to employ Putin's grandfather as a cook. The school is still there today, but is now a technical college. Since he was born in October, Putin did not begin to go to school until he was almost eight (in Russia children usually start school aged seven). The Russian president has the photo of his first day at school in his family album. 'I am in an old-fashioned, grey school uniform,' he recalled. 'It looks like a military uniform, and for some reason I'm standing with a flowerpot in my hand. Not a bouquet, but a pot.' At the beginning of the school year, on 1 September, schoolchildren traditionally brought their teachers a bouquet of cut flowers. But some parents, being more practically minded, used to send their children to school with potted plants. They lasted longer, and many schools in the early postwar period didn't have the budgets to buy potted plants for their classrooms. Hence the photo of Putin with his flower pot, a gift for his first schoolteacher, Tamara Pavlovna Chizova.

Putin was not top of his class, and was always late for school. His father had given him a watch when he was young to encourage punctuality, but throughout his life it was a recurring failing. In his early school days he was a poor pupil. By his own admission, the young Putin was a 'pretty haphazard student', right up to the sixth class and his teens. He was hyperactive, fidgeting in lessons and always looking out of the window. But he was not stupid, in fact he could appear clever although deeply self-contained, with a good memory and a quick mind. His marks were average, 3s and 4s (the highest is a 5), and he usually skimped on his homework. Tamara Stelmakhova, his retired history teacher, recalls a pretty bright boy taking part in debates on topical issues in class. 'This was a very patriotic school. Volodya showed strong character, an acute sense of justice, and unusual responsibility,' she said. But another teacher recalled Putin as being 'sneaky and disorganized'. Some of his classmates had a similar impression, of someone who was always watching but never leading from the front. Sergei Kudrov, a classmate, said Putin was never the centre of attention, and deliberately so. 'He preferred to influence events from a distance, a sort of "grey cardinal" as the saying goes . . . He's an introvert.'

Putin hadn't been accepted into the Pioneers, the Communist youth equivalent of the scouts, because he was viewed as a hopeless case. Usually, pupils were admitted in the third grade unless their behaviour was regarded as wholly unsatisfactory, but for three years the Pioneers refused to admit Volodya. Nevertheless, the young Putin evidently felt the need to impress his peers. On one occasion, a friend recalls him hanging upside down on the fifth-floor balcony outside his school for a bet. He used to play football and played the *bayan*, a type of accordion, badly, at his father's insistence. He would have preferred to play the guitar, like his idols the Beatles. Volodya, rebelling against his father, also started carrying around a hunting knife, which was confiscated by the police. The future president's name was placed on a list of juveniles requiring constant attention. 'I was a hooligan . . . Seriously, I was a real ruffian,' Putin reminisced.

Instead of concentrating on his homework, Volodya used to hang about on the fringes of an older group of undesirables, teenagers who used to fight, swear, drink alcohol and stand around the local courtyards. He wasn't very big or strong then, and if anyone upset him he would jump on them, scratching and biting them, and trying to pull their hair out. In these early encounters, Putin made up for his lack of strength by his determination to win a fight.

Many of the gang ended up in prison. Several times Volodya was hauled before a Comrades' Court, a formal quasi-judicial body of residents covering several blocks of flats. The Comrades' Court regulated bad behaviour, and regularly heard cases involving wife-beaters, alcoholics and juvenile delinquents. They could censor individuals and send their reports to a person's school or workplace. As related in Oleg Blotsky's biography, young Putin was threatened with borstal, or what was called a 'special boarding school for difficult children'. His father begged the Comrades' Court not to pursue the matter, and promised to deal with his son's problems himself. Out came the belt again.

So far all the toughness was just show. Putin only really toughened up when he took up sport in a big way around the age of ten or eleven. Small and delicate in appearance, Volodya decided he needed to be able to defend himself properly. The courtyard was a jungle. He initially took up boxing. However, his new passion didn't work out. After his nose was broken, he decided to switch to *sambo*, a Soviet combination of judo and wrestling. Vera Dmitrievna Gurevich, his class teacher from the fifth grade (who also taught him German), recalled his early sporting days. 'He didn't like socializing much. He preferred sports. He started doing martial arts in order to defend himself.' Putin had by then turned thirteen. Two to three times a week, for almost two hours, he took classes near the Finland Railway Station, on the right bank of the Neva, in a plain gym belonging to the Trud athletic club (*Trud* means labour in English). His trainer was Anatoly Semyonovich Rakhlin, who still trains boys and girls today. His parents were initially sceptical about the sport, but Rakhlin had a word and convinced them it would be good for their son. In his first year, Putin couldn't afford training shoes, and practised in woollen socks and a kimono made by his mother. He got hold of a real kimono the next year, when a mate dropped out.

Years later, when Putin was already twenty, Rakhlin then persuaded his pupil to switch to judo, a sport very similar to sambo. Unlike sambo, judo was an Olympic sport and would give Volodya the chance to try for the Olympics. The judo, like sambo, not only fulfilled the young Volodya's need for personal security, but perhaps subconsciously provided him with the physical contact he lacked at home. Putin excelled at the sport, later winning a black belt by training hard and regularly jogging at 5 a.m. Once he entertained his whole school, seeking the approval of his peers and teachers, performing his sambo moves on stage when a visiting gymnastic team failed to turn up. Sport also helped Putin focus on his academic studies. If his school marks were too low, he would not have been allowed to continue as a Trud club member.

In 1976, when Putin was twenty-four, he became the city's judo champion. He had already become a Master of Sports in both sambo and judo. These were serious sporting achievements for a young man in his early twenties. Years later, Vladimir would recall his daily 17-kilometre morning runs around Lake Khippiyarvi in the athletic centre outside Leningrad, and his many matches held around the vast USSR. Putin was always calm in victory and defeat, and had the endearing quality of only blaming himself if he lost a bout. Anatoly Rakhlin, now aged sixty-two, and Putin's coach thirty years ago, says Putin could have made the Olympic judo team. 'He could throw with equal skill in both directions, left and right. And his opponents, expecting a throw from the right, would not see the left one coming. So it was pretty tough for his opponents to beat him because he was constantly kind of tricking them,' Rakhlin said. Putin's ability to read his opponent's moves, and conceal his own intentions, proved invaluable in his later career. Judo and Putin's inherent inscrutability were perfectly matched. As Putin said, 'Judo is not just a sport, you know. It's a philosophy.' He later co-authored a book on the subject. It was a philosophy which helped guide Putin's passage through life, as he sized-up his opponents and friends alike.

The Putins had bought a small three-roomed dacha in Tosno, about 25 miles south-east of Leningrad, when Volodya was seventeen. People don't have to be rich to have dachas; many inherit them from elderly relatives, and some are just large sheds with a small piece of land. Some are old village houses. Dachas are not just weekend cottages in Russia, they are a way of life. Some families spend most of the summer camped on their dachas, work allowing. Many wives take their children to their family dachas for the long summer school holidays, which stretch from the end of May until September. Dachas are also a welcome relief from the congestion, heat and cramped living conditions in the cities. The Putins' dacha was modest but adequate. They had a simple wooden banya, built by Putin's father, where the family would have a sauna. They would take it in turns to beat each other with *venik*, bunches of small leafy branches of silver birch. A wood-burning banya produces steamy heat which is a cross between a sauna and a Turkish bath. The banya is a great Russian tradition, and many friendships and business deals are made there (usually assisted by beer and vodka). Friends would come out to visit and have a sauna, and Vladimir senior would cook fish in tomato sauce afterwards. Not a natural early bird, his son would lie-in late when he got the chance. The dacha created a lot of work for the Putin family and tasks were divided along traditional lines. The males, Volodya and his father, would do any manual tasks like repair and maintenance work, digging, chopping wood for the house fire and banya, carting-away rubbish and bringing water from a standpipe. Volodya would simply do the tasks his father set him. There was no avoiding work, even for young *dachniki* (dacha dwellers). The women (Maria in this case) would perpetually have their bottoms in the air doing weeding, or spend time cleaning, washing and cooking.

As with many dachas, the house didn't have running water, and the toilet was outside in a little wooden cabin the size and shape of an old phone box. Its organic contents had to be cleared by hand, but provided useful fertilizer for the garden. The dacha provided a useful supplement to the family diet and budget, producing vegetables like potatoes, apples and seasonal berries. Every other year, the gnarled apple trees would produce a bumper crop of succulent small green apples. Putin's mother liked the homegrown wild flowers.

During the period of the 'White Nights' in June, night never closes in, with the sky gradually becoming a deeper shade of blue for a few hours in the early morning. The Putins could cook *shashlik* (chicken, lamb or pork kebabs) over a charcoal fire late into the pale light night sky, staring up at the spectacular wisps of shaded white, blue and pink clouds scudding across the Arctic horizon. Although weekends and evenings on the dacha were thus often relaxed affairs, Volodya didn't really drink and never smoked. One glass of wine was about his maximum. Even so, one neighbour, Vera Brileva, recalled that Vladimir junior loved celebrating New Year and other Soviet holidays on the dacha in Tosno. Volodya used to entertain his family and guests with an earnest rendition of his favourite song, 'The Dashing Troika This Way Comes'. While his family were not well off, Putin's parents weren't mean and young Volodya didn't feel poor. Everyone around him lived in communal flats, and some were lucky enough to have small dachas like theirs which enabled them to get out of the city. They all lived more or less the same way, with the same low standard of living. No one that Volodya knew had lots of money. But on the whole, they didn't live too badly.

At school, Volodya had a narcissistic streak. He used to give out photos of himself with inscriptions such as 'a healthy spirit in a healthy body'. In one young girl's school-leaving report he wrote: 'Never live for yourself or for others only. Remember that any exaggeration is ugly.' The young blond sporty Volodya undoubtedly fancied himself. With his hair casually flicked over his high forehead (inherited from his parents) and his dreamy eyes, he rightly imagined himself attractive boyfriend material. But he wasn't generally interested in girls; he just wanted them to like him. Something seemed to click inside Putin in the sixth grade when he was thirteen, and he decided to start taking his schoolwork seriously. He began to get better grades. His old teacher, Vera Dmitrievna, thought he had decided to make something of himself, rather than drift along as a street urchin. 'Most likely he had understood that he had to achieve something in life,' she said. He joined a German language class, and surprised his teachers with his good memory and eagerness to learn. He stopped hanging around with the Kovshov brothers, who used to spend their time on the streets and jumping off garage roofs. Volodya was finally admitted to the Pioneers, and became chair of his unit's council. Still reluctant to join in the school dances, he enjoyed strumming on his guitar and singing popular Russian folksongs. Sport remained his primary love. But by the eighth class, Putin was no longer getting 3 for his schoolwork. Now all his marks were 4s or 5s.

What was it that made the young Putin decide to stop wasting his life on the streets and start taking his schoolwork seriously? Why had he suddenly become ambitious and focused? When he was younger, Volodya wanted to become a seaman or a pilot. Now in his early teens, he started to have other ideas. Putin says it was books and films like the *The Sword and the Shield* which filled his head with romantic notions of becoming a spy for his country. The novel version of *The Sword and the Shield* was published in 1965, when Putin was thirteen. It was almost certainly *The Sword and the Shield* and other books and films which stimulated his interest in studying German and gave him the notion that he should work hard and join the KGB. He and his friends read *The Sword and the Shield* several times. When the film came out three years later, it was a big hit. The story line was based on the true account of a double-agent serving in wartime Germany who stole secret documents to sabotage German operations. The Russian spy, named Alexander Belov, posed as a chauffeur, a role Putin briefly adopted himself in Leningrad after the fall of the Berlin Wall. Putin recalled: 'What amazed me most of all was how one man's effort could achieve what whole armies could not. One spy could decide the fate of thousands of people. At least, that's the way I understood it.' As a boy Putin liked to visit the nearby cinemas on Nevsky Prospect, places like the October, which only cost him a few kopeks.

Putin's fascination with *The Sword and the Shield*, and the life-changing impact it had on him, would give psychologists a field day. It was not just a young boy being impressed with a book. The story struck other chords with the young Vladimir. His father had been attached to the NKVD in the war, the Soviet forerunner of the KGB, which had an aura of mystery and secrecy. Germany was doubly the enemy. The Nazis had wreaked destruction in Leningrad and the surrounding districts, killing hundreds of thousands of local Russian people. Now Western Germany was again Russia's enemy, as part of the capitalist, degenerate West. Putin settled down to learn German not out of a love for the culture, but because he needed to know how to speak the language to become an effective spy. Putin was also a keen reader of other books on espionage and Soviet spies. He would fight the enemy from within, just like the hero in *The Sword and the Shield*. There was no love for Germany in the Putin household; the Nazis had been responsible for the death of a son and brother, and for permanently disabling his father. Putin wanted to go one step further than his father's wartime service as a partisan attached to the NKVD; he wanted to serve abroad as a KGB agent, and he actively prepared himself to be ready to be sent to Germany. And he was serious and methodical about it. Teachers at Putin's school later remembered he borrowed a book about spying. He never gave it back.

Volodya moved on to school No 281 after his eighth grade, aged sixteen. The school specialized in chemistry. His choice initially puzzled his former teachers, but like many pupils it was apparent that Putin's choice was influenced by a school chum, Slava Yakovlev. Slava had persuaded Volodya to follow him to school No 281. The choice wasn't entirely successful, as Volodya found himself unpopular at his new school. He tried hard to become a model student, singing revolutionary songs and being awarded a commendation for summer work on a collective farm. He worked hard at keeping up his German. Like everyone else at school, he was a member of the Young Communist League or Komsomol. But somehow the pupils at the new school didn't take to the young Putin. Perhaps they found him too introverted and insular. He only seemed to really care about sport. Volodya said sport was only sport if it was 'connected with sweat, blood and hard work'. For many teenagers, such fanatical commitment was off-putting.

Around the time the Red Army crushed the Prague Spring in 1968, the sixteen-year-old Volodya plucked up courage and asked to join the KGB. By now, he had nurtured his boyish dream to become a KGB agent for several years. It had almost grown into an obsession. He decided to approach the KGB through a friend whose father was a lieutenant colonel in the secret police. Alexei Nicolaev remembered that his friend loved to listen to his KGB father talking about his adventures in the secret service. 'Volodya loved listening to my father talk of his travels to distant parts of the Soviet Union. He seemed to think it romantic,' Alexei said. Volodya asked his friend whether his father could fix up a meeting with a KGB recruiting officer. But after a few enquiries, he decided to simply walk along to the 'Big House' (*Bolshoi Dom*), the KGB's Leningrad head office at 4 Liteiny Street. Everyone in Leningrad knew where the 'Big House' was. Nowadays, its location is thoughtfully marked on tourist maps. Number 4 Liteiny is about ten minutes walk from where Putin lived, at the Neva end of the street near the Robespierre Embankment, on the right-hand side as you look towards the river. A large and deep nine-storey modern Soviet block, bristling with huge antennae, the 'Big House' sticks out a mile among the period buildings along Liteiny Street. Putin was seen by a KGB officer on his third visit. The first time he checked the opening times, the second time he met a receptionist and was told to come back at a certain time, and only on the third occasion met a desk officer named Yegorovich whose job it was to deal with the public. The officer had a certain world-weary attitude to members of the public who requested a meeting with the KGB. Many of these 'walk-ins' were cranks, who wanted to report on neighbours or saw foreign spies on every street corner. Most were a total waste of time. Sometimes, just sometimes, somebody would bring in some useful information. The officer didn't have any great hopes from yet another meeting with an impressionable teenager.

Putin remembers his encounter with the KGB officer well. 'A guy came out and listened to me. "I want to get a job with you," I said. "That's terrific, but there are several issues," he said. "First, we don't take people who come to us on their own initiative. Second, you can come to us only after the army or some type of civilian education." ' When pressed by the teenager about which was the preferred subject, the KGB officer replied 'Law'. After the brief meeting, the KGB officer requested a file on Putin's family and wrote up a report on the twenty-five minute encounter. The report would be filed away and forgotten about for now. Around this time the KGB had decided to recruit more of its people from universities, the army officer corps and other higher education establishments. Too many of the USSR's experienced spies had been liquidated during Stalin's purges and replaced with none-too-bright bulldogs who did his dirty work but were incapable of sophisticated human intelligence work. The KGB had come to be filled with party hacks and hatchet men, who with poor language skills stuck out in foreign countries like sore thumbs. Putin and his generation would represent a new breed of KGB agent, educated, linguistically capable, dedicated and able to blend in abroad. Volodya's visit to the 'Big House' on Liteiny Street showed he had a great deal of ambition, nerve and determination.

Although the KGB was starting to recruit direct from higher education institutes, they would also sometimes mark out the brightest kids at the best schools, quietly approaching teachers to sound out likely candidates. They would then be closely observed at university or during their service in the armed forces. No approaches were made in Putin's case, and as the KGB told the young Putin, the secret police were suspicious of anyone who offered their services. No one wanted to end up with a loony or a glory-seeker unsuitable for the secret services. Even so, the KGB officer's advice to Putin was sound. The preferred training for the KGB at the time was either the law or foreign languages. The law could verse a KGB recruit in the details of Soviet laws and regulations, providing a useful background for counter-intelligence work and preparing cases for court.

The KGB's actions against dissidents, foreign spies and those engaging in 'anti-Soviet activity' required a detailed knowledge of the Soviet constitution, even if it could be ignored when politically convenient.

Vladimir Putin decided there and then to study law at Leningrad University. He knew he would have to rely on his own efforts, as he had no connections which might help him get a place at university. Dropping physics and chemistry, he concentrated on those subjects he needed for university, including Russian language and literature. He had always liked Russian literature anyway. Once again, his teachers were mystified by his career choice. No one could explain his sudden interest in studying law. The year following his meeting with Yegorovich, he applied to Leningrad State University to study law. While he was there, he would also continue studying German. It was the ideal combination for a budding KGB agent. Leningrad State was one of the best and most prestigious universities in the country, and competition for places was intense. Vladimir Lenin was amongst those who had attended the famous law faculty founded by Peter the Great.

Putin admits it wasn't that easy for him to win a place. Years later, he told journalists just how tough it was. He recalled there were a hundred places and only ten of those were reserved for high school graduates. 'The rest were for army guys. So for us high schoolers, the competition was fierce; something like forty kids per slot. I had obtained a B in composition but had As in all other subjects, and I was accepted.' Putin added: 'By the way, at that time, they didn't take into account the total grade point average of the applicant. So in the tenth grade I could completely devote myself to the subjects that I would have to pass to get into university. If I hadn't dropped the other subjects, I wouldn't have got in.' Years later, the university changed the system so that the average grade of the pupil at school was taken into account. If that had been the system in Putin's day, he wouldn't have been accepted. Still, the fact that Putin worked hard to improve his grades to gain a university place showed that he had the drive and determination to succeed in life. His father in particular was very proud that Volodya made it into university, and 'jumped for joy' when he saw his son's entrance results. A late child and a late developer at school, he was catching up fast.

Incidentally, his parents and coach had been gravely concerned by his decision to try for a place at Leningrad State University. They begged him to choose an easier option, in a higher education technical institute where he would be guaranteed a place due to his sporting prowess and where he could continue his beloved judo. The reason was simple. If he failed to get into university, he would be eighteen and without a place in college at the start of the academic year. That meant he would be called up into the army. He could end up anywhere in the Soviet Union, or abroad. War was always a possibility; military training in the USSR was never without its dangers. But young Vladimir ignored the pleas and took a gamble. Luckily for him it paid off, and he avoided conscription indefinitely. Like many young men, he wasn't too upset by the prospect. Going into the army wasn't too much fun, but if the worst came to the worst, he had been prepared to bear it. After all, the army was another route into the KGB.

At university Putin devoted himself to his studies, and became generally more reclusive. He majored in international law, but, inevitably, also studied Communist history and dialectical materialism. Marx, Engels and Lenin became his bedtime reading. His only extra-curricular activity was sport, where he kept up his interest in sambo and judo. Volodya became a sambo black belt after starting university, and a judo black belt two years later. But as he became immersed in his studies, he spent less time doing his sport. He wasn't active in Komsomol, and as a rule kept his head down. His university grant was so pitiable he ate and lived at home with his parents. One vacation he worked in a construction crew in Komi, northern Russia, cutting down trees for the lumber industry and building houses. Volodya was paid 1,000 roubles for six weeks' work, a comparative fortune in those days, when a car cost around 3,500 roubles. He spent his earnings on a holiday on the Black Sea with university friends, where he went swimming and picked up a good tan.

Despite his insularity, Putin was not a loner and did manage to find time to have one romance with a pretty medical student named Lyuda; they almost married. But the relationship didn't work out. He called the whole thing off at the last moment, despite the fact that the couple had already applied for a marriage licence, and their parents had splashed out on the rings, a wedding dress and the groom's outfit. He said he felt like a 'real creep', but it was better to suffer then than both suffer later. He still won't talk about the failed relationship today. Sergei Roldugin, one of Putin's oldest friends, thought part of Putin's problem was that: 'He was a very emotional person but he simply could not express his emotions. I often used to tell him that he was terrible at making conversation.' It could be that the relationship floundered because Putin had a particular view of the wife he wanted. In a way he sought a traditional, even old-fashioned wife, who would fit in with his future plans to be a foreign intelligence agent. By all accounts his first love was a bit bossy, telling him what he should do and eat to stay healthy, and perhaps she was also just too wilful and independently minded. Characteristics that wouldn't necessarily fit in with Putin's career plans at all. Six months after the aborted relationship with Lyuda, he met his future wife. But this time, he wasn't going to be rushed into any hastily conceived marriage. His mother apparently preferred Lyuda to his eventual wife, and made the fact evident to his future spouse.

In the third year of university, Putin had a lucky break when his parents won the lottery. They could choose cash or a car, and they chose a car and gave it to Volodya. The car was a Zaporozhets, a terrible Soviet model which was small, boxy and tinny. But for twenty-year-old Putin the car was great. Relatively few adults, let alone youngsters just out of their teens, had their own car in the USSR of the early 1970s. He loved driving around town at high speed, and was generous offering his friends lifts hither and thither.

Putin knew owning a car was hugely prestigious, and he made the most of it. On one occasion someone jumped out in front of his car, he didn't know who, and he hit him. Perhaps the person was drunk, but in any event they disappeared when he tried to find out who or what he had bumped into. If that was a close shave with tragedy, real tragedy struck a year later when a friend was killed in a judo bout. Volody Cheryomushkin was a university pal whom Putin persuaded to take up judo. But before his friend was really ready, his coach put him into a competition in the spring of 1973. He landed headfirst in a bout, and dislocated his vertebrae, leading to paralysis and death ten days later. At the public funeral, Putin as usual didn't show any emotion. He was just sombre and quiet. But when he returned to the cemetery with Cheryomushkin's mother and sister, he cried over his friend's grave. The cool calm exterior could crack after all. Yet if anything, after his friend's death Putin became even more sombre and introverted.

Putin waited and waited for the KGB to make contact. Four years passed, and he began thinking he might have to find a job as a prosecutor or an attorney. Eventually, when he had almost given up hope, a KGB officer approached him in the law faculty and asked him whether he would join the secret service. He was delighted, and agreed at once. He admitted that he didn't think about the Stalin-era purges, including the infamous 'Leningrad Affair'. 'My notion of the KGB came from romantic spy stories. I was a pure and utterly successful product of Soviet patriotic education,' he said later. Aged twenty-two, Putin accepted the KGB's job offer, his head filled with romantic images of espionage and serving his Motherland. Before offering him the job, the KGB had been watching his progress for several years, as was their normal practice. They talked to his teachers, checking his background, his personnel files at school and university, and his Komsomol membership. A KGB officer, Dmitri Gantservov, had also been to see Putin's father in the final year of his studies to check out his family personally.

Putin couldn't keep his excitement to himself. Sergei Roldugin, a soloist in the Marinsky Theatre Symphony Orchestra and a future godfather to Putin's eldest daughter, recalls: 'Vovka told me right away that he was working in the KGB. Practically right away. Maybe he was not supposed to do that. He told some people that he was working in the police. On the other hand, I treated these guys with caution, because I had had some run-ins with them. I had travelled abroad and I knew that there were always people posing as inspectors or officials from the Ministry of Culture. You had to keep your mouth shut when you were around them.'

The word in Leningrad was that the more you came into contact with the KGB, the more dirt they would file on you, perhaps to be used against you at a later date. Many students were wary of getting too close to the KGB, or falling into their clutches. There was always the danger that they could blackmail you to work for them, with the result that you could end up informing on your colleagues, friends or even family. Initially, Putin was not too discreet about joining the KGB, although that changed after a while when he started serving as an intelligence officer. His father certainly knew and approved of his decision to join the KGB. In the tenth grade, he confided in his sports coach that he wanted to be a KGB agent. He told one friend, Vasily Shestakov, that he was preparing for exams to enter Leningrad University Law Faculty, so he could later work in intelligence. Victor Borisenko, another friend, went with Putin to a Caucasian restaurant near Kazan Cathedral to celebrate his acceptance into the KGB. It was typical of Putin that although he didn't openly talk about it, all his close friends knew he had joined the KGB. He just couldn't contain his excitement that he had finally achieved his ambition. Of course, being a KGB officer was meant to be a secret. Some intelligence officers didn't tell their wives and family, let alone their friends. But Putin couldn't resist letting his friends know he had been recruited into the KGB. He had at last joined what he and other KGB officers called the *Cheka*, a word formed from the Russian acronym for Lenin's Extraordinary Commission, or secret police.

During the 1970s, being a KGB officer was a very prestigious and privileged position. KGB personnel had priority when it came to flat allocations, or when they wanted phones installed. Both caused most ordinary citizens major headaches. Foreign intelligence officers had the opportunity to travel, buy foreign goods (like cars) and be paid partly in hard currency. Their children would be guaranteed places in good schools. A KGB identity card could help open doors and would impress the local police. Vladimir also sought the respect and esteem of his peers. He was proud of his achievement in joining the KGB, and being able to impress his friends reinforced his sense of self-worth and success. In keeping all his old friends after joining the secret service, Putin was unusual. Many intelligence officers ditched their old acquaintances because they thought they could hinder their career prospects or compromise their work. Yet Putin kept his former circle of friends, both as a reference point for his own success and out of his strong sense of personal loyalty. His loyalty can be seen as one of the great strengths of his character. In a politician, however, misplaced loyalty can also sometimes become a serious political handicap.

Putin later became more circumspect about his profession. When Roldugin tried to press him about his work, he elliptically replied, 'I'm a specialist in human relations.' And indeed, that is what the young Putin was to become. He was formally recruited into the KGB in 1975, after he graduated from university aged twenty-three. He worked initially in the KGB's counter-intelligence department in Leningrad, in the 'Big House' on Liteiny Street. Counter-intelligence worked on the fifth floor, and foreign intelligence worked on the sixth. His counter-intelligence training took place at School 401 in Leningrad, near the Okhta river, where they specialized in preparing recruits in covert observation work. Some of Putin's work involved monitoring religious and dissident groups in Leningrad. After six months, he was spotted by KGB foreign intelligence officers as a good prospect, and sent to Moscow for a year of special training. A posting in foreign intelligence, with its possibilities for foreign travel and the perks that went with it, was a much better career move than working behind a desk in the USSR as a counter-intelligence officer. 'Of course I wanted to go into foreign intelligence. Everyone did. We all knew what it meant to be able to travel abroad under the conditions of the Soviet Union,' Putin reminisced.

After his first stint in Moscow, Putin returned to Leningrad, where he was based for four and a half years in the KGB's First Chief Directorate as a foreign intelligence agent. The 'First Department' had subdivisions in all the Soviet Union's major cities, including Leningrad. The vast bulk of intelligence work is concerned with analysing information and writing up reports. Putin acted very much as a traditional intelligence officer, routinely analysing information and preparing reports for his secret service bosses. However, some of the work of his small department did involve making contact with foreign businessmen, visitors and academics, and recruiting some as agents and informers. Putin was regarded as calm, reserved, hard working and competent but in other respects unremarkable.

Valery Golubev, a former KGB officer who shared an office with Putin for three years, remembered his colleague as a self-confessed 'expert in human psychology'. Putin, he said, looked for people's weaknesses and was 'very sensitive to what people felt and thought and would pay great attention to details about their troubles'. The future president was learning the vital listening skills and awareness of others' needs that would later become so invaluable to him. A year after joining the KGB, Putin finally achieved his aim in judo by becoming champion of Leningrad. In the early 1970s, his judo record had steadily improved, but the city championship eluded him. After winning that title, as he pursued his career in the KGB, he trained less and less. By the late 1970s he had almost stopped training altogether. A few years on he would return to some light training, but this would be just to keep himself fit. From now on, any sightings of Putin in a kimono would be for the benefit of a photo opportunity.

On occasions, he found his judo training useful. His friend Sergei Roldugin remembers that Vladimir got into one or two scraps even after he joined the KGB. Once, he and Roldugin were waiting at a bus stop and some drunken students tried to pick a fight. One of them took a swing at Putin and ended up flying through the air after being thrown by the judo black belt. He and Roldugin then simply walked away. Another time, a thug went for him on the Metro and he broke his arm defending himself. But Putin usually kept his sporting prowess to himself after he joined the KGB. Later in his political career he would find it useful to compare his athletic fitness with the ailing sot Boris Yeltsin.

Four and a half years after joining the KGB's First Department in Leningrad, Putin was sent to Moscow for further training at the Andropov Red Banner Institute, which became the Academy of Foreign Intelligence. This was the KGB's elite school for foreign agents, where the USSR's top spies were trained. Located in woods outside Moscow, the Red Banner Institute is isolated and fenced-off with barbed wire. For a year or sometimes more, its students are taught all the arts of espionage, including how to jump with a parachute at night, arrange dead-letter drops, lose a tail and run agents. In addition, they learned foreign languages, diplomacy, philosophy, literature and social etiquette. Putin had already risen to the rank of major in the KGB before being sent to the spy school. Once there, he was made a section or group head, and was designated to study Austria, Switzerland and East and West Germany in depth. It was logical that with his knowledge of German he would be assigned to work in a German-speaking country.

KGB Colonel Mikhail Frolov taught him at the Red Banner Institute, where like all trainees, he was given a pseudonym. Comrade Putin became Comrade Platov. Putin came across as organized, businesslike, tactful, honest and displayed personal integrity. He was always ready with a quip or joke. But his KGB appraisals were not wholly positive. Colonel Frolov reported that Putin was 'somewhat withdrawn and uncommunicative'. He added:

'I also cited a certain academic tendency among his negative aspects.' Frolov's assessment implied that Putin lacked some of the social skills possessed by the very best agents. These were the ability to communicate fluently with people, and interact well on a personal and social level. Foreign intelligence agents have to have the ability to woo their 'targets', and talk them into perhaps betraying their country. Putin was good at observing and understanding people, but the academy indicated that his communication and inter-personal skills let him down. In their opinion, he could be a good agent, but not an outstanding one. As one senior Western diplomat put it, he seemed and acted more like a policeman than a foreign intelligence agent.

During his early years as a KGB officer in Leningrad, Putin met his future wife. Her friends and family called her Lyudik or Lyuda for short. Lyudmila Alexandrovna Shkrebnyova was five years Putin's junior. He first met her on a blind date at a theatre organized by a friend on 7 March 1980, while she was still working as a domestic air hostess for Kaliningrad Airlines. Putin had used his KGB contacts to get four rare tickets to see the popular comedian Arkady Raikin. It was Lyuda's first visit to Leningrad from the 'closed' or secret garrison city of Kaliningrad, and she loved it at first sight. Kaliningrad, the former East Prussian city of Konigsberg on the Baltic Sea and birthplace of Kant, was reputedly the most militarized area in the USSR. The once picturesque city, nestling on the Polish and Lithuanian borders, had been occupied and depopulated by Stalin's Red Army. A base for 200,000 Soviet troops, the indigenous German population had either been killed or fled. Lyudmila was understandably glad to leave Kaliningrad, and the contrast even with Soviet Leningrad must have been dazzling.

Lyudmila was not overly impressed with her first sight of Putin. 'Volodya was standing on the steps of the ticket office. He was very modestly dressed. I would even say that he was very poorly dressed. He looked very unprepossessing. I wouldn't have paid any attention to him on the street.' Lyudmila on the other hand made a big impression on him. With her fair hair, large blue eyes and sensuous lips, Lyuda was an attractive woman with a determined personality. He saw her every day on her three-day visit to the city, impressing her by obtaining tickets to different theatres on every successive evening. Less impressively, he was constantly late. Unusually for him, he had given Lyuda his phone number before she left Leningrad. Putin started a courtship that was to last longer than three years, with Lyudmila flying from Kaliningrad to meet up for dates. Since she didn't have a phone at home, she used to ring him. For the first eighteen months he told Lyudmila he worked as a police inspector in the criminal investigation department, until she found out through a mutual friend he actually worked in the KGB. Working in the criminal investigation department was a standard cover given to intelligence officers in the 'Big House'. Lyudmila didn't mind either way. For many Russian women Putin was quite a good catch, a graduate from Leningrad University with a *propiska*, or permit, to live in the city. Under the Soviet system these were highly sought-after documents. Without a *propiska* people weren't free to live in the city of their choice. They could only dream about living in Moscow or Leningrad. As Putin's wife Lyudmila would have an automatic right to live in Leningrad with her husband. He was fit, decent looking and looked as if he had a good career ahead of him. Now Lyuda says it was his 'inner strength' that finally won her around. On her own admission, she then spent three years winning him around to the idea of marrying her.

Putin easily persuaded Lyudmila to move to Leningrad that summer, where, at his suggestion, she joined the Spanish Department and studied Spanish and French at university. He helped her find a job, and she managed to enroll as an external student before becoming a full-time student the following year, aged twenty-three. He also helped her find a room in a communal flat, where she lived. Again, at his prompting, she took a typing course, which he thought might be useful for his career. In Kaliningrad, Lyudmila had dropped out of technical college after a couple of years before becoming an air hostess. She only came to Leningrad to be near him. All Lyudmila wanted to do was settle down and have a family. Vladimir, however, had other ideas. He wanted his wife to have a university education and be a social and career asset. He clearly had a definite idea of the sort of wife who would fit in with his future as a KGB foreign intelligence officer. At one stage it looked as if the relationship might founder. Putin thought Lyudmila had acted too 'freely' at a party, and feared she might be too high-spirited for him to handle. The crisis blew over, and the courtship continued. For the time, Lyudmila was socially adventurous. They went on holiday together to the Black Sea several times. For the Soviet Union of the early 1980s, this was heady, permissive stuff. Couples didn't normally go away on holiday together unless they were married.

Over three years, Putin had plenty of time to size Lyudmila up, and assess for himself whether she would cope well with being a KGB officer's wife. Sometimes, Lyudmila would get the feeling he was testing her. He would turn up for meetings over an hour and a half late, and offer no apology or excuse. She felt she mustn't talk about his work, even though she wanted to. His marriage proposal totally unnerved Lyudmila at first. He sat at his home one night, and started saying that he wasn't an easy-going person, that he was the silent type and could be abrupt. He added: 'In three and a half years, you have probably made up your mind.' Lyudmila thought they were breaking-up, and blurted out, 'I need you.' He continued, 'Well, then, if that's the way it is, I love you and propose that we get married.' And they did. The marriage started as it was to continue. Putin chose and named the date, 28 July 1983. He was thirty, and for those days, he was getting married quite late in life. They had their wedding reception at the Poplovok restaurant, a floating restaurant next to the Lieutenant Schmidt Bridge on the Neva. The next day, they had another do for Putin's KGB work colleagues at the Hotel Moscow, near the city's Alexander Nevsky Monastery. Like many Leningrad newly-weds, they had their photo taken next to the famous bronze statue of Peter the Great on a rearing horse ('The

Bronze Horseman') in Decembrists Square behind St Isaac's
Cathedral. For their honeymoon they drove down to the baking
Black Sea, in Russia's deep south. When they came back, they went
to live with his parents, who had by now moved to a small two-
roomed flat in Avtovo, near the old Kirov works in the south-west of
the city. The flat was in an area of new purpose-built apartment
blocks. Vladimir senior had received the flat because of his status as
a disabled war veteran. The elder Putins lived in a 15-square-metre
room with a balcony, while the young couple shared a smaller, 12-
square-metre room. The first year for Lyudmila was absolute
married bliss. 'There was a continuous sense of joy, as though we
were on holiday,' she later remarked.

When Putin's foreign posting eventually came through, it was
to the German Democratic Republic (the GDR). A posting to East
Germany was not what an intelligence officer's dreams were made
of. A high-flyer would hope and expect a posting to the West, perhaps to Washington, Bonn, London or Paris. Being sent to the
intelligence backwater of Dresden was not a thrilling prospect. It
confirmed the overall evaluation he had received after a year at the
Academy of Foreign Intelligence in Moscow. A special commission
at the academy had evaluated every student, and decided where to
send them. The commission had comprised staff from the academy
and representatives from various KGB departments, who interviewed each student and looked at their performance, personal files
and end-of-year reports. The only question in Putin's case was
whether he was to be sent to East Berlin in the GDR, or somewhere
else in East Germany. East Berlin was clearly preferable since it acted
as the KGB's headquarters in the GDR, with the other KGB stations
across the country in Dresden, Leipzig and Karl Marx Stadt reporting to it. Berlin would then report direct to Moscow Centre. Being
based in the provinces meant that an agent's report would be read
first in Berlin, with the result that it might never reach Moscow. In
the event, Putin was selected to go to Dresden, not Berlin. Dresden
was obviously a second-tier residency, and being sent to the GDR at

all was similarly a second-tier posting. However, there were worst places an agent could be sent abroad. Although improbable (because of his German), he could have been sent to Afghanistan, at the height of the conflict following the Soviet invasion. Or he might have been sent to somewhere miserable, like Albania or Mongolia.

In the Soviet system, as Putin now knew, many of the foreign intelligence officers were the children of the elite. You had to know the right people or be exceptional to get one of the best jobs based in the West. *Blat* – cronyism – and connections ruled in the Soviet Union. As an outsider with modest family roots, Putin's chances of a top job in foreign intelligence were slim to start with. General Oleg Kalugin, former head of Soviet counter-intelligence and deputy head of the KGB in Leningrad, is brutal about Putin's career in the secret police. 'Any assignment to Eastern Europe,' Kalugin said, 'East Germany including, was a sign of someone's failing or lack of abilities. His record in the KGB is zero, he is a non-entity in the KGB.' Putin would seriously demur at Kalugin's assessment; with his German language skills he had undoubtedly hoped to duel with foreign spies in West Germany, perhaps in Bonn or Berlin. Instead, he ended up working with provincial plods in deadly dull Dresden. Although the German city on the Elbe retained some of its Baroque city centre, the RAF had done its best to obliterate the city in 1944. Thirty-five thousand civilians were killed in the process, as the RAF's Air Marshal 'Bomber' Harris sought to bomb the Germans into submission or the stone age, whichever came first. The wrecked skeleton of the Frauenkirche in the centre of the city stands as a monument to 'Bomber' Harris and his controversial terror tactics.

Nevertheless, Putin could console himself with the thought that a posting to East Germany wasn't that bad. Arriving in the summer of 1985, he came to Dresden a competent German-speaker. It had taken him ten years in the KGB to get a posting overseas, and although that wasn't the sign of a meteoric career in the security services, at least he made it. Many in the KGB at home never made the grade to travel abroad at all. During four and a half years in

Dresden, the Putin family sat out the chaos of *perestroika* (restructuring) and Mikhail Gorbachev's ultimately unsuccessful attempts to reform Communism. Gorbachev had become leader the previous March, and over the next five years economic conditions in the USSR steadily deteriorated, with consumer shortages commonplace. Queuing became the new obligatory pastime for Soviet citizens. In many cases, people just joined a queue with the hope of buying something. Anything would do; you could always barter it later. Germany, even Eastern Germany, was a different world. There the standard of living was better and everything was still orderly. For now.

3

THE SPY WHO LOVED ME

Question to Russian businessman: 'Do you pay the mafia?'
Answer: 'Oh no. I pay the police, my partner pays the mafia.'

Vladimir Putin travelled ahead of his family to East Germany. Lyudmila and Masha, now six months old, followed Putin to Dresden that autumn. When Putin arrived in Dresden, a KGB colleague described his spoken German as 'average', although by the time he left it had become pretty good. Lyudmila also learned German while living in Dresden. Learning Spanish and French at university gave her the linguistic skills to pick up the language relatively easily. By this stage, Putin had risen to the rank of KGB major, which was steady if unspectacular career progress. They lived in a decent two-bed flat in Radeberger Strasse next to a Soviet army tank base and some woods, had a car, driver, and access to good food. They shared the apartment block with members of the Stasi, German State Security, the GDR's equivalent of the KGB. The block didn't have a lift, which was a particular burden for the pregnant Lyuda, who sometimes would traipse up and down the stairs three times a day to their sixth-floor apartment. As usual, she was left to do all the housework and cooking on her own. Her husband thought all that was 'women's work', a not untypical Russian male viewpoint. She called him a 'despot' at home, and was so run-down at one point she was admitted to hospital for a blood transfusion.

Frustratingly for Lyudmila, KGB rules circumscribed the kind of paid work she could do, and she was restricted to some seasonal fruit picking. Nevertheless, the flat on Radeberger Strasse was the first flat they could call their own. Beforehand, they had lived with Putin's parents, and after that Lyuda had moved into a one-room flat in Komendantsky Aerodrome, in Leningrad's north-western suburbs, from where she visited Vladimir at the Academy of Foreign Intelligence in Moscow. She had gone through her first pregnancy virtually alone while Putin was studying advanced espionage in Moscow, and must have been relieved to be at last living as a proper family with her husband in Germany. Lyuda became pregnant with Katya, the Putins' younger daughter. Vladimir put on 25 pounds (weighing 165 pounds in all) and started developing a small beer gut, which was the first time in his life he had ever been out of shape. Lyudmila was amazed that the streets were so clean and that the windows were washed weekly. The contrast with living in the USSR was painfully apparent. The Germans who worked with the tight-knit group of Russians in Dresden were better paid than their KGB counterparts and generally the standard of living in the GDR was higher than back home.

Vladimir Putin was one of a group of eight KGB officers based in Dresden, who were under the command of Colonel Lazar Matveyev. While Matveyev was responsible for his officers, his wife made sure she kept the other Russian KGB wives in order. Each wife was instructed to cook a hot lunch for their husband every day, and the whole group would go on regular outings together. Matveyev was a KGB veteran, who served thirty years on and off in Germany by the time he left in 1989. The Dresden KGB station worked on political intelligence and analysis, counter-intelligence and acquiring useful technical information. In practice, the Russian KGB agents often spent their days recruiting Stasi and East German policemen, and trying to engage or compromise foreign visitors to the city. The

KGB regularly bugged hotel rooms where foreigners stayed. The rooms were all wired so that any calls could be tapped.

One favourite ruse was the 'honeypot' trap, whereby a foreign businessman or visitor was compromised by being filmed in bed with a beautiful woman. Or several beautiful women. The KGB had caught out British diplomats in Moscow in the same way. One diplomat had been compromised after having an affair with a chambermaid. Sexual blackmail was often effective. Failing that, there were other forms of entrapment, or the KGB could try plain bribery and rely on personal greed. It had worked well with some of the USSR's best US agents, including Robert Hanssen of the FBI. Arrested in early 2001, the American counter-intelligence officer was paid $600,000 to betray his country. Some Western academics visiting Dresden or Leipzig University could be recruited on the basis of their far-left ideological leanings. However, there is little evidence that Putin himself worked on turning foreigners. With his fluent German, he generally stuck to easier East German 'targets', concentrating on people who were already working in the GDR's security apparatus. The Russians nicknamed the GDR security officers 'our friends'. His task was to ensure that they switched their primary loyalties from Communist East Germany to the KGB and the USSR. Since most of these men were already committed Communists, his task wasn't too demanding.

Vladimir Putin's official job in East Germany was as deputy director of the Society of German–Soviet Friendship based in Dresden and Leipzig, but as indicated one of his main roles was to develop ties between the secret police in the Stasi and their KGB counterparts. Through Operation Looch (sunbeam), the Soviet Union hoped to build a network of spies which could supply the USSR with intelligence even if the Communist regime in East Germany collapsed. Although Putin denies being part of Operation Looch, a statement contradicted by a KGB officer who worked with him in Dresden, he was certainly involved in agent recruitment. As he admitted in his autobiography, First Person, he was involved in all

the normal intelligence activities: 'recruiting sources of information, obtaining information, analysing it, and sending it to Moscow'.
Putin collected material on Western political parties and any information on the 'main opponent', or NATO. While in Dresden Putin
was well thought of and popular among his group, especially with
the older KGB officers, and his boss, Colonel Lazar Matveyev. Putin
appeared to be developing the ability to charm those around and
above him. Colleagues respected his hard work, tact and politeness.
He seemed happy in his work and not overly ambitious, spending
much of his little spare time reading Russian classics like Gogol's
Dead Souls, and works by Bulgakov and Saltykov-Schedrin.

Klaus Zuchold was a lieutenant in the Stasi when he was
recruited by Putin, formally joining the KGB on 16 January 1990. To
Zuchold's children, the KGB officer was remembered simply as
'Uncle Volodya'. Putin dictated Zuchold's letter of allegiance to the
KGB in the latter's Dresden flat, after giving his twelve-year-old
daughter Cindy a book of Russian fairy tales. The written formal
declaration of allegiance to the KGB was a quaint Soviet practice,
which also ensured that there could be no going back. If anyone had
second thoughts, the letter could be used to blackmail the KGB's
new recruit to stay on side. However, in Zuchold's case the 'letter of
allegiance' ploy didn't work. Less than a year later he defected to the
West, exposing a ring of fifteen agents working for Moscow.
Zuchold's defection seriously compromised Putin's network in East
Germany, which was wound-up as a result. Putin's supposedly 'soft'
Stasi targets had gone sour, partly as a result of the fall of the Berlin
Wall and the implosion of the GDR.

Klaus Zuchold's contacts with Putin give some interesting
insights into the KGB officer's character. 'He had a great admiration
for German culture and discipline,' Zuchold recalled. 'He was clearly
proud of belonging to the KGB. That was his life. He showed me his
wristwatch, which had an inscription from some KGB bigwig. He
loved patriotic stories of Russia's great past and popular heroes.'
Putin showed Zuchold a new stereo he had bought during a trip to

KaDeWe, an upmarket store in West Berlin. At the time, the shopping trip was as close as Putin got to working in the West. A respect for discipline and his strong patriotism reflected Putin's upbringing and his youthful idealism. Zuchold also revealed that Putin had a penchant for Jewish jokes, but in this regard he was no more anti-Semitic than the average Russian (who is generally pretty anti-Semitic). Putin also shared many conversations about history, literature and philosophy. Although he was getting better at the art of conversation, the talking tended to be one-sided. 'He'd perfected the hour-long conversation of letting the other person contribute maybe 80 per cent when he added only 20 per cent,' Zuchold said.

For some, such a flattering ability to listen attentively for hours on end proved just how good a conversationalist Putin was. Nevertheless, Zuchold found Putin a man of few words, inscrutable and largely 'impenetrable'. The Russian KGB intelligence officer gave the impression that he was very driven and determined, and always in control. 'Whenever we drank together he always made sure he was at least three glasses behind everyone else,' said his old German colleague, revealing that Putin was also a 'very good poker player'. Putin had been spotted on another occasion quietly tipping away a full glass of vodka. His reluctance to drink marked him out from other Russians, who often need no excuse to become blind drunk. Putin's capacity to stay sober and closely observe those around him was one of his strengths as a secret service officer. KGB officers are trained not to drink on the job, or at least to resist drinking heavily, so they can remember everything that was said in a given 'social' situation, and go away and write up their reports verbatim. As virtually teetotal by Russian standards, this part of the job came easily to him.

Whatever his problems in Germany, he never discussed them with his wife. Lyudmila says they didn't discuss work at home. 'There was always a principle at the KGB: do not share things with your wife. They told us that there had been incidents when excessive frankness had led to unfortunate consequences,' Lyudmila said.

'They always proceeded from the premise that the less the wife knew, the better she'd sleep. I socialized fairly often with the Germans, and if one of my acquaintances was undesirable, Volodya would let me know.' There were no sports facilities, and the hours were long, so Putin himself had relatively little time for socializing. Sometimes German or Russian friends would come round after work, and the Putin family would go picnicking in Saxony over the weekends. When they had guests, Vladimir's speciality was telling Russian anecdotes and jokes. Putin fitted in well, but was not a natural leader in company or in the office. Despite his natural abstemiousness and commitment to his work, he did like drinking the local German beer. It was so good, it was difficult for him to resist. He used to imbibe a three-litre keg of beer about once a week in the small town of Radeberg, which had one of the best breweries in East Germany. Starting to approach forty, putting on weight and knocking back the German beer, Putin seemed to be losing some of his former edge. He lived a comfortable, not too demanding life.

Putin's second daughter, Katya, was born in Dresden in August 1986, a year after Vladimir first arrived in the city. She learned to speak German before Russian. By early 1990, after over four years in the GDR, the family was packing up to return to Leningrad. Putin admitted to his friends that the period after the fall of the Berlin Wall had been stressful. Although he could see that the whole East German Communist system was rotten, he didn't anticipate how quickly the Berlin Wall and the GDR would fall apart. In fact, he was deeply shocked and scarred by the whole experience. 'It was hard to imagine that such abrupt changes could take hold in the GDR. No one could have ever imagined it! And we didn't know how it would end,' Putin remarked of those fateful days. His sense of bewilderment was shared by his wife, who said years later, 'Four years passed, and in four years a foreign country and a foreign city can become almost like your own. When the Berlin Wall fell and it was clear this was the end, we had the horrible feeling that the country that had almost become our home would no longer exist.'

For Putin and his KGB colleagues, the precipitate collapse of the Wall and all it stood for caught them totally unprepared. No one had predicted it. Putin destroyed all his secret communication equipment, his lists of contacts and confidential files. He walked around for days with secret papers hidden inside his clothes. The KGB station was burning so much paper that the furnace over-heated and blew up. Some top-secret material was sent back to Moscow. Putin watched angry crowds break into the local offices of the Ministry of Security (MGB). The mob next moved on to the KGB's compound. The Russian intelligence officers armed them-selves and prepared to defend their building. Putin went outside and calmed the crowd, claiming he was a German translator, and that the KGB office was in fact a Soviet military facility. The crowd's mood looked ugly, but Putin's protestations of innocence did the trick for a while. In the meantime the besieged KGB agents con-tacted the local Soviet garrison. Putin was shocked to be told: 'We cannot do anything without orders from Moscow. And Moscow is silent.' For the first time in his life, Putin felt abandoned by the Motherland. He instinctively felt this was the beginning of the end, not just for the GDR but also for the Soviet Union as he had known it. 'I got the feeling that the country no longer existed. That it had disappeared,' he said. Eventually, the Soviet garrison sent some vehi-cles filled with paratroopers to the KGB compound, and the mob dispersed. But Putin's sense of disillusion stayed with him.

Lyudmila saw the immediate effect on her friends in the German secret services. She recollected: 'I saw what happened to my neighbours when all those revolutionary events started in the GDR. My neighbour, who was my friend, cried for a week. She cried for her lost ideals, for the collapse of everything that she had believed in her whole life. For them, it was the collapse of everything – their lives, their careers. They were all left without jobs. There was a ban on their profession.'

The Putins had glimpsed the future of the USSR itself, although they were not yet ready to acknowledge that the old life was over. Vladimir's main regret at the time was that the Soviet Union had lost its position in Europe. Talking to Henry Kissinger years later, Putin agreed with Kissinger's analysis that the Soviet Union should not have abandoned Eastern Europe so quickly. The former US Secretary of State found Gorbachev's hasty retreat from Eastern Europe inexplicable. 'Kissinger was right,' Putin believed. 'We would have avoided a lot of problems if the Soviets had not made such a hasty exit from Eastern Europe.' However, as the Putin family started to head back to Leningrad, even worse was to come. The entire Soviet Empire was about to unravel in record time, leading to the disintegration of the USSR.

Returning home to Leningrad in January 1990 seemed a mixed blessing for the Putin family. Coming back to the USSR after four and a half years was six months short of the usual five-year GDR posting. The fall of the Berlin Wall and its aftermath were largely to blame for the Putins' early return. In career terms, Putin's stint in East Germany had gone quite well. While there, he had been promoted twice, which was unusual and a sign of some success. He arrived as a senior case officer and major, and was promoted to assistant to the department head (and lieutenant colonel) in 1987, and again two years later to the post of senior assistant. He was effectively number two to Colonel Matveyev in Dresden, and his next promotion would have been to the rank of full colonel. In some ways he was promoted because of his good relationship with Matveyev. Also, his promotion was partly due to the appraisal system operated by the KGB. Promotion to the next rank was based on the volume of information passed on up the chain of command. Providing Putin worked hard and produced a sufficient amount of intelligence information from his sources and agents, he was practically guaranteed promotion. Some KGB officers abused the system by reproducing material from academic or public sources and passing it off as secret intelligence. They knew that their bosses in Moscow Centre rarely double-checked the source of the information. A chat with a journalist or politician could also be presented as incisive intelligence work, which sometimes led to examples of unwitting individuals on the diplomatic cocktail circuit being cited as 'agents of influence' by the KGB.

In any event, the general principle applied by KGB agents was that for personal advancement, volume counted for more than quality. Putin exploited the KGB evaluation system, and did well as a result. But by the time he returned to Leningrad, his career as a foreign intelligence officer seemed in the doldrums. Hundreds of thousands of military and KGB officers were coming home to the USSR as the outposts of the Soviet Empire were scaled down or abandoned one by one. After the GDR came Czechoslovakia, Hungary, Poland, Bulgaria, Romania and the rest of Eastern Europe. The USSR had withdrawn at last from Afghanistan, and was reducing its presence in Africa, Cuba, Mongolia, Vietnam and the Far East. In effect, Putin didn't have a job to come home to, and he was placed in the 'active reserves'. There was some talk of him going to the KGB's Moscow Centre and getting a job there, but nothing came of it. Putin also knew that if he were to go off to Moscow he wouldn't have been provided with a flat, or had any relatives to stay with. More importantly, all his friends and contacts were in Leningrad, and in Russia it was usually your friends who helped to fix you up with a job. Staying in Leningrad meant that at least he would have somewhere to live, and some friends to help him make his next career move.

Putin and his family thus moved in once more with his parents, which was uncomfortable for everyone concerned. Lyudmila had had her own small place even while Vladimir was away training in Moscow, and was reluctant to move back in with her in-laws. They now had two young girls, and all of them lived together in the one flat. The family had no choice for the time being. With the end of his service in East Germany, Putin had lost his KGB flat. They did not provide him with another in Leningrad, nor were they ever likely to. One small consolation was that Putin's parents had been allocated a new three-roomed flat on Sredneokhtinsky Prospect, near the Okhta river in the east of the city. Once again, Putin's father's status as a Second World War invalid veteran helped the family get a better flat. They now had an extra room for the two girls. But overall, it was not an ideal situation. Putin had time on his hands for the first time in years, and spent hours tinkering with his Volga car. The Volga and a twenty-year-old, second-hand washing machine were all the Putins had to show for their four and a half years in Dresden. All their savings had gone on buying the car.

Finally, Putin took up an administrative post as vice-rector at Leningrad University, responsible for international liaison and looking after foreign students, and started preparing a doctoral dissertation. The post was a traditional KGB foreign intelligence job, which was earmarked for a member of the secret services. The KGB had their people planted throughout Soviet civil and security structures, and this was a post that was always held by a member of the KGB. The KGB's vice-rector could use the post to keep an eye on goings-on in the university, and report back on any interesting foreign contacts. In Putin's own words, he went 'undercover' at the university. Describing his role as undercover is perhaps imbuing the job with more mystery than it really warranted. Many of the university's staff would know he came from the KGB. At the same time he stayed on the KGB's payroll, although by now his salary was falling into arrears, something millions of Russians were starting to experience. With so much free time, Putin also offered to be a voluntary chauffeur for Galina Starovoitova, one of Leningrad's leading reformist politicians. Up to that point, he had shown no interest in the USSR's democratic movement. His role as a chauffeur ironically mirrored the career of the Russian secret agent in the film *The Sword and the Shield*, so idolized by Putin as a boy. Tragically, Starovoitova was murdered years later in the stairwell of her flat in central St Petersburg near the Moika river, around the time she was gathering a dossier on corruption in the city. Her assassin or assassins are still unknown. As head of the Federal Security Service (FSB) at the time, the KGB's domestic successor, Vladimir Putin was responsible for ordering the investigation into her death.

Things were not looking particularly rosy for Putin as he faced the future with only a university sinecure and his intelligence career drifting into uncertain waters. He was thirty-eight, with a wife and two children but no obvious sense of direction. In Lyudmila's words, Putin 'felt that he had lost touch with his life's real purpose'. It seemed that the KGB's Moscow Centre and even Leningrad's 'Big House' had lost interest in its former foreign intelligence officer. In the normal run of things, after nine months or so at home, a successful KGB agent would be expected to be sent abroad for another tour of duty of three to five years, depending on the country and the post. In Putin's case, there was no suggestion that he could expect another imminent foreign residency. After the chaos of the fall of the Berlin Wall and the retreat from the East, Putin had no chance of being one of the few well-connected or brilliant agents who managed to find themselves a juicy foreign posting.

Putin didn't even try. He saw that for KGB officers like him, the future looked grim. No one at the centre seemed to care any more, as the old spy networks in Eastern Europe and elsewhere were wound up or abandoned. He briefly toyed with the idea of teaching or starting a law practice. Many of his KGB colleagues went into 'business', but according to Oleg Blotsky's biography, he felt that with his security/military background, business was not for him. Foreign intelligence officers were meant to have high moral standards, and Putin would have felt uncomfortable in Russia's brash commercial environment: 'It was quite difficult in those days to do business within the parameters of the law,' he said in his usual understated manner. His only option now seemed to be to hold on to his university job, and wait for his pension. To help the family budget, Putin helped Lyudmila get a job at the university teaching German, a job for which she was technically unqualified. Although she spoke the language well, her grammar was weak. Nonetheless, after a break of many years, Lyudmila was glad to be back doing an interesting job. It was better than picking peaches in East Germany, although that job had had its moments.

For once *blat*, or Russia's traditional cronyism, worked in Vladimir's favour. In May 1990, following the city's first ever set of free elections, the deputies of Leningrad's city council (*Lensovet*) elected the reformist politician Anatoly Sobchak as their chairman. A year later he was elected mayor of Leningrad in a citywide poll. Sobchak was a former law lecturer at Leningrad State University, and Vladimir Putin had been one of his students. One of Putin's university friends said Sobchak was looking for administrative staff and recommended him to the city leader. The two men met at the Marinsky Palace (where the city assembly was based), and Putin told his potential new boss straight away he was still officially a KGB staff officer; correctly assuming Sobchak would be impressed with his new recruit's honesty. Sobchak expected many of those around him to have security service backgrounds; at least with Putin he knew where he stood. KGB contacts could always be useful for the city leader's office, and sometimes they were invaluable. At the same time as coming clean with Sobchak, Putin also cleared his appointment with his KGB superiors. Unsurprisingly, they didn't object. The KGB probably calculated they could turn his close proximity to the mayor to their own advantage.

According to Putin the KGB did approach him to compromise Sobchak, but he rebuffed the attempt. At the same time he continued to receive his KGB salary, which was higher than the salary paid by Leningrad City Hall. Some politicians accused him of being a KGB plant to his face, while other businessmen pressed him for favours while trying to blackmail him over working for the secret services. He countered by admitting his past, even going on local TV to say he had worked for the KGB as a foreign intelligence officer. Sobchak publicly defended him as a *former* KGB intelligence officer, but glossed over the fact that he was still a *serving* secret service agent, even if he was technically in the 'active reserves'. Around this time Putin also claimed to send his first resignation letter to the

KGB, although it wasn't technically possible to 'resign' from the secret services in the Soviet Union. Nevertheless, his public 'outing' as a former KGB agent and his display of frankness successfully disarmed his opponents.

During the hardline coup against President Mikhail Gorbachev in August 1991, Putin was on holiday in the Kaliningrad region. In his own words he was 'still an active KGB officer' because his resignation letter had got 'stalled somewhere'. In fact, there was no evidence he had as yet quit the KGB. The attempted putsch set off widespread political protests in what was then still called Leningrad, and the City Duma (or council) hastily established a defence headquarters. 'Putin never came near,' said Alexander Vinnikov, an elected city deputy. 'His role was absolutely zero. He says now that was when he quit the KGB, but that's pure propaganda. Besides, you can't quit.' Recalled to Leningrad by Sobchak, Putin maintained a low profile. In his finest hour, Boris Yeltsin showed his mettle by standing atop a tank at the height of the attempted putsch outside the White House in Moscow, home of the State Duma, or lower house of parliament. Shielded from snipers by a hand-held bulletproof vest, Yeltsin's stand was undoubtedly courageous and perilous. As usual, Yeltsin's initiative was also histrionic since his tank escapade shamelessly emulated Lenin's famous speech on his return from exile in 1917 from on top of an armoured car, parked outside Leningrad's Finland Railway Station. The difference was that Lenin was to lead a putsch; Yeltsin sought to stop one.

Putin claims he finally left the KGB only when it became clear that the plot to overthrow Gorbachev had failed. But even after the attempted coup, Putin remained an officer in the KGB's reserve. When he was appointed FSB Director some years later, he proudly told President Boris Yeltsin he was still a lieutenant-colonel in the Federal Security Service's reserve. Legally, it was dubious that any KGB officer had the right to quit the secret service – in Soviet times anyway. In the Soviet era, once you were a member of the KGB, you were a member for life. It was a bit like the 1960s TV cult classic

The Prisoner with Patrick McGoohan; once in the KGB, there was no escape. Nor is there any evidence that Putin resisted or resented being placed in the KGB's reserve. In his autobiography, *First Person*, he did say that the attempted coup changed his outlook. 'All the ideals and aims I had when I went to work for the KGB collapsed in the days following the putsch,' he remarked. It was a bit like his Dresden experience all over again, although a hundred times worse. Now it was the USSR and his beloved KGB that was falling apart. 'Look what happened to the Soviet Union,' he later exclaimed. 'Who could have imagined that it would simply collapse? No one saw that coming – even in their worst nightmares.' Putin was quite open about maintaining good relations with the KGB boss and coup leader General Vladimir Kryuchkov, whom he later told journalists was 'a convinced Communist who thought everything the plotters were doing was right. He was a very decent chap for whom I still have a lot of respect.' The fact is that Putin still had more in common with the plotters than the democratic movement which marshalled its forces to prevent the coup. According to him, the plotters' aims were 'noble' since they sought to prevent the disintegration of the USSR, which he also personally bitterly regretted. At the same time, he thought Gorbachev had been guilty of carrying out a policy of 'unilateral disarmament'. Putin only questioned the means the plotters had chosen, which had the unfortunate result of hastening the very collapse they had sought to avoid.

Looking back at the coup attempt, he admits he was uneasy about the direction of the democratic movement at the time. 'I was from the democrats' milieu. But it got worrying. Remember what kind of situation the security organs were in then. [The democrats] wanted to destroy, to break, to lacerate them, they called for the agency's lists to be opened up, for the secrets to be revealed.' At heart, there can be no doubt that he remained a KGB man. But he also watched the way the wind was blowing, and could sense the Soviet system had no future even if he was taken aback by the pace of its decomposition. The attempted putsch put him in an awkward position. Did he follow his nominal KGB masters, or his new bosses in Leningrad City Hall?

In keeping his head down but sticking with Mayor Sobchak, he was clearly taking a risk. If KGB General Kryuchkov had come to power, he might have found it very difficult to explain why he didn't come out openly in support of the coup leaders and their State Committee on the Emergency Situation. While he could try to convince the KGB that he had been their man in City Hall all along, it was also very possible they wouldn't believe him. He admits his dilemma was acute. 'I believed that for moral reasons, I couldn't fulfil any orders against the authority I was part of.' But he also realized the personal consequences could be dire: 'I thought then, if the coup plotters triumph and they don't put me behind bars, how am I going to feed the family?' Oleg Blotsky's biography quotes him as saying. Putin knew that if the plotters succeeded, he might at best become unemployable. 'Honestly speaking,' he added, 'I thought about becoming a taxi driver.' He could have used the Volga he brought back from East Germany as an unofficial 'black taxi'. Thousands of Russian men use their private cars as unlicensed taxis, roaming the streets waiting to be flagged down by potential customers. Some are moonlighting from other jobs, others do it for extra cash or because they have no alternative. As in the West, taxi driving in Russia is the last refuge for the middle-aged man whose career has run out of steam.

Putin felt a sense of real loss but also a certain finality on the ultimate demise of the USSR. 'You would need to be heartless not to regret the disintegration of the Soviet Union. You'd need to be brainless to want to restore it,' he would say years later. It was time to move on, albeit with a heavy heart. When it was clear that the coup had failed and there was no future for the USSR, Putin believed he had little option but to quit his post as a serving KGB secret intelligence agent. He sent in another resignation letter, standing down as an 'active' KGB officer. By that time, the KGB was in chaos and probably no one in the KGB cared whether Putin resigned or not. His decision to leave the active ranks of the KGB, while still staying in the secret service's reserve, was undoubtedly one of the hardest of his life. In a sense, the KGB had left him. It had no career left to offer him, and he didn't have the necessary connections to salvage something from the wreckage of what was left of the intelligence agency. As a member of the reserve, Putin would normally only be recalled to active service in the event of a state of emergency or war. When he became a member of the KGB, it was also obligatory to be a full member of the Communist Party. In classic Putin style, he kept his options open by retaining his Communist Party membership until the party was banned by President Yeltsin in November 1992.

Working with Anatoly Sobchak in his new job, Putin was always standing so close to the mayor at public meetings that he was often mistaken for a bodyguard or interpreter. He learned early to stick close to his boss, almost literally hanging on to his political coat-tails. He would later describe Sobchak as his friend and mentor, although in the early years the relationship was less equal. Putin's office was in Smolny, the same beautiful early nineteenth-century classical building next to the Neva river where his naval uncle had been based during the war. The building, once Lenin's HQ and residence, now housed the city's administrative headquarters. Installed in his new office, Putin hung a portrait of Peter the Great on the wall where previously there had been pictures of Lenin and Kirov. Tsar Peter, the autocratic reformer, was now more to his taste. Between his appointment in June 1990 and the following May, Putin worked as Sobchak's adviser. He took an active part in the mayoral campaign of June 1991, and by his own account was instrumental in getting the new elective post of mayor passed by the city council. Since Sobchak was at the height of his popularity (despite the city's difficulties), the election was a pushover. Shortly after Sobchak was elected mayor, Putin was appointed chairman of the city's new foreign relations committee, and one of three deputies to the mayor. Three years later, he was appointed first deputy mayor and effectively Sobchak's second-in-command, whilst keeping his chairmanship of the foreign relations committee. Being deputy mayor was an unelected position, which reflected Putin's role as a competent technocrat rather than a politician. Keeping his job depended on the grace and favour of the mayor.

He seemed to be the perennial deputy. He had been deputy KGB chief of station in Dresden, university deputy or vice-rector and now deputy mayor. However, being a deputy suited his style and temperament. He wasn't a good orator like Sobchak, and didn't share his boss's enjoyment of the endless receptions that went with the post of mayor (neither, incidentally, did Lyudmila). Nor was he used to leading from the front; he preferred staying in the background. Mayor Sobchak and his wife, Lyudmila Borisovna, were the public face of the city administration, and Putin just got on with the day-to-day work. Vladimir continually had to assuage the elected city council deputies, who found the mayor difficult and autocratic. Sobchak – impulsive, argumentative and mercurial – couldn't be bothered with the day-to-day drudgery of city administration. He had Putin and others to carry that load for him. Once Sobchak enraged the Leningrad military district heads by skipping a meeting to greet the famous Russian singer Alla Pugacheva at St Petersburg airport. He preferred attending her concert to another boring meeting with Russian generals.

Vladimir Putin felt he virtually ran the city as the flamboyant Sobchak wooed Western politicians, and was feted in return as a leading democratic reformer. Sometimes the two went on foreign trips together, and Putin acted as Sobchak's adviser and interpreter on his frequent visits to Germany. Meanwhile, Putin had done well as head of the city's foreign relations committee, opening branches of the Dresdner and Banque Nationale de Paris in the city, attracting Coca-Cola and Gillette, and completing a fibre-optic cable link to Copenhagen. It remains the city's most successful period for attracting major Western investment. 'The entire system of government for this city of five million had to be built from scratch in the early

1990s. It's the system we still have and was created by Sobchak and Putin,' said Yury Novolodsky, a St Petersburg lawyer who studied with Putin for four years and served with him in city hall. Putin consolidated his reputation as a competent technocrat. He felt he was doing a very important job, and saw himself as the second most important person in St Petersburg. If Sobchak had won re-election in 1996 and subsequently, Putin would almost certainly have stayed on as his deputy, and would probably be in the same job today. He liked his role enormously, even if it did involve him working from early in the morning to late at night.

Many rumours have circulated about the extent of corruption in Anatoly Sobchak's administration. Inevitably, Putin was linked to some of the stories implicating him, but none have been substantiated. Sobchak himself came under criminal investigation for allegedly buying an apartment with city funds, and procuring other desirable state-owned flats for his relatives. His wife, Lyudmila Borisovna, was prominent in St Petersburg business circles and was known to offer 'introductions' to the right people, which raised eyebrows amongst the Western diplomatic corps. Even Boris Yeltsin, notoriously reticent to identify corruption, said, 'Of course not everyone in his [Sobchak's] entourage was clean.' Some reports alleged that Putin himself had made money from the sale and privatization of the 11th St Petersburg TV channel to the 'Russian Video' channel and company, but this remains highly tendentious hearsay. Putin does acknowledge, however, that he was involved in regulating the city's casinos (with the city maintaining a 'golden share' of their businesses), which in the early 1990s was tantamount to working hand-in-hand with the mafia.

Around this time he once conducted a 'fact finding' visit to Hamburg's Red Light district. If nothing else, managing St Petersburg's gambling dens put Putin in a seriously vulnerable position. The city had already established the reputation of being the 'crime capital' of Russia, and contract killings of 'businessmen' or officials were almost a weekly occurrence. Misha Manevich, one of

Putin's friends and colleagues and also a deputy mayor, was shot in his car by persons unknown while working for Sobchak's successor, Vladimir Yakovlev. Years after Putin had moved on, St Petersburg legislative assembly deputy speaker Victor Novoselov had his head blown off when a bomb was placed on his car at some traffic lights. It was always the same when an individual had influence over business and financial matters in St Petersburg. A financially important decision could end up upsetting dangerous people. The spate of contract killings seemed endless. It's not surprising that by the end of his term as deputy mayor in St Petersburg, Putin had taken to sleeping next to an air gun. He knew it offered precious little protection, but it helped him sleep better at nights.

Another dubious enterprise which the city administration and Putin became involved in was a deal with businesses to support the export of raw materials in return for food supplies for St Petersburg. In the desperate circumstances of 1991, when food supplies were drying up in the city as the USSR's command economy imploded, it seemed like a reasonably good idea. Putin said in a TV interview years later: 'It was the most difficult time, because all the economic ties of the former Soviet Union had collapsed, and nothing was running. The five-million-strong city was on the brink of a catastrophe. We even had to open the strategic reserves of canned food.' I remember visiting Gostiny Dvor, one of the city's major department stores on Nevsky Prospect in the spring of 1991, and there were endless lines of *babushkas* but virtually nothing to buy. People queued for hours in the hope of buying something, anything, in order to barter or re-sell it later on. It was not quite as bad as the blockade, but the empty shops and long lines at Gostiny Dvor were symptomatic of a city near the edge. Perhaps predictably, in the chaotic conditions of 1991, the companies largely reneged on their side of the bargain and walked away considerably richer. Although the city wasn't responsible for issuing the final export licences, the scope for corruption was obvious.

Undoubtedly, given the times and his position involving

foreign investment, casinos and local businesses, Putin could have made millions of dollars for himself. Yet in none of these cases has there appeared any evidence that he personally enriched himself. Ten or so years on, there is still no 'smoking gun', which would seem to indicate that the rumours were unfounded. Putin's reputation as deputy mayor in Western diplomatic and business circles was as an efficient, competent and honest operator. This was at a time when many other city hall officials were demanding a cut from any business deal involving Westerners, or Russians for that matter. Many other corrupt Russian officials and senior politicians, otherwise skilful in covering their tracks, have not been able to keep their personal reputations intact. So far Putin has. He prides himself on his probity, patriotism and integrity. Besides, as a top city official, there were many other perks of the job, which would mean that it wasn't necessary to compromise himself by accepting wads of hard currency stuffed in brown envelopes.

A couple of stories during Vladimir Putin's period in St Petersburg's city administration give an insight into his character. Sometimes it seemed that Putin's feelings deserted him completely, leaving a vacuum where his humanity and empathy should have been. The most appalling events could seemingly wash over him, even those close to home, leaving him apparently unmoved. His secretary, Marina Yentaltseva, who worked with him from 1991 to 1996, described an incident which puzzled and disturbed her. Lyudmila rang from the dacha to say their pet Caucasian sheepdog, Malysh, had been run over and killed by a car. Marina told Putin the bad news, expecting he would be upset. 'I looked at him, and there was zero emotion on his face. I was so surprised at the lack of any kind of reaction that I couldn't contain myself and said, "Did someone tell you about it?" And he said calmly, "No, you're the first to tell me." And I knew I had made a blunder.' A similar lack of any public display of empathy or humanity deepened Putin's first major crisis as president in August 2000, when the *Kursk* nuclear submarine sank with the loss of all 118 crew.

The second story concerns Lyudmila and a serious car crash in St Petersburg in October 1993. Things had started looking up for the Putins. The couple had purchased a new Lada, a Zhiguli, and were refurbishing a flat on Vasilevsky island, which was just across the Neva from the Winter Palace. Although only 63 square metres, it would be their first wholly-owned flat in St Petersburg, and the refurbishment was taking some time and a lot of money. In the meantime, the Putins were staying in a smart, official, city-owned dacha in fashionable Zelenogorsk, outside the city and near the Gulf of Finland. Vladimir's parents still had the flat on Sredneokhtinsky Prospect. The area around Zelenogorsk was surrounded by exclusive dachas and the city's elite. Lyudmila was taking seven-year-old Katya to school in the city when her car was struck side-on by another, which had jumped a red light. While Katya was taken to Smolny by one of Putin's assistants, Lyudmila was taken conscious but sedated to the city's October 25th Hospital. It was a dreadful place, full of dying people and dead bodies in the corridors.

The memory of the hospital still fills Lyudmila with a sense of horror. It was a typical emergency hospital of the time, barely functioning because of the horrendous cuts in the health service. A stay in one of these hospitals was often tantamount to a death sentence. Life was cheap, and treatment was expensive. Lyudmila was left naked in a freezing operation room. Staff at the October 25th Hospital said that she didn't need anything, and just sewed up her ear and left her where she lay. Despite phoning and checking with the hospital, Putin's staff were left unaware of Lyudmila's true condition. When Vladimir eventually got away from one of his meetings, the hospital staff told him she was all right and recovering from her ordeal, so he left without seeing her. Putin stayed in a series of meetings with Ted Turner and Jane Fonda all day discussing the holding of the Goodwill Games. But he did ask for his staff to arrange for Lyudmila to be transferred to St Petersburg's elite Military Medical Academy, which managed to maintain excellent standards of treatment and care. The Military Medical Academy staff discovered that in fact Lyudmila had a crack in her spine and a fracture at the base of her skull. Lyudmila has no doubt that the hospital transfer saved her life. 'I realize now that the doctors had great doubts about whether I was going to survive. I was lucky to make it out in one piece,' she recalled.

Putin at last visited Lyudmila in intensive care at the Medical Academy, but after a short while he left, saying that he would try to come back later, but probably wouldn't make it because his meetings would be going on late into the night. From then on, Putin and the two girls (who were looked after by Lyudmila's mother, Ykaterina Tikhonova) visited Lyuda regularly in hospital. Lyudmila was in hospital for over a month, and took almost three years to fully recover from the accident and the operations on her spine and skull.

Did Putin act appropriately in this domestic crisis, or did he again display a certain lack of human empathy? It comes down to a matter of personal judgement. He did check on his wife's condition several times, and made sure his staff did the same. Crucially, he arranged her transfer to a decent hospital, under the care of the highly skilled Dr Leonidovich Shevchenko, who perhaps not coincidentally became Russia's Health Minister under Putin. Others would criticize Putin for not breaking off from his meetings completely, to be by his wife's bedside. Many politicians and senior figures might have done the same (Prince Charles was criticized for attending the opera when one of his children was seriously ill), but the incident does leave a question mark over Putin's natural sense of humanity in a crisis. The ability to display empathy and humanity is something which often marks out a statesman from the average politician, witness Bill Clinton's empathic skills and Tony Blair's identification of Princess Diana as the 'People's Princess' on the day of her untimely death. On the other hand, President George W. Bush's disappearance on 9/11 and flight to a US air base in Nevada jarred badly with New York Mayor Rudolph Giuliani's more humane and dynamic response to the Twin Towers tragedy.

Putin ran Sobchak's re-election campaign in 1996, but Sobchak

lost to Vladimir Yakovlev, who under the new system became governor of St Petersburg. Putin never forgave Yakovlev (who also
worked in the city administration) for standing against Sobchak,
calling him a 'Judas' on TV. The main charge against Yakovlev
seemed to be that as one of Sobchak's own deputy mayors, he should
not have had the temerity to challenge his increasingly unpopular
incumbent boss. Perhaps more woundingly for Putin, Yakovlev was
responsible for removing him from a very good job, which he loved.
The two men would clash again later, when Yakovlev supported the
rival Fatherland Party in the run-up to Putin's election as president.
Putin's reaction to Yakovlev's victory over Sobchak shows two further interesting facets of his character. First, he does not have a
traditional, Western concept of democracy. Legitimate political
opponents standing for elective office are not usually publicly
denounced as 'traitors' in the West, whatever the personal circumstances. Putin rather loosely applies the term 'traitor' to anyone who
threatens the state's stability or his immediate political interests.
This becomes a recurring theme in his early Kremlin career.
Western-style democracy, which frequently ousts the party of power,
is anathema to him. Second, Putin does not forgive or forget those
who have crossed him, although he tends to favour neutralizing his
political opponents rather than grinding them into the dirt. This
characteristic was noticeable even when he was a teenager. His
teacher in school, Vera Dmitrievna Gurevich, said of him: 'I think
Volodya is a good person. But he never forgives people who betray
him or are mean to him.'

The flip side of Putin's character is that he resolutely turns a
blind eye to his friends' weaknesses. He would put it differently; he
is intensely loyal to his friends, and sticks by them no matter what.
By 1996 Anatoly Sobchak's administration was mired in allegations
of corruption and criminality. The Tambov mafia, one of the country's most notorious and powerful organized crime groups, was
rampant in the city. The mafia were recruiting army officer cadets
with martial arts training direct from St Petersburg's military

academies. The infrastructure of the city had continued to deterio-
rate, despite Putin's success in attracting foreign investment.
Changing the name back from Leningrad to St Petersburg after a
1991 referendum had done little to arrest the city's relative decline.
Most elderly people still called it Leningrad; it was mainly the young
who had voted to dissociate the city from its Communist past.
Meanwhile, St Petersburg's imperial façades continued to rot, while
domestic investment flooded into Mayor Luzhkov's Moscow. The
people of St Petersburg became tired of Sobchak's endless democratic rhetoric, and dumped him as mayor. Sobchak lost by 2 per
cent. The shocking thing for Putin was that contrary to his later
protestations, he did not see defeat coming. Sobchak decided to
run the campaign with his own team of advisers and his wife, and
he and his people were too complacent. Putin was in charge of
Sobchak's campaign HQ, but spent much of his time preparing his
candidate's doctoral dissertation at the Gorny (Mining) Institute in
St Petersburg. His thesis was on the region's economic problems,
but the fact that he was doing it at all a month before the poll
showed his lack of campaign experience and casual attitude to the
elections.

The date of the poll had been brought forward by a month to
wrong-foot Sobchak's opponents, supposedly not giving them
enough time to organize themselves. The mayor attempted to
monopolize the local media and prevent his opponents from getting
any coverage. The move backfired. When Putin finally realized that
Sobchak could actually lose May's election, it was already too late.
He and Alexei Kudrin, another deputy mayor who was to join
Putin's future government, tried desperately to turn the campaign
around in its last weeks. But as anyone who knows anything about
elections will tell you, an election is usually decided months if not
years before the final poll. Putin simply didn't have any experience of
the party in power losing; at the outset of the campaign he probably
didn't think it was even possible. He had, after all, been brought up
in the old Soviet system of pre-determined elections. Things were

going so well in his life he just didn't contemplate defeat. His experience in running and losing Sobchak's 1996 campaign taught him that democracy could have unintended unpleasant results. Elections could be lost and everybody could lose their jobs. He was determined to avoid such unpleasantness in the future. After losing the election, Sobchak himself fled the continuing criminal investigations and went into self-imposed exile in Paris, aided by his former pupil, Vladimir Putin.

Looking back at the election, Putin tried to say Sobchak had been unfairly robbed of victory. He had been 'betrayed' by Yakovlev, who had been backed by 'dark forces' in Moscow, like Yeltsin's shady bodyguard General Alexander Korzhakov, and the hard-line deputy premier Oleg Soskovets. The security services, prosecutor's office and the Interior Ministry were ganging up to blacken Sobchak's name, linking him to criminal investigations. Leaflets exposing Sobchak's supposed criminality and corruption were dropped on the city from the air. It was all an unfair crusade to remove a democratic liberal reformer from Russia's second city. Maybe. But the fact remained that Sobchak's administration failed because of poor leadership from the top, ramshackle infrastructure, the widespread perception of corruption and criminality, and an inability to improve the standard of living of the average citizen. For any politician, these are 'bread and butter' issues. Sobchak's failure wasn't as a democrat or an orator, it was as a city manager.

The relationship between Putin and Sobchak was one of mutual admiration. Putin insisted, almost right up to Sobchak's death in February 2000, that he was 'a decent man with a flawless reputation'. On another occasion, he told Russian television, 'I always had very warm feelings towards him and respected him greatly.' In December 1999, Anatoly Sobchak was seeking election and political rehabilitation as a member of the Russian Duma. He was addressing public meetings with his usual panache and living in a very expensive flat on the Moika river, in the city centre. It was unclear where and how he had amassed his obvious personal wealth. With his protégé now acting-president, Sobchak found it safe to return to St Petersburg, knowing that the corruption charges against him would not be pursued. He was clearly proud of his association with Putin, and supported the latter's initiative to launch a second war in Chechnya. He considered Putin a man of integrity, and backed his bid for the presidency. Putin in turn liked to reminisce about their foreign trips together, when they would sometimes be left virtually alone for several days. In a way, Sobchak was Putin's first real political mentor and supporter. Before meeting Sobchak, Putin had struggled through life without a guiding patron. It had sometimes been a lonely and difficult struggle.

When Sobchak lost the election to Yakovlev, Putin once more found himself out of a job. These were some of Putin's hardest times, and he was filled with self-doubt and worry. Earlier in the campaign, Yakovlev had offered him the chance to stay in his old job and join the new regime. Putin disdainfully rejected the offer, and organized a statement by Sobchak's staff saying that they would all leave Smolny if their boss lost. It was perhaps a rash move, but Putin insists that his sense of loyalty prevented him from deserting Sobchak at his time of need. After the election, Putin clung on to his office in Smolny, under the guise of working with Boris Yeltsin's presidential campaign headquarters in St Petersburg. When that election ended with Yeltsin's re-election, Putin was none too subtly told it was time to leave his office. But before he went, he received a call from Pavel Borodin, who headed the General Affairs Department in the Kremlin. Borodin suggested Putin might be able to get a job in the presidential administration in Moscow, under Nikolai Yegorov, the former governor of Krasnodar. In a way, Borodin's telephone call was strange. He didn't know Putin very well, and didn't owe him any favours. It is almost certain that Borodin's call came because Yakovlev wanted to remove Putin from Smolny, and preferably St Petersburg. The new governor wasn't keen on having Sobchak's former deputy hanging around making a nuisance of himself. It was a classic case of kicking someone upstairs. Governor Yakovlev was close to the Yeltsin family (unlike Sobchak), and proud that Naina Yeltsina, the president's wife, was godmother to one of his grandchildren. Yakovlev clearly had the influence to get Putin offered a job in Moscow. After Borodin's phone call, Putin rushed off to Moscow to meet Nikolai Yegorov, who offered Putin a job as deputy head of the presidential administration, and everything seemed to be going well. But a few days later, Yegorov was replaced as head of the presidential administration by Anatoly Chubais, and there was no news for about two months. Putin didn't hear anything more about his promised Moscow job.

As Putin waited to hear from Moscow, the family moved out to a dacha they had been building for over five years, sixty miles outside the city. Disaster struck when the family *banya* or sauna caught fire and burnt the house down. As could only happen in Russia, fire engines came three times but didn't have a hose to put out the fire. The dacha sat right next to a lake, and slowly burnt to the ground. Putin, his family and some friends safely evacuated the house, but Vladimir decided to re-enter the building to save some money stashed behind a bed head. Like most Russians, the former deputy mayor of St Petersburg didn't trust banks, and had his life's savings hidden in dollars in a briefcase in his bedroom. There was about $5,000 dollars in cash, and together with the family car, dacha and flat in St Petersburg, this comprised the Putins' total wealth. When the thickening smoke threatened to overcome Putin, he decided the cash wasn't worth dying for, and escaped over a balcony.

The scene was desperate but comic. Putin lowered himself from the balcony wrapped in a sheet from the *banya*, which billowed in the wind as concerned and curious neighbours watched. As the sheet flapped about, the future president's naked body was exposed to the crowd thronging below, who were evidently engrossed in the whole drama. It was not a dignified spectacle, and as Putin and his family stood by and watched their house burn down, he must have wondered if things that summer could possibly get any worse. He had lost his job, and now the house they had spent six years building and waiting for. It was an expensive double whammy. The expected Moscow job offer had not materialized, and no one else seemed to be queuing up to offer him a job. Putin worried about his future, and the future for his wife and children.

The fire at the dacha was also memorable for Putin for another reason. Before going into the sauna, he had taken off the aluminium cross that his mother had given him, and which he had taken to be blessed at the Lord's Tomb on a 1993 visit to Israel. It was the very cross with which he had been baptized at the Cathedral of the Transfiguration, over forty years before. After the ferocious fire, Putin was amazed when the cross was found intact in a pile of ashes. Displaying a mixture of superstition and religiosity common in Russia, Putin confided on the *Larry King Live* television programme in September 2000 that he had never taken the cross off since. One devastating fire, it seems, is more than enough for a lifetime.

Months passed, and Putin continued to lobby for a job in Moscow, in the Kremlin. Alexei Kudrin, former deputy major of St Petersburg and Putin's old colleague, put in a word with other St Petersburgers based in the presidential administration. Putin affectionately called Kudrin Lyosha, the diminutive for Alexei. Kudrin himself was now chief of the president's Main Control Directorate, and had been repeatedly promoted by Anatoly Chubais. Later Kudrin was appointed deputy prime minister and finance minister under Putin. Ironically, Putin's way was initially blocked by Chubais, another former resident of St Petersburg and newly appointed chief of the president's administration. Chubais was a former assistant professor at Leningrad's Institute of Engineering and Economics, and head of the city's Committee on Economic Reform. He had moved on to become head of the Russian Federation's Committee on State Property Management, led the much criticized 'voucher privatization' of state enterprises and became first deputy prime minister. He was later sacked from the government, but reinstated as Yeltsin's chief of staff on 15 July 1996. He was then the most prominent St Petersburger in the country. As discussed, Putin was due to be appointed as deputy to Chubais's predecessor, Nikolai Yegorov, but Chubais abolished the post, leaving Vladimir without a job. Perhaps Chubais saw Putin as a rival, but it is more likely that he just didn't think much of him. Chubais had been a deputy prime minister as far back as 1992, and as far as he was concerned, Putin was just a former minor local government official. A great distance separated the two men in terms of their respective careers, their standing in the country, and their political influence. Vladimir and Lyudmila never forgave Chubais for leaving Putin out in the cold. The two would clash again, as Chubais tried and failed to block Putin's appointment as prime minister. By this time it was Chubais's star which had waned.

In spite of his unhelpful attitude, Chubais had indicated to Kudrin that he wouldn't object to Putin working elsewhere in the administration, albeit at a lower level. It was suggested he might work in the Public Relations Department, which wasn't really Putin's area of expertise. Vladimir once more made the journey to Moscow in search of a job. It was another St Petersburger, deputy prime minister Alexei Bolshakov, who came to Putin's aid. Bolshakov was a former first deputy of the executive committee of Leningrad City Council, under the old Soviet system. Putin was careful to cultivate Bolshakov when he was deputy mayor of St Petersburg, on the basis that he could be a useful contact in the future. Many of the former Soviet bosses turned up in influential positions in the new Russia. Bolshakov's appointment under Prime Minister Victor Chernomyrdin was fortuitous for Putin, as he now had a contact at the heart of government. *Blat* helped Putin for a second time in his career. Bolshakov got on to Pavel Borodin, head of the president's General Affairs Department, who offered Putin a job as his deputy. It was a much better prospect than working in public relations. Putin was to be head of the Law Department and would deal with foreign economic relations and state property owned abroad.

Despite Chubais, whom the Putins now despised, Putin ended up serving the government in the Kremlin's Old Square in a meaningful job.

Vladimir Putin never established cordial relations with Chubais after being snubbed as his deputy. He was scornful of Chubais's privatization record, later describing him as a 'hardnosed Bolshevik', pointing out that 'he has a bad credit record', meaning the public trust in him is low, and damning him with faint praise as a 'technocrat' and 'very good administrator'. Lyudmila clearly dislikes the man. She complained that 'he doesn't take women seriously. He treats them with a certain contempt. I'm not a feminist, but I want women to occupy the place that they deserve in this world.' Significantly, Chubais was never offered any post in government under Putin, and went off to head the giant Russian electricity monopoly, UES.

The St Petersburg 'mafia' (in the broadest sense) generally tried to look after its own. Chubais excepted, St Petersburg people tended to promote people from their native city, and remove those from Moscow. The same was true in business circles, where there was a strong but unspoken rivalry between the capital and its imperial sister. People from Leningrad/St Petersburg consider themselves the intellectual elite, and regard Muscovites as vulgar monied parvenus. Muscovites regard themselves as living in the centre of the universe, and entrepreneurially sublime. They think St Petersburg is a decaying backwater, full of intellectual snobs who spend all the time at the ballet, theatre and the Hermitage. Of course, this is a broad generalization, but even Putin acknowledged that politically St Petersburg could be said to be 'provincial'. It was why he moved to Moscow in the first place, despite preferring St Petersburg.

Pavel Borodin, Putin's new boss, was in charge of the General Affairs Department, which managed the Kremlin's property holdings. It was a job which saw Borodin in overall charge of a huge and expensive property portfolio, with all the financial responsibilities and possibilities that that implied. As his deputy, Putin had started his ascent up the greasy pole in earnest. The Swiss authorities later issued an international warrant against Borodin, who was arrested for alleged money laundering and bribery at John F. Kennedy Airport in New York in January 2001, and extradited to Switzerland. The warrant had been requested by Bernard Bertossa, Geneva's chief prosecutor, and issued through Interpol. Borodin had been attending President Bush's inauguration, as secretary of the Russia–Belarus union. Pavel Borodin's appointment to the latter post was one of Putin's first steps as acting-president when Yeltsin resigned on New Year's Eve 1999, conveniently removing Borodin from the Kremlin. Putin didn't want to be associated with the growing stench of scandal surrounding his former colleague, but also had no intention of abandoning the man who gave him his first job in the Kremlin.

The Swiss alleged that Borodin and his family had received kickbacks totalling $25 million on contracts worth $492 million to the Swiss-based Mercata Trading and Engineering Company, to refurbish the Kremlin and other government offices. Mercata was a shell company owned by a Russian businessman, Viktor Stolpovskikh. The so-called Mabetex affair, named after Mercata's sister company which carried out the work, also touched President Boris Yeltsin and his family. Allegations published by the *St Petersburg Times* suggested Borodin and Tatyana Dyachenko, Yeltsin's daughter, transferred millions of dollars to their own accounts via Mabetex. The US magazine *Newsweek* later linked Yeltsin and his daughter to $15 million frozen in Swiss bank accounts. Yeltsin and his immediate family also allegedly gained guarantees from a Lugano-based Swiss bank for five credit cards, which were supposedly duly issued. Lugano is a known haven for members of Russia's criminal fraternity and their 'dirty' money.

Beghjet Pacolli, Mabetex's chief, told Russia's *Literaturnaya Gazeta* in December 1999 that his company had indeed opened credit card accounts for Yeltsin and his daughters, a statement emphatically denied by Russia's outgoing president. Borodin's arrest in New York led to a formal diplomatic protest from Russia's Foreign Minister Igor Ivanov, who said his country would take 'all necessary steps' in the US and Switzerland to free him. Borodin subsequently refused to cooperate with the Swiss authorities, and the Russian state paid his bail to enable him to return to Moscow. Russian prosecutors unsurprisingly shelved a corruption investigation against Borodin for lack of evidence, and the case against him was dropped. Pavel Borodin continued to deny any wrongdoing. The order to protect Borodin came from the very top. He knew too much about the Kremlin's murkier dealings to be abandoned to the wolves. Furthermore, as Putin had shown with Sobchak, he never deserted his friends.

Loyalty is one of Putin's more admirable qualities, although on occasions his judgement could be questionable. His view of friendship is recorded in his autobiography: 'I have a lot of friends, but only a few people are really close to me. They have never gone away. They have never betrayed me, and I haven't betrayed them, either. In my view, that is what counts most. I don't even know why you would betray your friends.' Morally, this begs the question whether it is right to stand by a friend whose behaviour has been reprehensible, or perhaps even criminal. Putin's personal credo, with its emphasis on loyalty and abjuring betrayal, seems to imply that real friendship transcends all else, including any abstract concept of morality. For Putin, as he had learned in the KGB and subsequently the Kremlin, personal loyalty was his guiding, over-arching principle. It was an ever-present theme in Putin's career, and one which would ultimately propel him to the presidency.

4

ON THE WAY UP

Babushka on entering swanky new Russian bank with expensive marble cladding: 'Now I understand why I can't afford my sausages any more.'

The Putins bade farewell to St Petersburg with mixed feelings. Lyudmila hadn't wanted to go to Moscow and was 'wild about St Petersburg', but when she came to the capital, she soon got over it. She preferred the city's atmosphere and the bustling streets, and the fact that unlike St Petersburg, the city was so well kept. The people seemed friendlier and more open than in Russia's 'northern capital'. Lyuda 'fell in love with Moscow right away'. Putin found it more difficult to adjust. Whereas Lyudmila had been brought up in grim Kaliningrad, and found it easy to switch allegiances, he had spent all his life in St Petersburg. He said that it wasn't that he actually disliked Moscow, 'It's just that I like Piter more.' One day, he intended to return to his home city on the Neva. A true son of St Petersburg, he secretly felt contempt for Moscow. No self-respecting denizen of St Petersburg, used to its imperial grandeur and aesthetic beauty, prefers Moscow. Most Petersburgers think Moscow has the feel of a large railway station or over-populated village. They virtually always prefer 'Piter', as it is affectionately known by its residents. But Putin is always the pragmatist. He knows that Moscow is where Russia's political power and wealth is concentrated. Most of the best jobs are based in the capital. To reach the top in Russia, you have to go to Moscow.

The Putin family moved to a state dacha in Arkhangelskoye, just outside Moscow. It was an old, semi-detached house on two levels, with two rooms and a kitchen downstairs and four rooms upstairs. There was plenty of space for the girls and any visiting guests to stay over. Lyudmila was delighted with their new government-allocated home, and was enthralled by Moscow city life. For her, the contrast between St Petersburg and Moscow was like the difference between Manhattan and Boston. Boston may be nice and all that, but it hasn't got New York City's round-the-clock buzz. At first, the Putins used to travel back to St Petersburg regularly, keeping in touch with all their old friends. But as time wore on, they inevitably started going back to Piter less and less. There was just too much to do in Moscow, and not enough time to do it all. Besides, the shops are better.

In the Kremlin, Putin found himself in his element. After eight months as Borodin's deputy between 1996 and 1997, Putin was on his way up. 'Putin's great talent is knowing how to please his bosses and getting noticed and trusted by them,' said Dmitri Travnin, a St Petersburg analyst and veteran Putin-watcher. During the course of 1997 Putin was appointed head of the Main Control Department, replacing Alexei Kudrin, who had recommended him for the job. Kudrin had left the presidential administration to join the government with Chubais (who became first deputy premier).

The following year, Putin was appointed deputy head of management in the presidential administration, under President Yeltsin's senior aide, Valentin Yumashev. He was put in charge of relations with the 89 Subjects or constituent parts of the Russian Federation, and was firm in his dealings with Russia's elected governors. Using his now well-honed skills as a courtier, Putin was starting to come to the attention of Tsar Boris Yeltsin's 'family', the president's inner circle of close relatives, advisers and confidants. Putin had already been noticed by Yumashev, a 'family' member, thanks partly to Kudrin.

Putin was also spotted by Yeltsin's daughter Tatyana Dyachenko, who was also increasingly becoming the focus of allegations of corruption. At this time, she worked in the Kremlin as an adviser to her father, and had been part of the campaign team which had overseen his re-election back in 1996. Her husband, Valery Okulov, previously a pilot, ended up heading the state airline Aeroflot, and was close to the tycoon who controlled the company, Boris Berezovsky.

Berezovsky was in turn close to Tatyana Dyachenko and the Yeltsins, although President Yeltsin tried to distance himself from the oligarch subsequently. But there was no escaping that it was Berezovsky who had ensured Yeltsin's son-in-law was appointed to the job of heading the national airline, so cementing the link to the president's blood relatives. Berezovsky had also been instrumental in publishing Yeltsin's earlier memoirs, *Notes of a President*, for which the president received more money than apparently justified by his royalties. Yumashev, who had worked as a journalist and deputy editor for the magazine *Ogonyok* (supported and later owned by Berezovsky) ghosted the memoirs, and later introduced the oligarch to the Kremlin's first family. According to the late Paul Klebnikov's book, *Godfather of the Kremlin*, Yeltsin's book made about $200,000 outside Russia, although Berezovsky allegedly topped up the president's royalties to around $3 million, channelling the money to Yeltsin's London-based Barclays account. It was an expensive but ultimately profitable way to get an introduction to the Kremlin's inner circle.

General Alexander Korzhakov, Yeltsin's former bodyguard, records seeing the scruffily dressed journalist Valentin Yumashev turning up every month in Yeltsin's office between 1994 and 1995, with a suitcase full of $16,000 in cash, the interest from Yeltsin's London account. After a private meeting lasting a few minutes, the president stashed the cash in his personal safe. Yumashev went on to become head of the presidential administration under Tsar Boris. Such were the goings-on at the Kremlin during Yeltsin's tenure, and these were also the same people responsible for Putin's rapid series of promotions. As Yeltsin continued to deny any impropriety in the relationship with the swarthy tycoon (denying even its very existence), Berezovsky became embarrassingly embroiled in a $900 million alleged case of embezzlement involving Aeroflot's foreign hard currency earnings. Further charges of malfeasance would continue to be brought against Berezovsky over the coming years. Berezovsky vociferously denied and denies all culpability, usually rattled out in his trademark stream of consciousness.

Putin had to pinch his nose tight to ignore the stench of corruption surrounding Boris Yeltsin's administration. As one of Tsar Boris's courtiers, Putin concentrated on working competently and quietly in his usually understated style, whilst getting noticed by the right people. His inexorable rise continued. In July 1998 he was appointed head of the FSB, domestic security successor to the KGB. Putin's immediate predecessor was Nikolai Kovalev, a career KGB man, who had shown (in Yeltsin's view) an unhealthy interest in investigating corrupt banks and businessmen. President Yeltsin had a huge personal antipathy towards anyone who showed too much interest in rooting out corruption among Moscow's business and political elite. Putin on the other hand didn't have a record of challenging authority. Like a true military man, he obeyed and carried out orders with admirable efficiency. After all, the KGB had always been under the control and funded by the Ministry of Defence, with military ranks and uniforms. KGB officers were trained above all to obey orders, and Kovalev's freewheeling investigations truly disconcerted the 'family'.

Boris Yeltsin describes in his memoirs, *Midnight Diaries*, how he offered Putin the rank of general to head the FSB. But Putin demurred, reminding his boss that he was still a lieutenant-colonel in the FSB's reserve, and requested that he stay a civilian. He had no desire to go back into uniform. After all, Putin had left the KGB seven years before, making a career for himself as a technocrat. He didn't want to go back to a full-time career in the secret services; in some ways he felt it was a step backwards. The post of FSB director was not his ideal job at all; he would have preferred instead a mainstream post in the presidential administration or government. Yeltsin didn't give Putin a choice, and in any case it was a promotion that he would have been foolish to decline.

Putin's return to his once-beloved KGB saw him take an office in Moscow's notorious Lubyanka, where so many of Stalin's victims were tortured and shot. The KGB's old headquarters, now occupied by the FSB, had doubled as a prison and execution block. The statue of Felix Dzerzhinsky, the founder of the feared *Cheka* (Bolshevik precursor of the KGB) had been pulled down in the euphoria following the collapse of Communism, but the building retained its imposing and brooding presence. Some wanted to put Dzerzhinsky's statue back up in the square. Putin did restore a plaque in the Lubyanka, taken down in 1991, honouring Yury Andropov, long-time KGB chief and then Communist Party general secretary. Andropov was head of the KGB when Putin joined, and was respected by fellow Chekists for his determination to reform the KGB, instil discipline and modernize the USSR. To confound his critics, Putin also laid a wreath at the grave of the dissident nuclear scientist Andrei Sakharov, who was persecuted by Andropov's KGB. Putin respected Sakharov for his intellect and integrity, his work on developing the hydrogen bomb, for his belief in reforming the USSR and in the KGB as the country's least corrupt institution. Although Sakharov had been on the other side when he worked for the KGB in Leningrad, he was a man Putin felt he could relate to, just as he could Yury Andropov. He saw no contradiction between admiring the two very different men.

Putin's period as FSB boss was largely unremarkable; he instituted no reforms and no major changes. He was the Federal Security Service's seventh boss in eight years. His main contribution to the FSB was to clear out some of the dead wood at senior management level and bring in a number of former KGB colleagues from St Petersburg. A notable appointment was Sergei Ivanov, a close KGB friend from Leningrad, who became deputy director of the FSB a month after Putin took over the agency. Ivanov later went on to head the Security Council and become Russia's first civilian defence minister. Viktor Cherkesov, another KGB man from Putin's home town, also became a deputy director of the FSB. He went on to become Putin's presidential representative (or plenipotentiary) in north-west Russia. Cherkesov, like Putin, had studied at Leningrad Law Faculty, and then served in the city's KGB, gaining a reputation as a harsh illiberal character, fond of persecuting dissidents. St Petersburg's liberal intelligentsia loathed him. They loved him even less when he came back to St Petersburg in 2000 as Putin's personal representative. His sole purpose seemed to be to remove Governor Vladimir Yakovlev, the city's popular if flawed leader. Nikolai Patrushev, another veteran KGB officer from St Petersburg, was appointed to head the FSB after Putin left and subsequently took over responsibility for the Chechen 'counter-terrorist' operation in the breakaway republic. Ivanov, Patrushev and Cherkesov were all born in Leningrad in the 1950s, within a year or two of Vladimir Putin, and like him they also had been based in the KGB there.

As FSB Director, Putin found himself in a position to help his old boss, former St Petersburg mayor Anatoly Sobchak. Under investigation for corruption and misuse of city funds, Sobchak had been admitted to hospital with cardiac problems. Yury Skuratov, prosecutor-general, was pursuing the case against Sobchak as part of his anti-corruption drive. Although based in Moscow, Putin visited Sobchak in his St Petersburg hospital in November 1998. Within days, although Sobchak was the subject of an arrest warrant from the general prosecutor's office, the former mayor was whisked out of the city in a private plane. Sobchak fled to Paris, where he stayed until Putin came to power and it was safe for him to return to St Petersburg. Although Putin denies it, Boris Yeltsin has no doubt that Sobchak's former deputy arranged for his mentor to be spirited out of the city. The day of Sobchak's flight was 7 November, a national public holiday. The whole thing looked meticulously planned. If Putin was involved as Yeltsin claims, it would mean that he was aiding a fugitive to evade justice. Since he was a member of the government and director of the FSB at the time, that is quite a charge. But Yeltsin was quite categorical about Putin's role, as related in his memoirs, *Midnight Diaries*: 'Thanks to the holidays, the city was quiet. Using his connections in St Petersburg, Putin made a deal with a private airline and brought Sobchak out to Finland. From there Sobchak made his way to Paris. Sobchak was ordered not to leave town, so he was being followed. But they were not watching too carefully, probably because they didn't think anyone would help a man who was five minutes away from finding himself behind bars in Kresty Prison . . .'

Kresty Prison is St Petersburg's main prison – a huge, old and intimidating red brick monstrosity which makes some of Britain's Victorian jails look positively palatial. With six or more to a cell and violence and disease rampant, it's not the sort of place Anatoly Sobchak would care to visit, let alone stay in for a long spell. For Boris Yeltsin, Putin's actions in saving Sobchak's neck were highly commendable. He couldn't praise him enough. 'Later, when I learned about what Putin had done,' he gushed, 'I felt a profound sense of respect for and gratitude towards him.' For Yeltsin, helping one's former boss escape from justice was a cardinal principle and a touchstone of loyalty, recommending the person concerned for the highest of offices. Putin certainly went up in Yeltsin's estimation after the Sobchak affair. When Anatoly Sobchak died of a heart attack in February 2000, his funeral was one of the rare occasions when Putin allowed himself to be seen weeping publicly. He was loyal to his old mentor to the very end.

While installed in the Lubyanka, Putin did carry out one outstanding secret operation. The FSB had videotaped the then prosecutor-general, Yury Skuratov, allegedly cavorting with two prostitutes in a sauna. Putin ensured the tape was given to a TV station and the press, torpedoing Skuratov's investigation of corrupt government officials, the Swiss Mabetex scandal involving Pavel Borodin, and kickbacks to the Kremlin and Yeltsin's relatives.

Skuratov's investigations were also looking at the role of 800 government and Central Bank officials speculating on the GKO domestic treasury debt market, which partly prompted a financial collapse in August 1998. The GKO bills paid unsustainably high interest rates, and rapidly became a pyramid scheme dependent on ever-increasing new funds to pay off old debt. One of those under investigation was Anatoly Chubais, the former deputy prime minister and head of the presidential administration. It also emerged that Fimaco, an obscure fund management company on the island of Jersey, had been used as a vehicle by Central Bank staff to re-invest billions of dollars of IMF loans and hard currency reserves in the speculative GKO market. In one fell swoop the economic debacle had once again wiped out middle-class savings as banks lost their depositors' money, undermined the rouble, foreign investment and confidence in the country's economy.

The IMF demanded an investigation into Fimaco's activities and accused the Russian Central Bank of lying about the level of the country's hard currency reserves. Government officials and central bank staff had colluded in a massive insider trading fraud which almost bankrupted the country. Skuratov and Prime Minister Yevgeny Primakov were determined to go after the bankers, oligarchs and officials responsible, including those close to Boris Yeltsin. Along the way, they wanted to nail those close to the Kremlin who profited as the country sailed close to the abyss. Skuratov, who had failed in his years as prosecutor-general to bring one major corruption case to a close, had been galvanized and emboldened by Primakov's anti-corruption drive. After a Duma amnesty freed almost a hundred thousand convicts early in 1999, Primakov had ominously warned the cabinet he was clearing out the prisons to make way for those who had committed economic crimes. Within days, armed police raided Berezovksy's companies in Moscow. That spring, the prosecutor's office issued a warrant for his arrest on the grounds that he had fraudulently diverted Aeroflot's foreign ticket sales. Primakov, in spite of Yeltsin's obvious hostility to his prime minister's anti-corruption crusade, was showing that he meant business. Yet neither Skuratov or Primakov would politically survive to continue their task. President Yeltsin and his family couldn't be rolled over that easily.

The titillating tape exposing Skuratov was shown on RTR state television on 16 March 1999. Skuratov and many others claimed the tape was a forgery. Whatever the compromising material held on Skuratov (called *kompromat* in Russian), the corruption trail led to the Kremlin and up to President Yeltsin and his immediate family. Putin attended a crucial meeting between Yeltsin and Skuratov to force the latter's resignation. By destroying Skuratov's credibility and career at a crucial moment, Putin earned the gratitude of the Yeltsin 'family' and proved his unquestioning loyalty. Here was a man who had shown he could be depended upon to look after the family's vital interests. It was the only recommendation Putin needed. Less than two weeks later, Vladimir Putin was appointed secretary of the powerful Security Council, while keeping his post as director of the FSB. His predecessor on the Security Council, Nikolai Bordyuzha, had committed the cardinal sin of becoming too close to Yevgeny Primakov, Yeltsin's prime minister and potential rival. With the support of the upper chamber of parliament, the Federation Council, Prosecutor-General Skuratov hung on in office for another year. Throughout his struggle with the Kremlin, Skuratov had also received the vocal support of Moscow's populist and ambitious mayor, Yury Luzhkov. But when Putin was elected president, the game was up and Skuratov quietly relinquished his post. Primakov didn't last that long; he was sacked by Yeltsin as prime minister less than two months after the Skuratov video was first aired.

Around the time the Skuratov scandal broke, Boris Yeltsin was getting desperate to find a loyal and dependable successor. In May the Communists in the Duma had launched impeachment proceedings against him, which reputedly cost the Kremlin and its allies $30,000 a vote to head off. Prime Minister Yevgeny Primakov was fast becoming by far the most popular politician in the country, and started looking like a future president. Primakov was on the cusp of forging an alliance with Moscow mayor Yury Luzhkov, and the Kremlin feared that a Primakov–Luzhkov axis would be an unbeatable political combination. Yeltsin's immediate reaction had been to sack Primakov on 12 May and replace him with Stepashin, which not only wrong-footed Primakov but distracted attention from the Duma's attempted impeachment. However, Primakov's dismissal only brought Yeltsin and his family a short breathing space. Primakov and Luzhkov could be expected to re-double their drive for power. Yeltsin had suffered five heart attacks and a triple heart by-pass, so even if he could somehow manage to win his third election as Russia's president, he might not survive much beyond the campaign. In the summer of 1999, a national opinion poll survey by VCIOM (a polling organization) gave him an approval rating of just 18 per cent. Dragging the unpopular 'Boris the Boozer' through another election battle was too much of a risk, both politically and physically.

During the presidential campaign of July 1996, President Yeltsin was so unwell that he had failed to turn up to cast his vote at his local polling station at Osennyaya Street, in Moscow's western suburbs. Prime Minister Victor Chernomyrdin assured the waiting world's press that Yeltsin was in good form and working at home. In fact, he and his wife had arranged for a transfer vote the previous day, enabling him to cast his vote at the Barvikha sanitarium, where he was recovering from a heart attack. Inviting four busloads of the international press to watch the president cast his second round vote had misfired. Yeltsin had been too poorly to attend, and was briefly filmed by his private camera crew voting at Barvikha ten miles away. Some cynics darkly joked that Russia was electing a corpse as president. Yeltsin and his family couldn't hope to pull the same stunt twice in the 2000 presidential elections.

To secure the interests of the 'family' this time around, an heir apparent had to be selected and groomed for office. Of course, they would have to have the right attitude, and guarantee that there would be no retribution after Tsar Boris abdicated. He thought he might have found his man in Sergei Stepashin, a St Petersburger with democratic credentials who had headed the FSK, the counter-intelligence agency which preceded the FSB. He had also been a hawkish minister of the interior, preparing a plan for an incursion into Chechnya, which had effectively declared independence and was beyond Moscow's control. Yet the 'family' quickly decided that Stepashin was disappointingly weak, with an unfortunate inde-pendent streak and a tendency to criticize the oligarchs. On a visit to the USA he made the mistake of saying he would take on Russia's business tycoons. Worse still, from the Kremlin's point of view, he refused to stop the various criminal investigations into members of President Yeltsin's 'family'. Two weeks later he was sacked. He had been prime minister for less than three months.

At the beginning of August 1999, to general surprise, President Yeltsin appointed the virtually unknown Vladimir Putin as his fifth prime minister in seventeen months. Stepashin had been shocked at his summary dismissal, but was powerless to resist it. Putin and Stepashin knew each other, but were not close. Yeltsin simply invited Stepashin to his dacha at Gorky-9 and sacked him, with Putin look-ing on. Putin found the whole exercise of removing Stepashin brutal and distasteful, but at least he knew what to expect if his boss thought he was failing him. The weary public and Moscow political elite assumed Putin was joining a long-line of temporary prime ministers. During his presidency Yeltsin replaced five prime minis-ters, three foreign ministers, six prosecutors-general, seven heads of the security service (FSB), nine finance ministers and six interior ministers. His strategy to 'divide and rule' seemed completely out of control. President Yeltsin, most people believed, had simply lost the plot and was ruling Russia increasingly erratically, if at all. Yeltsin went further, and universally astonished Russia's politicians, public and media by declaring that Putin was his preferred successor as president. Naming Putin as his new prime minister in a televised address, Yeltsin told viewers: 'In one year's time, in exactly one year's time, there will be presidential elections. I have decided to name now the person who is, in my opinion, able to consolidate society and to ensure the continuation of reforms in Russia, drawing support from the broadest political base. He will be able to unite around himself those who will revive Great Russia in the new, twenty-first century. He is . . . Vladimir Vladimirovich Putin.' Political commentators remembered he similarly anointed General Alexander Lebed his successor in 1996, before sacking him as secretary of the Security Council three months later.

In private, Yeltsin was more circumspect, telling Putin he was a 'prime minister with a future'. Putin felt Yeltsin was implying that if he played his cards right and pleased the 'family', he would indeed become president. However, if he showed himself untrustworthy, or if he looked as if he wouldn't protect the Yeltsin family's interests after the president stood down, he could expect the same fate as Stepashin. Lyudmila sometimes found herself wondering at how fast her husband's career had progressed. 'I would catch myself thinking: "How strange; I'm married to a man who yesterday was really just an unknown deputy mayor of St Petersburg, and now he's the prime minister."' A few days after Putin was named prime minister, his father died of heart disease. He had been visiting his ailing father in St Petersburg every weekend, in spite of his heavy workload. His mother, Maria, had died a year earlier of cancer. His parents had been fiercely proud of his achievements, and their death left a void in his life. Apart from his wife and children, no one had come anywhere near being as close to him.

In other respects, life improved for the Putins now that Vladimir was prime minister. He was given a new state dacha outside Moscow, where they had a 12-metre pool. Putin would work out every morning for 20 to 30 minutes, and swim in the pool morning and evening. He was determined to keep fit, missing lunch because he was often too busy, and in the mornings eating just fruit for breakfast and drinking *kefir*, a type of yogurt. Sometimes in the evenings, he would find some time to watch cartoons with his two girls, Katya and Masha. Masha had ambitions to be a manager, Katya an interior designer. Unlike many politicians, Putin read Russian newspapers, not just the press clippings often prepared for prime ministers. He and Lyudmila never discussed people he worked with; she only met Boris Yeltsin twice in all the years Putin was in the Kremlin. Like a good traditional Russian wife, she remained in the background, cooking, looking after the children, and minding the family finances. When Putin became prime minister, they even had the luxury of their own cook, which must have reminded Vladimir of his grandfather's role as a chef to the party elite. Putin rarely brought his work home, and never raised his voice, although according to his wife he can answer rather sharply. At times, when under pressure, he can be in a bad mood. Lyudmila puts it this way: 'In general he's a composed person, but at certain moments it's better not to bother him.' He usually doesn't drink at home, but sometimes he can have a sip of vodka or cognac. Putin always seems in control, especially of himself and usually of his emotions.

The August invasion of the Russian republic of Dagestan by Islamic militants presented Putin with his first major challenge and his first opportunity to prove his mettle. The invasion also provided an immediate excuse for a second Chechen war and the unabashed promotion of Putin as a steely 'man of action'. The idea of launching a full-scale war in Chechnya to crush the Islamic separatists once and for all was taken by Yeltsin's inner circle. Sergei Stepashin, when prime minister, had developed a plan to invade Chechnya up to the Terek river, dividing the republic between the more pro-Moscow north and the separatists' bastions in the mountainous south. Stepashin's idea had been to create a *cordon sanitaire* around the rebels beyond the Terek, to hem them in and neutralize them by bombing their training camps. This had all been discussed at a Security Council meeting in July, prior to the rebels' attack and following intelligence of an imminent strike from across the border in Chechnya.

Earlier that spring an Interior Ministry general and President Yeltsin's personal envoy, Major-General Gennady Shipgun, had been kidnapped from Grozny airport and brutally murdered. Stepashin and the Russian military felt that Aslan Maskhadov, the titular president of Chechnya, had lost control of his fractious republic and its squabbling warlords. They seemed more intent on seizing hostages and trading in weapons and drugs than in creating order in the breakaway republic. In a two-year period, 1,300 hostages had been seized, with most being held for ransom. Many were abused, and according to the Russian Mothers' Committee, around 800 captured Russian soldiers were used as the guerrillas' private slaves. Vladimir Yepishin, whose case was highlighted in the London *Sunday Times*, made it back to his family after thirteen years of Chechen slavery, after he was abducted in the Russian city of Yaroslav, 200 miles north-east of Moscow. Sold on ten times and badly beaten, losing all his teeth and the sight in one eye, Yepishin was freed with the help of a Russian journalist from a Chechen enclave in Georgia's Pankisi gorge. 'To them I was nothing,' said Yepishin. 'For Chechens, having a Russian slave is a status symbol.' Ramil Gamilov, another Russian slave in Chechnya, was freed after seven years of captivity. He was unaware the USSR no longer existed.

Other victims included six foreign Red Cross workers and four Western telecom engineers (three Britons and one New Zealander), whose decapitated bodies were found beside a road in the breakaway republic. Two British charity workers, Jon James and Camilla Carr, were physically and sexually abused during their captivity by their Chechen captors. In the latter case, it was Boris Berezovsky who negotiated their release, apparently on payment of a ransom. The going rate was up to $2 million for foreign hostages. Following Shipgun's kidnapping, the Russian government threatened to tighten the noose around Chechnya, cutting off transport and energy links with the recalcitrant republic and warning that it might attack guerrilla training bases inside the territory. The rebels' attack on Dagestan ratcheted up the tension and made a Russian strike against Chechnya inevitable. Sergei Stepashin was sacked just as he was preparing to respond to the attack on Dagestan. Yeltsin's clan and Prime Minister Putin merely picked up Stepashin's plan and developed it.

The incursion by the rebels began when a large group of several hundred guerrillas crossed the border from Chechnya into Dagestan, an ethnically mixed Russian republic with a predominantly Muslim population. Shamil Basayev, the radical guerrilla leader, who had been responsible for the Budyonnovsk Hospital seizure in southern Russia in 1995 (when 150 people died), declared he wanted to create a trans-Caucasian Islamic republic. The Dagestanis were not particularly impressed, and despite some infiltration by Islamic militants into border village communities, resisted the Chechens' call to join them. In fact, many Dagestanis were armed and prepared to resist Basayev and his men. This was the same Basayev who was later to claim responsibility for the Moscow Dubrovka theatre siege in October 2002, when over 800 theatregoers were threatened with being blown up by Chechen suicide bombers. Among Basayev's immediate circle was Samer bin Saleh al-Suwailem, a Saudi known as Khattab, a notorious guerrilla commander who had joined the Chechen cause in 1995. Khattab led a small group of Arabs to the Caucasus after fighting in Afghanistan, where many of the Islamic rebel commanders cut their teeth thanks to funding from the CIA and support from Pakistan. A member of the extremist Wahabi Sunni sect, Khattab was linked to al-Qaeda and Osama bin Laden, another Saudi who knew him well. Unlike bin Laden, Khattab was from a poor desert settlement in Saudi Arabia. Russian intelligence claims bin Laden gave at least $25 million in support of the Chechen cause, and sent a number of fighters to join Khattab and other rebel groups. A fluent Russian speaker known for his ruthlessness, Khattab's speciality was severing his Russian captives' heads with a *kinzal*, a traditional Chechen sword. In Chechnya, he commanded up to 1,500 guerrillas, some Arabs but mostly Chechens. Fund-raising videos of his exploits, including one showing him marching triumphantly among the charred bodies of dead Russian soldiers, were circulated around the Middle East.

Khattab had been spotted in Dagestan's border areas, and even married a local girl from Karamakhi village to inveigle the inhabitants with his vision of a wider Islamic state in the Caucasus. After years of bribery and threats, the village had become an armed camp, dominated by Chechen and Arab guerrillas and filled with tunnels, trenches and stockpiled weapons. At first, villagers had been paid $30 to convert to the Wahabis extreme form of fundamentalism. By 1999, according to Magomed Makhideyev, a local imam, the rebels were saying, 'Join us or we'll cut your head off.' The village's fourteen Russian policeman were expelled and Islamic sharia law introduced. Those caught drinking alcohol were severely beaten with sticks. The separatists' infiltration into villages like Karamakhi was part of Basayev and Khattab's plan to create a trans-Caucasian Islamic fundamentalist state. In the end, all the planning did Khattab little good. The Russian FSB caught up with him in Chechnya in March 2002, killing him by passing on a letter sprayed with fatal neurotoxins.

When the war began, many experts thought Russia would stick to Stepashin's limited invasion plan, or were just bluffing. They couldn't believe Russia would re-fight the first Chechen war, with the huge human and financial cost that would involve. Some thought the Russians simply couldn't afford another war, and logic dictated that a second Chechen conflict was unthinkable. At the time, I felt the Russians might ignore the cost and go for broke, in a bid to wipe out the separatists and re-incorporate the rebellious republic. Political imperatives, Russian fury and the desire for retribution and revenge for the humiliation experienced in the first Chechen war outweighed all other considerations. The collective Russian political and military psyche couldn't give a fig about budgetary or humanitarian considerations in such circumstances, something Western liberal humanists are apt to misunderstand. As an incredulous world media watched, the Russians cranked up their lumbering war machine.

The Chechen war proved a dramatic backdrop to the coming election campaign. In the first stage of the war, Putin claimed the rebels would be ejected from Dagestan within two weeks. Indeed, Russia's response was initially so ferocious that the Chechen rebels abandoned Dagestan within a fortnight, a fact which made some claim that Berezovsky and the Kremlin had instigated the whole rebel incursion as part of a Machiavellian political plot. A newspaper reported a purported telephone discussion between Berezovsky and a rebel leader, which alleged that the tycoon had paid the Chechens to launch their ill-fated attack. Such an account seems wholly far-fetched. Although Berezovsky had business links with Chechens, and had mediated hostage releases with a number of Chechen warlords whom he knew well, there is no real evidence he had any part in the Dagestan operation. Basayev and Khattab had proved in the past they were capable of such audacity without the need for prompting or inducements from any oligarch. In any event, they received plenty of money from the Arab world, al-Qaeda, and their own highly lucrative trade, drug and arms deals. It's probable that Basayev and Khattab overestimated their likely support in Dagestan, and like many in the West, didn't believe the Russians had the stomach for another Chechen war. This time, however, the Chechen warlords had overplayed their hand. Events in Moscow and other Russian cities were shortly to take the Chechen crisis to another level.

A bombing campaign in Russia apparently launched by the Chechens in September 1999, but blamed by others on FSB provocateurs, claimed 300 lives in Moscow, Buinaksk and Volgodonsk. The apartment block bombings caused near hysteria and panic in Russia's cities, cementing support for the war, and Putin's leading role in its prosecution. Previously virtually unknown among the general public, Putin's profile grew exponentially. The Russian government and military launched a full-scale invasion of Chechnya at the end of September, involving some 80,000 Russian troops. The invasion plan was designed to expurgate the separatist rebels and subjugate Chechnya once and for all. Learning lessons from NATO's 70-day air campaign in Kosovo, and their previous losses in the first Chechen war of 1994 to 1996, this time the Russians completely flattened Grozny before taking the city. About the size of Manchester in the UK or Springfield, Massachusetts, Grozny was left with hardly a building standing untouched. The centre of the city became a bombed-out hellhole. Thousands of civilians died in the onslaught, and around a quarter of a million inhabitants of Chechnya were displaced. Refugees flooded into neighbouring Russian republics, particularly Ingushetia.

There are those who still maintain the apartment bombings were just too conveniently timed to be taken at face value. Stories quickly surfaced that Russia's own security services, in particular the FSB, planted the bombs. Boris Berezovsky and an FSB defector, Lieutenant-Colonel Alexander Litvienko (a Berezovsky associate), promulgated the theory from the safety of their London exile in March 2002. But in both cases, being wanted in their home country on criminal charges damages the credibility of their allegations. Nevertheless, certain unanswered questions about the apartment block bombings seem to remain. Just six months after the bombs went off in the three Russian cities, a joint UK *Observer/Dispatches* investigation aired some disturbing allegations. The allegations concerned the so-called 'Ryazan incident', when a bomb was found in the eponymous city 100 miles south of Moscow. The Ryazan incident occurred around the same time as the other apartment block bombings, and received widespread coverage in the Russian media.

A few days after the first terrorist bombing in Moscow, a resident of an apartment block in Ryazan at 14/16 Novosyolov Street alerted police as he saw three suspicious people unloading bags into the basement of his building. One of the three was a young blonde woman. Police Inspector Alexei Chernyshev was the first on the scene, and he realized at once that he was looking at a bomb, including sacks of sugar, an electronic device, wires and a clock. The local bomb squad was called, and the device was defused by Yury

Tkachenko, a bomb disposal expert. The live bomb used the same explosive material as the Moscow bomb, hexogen. The detonator, which was filmed by the bomb squad and published in the media, was set to go off at 5.30 a.m. the following morning, 23 September. The timing was designed to kill the maximum amount of people asleep in their beds, perhaps up to 250 residents. Like the Moscow bomb, the block was in a working-class neighbourhood. The difference here was that those who planted the bomb were caught red-handed by the local police. They tried to get away by flashing their ID cards. It turned out they were members of the FSB. When FSB headquarters in Moscow intervened, the two men were released.

The next day, the Russian Interior Ministry announced that police had defused a timing device after finding some explosives hidden in some bags. Later the same day, the FSB in Moscow announced that the whole thing had been a training exercise, designed to test the vigilance of the authorities. There had, according to Nikolai Patrushev, the FSB's new boss, never been any bomb. Officials claimed they knew who carried out the bombings, and blamed the atrocities on 'Chechen terrorists'. Nicolai Patrushev, as noted earlier, was Putin's old KGB colleague from Leningrad. They had entered the KGB in the same year, 1975. Putin had insisted that Patrushev replace him as head of the FSB when he went on to become prime minister. Patrushev's explanation of the Ryazan incident stretched public credulity to the limit.

Given the media's account of the Ryazan incident and the FSB's less than convincing rebuttal, it is perhaps understandable to imagine the terrorist apartment bombings as a massive plot to whip up popular support for a second war in Chechnya, and indirectly, support for Vladimir Putin. The claim by some, including Putin, that the FSB is not capable of such horrors, ignores some of the less salubrious activities of the old KGB during the Cold War. The KGB has had its fair share of calculating killers. The assassination of dissident BBC journalist Georgi Markov on Waterloo Bridge in London with a poisoned umbrella in 1978 springs to mind, a murder which was perpetrated by the Bulgarian secret service with the active support of the KGB. As the Mitrokhin archive of secret KGB documents shows, Vladimir Kryuchkov advocated Markov's assassination in discussions with Yury Andropov, who at the time was chairman of the KGB. This was the same Vladimir Kryuchkov who was later to head the KGB and became one of the leaders of the 1991 attempted putsch. In his autobiography, as previously noted, Putin described General Kryuchkov as a 'very decent man' for whom he has the 'greatest respect'. There have been many other victims of the KGB in the not too distant past. But even Berezovsky doesn't claim Putin ordered the Russian security services to carry out the apartment bombings; instead he claims the future president merely 'knew the FSB was involved'. Other conspiracy theorists might imagine he didn't have to be in on any such plot; others could do the dirty work on his behalf but without his knowledge.

But all these conspiracy theories remain totally unproven. Events since the apartment bombings have reinforced the belief that the Chechen Islamists were perfectly capable of perpetrating or organizing such atrocities. Repeated suicide bombings in Chechnya and southern Russia, together with the infamous Moscow theatre siege in October 2002, point to a growing terrorist threat from Chechnya. If anything, the Chechen separatists are becoming more radicalized and desperate with each passing year. Certainly, the advent of women suicide bombers is something new and disturbing in Russia. As a postscript to the Ryazan incident, the authorities subsequently sentenced a traffic inspector, Stanislav Lyubichev, to four years in a penal colony for aiding and abetting the terrorists who planted the Moscow bomb. According to the Russian prosecutors, Lyubichev had knowingly escorted an explosive-laden truck part of the way to Moscow. Two residents of Karachay-Cherkessia, Yusuf Krymshamkhalov and Adam Dekkushev, accused of planting the bombs, testified against Lyubichev. Although from the Caucasus, neither were Chechens. The two accused had been extradited to Russia after fleeing to Georgia after the terrorist outrages.

Putin saw the second Chechen war as a huge political risk. He was under no illusions that if it went wrong, he would carry the can and be sacked by Yeltsin, who would continue his search for a malleable successor. Putin saw it as his 'historical mission' to resolve the crisis in the northern Caucasus. The stakes were high. If he pulled it off, he would become president, if he failed, obscurity beckoned once more. He reckoned he had 'two, three, maybe four months – to bang the hell out of those bandits. Then they would get rid of me.' He saw the Chechen conflict as a 'continuation of the collapse of the USSR. Clearly, at some point it had to be stopped.' There was a real fear that the attack on Dagestan could lead to the final disintegration of the Russian Federation. 'If we don't put an end to this,' Putin said in his autobiography, 'Russia will cease to exist.' He continued: 'I was convinced that if we didn't stop the extremists right away, we'd be facing a second Yugoslavia on the entire territory of the Russian Federation – the Yugoslavization of Russia.' Chechnya would not limit itself to its won independence, it would, he added, 'become a beachhead for further attacks on Russia'.

There is no reason to doubt Putin's fear that the Chechen conflict and the invasion of Dagestan by Islamic separatists could have fatally fragmented Russia. He believed that after Chechnya's secession, the entire Caucasus could have followed, including Dagestan, Ingushetia, and then up the Volga river to Bashkortostan and Tatarstan. He felt the disintegration of Russia in such circumstances would be a 'global catastrophe'. Nevertheless, Putin's crusade to shore up Russia's sovereignty neatly coincided with his own political interests. After the apartment block bombings and the invasion of Dagestan, he had full public support in his campaign to re-establish Russian control over rebellious Chechnya. While the Western media looked on and pontificated that the Russians couldn't seriously be launching a second Chechen war to retake Grozny, Putin and the Russian armed forces did just that. It was pay-back time for the humiliating defeat in the earlier 1994 to 1996 war.

With relentless backing from most of the Russian media,

Putin's public standing went up from 2 per cent in September to over 70 per cent by the time of the presidential election the following March. Putin benefited from the fact that although he was Yeltsin's chosen successor, he was also his antithesis. Boris Yeltsin was a heavy drinker, charismatic and seriously ill. Putin was almost tee-total, an 'everyday bloke', and paraded his supreme fitness in mock judo bouts on TV. Putin's lack of political track record, and his awkward appearances on television compared favourably in the public's mind with the usual gaggle of corrupt and garrulous Russian politicians who regularly appeared in the media. He was obviously a non-politician standing for political office. As he told President Yeltsin on being appointed prime minister, he didn't really like campaigning or elections, and it showed. In the run up to the Duma elections in December 1999 he could therefore present himself as 'all things to all men'. As a former KGB officer, he simultaneously appealed to the nostalgic past, while promising a young and newly invigorated leadership for the country. As Yeltsin's chosen successor, he both represented continuity and the promise of a bright new future. Putin's war on the Chechens sought to wipe out the humiliations of the past, and restore Russia's self-esteem as a great military power. Russians loved his 'action man' image, as he was pictured in blanket TV coverage sitting in fighter planes, visiting Chechnya, instructing ministers on how to run the country better, and flooring opponents on the judo mat. For Russians, it was a relief to have a leader who could stand up straight and string a few sentences together without slurring his words. Putin was the tough, virile, assertive leader Russians craved for. And that was the message fed to the Russian public day after day before the Duma and presidential elections.

Putin had the Kremlin and the country's media supporting him, but that wasn't all. In addition to throwing the weight of Russia's ORT television behind him, Boris Berezovsky helped the 'family' create a new party, Unity. Apart from Berezovsky, the key figures in the family (always a slightly movable feast) were Tatyana

Dyachenko, Yeltsin's daughter; Alexander Voloshin, the presidential head of administration; and Valentin Yumachev, the president's former chief of staff and ghost-writer of his memoirs. Voloshin was a bald and bearded former train driver and economist who had worked with Berezovsky on one of his dubious money-making schemes in the early 1990s, the All-Russian Automobile Alliance (AVVA) securities project. The scheme had raised $50 million for Berezovsky, but none of the thousands of investors saw any of their money back. Voloshin, meanwhile, had gone on to work his way up and through Yeltsin's presidential administration, becoming its head in March 1999. The 'family' had created Unity as a counterweight to the bloc formed by Primakov and Luzhkov that summer, called Fatherland-All Russia (OVR). As the political elite saw no obvious alternative to Yeltsin as leader, Russia's regional leaders had been joining Fatherland at what the Kremlin saw as an alarming rate. They included regional heavyweights like Tatarstan's President Mintimer Shaimiev and Putin's arch-enemy St Petersburg Governor Vladimir Yakovlev. Berezovsky travelled the country signing-up supporters to the Kremlin's new creature, Unity, which the 'family' hoped would become the new 'party of power'.

Unity, or Medved (named after the bear which was its symbol), was a political movement cobbled together in a few weeks, with no structure, no ideology and no grass-roots membership. Its leaders were Sergei Shoigu, the popular emergency minister; world champion wrestler Alexander Karelin; and General Alexander Gurov, an Interior Ministry crime-buster known for taking on the mafia. Rather like some European parties using a proportional list system, Unity's leaders were chosen on the basis of their popularity and their recognition factor. The Kremlin hoped this would be enough to carry Unity's otherwise unknown parliamentary candidates to victory in December's forthcoming Duma elections. Half the 450 Duma deputies would be elected by individual constituency, the other half would be elected proportionally via a federal party list. Unity was unashamedly populist, with little political programme but to support Prime Minister Putin. The idea was to hang on to Putin's political coat-tails all the way to the elections. With Putin's poll support going through the roof, the strategy seemed foolproof. Governors who were worried for their personal futures, like Primorye Governor Yevgeny Nazdratenko, Kursk Governor Alexander Rutskoi and Kaliningrad Governor Leonid Gorbenko, flocked to the new Unity movement. Others dependent on the Kremlin for subsidies or patronage also lined up behind Unity.

There was, however, another strand to the Kremlin's family strategy. Yevgeny Primakov and Yury Luzhkov, Putin's only credible political rivals for the presidency, would be destroyed by smear and innuendo. If Fatherland-All Russia was heavily defeated in the Duma elections, the movement would unravel, and with it any chance of Primakov or Luzhkov becoming president. It was interesting to witness just how the Kremlin went about its business of destroying Primakov and Luzhkov. One of the Kremlin's secret weapons was the Berezovsky-controlled Channel 1, or ORT, and specifically the broadcaster Sergei Dorenko. Boris Berezovsky encouraged Dorenko to launch a series of vicious attacks on Primakov and especially Luzhkov on his Sunday programme. Yevgeny Primakov, an Arabic speaker, former head of foreign intelligence (SVR), past foreign minister and prime minister, had also been a candidate member of the Soviet politburo in the 1980s. Now seventy, Primakov was no spring chicken, and had undergone a hip replacement operation. Dorenko portrayed Primakov as an atavistic Soviet has-been of poor health, and gloried in showing a close-up of hip replacement surgery to ram his point home. Moscow Mayor Yury Luzhkov fared even worse on Dorenko's show. Short, bald, podgy and usually pictured wearing his signature leather cap, Luzhkov looked the archetypal Soviet bureaucrat that he undoubtedly was. Repeated programmes accused Luzhkov of being corrupt, associating with known criminals, and accused him of being involved in money-laundering and murder. The *Washington Post* journalist David Hoffman, meeting Yeltsin's head of administration Alexander Voloshin that summer, was given a similar line. Primakov, Hoffman was told, was 'a wily old spy', while Luzhkov mixed in 'semi-criminal' circles. The attacks on the two politicians were obviously well thought-out and coordinated.

Dorenko's programme specifically tried to link Luzhkov to the money-laundering scandal involving up to $15 billion illegally channelled to the Bank of New York. No evidence was produced to substantiate the claim. Even more damagingly, Luzhkov was charged with responsibility for the murder of American businessman Paul Tatum, who part-owned the Radisson-Slavyanskaya Moscow hotel. The Moscow city authorities also owned a significant part of the hotel, and the mayor's representative on the hotel's management was a Chechen called Umar Dzhabrailov. Dzhabrailov, general manager of what is popularly known as the Slavyanskaya-Chechenskaya Hotel, is a rich supremely confident character in his thirties, with long flowing dark hair. When I saw him in his hotel, unlike the unfortunate Tatum, he was always surrounded by his numerous stocky bodyguards. He has been interviewed by police a number of times in connection with Paul Tatum's contract killing, but no charges have ever been brought despite his reputed mafia connections. As an indication of his delusions of grandeur, and perhaps also his desire for immunity from prosecution, Dzhabrailov stood for the Russian presidency in 2000, gaining a derisory share of the popular vote. His natural constituency seemed to be limited to Russia's Chechen mafia clans, who specialized in contract killings, racketeering, prostitution, people-trafficking, drug- and gun-running, banking and other semi-legitimate 'business'. It was unlikely to garnish enough support to win Dzhabrailov a majority in the country.

The association with Dzhabrailov didn't look good for Mayor Luzhkov, who was also accused of working closely with Chechen and other mafia groups in Moscow. A probably apocryphal story doing the rounds in Moscow accused the city authorities of skimming millions of dollars from the city's Ring Round scheme by narrowing the motorway by 15 centimetres along its entire length. Luzhkov tried to sue Dorenko for defamation through the Moscow courts, which he largely controlled, but the damage was done. When Luzhkov came to England the previous autumn, I met him and it was clear he was testing the water for his run at the presidency. A few months later, he was standing at a respectable 15 per cent in the presidential opinion polls. By October 1999, after the disastrous Moscow apartment bombing and Dorenko's relentless weekly attacks on ORT, his standing had fallen to 5 per cent.

Supporters of Fatherland-All Russia couldn't jump ship fast enough. Meeting Governor Yakovlev just before the Duma elections for the lower chamber of parliament, he told me he had had enough. The pressure from the media and the Kremlin on the Luzhkov-Primakov axis was immense. No soft touch, Yakovlev made it plain that once the elections were out of the way, he too would abandon Fatherland-All Russia. Out of the mainstream media, only Vladimir Gusinsky's Media-Most empire stuck with the OVR. Gusinsky, another oligarch and bitter Berezovsky rival, had allowed his media holdings to be extremely critical of Yeltsin in the first Chechen war, but had swung behind him to keep the 'red menace', represented by Gennady Zyuganov's Communist Party, out of power. United media support had helped raise President Yeltsin's opinion poll ratings from 2 per cent at the end of 1995 to over 50 per cent by the following summer. Igor Malashenko, head of NTV, had even joined Yeltsin's election team to ensure his re-election.

But by 1999, Gusinsky was again getting restless and trying to flex his political muscles. He felt he was losing influence and not benefiting sufficiently from the post-privatization carve-up. Having worked with Luzhkov for years to build up his personal fortune, he naturally inclined towards supporting Fatherland-All Russia. NTV, his flagship independent television channel, strongly backed the Luzhkov–Primakov alliance. This time around, however, NTV was less critical of the war in Chechnya, partly because of public opinion and partly because it was virtually impossible to cover the fighting from within the republic. Censorship and the dangerous conditions inside Chechnya made objective reporting extremely difficult. Three NTV staff had been kidnapped and ransomed in Chechnya in 1997, which made journalists even more wary of reporting from the war zone. The constant threat of kidnapping, the invasion of Dagestan, and the series of terrorist bombings in Russia had considerably eroded any lingering sympathy for the Chechen guerrillas. Few journalists rushed to portray the Chechen fighters as the plucky separatists often depicted in the first Chechen war.

Even so, the second Chechen war was just as bloody as the first. The Russians established 'filtration' camps to separate the terrorists from ordinary civilians. Reports of murder, rape of men and women, and physical brutality continued to seep out from Chechnya, especially in the Western press. The one or two independent Russian journalists who reported on the allegations of Russian brutality were vilified for their troubles. Vladimir Putin, using prison jargon, caught the mood of the country when he threatened 'to wipe the bandits out in the shit-house' (*mochit v sortire* in Russian). Some well-educated Russian liberals were shocked that their prime minister was using criminal slang, but most of the public lapped up their prime minister's earthy language. No doubt such use of language was all part of Putin's advisers' strategy to brand the prime minister as an 'ordinary common bloke'. Pollsters like Dr Alexander Oslon, described by Yeltsin as part of his 'family', were carrying out regular and detailed polling to gauge the public's reaction to Putin and all he represented. They were pleased by the results. Putin seemed to appeal to a wide cross-section of Russian society, because he could appear to be all things to all people. Women liked him. Behind the scenes, the Kremlin pumped huge amounts of money into the economy to ensure that for the first time in years, pensions and federal salaries were paid on time, and arrears paid off. Detailed polling showed that whilst Chechnya monopolized the headlines, the fact that people's wages and pensions were paid regularly had a greater influence on voting intentions than war in the Caucasus.

Meanwhile, Putin refused to define his political or economic programme, but looked determined, vigorous, healthy and strong. Constantly pictured on television surrounded by ministers, he promised ill-defined action and improvement. For most Russians this would definitely be an improvement on President Yeltsin. Frustratingly for Unity, Putin stayed aloof from party politics and the election campaign, and initially refused to endorse them. He wanted to look too busy running the country to be bothered with petty party politics. The prime minister finally grudgingly endorsed Unity in November, but seemed to keep his options open by also meeting with Sergei Kiriyenko, one of the leaders of the liberal reformist Union of Right Forces (SPS). The prime minister was indicating he would not be beholden to any political party, not even one created by his Kremlin allies. It also put some distance between him and Unity, should the bloc not do as well as expected in the forthcoming elections. His advisers had squabbled over whether he should publicly support any of the political groups fighting for seats in the Duma at all. Alexander Oslon, Kremlin campaign veteran, had been one of those pressing Putin to back Unity openly. Putin continued to agonize over whether he should come out in support of the Unity bloc, as other advisers voiced fears the ploy might backfire and undermine his credibility. The upshot was his half-hearted pledge to vote for Unity 'as a citizen' and friend of Sergei Shoigu. In answer to a reporter's question, he volunteered that only Unity unequivocally supported the government's position.

Putin's apparent disdain for the political process paid dividends in the Duma elections held on Sunday 19 December 1999. Parties aligned with Putin, such as the Unity election bloc, spectacularly triumphed at the polls, giving the Kremlin an effective majority in the lower house. Unity, which had ratings of below 4 per cent at the end of October, won a 24 per cent share of the vote in December, just below the Communists, who did worse than usual. Fatherland-All Russia obtained 13 per cent of the vote (on a 60 per cent turn-out), less than expected, with other opposition blocs like the liberal Yabloko Party and Zhirinovsky's extreme far-right Liberal Democratic Party faring much worse. The Kremlin described the election as 'a quiet revolution'. For the first time since the collapse of the USSR, the 'Red–Brown' alliance of Communists and nationalists would not dominate the Duma. Unity, with its allies the People's Deputy Party, the SPS and the pro-government Russian Regions, outnumbered the Kremlin's traditional opponents. When Fatherland-All Russia later merged with Unity, the Kremlin's stranglehold on the Duma was assured. Unity had scored a remarkable electoral success. Like Italian Prime Minister Silvio Berlusconi's Forza Europa, Unity had come from nowhere to dominate the political landscape. The results of the election not only effectively packed the Duma with the prime minister's craven supporters, but also acted like an effective referendum on Putin's leadership. With Primakov and Luzhkov's OVR crushed, and the Communists humbled, Putin looked like he had a clear run at the presidency.

Vladimir Gusinsky and NTV, which had backed the Fatherland opposition, were soon to face the Kremlin's wrath. Yevgeny Kiselyov, anchor-man and general director of NTV, said that during the previous summer, managers and editors of Media-Most had been invited to a number of meetings with Kremlin officials. 'They made it clear that we either support the candidate that the Kremlin was going to choose or we would have trouble,' Kiselyov recalled. Gusinsky and NTV opted for trouble. Vladimir Gusinsky, an arrogant and volatile character, had seriously overestimated his capacity to defy the Kremlin. Putin, never one to turn the other cheek, would not forget Gusinsky's defiance.

According to Boris Yeltsin, he first discussed resigning and handing over to Putin at a meeting on 14 December, several days before the Duma elections. The meeting took place at Yeltsin's presidential dacha at Gorky-9, outside Moscow. Gorky ('the hills' in English) had become Yeltsin's almost permanent residence over the past year. Putin reportedly showed the requisite modesty, telling the president, 'I'm not ready for that decision, Boris Nicolayevich.' Explaining his apparent misgivings, he continued: 'It's a rather difficult destiny.' Both men knew that the last few months had been all about preparing Putin to take over the reins of power, but his reticence nevertheless reassured Yeltsin. Throughout his eight years as president, Yeltsin had ruthlessly jettisoned any politician who had shown the remotest ambition to succeed him. General Alexander Lebed, Victor Chernomyrdin and Yevgeny Primakov had been just three high-profile victims of Yeltsin's suspicion of ambitious men. The Siberian bear had jealously guarded his power. Putin, a natural courtier and seemingly reluctant political careerist, posed no threat to Tsar Boris. He was in a way Yeltsin and the family's creation. The 'family' had held meetings over the summer at their dachas planning Putin's ascent to power. The key figures were again Dyachenko, Voloshin and Yumashev. As President Yeltsin disarmingly wrote in his autobiography, he 'deliberately and purposefully began to get the public used to the idea that Putin would be the future president'. The presidential election, it seems, was a mere formality. Tsar Boris would introduce the people to their next president, and they would accept the candidate proposed gratefully.

Yeltsin met Putin again in his Kremlin office on 29 December, to finalize the details of the handover of power. There can be no doubt that agreement had been reached on what would happen to Yeltsin, his immediate relatives and his entourage. Some of Yeltsin's inner circle would remain *in situ*, including Alexander Voloshin, head of the presidential administration. Voloshin, forty-three, slim and bald with a high forehead and beard, is an intelligent chain-smoking workaholic. A soft-spoken man who rarely gave interviews, he was known as the 'Grey Cardinal' for his mastery of the Kremlin's Byzantine intrigues.

Yeltsin's claim that he didn't tell his daughter of his decision to resign until a few days beforehand seems disingenuous. Tatyana Dyachenko had been working in the Kremlin for the last four years, and was at the heart of the president's 'family'. It was the family, rather than the sick Yeltsin, who was really running the country and the government. Since the beginning of his second term in 1996 and his quintuple heart by-pass operation later that year, the increasingly erratic and unpredictable Yeltsin tended to be merely a figurehead. When he was well, Yeltsin mainly concerned himself with international summits involving world leaders, and with rubber-stamping the frequent changes of government. He was totally uninterested in the detail of government, which would have probably have been the case by his second term even without his drink and associated health problems. Mikhail Gorbachev told the Italian newspaper *La Stampa* that he thought Boris Berezovsky, Alexander Voloshin and Tatyana Dyachenko were key figures in persuading Yeltsin it was time to go. 'It's those three who devised the Putin operation and they have now made the decisive move,' he was quoted as saying.

President Yeltsin, advised by the 'family', was determined to pull off a dramatic resignation stunt and catch the country completely by surprise. The 1993 constitution, which he had imposed on the country, stipulated that the presidential election should have taken place in June 2000. But Yeltsin and the 'family' didn't want to risk holding off the presidential elections until then for two reasons. First, there was a danger that the war in Chechnya could start going badly, which would weaken Putin's popularity and undermine his bid for the presidency. Second, although Primakov and Luzhkov had been cowed, the family didn't want them or any other candidate to have enough time to organize an effective campaign. If Yeltsin resigned, according to the 1993 constitution, presidential elections had to be held within three months. Furthermore, the prime minister would also become acting-president, giving Putin all the advantages of incumbency. He would hold both posts simultaneously, giving him an immense advantage over any challengers. His every move would be covered by a generally supportive media, as he went about his business as the country's acting head of state. The public would be treated to the spectacle of wall-to-wall coverage of Acting-President Putin, backed by the entire machinery of government. The transition from Acting-President Putin to plain President Putin would be seamless.

An armoured car, escorted by police vehicles, carried Yeltsin's New Year message to the Ostankino TV tower, in Moscow's northern suburbs. The taped video resignation speech was to be broadcast that day at noon, so it would be shown at midnight in Russia's far east. As Russians toasted the coming of the New Year, they could also say farewell to Russia's first post-Communist elected president. Meanwhile, Yeltsin and Putin were having a number of handover meetings in the Kremlin. When the meeting with Patriach Alexei, leader of the Russian Orthodox Church was concluded, the patriach bowed to Putin. The religious authority was acknowledging the superiority of the secular power. Next, Yeltsin and Putin met the heads of the 'power ministries' (*siloviki*), so-called because they represented the power of the state. They included the Defence, Interior and Justice Ministries, the Federal Guard Service, the Federal Security Service (FSB) and the Foreign Intelligence Service (SVR). It was crucial to have these men, and their ministries, onboard for the handover of power. Before leaving the Kremlin at about 1 p.m., former president Yeltsin gave into Putin's safekeeping the nuclear briefcase which contained the launch codes for Russia's strategic nuclear arsenal. All this was filmed by the TV cameras for public consumption. Putin looked pensive and drained, with a glazed look in his eyes. As usual, it was impossible to see what he was thinking or feeling. His KGB training and background once again came to the fore. Yeltsin looked wooden, stiff and puffy. He didn't look a well man. Out of office, he would look much fitter than his last few years in the Kremlin. All the decrees confirming the handover had been prepared in advance, and as he left his Kremlin office for the last time, Yeltsin turned to Putin and said: 'Take care of Russia.'

President Yeltsin's New Year's Eve speech was an emotional affair. He told the Russian people he was leaving early to ensure the country entered the new millennium 'with new politicians, with new faces, and with new, intelligent, strong, energetic people. And we who have been in power for many years must stand down.' The Duma elections had shown that Russia would no longer return to the past, and that meant that he had achieved his life's goal. Why should he hang on to power, he argued, when there was such a strong person in the country worthy of becoming president? In an emotive passage, he also asked the Russian people to forgive him. 'I want to ask your forgiveness. I want to apologize for not making many of our dreams come true. What seemed easy turned out to be extremely difficult. I apologize for not justifying some of the expectations of people who believed that we could jump in one swoop from the grey, stagnant, totalitarian past to the bright, prosperous, civilized future. I believed in it myself.' He had, he admitted to his national audience, been naive. Wiping away a tear, Yeltsin concluded by wishing his 'dear Russians' a Happy New Year and century. The country reacted calmly, most thought it was about time he should go in any case.

There can be no doubt that Putin, described by one analyst as a 'nobody, from nowhere' was given Russia's presidency on a plate. Unlike Russia's other leading figures, Putin had never before been elected to a single post or public office. He had come from practically nowhere to become the most powerful man in the country, and arguably one of the most powerful in the world. Why had Yeltsin done it? He did not have a particularly close relationship with Putin, and up to this point, they had rarely met outside the working environment. The reason was almost too simple. Yeltsin was too ill to carry on as president for much longer. His heavy drinking had almost killed him several times. He had only just survived his heart by-pass operation in 1996, and had been re-elected president while he was secretly in intensive care. No one knew how long Yeltsin could survive. But before he retired, he needed to find a successor he could trust to protect his family and his interests once he stood down. Russia had not been particularly kind to its ex-leaders, and there had never before been a peaceful democratic transfer of power.

Yeltsin wanted immunity from prosecution on corruption or any other charges for himself and his immediate family. He also wanted a decent pension and lifestyle after he quit. Prime Minister Sergei Stepashin had made the mistake of publicly stating he would take on the corrupt oligarchs. When I met Stepashin in late 1999, he was still shellshocked by the speed of his dismissal. Sadly, from Yeltsin's perspective, Stepashin had shown himself to be untrustworthy. As Yeltsin saw it, his prime ministerial appointee was there to protect the 'family' and those connected to it. Yeltsin couldn't afford to have a loose cannon attacking important vested interests. Stepashin didn't understand this unspoken pact, and was punished for it.

Vladimir Putin, on the other hand, was more circumspect and his loyalty was unquestionable. Some critics would say it was also unquestioning, a military quality which Yeltsin and his 'family' found appealing. From President Yeltsin's point of view, it was swiftly apparent that he had made the right choice. Following Yeltsin's dramatic New Year's Eve resignation, Putin's very first act as acting-president was to sign a decree granting immunity to Yeltsin and his immediate family. Yeltsin was awarded a generous pension, state security protection, medical care for him and his immediate family, and retained the Gorky-9 state dacha for his personal use. The cost to the Russian taxpayer of looking after the Yeltsin family is over $1.4 million per year. Almost a year on, Putin's supporters in the Duma introduced a bill guaranteeing a similar package and immunity from prosecution for the current and all future Russian presidents.

Boris Yeltsin had been less than forthright about the immunity deal he received from Putin. In his ghosted autobiography, *Midnight Diaries*, Yeltsin claims: 'Immunity has not been conferred upon my family.' In the face of overwhelming evidence to the contrary, this statement should be taken with a large pinch of salt. The decree of 31 December granting Yeltsin immunity is officially entitled: 'On Guarantees for the President of the Russian Federation and His Family Members after Completion of His Exercise of Power in

Office.' Yeltsin's assertion that the decree was only designed to prevent political persecution after his resignation should perhaps be regarded in the same light as his claim that all his wife's jewellery was paste. As the flawed but charismatic Boris Yeltsin shuffled off centre-stage, his place was taken by a sandy-haired ex-KGB man with cold, steely eyes.

5

PRESIDENT PUTIN GETS ELECTED

*Question to Russian diplomat: 'Describe the situation in
your country in one word.' Answer: 'Good.' And in two
words? 'Not good.'*

The Putins took a personal risk in visiting Chechnya on New
Year's Eve, 1999. Whilst politically astute, it was a hair-raising
experience. At first, Lyudmila decided she wouldn't go. Then she
changed her mind, although she was still extremely apprehensive.
'No one could guarantee that something wouldn't happen. Things
were unpredictable,' she said later. After a failed attempt to reach a
garrison in Chechnya by helicopter, usually the safest form of travel
in the war zone, the Putins finally made a visit to Gudermes in a land
convoy in the early hours. The Russian-held town was 18 miles east
of war-torn Grozny, Chechnya's capital. Lyudmila recalled: 'You
should have seen the surprise and amazement in the eyes of our boys
when we arrived. They looked tired and a little disorientated – as
though they wanted to pinch themselves: Was it really Putin who
had come to see them and celebrate New Year's Eve with them? Were
they dreaming?' Presenting hunting knives to soldiers in a live televised ceremony, Putin told his troops that the war was 'not just
about restoring the honour and dignity of Russia. It is rather more
than that. It is about putting an end to the break-up of the Russian
Federation.' Russia, he said, was grateful to them. There would be no

change in military tactics. 'We are going to do everything in an optimal way. Optimal means lowest possible casualties among our troops and absence of casualties among civilians,' he assured the assembled reporters. A few hours later, the acting-president's fleet of cars returned to Makhachkala, Dagestan's capital. The road they travelled on was bombed by Chechen separatists the next day. With a sense of relief, but with a morale-boosting photo opportunity under their belts, the Putins returned to Moscow.

With backing from most of the country's media, Putin's favourable opinion poll ratings started to go through the roof. Nearly three-quarters of the electorate thought he was doing a good job as acting head of state. There was never any doubt that Putin would win the presidential election. In a way, the result was a non-election. Vladimir Putin continued in much the same manner as he adopted during the run-up to the Duma elections. He affected a nonchalant disinterest in the election process. The acting-president was portrayed as too busy with his official duties to sully his hands with grubby campaigning. There would be no campaign rallies or speeches on the stump. Every evening Putin was seen in different parts of the far-flung Russian Federation, visiting villages, schools, factories and hospitals, giving awards and taking part in events for International Women's Day. He would be pictured in the Kremlin, hearing reports from grave-looking ministers. Visiting Chechnya again, this time being flown into a Russian base in a fighter plane, Putin denied the whole thing was a publicity stunt. Using a combat jet was the safest way to visit the embattled republic, he later told journalists. Putin's itinerary and whole body language seemed to be saying he was above petty politicking.

In his autobiography, Putin says that he envied the Romanov Tsars their ability to avoid elections: 'The sovereign does not have to think whether he will be re-elected. He can think about the destiny of his people without being distracted by trifles.' He had a cynical attitude towards political campaigning and disliked the whole process. 'You have to be insincere and promise something that you cannot fulfil,' he said. 'So you either have to be a fool who does not understand what you are promising or deliberately lie.' It doesn't seem to have occurred to Putin that some politicians actually make electoral promises which they mean to keep. On another occasion he compared television campaigning to selling 'Tampax or Snickers bars' and announced his campaign was relinquishing TV advertising spots. When a group of journalists had the temerity to ask Putin about his political programme, he replied: 'I won't tell you.' Such a response from a politician in the West would beggar belief, it might even raise an eyebrow in Turkmenistan or Tibet. Putin's response showed that he hadn't yet learned the experienced politician's manner of suavely evading a specific question. But what Putin really meant was that the electors had to take him as he was; he wasn't prepared to hustle for their votes like other presidential candidates. If the public thought he was doing a good job, and liked what they saw, they should just go out and vote for him. Lack of precise definition worked in his favour. If he didn't seem to have a detailed programme as such, he couldn't offend anyone.

The irony was that the Kremlin did produce a ten-year development strategy paper, but consciously decided not to publish it widely. The fear was that once Putin's programme became known, he would immediately alienate some sections of the electorate. Entitled 'Russia on the Brink of the Third Millennium', the paper was produced by German Gref's Centre for Strategic Studies, and endorsed by Vladimir Putin at the end of December 1999. It was only available on the internet. Gref, a thirty-five-year-old ethnic German from Kazakhstan (his family were deported from Leningrad during the blockade), was a liberal economic reformer who wrote his postgraduate dissertation at Leningrad University's law faculty. He knew both Putin and Sobchak, and went on to become trade minister under his fellow Petersburger. Supposedly a document on economic policy, the Millennium paper was more a statement of how Putin and his team saw Russia's future. Although put together by Gref and his team, the paper was written mainly in the first person, as if it were all Putin's own words. This was as close to Putin's personal manifesto as the electorate were likely to get, although of course most weren't privileged to read it.

Russia's market and democrat reforms, Putin wrote in the Millennium paper, should only be implemented by 'evolutionary, gradual and prudent methods'. But economic reform and efficiency were designed to underpin and strengthen Russia's status as a world power. 'If we lose patriotism and national pride and dignity, which are connected with it,' Putin wrote, 'we will lose ourselves as a nation capable of great achievements.' According to him, 'Russia was and will remain a great power.' While people had got used to freedom of expression, freedom to travel and other political and human rights, including democracy, all this was based on the belief in the state as the guarantor of order and the driving force for any change. People still looked to the state for an improvement in their conditions. Paternalism was deep-rooted in Russian society, Putin reasoned, and would not dissipate easily. 'Russia,' he therefore argued, 'needs a strong state power and must have it.' He was not calling for totalitarianism but a 'democratic, law-based, workable federative state'. He then listed much of what he would set out to achieve. This included a fight against crime and corruption; reform of the judiciary and budget; tackling anti-constitutional laws; and enhancing relations between the executive and civil society.

Putin also outlined a whole raft of economic reforms required to overhaul the economy. The country needed a long-term development strategy, with the state coordinating and regulating the economy. Investment should be encouraged, with industrial policy promoting the high-tech sector. Natural monopolies would be regulated; taxes reformed; non-payment and barter would be phased out; the banking system would be restructured; financial and stock markets overhauled; abuses in the shadow economy combated; and low inflation and a stable rouble maintained. A modern agrarian policy would embrace land ownership reform. Integration of Russia's economy into world economic structures, particularly the

World Trade Organization, was seen as a particular priority. Science, education, culture and health care would all be supported, and an incomes policy introduced to improve real disposable incomes. In a Blairite flourish, the paper added: 'The state must be where and as needed; freedom must be where and as required.' It was an impressive wish-list, but could Putin succeed in implementing all these ambitious policies? Over the coming years, he and his team would certainly try.

Yet the interesting point about the Millennium paper is whether Putin sees economic reform as a means in itself, or as a means to an end. The evidence points to his belief that economic reform is necessary to prevent Russia slipping down the league of great nations. In the section on 'economic efficiency', Putin began, 'to put it mildly, it is too early to bury Russia as a great power'. He came back to the theme at the end of the paper: 'For the first time in the past 200 to 300 years, it [Russia] is facing a real threat of sliding to the second, and possibly even third, echelon of world states. We are running out of time left for removing this threat.' So for Putin, economic reform was necessary to bolster Russia's claim to be a great power. Without it, Russia would continue declining and become a third-rate country. If on the other hand the country pursued the course of economic reform, people's prosperity would increase, and this was undoubtedly important for Russia and for Putin. Yet the starting point for Putin was making Russia more efficient and stronger, both domestically and internationally. From this, everything else flowed.

Putin's whole upbringing and background instinctively focused on the need for a strong state. As president-to-be, Putin felt he epitomized the strength and vitality of the state. *L'etat, c'est moi*, as Louis XIV said. He wanted to re-create a 'Great Russia', with a revitalized state apparatus. Even before the presidential election there were moves afoot to strengthen the power of the state and specifically the institution of the presidency. During the campaign, Putin had caused some observers to fear a return to authoritarianism. 'From the very start,' Putin had said in his autobiography, 'Russia was created as a supercentralized state. This is part of its genetic code, traditions and people's mentality.' Familiar pledges to uphold a liberal economy, the free market, human rights and respect for Russia's neighbours and global partners, were not universally accepted. Putin had also spoken darkly of imposing a 'dictatorship of the law'. It was an unfortunate phrase for those who remembered Soviet dictatorship and the USSR's scandalous disregard for the rule of law. The ITAR-Tass news agency issued a statement from Putin on New Year's Eve, quoting the acting-president as warning that 'any attempt to exceed the limits of law and the Russian Constitution will be decisively crushed'. There would be no power vacuum 'even for a moment'. He guaranteed freedom of speech, freedom of conscience, freedom of the mass media and property rights. On Thursday 30 December, the day before being anointed acting-president by Boris Yeltsin, Putin talked to CNN about the need for strong government to crush widespread lawlessness and corruption. Repeating his commitment to a liberal free market economy and human rights, he told his CNN audience: 'We don't need a weakened government but a strong government that would take responsibility for the rights of the individual and care for society as a whole.' Russia, he concluded, had only one ambition, to 'enjoy respect from other nations'.

Corporate, collective forms of activity had always prevailed over individualism in Russia, Putin had argued in the Millennium document. Individual rights and liberal humanism were not entrenched in the Russian psyche, or part of the country's rich and often tragic historical experience. For that reason, as he put on record in German Gref's paper, he believed that Russia was unlikely to become a second edition of the US or Britain with its liberal values. This style of state paternalism puts the interests of 'society' and the collective above the rights of the individual. The danger of this philosophy, predominant in Russia during Communism and Tsarism, is that the rights of the individual can be ridden roughshod over in the interests of the state.

Following criticism of Putin's lack of engagement with the voters, he took part in a half-hour phone-in with the *Komsomolskaya Pravda* newspaper on 11 February 2000. The acting-president answered questions from thirty-eight callers. Although not particularly illuminating, Putin again broadly stressed his commitment to the ideals of democracy and the market economy. He pledged to gradually professionalize the army; justified the intervention in Chechnya in terms of rooting out crime; and reiterated that oligarchs like Berezovsky would be treated equally before the law. On the break-up of the USSR, he rehearsed his favourite argument: 'he who is not sorry about the collapse of the Soviet Union has no heart and he who wants it recreated in its former shape has no head'. Asked why people should vote for someone put forward by Yeltsin, Putin stuck to his take-me-or-leave-me approach. 'If the people vote for me, I'm worthy and if they don't I'm not,' he said, adding 'a man is judged not by what people say about him, but by what he does.' Canvassing for votes was not really Putin's style. On a personal note, he revealed that his teenage daughters' German was better than his. They both attended a German school in Moscow.

The Kremlin's second and last major attempt to explain Putin's future direction and policies came with the publication of his 'Open Letter to Russian Voters', printed in the newspaper *Izvestiya* on 25 February. His letter admitted there were no special electoral events on his daily work schedule; he was determined to keep out of the political fray. Putin and the Kremlin attempted to popularize the ground already covered in the Millennium paper. A strong state was again a primary theme. 'In a lawless and, consequently, weak state man is defenceless and unfree. The stronger the state, the freer the individual,' Putin controversially explained. He didn't seem to think that the state could be too strong. On the contrary, he said the answer was 'a dictatorship of law and not of those whose official duty it is to enforce the law'. His relationship with the oligarchs would be the same as with anyone else, he wrote: 'The same as with the owner of a small bakery or a shoe-repair shop.' The implication was that unlike under Tsar Boris, the oligarchs could expect no favours from Putin. Elsewhere, Putin promised to eliminate the hated oligarchs as a class. Again, he promised to overcome poverty, and protect property rights and the free press. 'Our press is free and forever will be,' he pledged.

Unlike the Millennium paper, his *Izvestiya* letter outlined his attitude to foreign policy. For Putin, foreign policy priorities flowed from domestic priorities: 'Our priority is to fashion a foreign policy proceeding from the national interests of our country. In effect, we should recognize the supremacy of internal goals over external ones.' Russia's place in the world depended on how it rose to its internal challenges. But fundamentally, pragmatism and canny self-interest were the rule. 'Only the real interests of our country, including economic interests, should be the law for Russian diplomats.' Those who were puzzled by Putin's vigorous opposition to the war in Iraq, or his attitude to maintaining arms and nuclear contracts in the face of US opposition, need look no further for an explanation of Putin's core beliefs. Putin's Russia would put its own interests first, even if that meant clashing with the West on occasion: 'Domestic economic interests would determine Russia's external policies, and not vice versa, as was often the case with the USSR.' Nevertheless, Russia had 'zones of vital interest', the same as other countries. Although Russia wasn't a threat to any state, in Putin's view it was still a great power. It would be unreasonable to be afraid of a strong Russia, Putin argued, but added: 'One can insult us only at one's own peril.' Pragmatic Putin has a touch of the nationalist in his make-up. Despite the implosion of the USSR, Russia's leaders still hanker for their country to be taken seriously as a key player on the world stage. They would love Russia to be feared again, just a little.

Putin soon put some of his ideas into action. After granting Boris Yeltsin immunity, one of his first acts was to sack Yeltsin's daughter and one-time ally Tatyana Dyachenko from the Kremlin. Dyachenko had installed herself in the Kremlin as an 'adviser' to her father and the administration. Some people thought she, not Yeltsin, effectively ran the government. Dyachenko sat in at high level meetings in the Kremlin, giving the impression to foreign diplomats that she was taking key decisions. Putin also astutely removed his former boss Pavel Borodin from the Kremlin, giving him the sinecure of secretary of the Russia–Belarus union. Allegations of corruption pursued Borodin in his new job, but at least he was no longer closely associated with Putin's new administration. Dyachenko too was facing investigation by the Swiss authorities looking into the Mabetex affair, and was considered a political liability in the run-up to the presidential elections. Putin also dismissed Dmitri Yakushin as presidential spokesman, although he was given a job elsewhere in the presidential administration. Perhaps more shockingly, Putin prepared to move against the oligarchs in a populist move designed to bolster his image as his own man. Boris Berezovsky, whose media interests backed Putin in the Duma and presidential elections, found himself once again facing embezzlement charges involving Aeroflot foreign ticket sales. Berezovsky had previously faced such allegations under Yevgeny Primakov's premiership in late 1998, but these had been brushed aside when Primakov was subsequently sacked. By the summer of 2000, five of the country's leading oligarchs found themselves under investigation from government prosecutors and tax police.

Working through the New Year holiday, Putin continued his minor reshuffle by promoting Sergei Shoigu, who led the successful Kremlin-backed Unity Party in the Duma elections, to deputy prime minister. Two Yeltsin ministers, Nikolai Aksyonenko and Victor Khristenko were demoted, while another, Mikhail Kasyanov, became the sole first deputy prime minister in the cabinet. Kasyanov, a forty-two-year-old English-speaking technocrat and former deputy prime minister and deputy minister of finance under Yeltsin, was close to the 'family' and had led negotiations with the International Monetary Fund. Clearly groomed for the prime minister's role in a Putin presidency, Kasyanov was commonly known as 'Misha two per cent'. The nickname referred to allegations circulating about Kasyanov's supposed cut from the debt deals he organized, including Russian and Soviet sovereign debt. The allegations of bureaucratic graft remain unproven, but Kasyanov was undoubtedly a member of the Yeltsin 'family', if not of its inner core. Mikhail Kasyanov's continued seniority in Putin's government was seen as part of the agreement with the 'family' to keep some of its key players in place. After Putin's presidential inauguration, Kasyanov was confirmed as prime minister, a position he retained until just before the 2004 presidential election.

The Babitsky case didn't augur well for the future of press freedom in Russia. Andrei Babitsky, a Russian journalist who worked for the US-funded radio station Radio Liberty, was arrested by Russian forces outside Grozny in mid-January 2000. His reports from rebel-held areas had reportedly infuriated the Kremlin, who saw him as unduly sympathetic to the Chechen guerrillas. Babitsky's coverage also made a mockery of the Russian authorities' attempt to control media coverage of the war inside Chechnya. Strict conditions were imposed on the movement of journalists and television crews in the territory, and the government had appealed to the media not to put the voices of 'Chechen terrorists' on air. Andrei Babitsky was initially arrested for allegedly not having proper accreditation to work inside the breakaway republic. In a bizarre twist, he was then shown on Russian TV being handed over to Chechen guerrillas in 'exchange' for three soldiers. Doubts were expressed about whether the exchange was genuine, and fears grew for Babitsky's safety, leading to a demonstration in Moscow by fellow journalists, and expressions of concern from the US State Department and the European Commission for Babitsky's well-being.

Acting-President Putin promised to personally look into the Babitsky case, and under intense international pressure, asked Russia's security services to ensure the journalist's safety. It had taken the Russian authorities two weeks to acknowledge they had arrested him in the first place. Babitsky was eventually released after more than a month of captivity in Chechnya. It appeared that the whole prisoner exchange exercise had been an attempt by the Russians to paint Babitsky as a member or supporter of the Chechen rebels. Savik Shusters, of Moscow's Radio Liberty, said: 'I think people should be really frightened because it is absolutely clear that the powers that be are now dividing the people into two categories – ours and not ours.' Babitsky believes he was handed over to pro-Moscow Chechens in an attempt to discredit him. It also transpired that he had been held by Russian forces in the notorious Chernokozovo detention camp in northern Chechnya. During his two weeks there, he claimed he had been beaten and heard the screams of a woman being tortured. According to the journalist, he also saw another man had been beaten black and blue. Babitsky claimed torture methods included victims crawling along a corridor under a hail of blows from batons; threats of amputation; and filling prisoners' cells with tear gas. Human rights groups reported allegations that Chernokozovo detainees had been beaten, raped and killed. 'We've all read about concentration camps during the Stalin era, we all know about the German camps – it's exactly the same there,' Babitsky said after his release.

Babitsky was freed after travelling in the boot of a car, and following the removal of his internal and foreign travel passports (Russians have two). All along, Babitsky wondered whether he would survive his ordeal. Crossing into Dagestan, he was re-arrested for travelling with false documents, and belonging to an armed group. Released and returned to Moscow on President Putin's orders, the latter charge was dropped. The Radio Liberty journalist was later fined $300 on the first charge, which became void due to an amnesty. Commenting on the whole sorry saga in his autobiography, Putin displayed an alarmingly hardline attitude towards Babitsky, saying of the journalist: 'He was working directly for the enemy. He was not a neutral source of information. He was working for the bandits.' In his view, what Babitsky did was 'much more dangerous than firing a machine gun'. Putin defended the apparent prisoner exchange, saying it was worth handing Babitsky over for just one Russian soldier, let alone several. This had all been with Babitsky's permission, and in any case, 'the bandits wouldn't do anything to Babitsky because they thought of him as one of their own'. The whole episode underlined Putin's hostile attitude to a critical, independent media, especially where the hyper-sensitive question of Chechnya was concerned. This was in stark contrast to Boris Yeltsin, who had been frequently criticized by the independent media, but despite all his faults had never tried to gag it. Yeltsin had on the whole just ignored the opposition media. The only time the Russian media had reined itself in was to support Yeltsin during the 1996 presidential elections, with the express purpose of keeping the Communists out of power.

Reacting to some critical coverage from oligarch Vladimir Gusinsky's media empire, the Kremlin launched a savage attack on the independent media in early March. Singled out for special treatment was Gusinsky's *Segodnya* newspaper, which it accused of 'one-sided' and 'tendentious' coverage of the presidential election race. The Kremlin said darkly that it would respond to acts of provocation with all the firepower it could muster, and accused the paper of sowing 'doubt among those who had already decided who to vote for', which would 'rock the boat of public accord and calm in our country'. The newspaper's crime, it turned out, was alleging that the acting-president had abused his position as incumbent to promote himself before the official start of the 2000 election campaign. This would be in breach of electoral law. *Segodnya* editor Mikhail Berger said the Kremlin response sounded like 'threats from bandits'. In fact, the Central Electoral Commission said the Putin campaign had broken electoral rules on three occasions. The first concerned a pro-Putin puff by the state-owned *Rossiiskaya Gazeta* newspaper, before the election campaign officially started; a lengthy interview on ORT state television in early February, when a family-friendly Putin was seen stroking his pet poodle; and *Izvestiya*'s 'Open Letter to Russian Voters'.

The mysterious death of Artyom Borovik, a Russian TV and print journalist and media magnate critical of Putin and the war in Chechnya, added to the air of mutual suspicion surrounding coverage of the election campaign. Borovik and eight others died in a plane crash on take-off at Moscow's Sheremetyevo Airport on 9 March. The journalist had specialized in investigative exposés of corruption amongst the Kremlin elite, which appeared on his TV programmes or in his newspapers *Top Secret* and *Versiya*. Pilots told Russian television that the small Yak-40 on which he was travelling was regarded as a reliable aircraft, and even if all three engines failed on take-off, it should have been able to land safely. Earlier in the year, police had sought to detain Alexander Khinshteyn, another leading investigative journalist, and send him to a psychiatric clinic run by the Interior Ministry outside Moscow. The incident smacked of old Soviet KGB tactics, when dissidents were regularly declared insane and locked away in state mental asylums. Warnings from the Kremlin, the Babitsky case, Borovik's untimely death and Khinshteyn's treatment all sapped the confidence of Russia's beleaguered independent media. From their point of view, it looked as if there was a sustained attempt to intimidate journalists and suppress criticism of the war in Chechnya, the Kremlin and Acting-President Putin. Putin may not have been the architect of this strategy, but it was certainly the effect of the combined weight of the Kremlin and the government apparatus bearing down on the press. The Kremlin and Putin's campaign team were attempting to whip the media into line behind their man, just as Russia's TV and press had lined up behind Yeltsin in 1996.

A plan to distribute Putin's autobiography, *First Person*, widely throughout the country was deemed illegal by the Central Electoral Commission, and scrapped. The original idea had been to print 500,000 copies of the book and sell it for 20 to 25 roubles (70 to 88 US cents) across Russia. There was a fear that the books could even be given away free to the electorate. After the country's election commission deemed the book 'campaign propaganda', the plan was scaled down so that only 50,000 copies of the autobiography were printed, and sold to Putin's campaign HQ for 17 roubles each. The 50,000 copies of the acting-president's autobiography were then distributed free to the electorate. The book consisted of 24 hours of interviews with three selected Russian journalists, extracts of which were published by the *Kommersant Daily* newspaper on 10 March, around a fortnight before the polls opened. All these questionable attempts to boost Putin's media coverage highlighted the Kremlin's tendency to go in for unnecessary overkill. Eighty-five per cent of Russians gained their information from the television, and two of the three main TV channels were state controlled. The third, Gusinsky's NTV, didn't really have an alternative presidential candidate to back once Yevgeny Primakov had made it clear he would not be putting his name forward. Putin was the only serious champion the media had to support.

Putin's presidential campaign was run from the marble-cladded Alexander House in Moscow. Apart from Dmitri Medvedev, a young former Leningrad lawyer, head of the campaign and a presidential official, Putin's campaign team comprised a mixture of Petersburgers and Yeltsin's 'family' members who had ensured the old president's re-election in 1996. German Gref, the economic brains behind the Putin team, based his Centre for Strategic Studies at the Alexander House campaign HQ. There was also Mikhail Margelov, head of Rosinformcentre, the state information body; Alexander Voloshin, Yeltsin and Putin's chief of staff; Gleb Pavlovsky, a political consultant running the Foundation for Effective Politics (also based at Alexander House); and Dr Alexander Oslon, head of the Public Opinion Foundation polling group. Oslon had also been at the heart of Yeltsin's re-election team. Vladislav Surkov and Alexander Abramov were two Kremlin campaign secondees, and were both former executives of the Alfa Group, which includes the large private Alfa Bank. The Alfa Group is controlled by an oligarch favoured by the Kremlin, Pyotr Aven. Alexander House itself was formerly owned by another oligarch, Alexander Smolensky, whose SBS-Agro Bank went belly up in the financial crisis of 1998. Thousands of depositors lost their life savings in the debacle.

Six weeks before the presidential election on 26 March, seventeen key Kremlin posts were already filled by people who were from St Petersburg and knew Putin when he was deputy mayor there in the early 1990s. Some had known him since the 1970s. The seventeen included two deputy prime ministers and the head of the FSB, Nikolai Patrushev. Among this group were Alexei Kudrin, first deputy minister of finance; Victor Cherkesov, deputy head of the FSB; Sergei Ivanov, secretary of the Security Council; Victor Ivanov, head of personnel in the Kremlin, and the economist German Gref. Gref was deputy privatization minister when Putin became acting-president, and also became head of the Centre for Strategic Studies, with a two-month deadline to draw up a plan for Russia's economic revival. Gref said the plan was to follow a 'liberal model of development', while preserving state regulation and a wider social safety net. Dima Medvedev, an academic who taught civil law at Leningrad University and advised Putin when he was deputy mayor, was brought in to run the acting-president's election campaign. Fyodor Gavrilov, a St Petersburg columnist, said Putin was 'using the St Petersburg people first of all because he knows them'; adding, 'At best, he will use the intelligentsia for ideas and the ex-KGB men to put them into practice.'

The practice of bringing cronies from one's home town was well-established in Russia. Yeltsin had brought a number of people with him into the Kremlin from Yekaterinburg in Siberia; Stalin had brought in some thugs from Georgia, including Lavrenti Beria, head of the secret police. Partly it was about rewarding friends, but more importantly Putin's appointments reflected the age-old desire to have about him people he knew and could trust. Many of the bureaucrats hanging around the Kremlin were badly tainted from association with the 'family', corrupt, incompetent or simultaneously all three. Putin's Petersburgers were usually competent if not outstanding, and had had little opportunity to be corrupted by the endemic Kremlin infighting prevalent during Tsar Boris's reign. Later on in his presidency, Putin would appoint more Petersburgers to his government, and promote others.

Vladimir Putin's first television interview with a foreign journalist while he was acting-president had caused quite a stir. Sir David Frost interviewed Putin in Moscow on 29 February for the BBC's *Breakfast* programme, and the most surprising aspect was Russia's apparent willingness to consider NATO membership. In response to a question from Sir David, Putin said he could envisage a closer relationship between Russia and the alliance. 'We believe we can talk about more profound integration with NATO, but only if Russia is regarded as an equal partner.' Pressed on whether Russia might ever join NATO, Putin replied: 'I do not see why not.' He said he could not view Russia in isolation from Europe or the 'civilized world', and it was therefore hard for him to see NATO as an enemy. Putin went on to say that attempts to exclude Russia from the debate over the Atlantic Alliance's eastward expansion had led Moscow to oppose NATO's enlargement. 'If an attempt is made to exclude us from decision-making, that concerns and irritates us,' he added. But the media's interpretation that Russia was preparing the ground to apply for NATO membership was wide of the mark. Although Putin wanted to improve cooperation with NATO, he had been accidentally drawn into overstating Russia's position. The idea of joining NATO horrified many in Russia's military-industrial complex and the security services. For many (including Putin), NATO had been the 'main opponent' for most of their careers. They couldn't imagine Russia being overruled in security discussions by other NATO countries, despite the fact that decisions were made by consensus. In Chechnya, for example, the Russians would not countenance any political or military NATO involvement.

The response from the Russian military was swift. General Leonid Ivashov, head of international relations at the Defence Ministry, swiftly 'clarified' Putin's remarks on the programme. Ivashov said it was 'hypothetically possible' that Russia could one day join NATO, but only if the Atlantic Alliance offered it a right of veto. 'But for that to happen, NATO, which is a military bloc, would have to transform itself into a European security institution and

Russia would have to have an equal voice and the right of veto,' he said. Russia still opposed NATO enlargement, and according to Ivashov, 'the prospect of collaboration between Russia and NATO depends on cooperation in Kosovo'. Moscow had bitterly accused NATO and the UN of favouring the ethnic Albanian majority over the Serb minority.

What most Russian policy-makers ideally wanted was a relationship where Russia could veto NATO's military decisions, and where Moscow was equal to the entire weight of the Atlantic Alliance countries put together. A bilateral arrangement between equal partners was what Russia sought (with veto powers), and it was this relationship which NATO naturally resisted. Even when the USSR was a superpower, it had struggled to achieve parity with NATO, and post-1991 Russia's claim to be a global force had dramatically diminished. The outcome of this seeming stalemate would be enhanced cooperation between the two, building on the 1997 agreement to establish a permanent joint council, and something which both NATO and Russia could live with politically. In the face of hostility from the Russian military and security establishment, Putin subsequently back-tracked on his seeming willingness to join the West's most powerful military alliance. A few days after the Frost interview was broadcast, he said that while he wanted to see closer political ties with NATO, Moscow would not be rushing to join the organization because of its role in Yugoslavia. The following year, President Putin went further when he told Russian deputies of the International Affairs Committees of both chambers of parliament: 'Russia does not intend to stand in line for NATO membership. With its economic, human, military, territorial, scientific and technical potential, Russia is a self-sufficient state, capable of securing its own defence.' There had, after all, been no change in Russian policy on NATO. Putin had just been caught out by Sir David Frost's question, again showing his early lack of political experience.

In an extraordinary move, British Prime Minister Tony Blair

travelled to St Petersburg to meet Acting-President Putin on 10 March, slightly more than two weeks before the presidential elections. There was some adverse press coverage in the UK because the trip was seen as endorsing Putin's presidential bid in the immediate run-up to the elections, particularly controversial given the background of the bloody conflict in Chechnya. In the course of one week, federal forces reported the loss of 156 Russian servicemen in heavy fighting around the village of Komsomolskoye. Putin had just announced that he would impose direct presidential rule on Chechnya for 'a couple of years'. Human rights groups criticized the visit as they felt it condoned Russian human rights abuses in the breakaway republic. Amnesty International urged Tony Blair to 'tell Mr Putin that the world will not accept a Russia that turns a blind eye to systematic human rights abuse in Chechnya'. The New York based Human Rights Watch was more outspoken in its criticism of the trip. 'This is absolutely the wrong signal to be sending, making a private visit to the opera at a time when war crimes are being committed with impunity by Russia forces in Chechnya,' said spokesman Malcolm Hawkes. 'There are mass executions of civilians, arbitrary detention of Chechen males, systematic beatings, torture and, on occasion, rape. There is the absolutely systematic and rampant looting of Chechen homes by Russian troops; these acts need to be condemned publicly in the strongest terms.'

In response, the British prime minister promised to raise the issue of human rights in Chechnya. 'We have always made clear our concerns over Chechnya and any question of human rights abuses there, though it is important to realize that Chechnya isn't Kosovo,' Mr Blair said. 'The Russians have been subjected to really severe terrorist attacks.' From Britain's point of view, it was an opportunity to size up the new Russian leader and develop a personal relationship between the two heads of government. At this juncture, Russia's new leader was a lonely figure on the world stage. President Bill Clinton was in the last year of his second term, playing the traditional role of a 'lame-duck' US president. He wasn't focused on

Russia, and in any case he had had a close relationship with President Yeltsin during the early post-Soviet years.

The 'Bill and Boris' friendship had been strained somewhat by the war in Kosovo, and the previous year had not been good for US–Russian relations. Gerhard Schroeder, the Social Democrat German Chancellor, seemed more preoccupied with domestic issues and had little time for Russia. Like France, Germany had also been very critical of Russian human rights abuses and the war in Chechnya. President Jacques Chirac, the Gaullist leader, was of a different generation to Putin and seemed slow to develop relations. Among the West's leaders, one of the few to show any real interest in developing relations with Russia was Tony Blair. He could act as Putin's bridge to the West, including Europe, and avoid Russia's international isolation. There was always the danger Russia could slip back into isolationism and authoritarianism, neither of which would be good for the West. On a personal level, the leaders were both around the same age, Blair forty-six and Putin forty-seven, and both lawyers. Since Tony Blair had been elected back in 1997, he was the more politically experienced of the two, especially since he had been a professional politician since the early 1980s. Putin had been a professional politician since the previous August. After taking over from Yeltsin on New Year's Eve, Putin had not ventured out of the country.

The British Foreign Office saw the opportunity of engaging Russia's new leader, and the risk of doing nothing, and decided critical engagement was better than isolation. On the issue of whether Blair should be meeting Putin on the eve of an election, the British government's line was that it was perfectly proper for Prime Minister Blair to meet Prime Minister Putin, who also happened to be acting-president. From Her Majesty's Government's perspective, it was business as usual; it was considered obvious that Putin would be elected president. Once Blair had met Putin, there would be a queue of other leaders lining up to meet him, especially after the election. Britain, however, had got there first, and felt pretty smug about it.

Before meeting Putin, the British prime minister's spokesman made all the right noises. 'The prime minister's key objective is to build a personal relationship with Putin and assess for himself where Putin is coming from and what he wants to achieve,' he told the press. 'Russia is too important a country to ignore or isolate over Chechnya,' he added. 'We need to engage. This opportunity should not be turned down.' However, the prime minister would express concern about human rights in Chechnya and call for a political settlement to the conflict. The use of force in Chechnya should be in proportion to the threat facing Russia. Before leaving for St Petersburg, Tony Blair told the BBC that 'the way to conduct ethical foreign policy in these circumstances is to complain about abuses that occur and make sure action is taken'. Blair's trip to St Petersburg followed a visit to Moscow the previous month by Robin Cook, the foreign secretary, who enthused that Putin was a 'refreshingly open' man who would pursue economic reform and a better relationship with the West. Cook added that the acting-president's 'priorities for Russia are ones we would share'. This was perhaps a precipitate rush to judgement, but at least Cook had avoided the American secretary of state Madeleine Albright's sanguine description of Putin as a 'liberal democrat', following a three-hour meeting with him in Moscow. Her assessment of Putin was perhaps a momentary triumph of hope over experience.

Some Russian commentators were wary of Blair's pre-election summit with Putin. Andrei Piontkovsky, director of the Strategic Studies Centre in Moscow, felt the visit was an interference in Russia's domestic politics. The visit, Piontkovsky argued, would embellish Putin's image as a politician who stood up for Russia's interests while earning the West's respect. 'I do not understand why the leaders of the Western world are behaving like governors of Siberian regions, especially considering they do not receive credits from the Kremlin but give them instead,' he said. *The Times* believed the visit would lend Putin 'some badly needed charisma and enhance his claim that he is a man who can do business with the

West'. Moscow's *Nezavisimaya Gazeta* reported that Britain knew that the visit of a European leader on the eve of the presidential elections in Russia 'will lead to the growth of Putin's popularity, not only in Russia but also in the West. At the same time, the UK thinks that the establishment of relations with Russia is a more important task.' The argument was that the Blair visit would boost Putin, but since he was bound to win anyway, building up Anglo–Russian relations and links with the West were far more important than electoral niceties.

Tony Blair arrived in St Petersburg late on the Friday night, 10 March, accompanied by his wife, Cherie, who was heavily pregnant with their fourth child. Diplomats were concerned that Cherie might find being driven around St Petersburg in a green minibus extremely uncomfortable, but she bore up very well. Topics on the agenda for the following day's talks included the Balkans, Chechnya, organized crime and the forthcoming G8 summit of the leading industrialized nations and Russia. In particular, Britain wanted to discuss greater cooperation with Russian peacekeeping forces in Bosnia and Kosovo; closer economic ties; and better coordination between criminal investigation agencies.

After the two-hour meeting at Peter the Great's splendid Peterhof summer palace outside the city, Blair and Putin both emerged satisfied and exchanging pleasantries. Blair rejected suggestions that he shouldn't be meeting Putin two weeks before the election and against the backdrop of a vicious war in Chechnya. Rather, it was in his view 'a privilege' to be in St Petersburg. 'It is in the interests of the whole world that Russia is a successful and engaged nation,' Blair said. 'We had a very good and full discussion . . . I want to say how much I have enjoyed the dialogue.' For his part, Putin described the prime minister as a 'very pleasant and a very appropriate partner. We're both law graduates and of the same generation . . . We consider the prime minister's visit very significant . . . Our countries are natural partners and at critical periods in world history they always stood together.' Vladimir and Lyudmila then accompanied Tony and Cherie to a performance of Sergei Prokofiev's opera *War and Peace* at the world renowned Marinsky Theatre. The Marinsky was known as the Kirov Theatre in Soviet times, and still maintains the Tsar's old imperial box. The *Chas Pik* newspaper complained that the attendance of Putin and Blair pushed up prices in the stalls to 3,000 roubles ($100), about two thirds the average monthly wage.

In Peterhof, behind closed doors, Tony Blair and Vladimir Putin had discussed the thorny issue of Chechnya. Each leader had one adviser and an interpreter present throughout the talks. As trailed beforehand, Blair told Putin there should be an 'objective' investigation of the alleged human rights abuses taking place in Chechnya, and complained that Russia's response to secessionism seemed 'disproportionate'. But the British toned down their criticism of the conflict, with a Downing Street official largely accepting Putin's version of events. 'There is a terrorist insurrection on their territory,' the official said, taking a position which undoubtedly delighted Blair's hosts. Putin went to some lengths to appear conciliatory and reasonable. After the meeting he told the press Russia was ready to listen and 'make adjustments', and would consider whether to allow the Red Cross and international observers into the Chechen war zone. British officials felt there had been no substantive change in Russia's policy towards Chechnya. A political solution to the crisis was nowhere in sight.

A request from Putin for assistance in combating terrorism was politely declined. For years Russian diplomats had tried to make a link between Britain's efforts to fight terrorism in Northern Ireland with the struggle in Chechnya. Russian diplomats have made the same point to me in the past. The argument was that the British could share their anti-terrorist expertise and so help the Russians fight Chechen guerrillas in what they insisted on calling an 'anti-terrorist operation'. Privately, British officials pointed out that the UK's anti-terrorist operations had not involved obliterating Belfast and displacing hundreds of thousands of people. The 11th of

September 2001 would change attitudes about cross-border anti-terrorist cooperation, but the British continued to disavow any comparison between Northern Ireland and Russia's war in the Caucasus.

From the points of view of the British and the Russians, Blair's summit meeting with Putin was a great success. Leaving St Petersburg, Blair told the British press on his flight home that he found Putin 'impressive'. The acting-president's two priorities seemed to be to reform the economy and open up Russia to the outside world, Blair indicated. He declared that Putin was 'highly intelligent with a focused view of what he wants to achieve in Russia'. Blair believed Putin wanted a Russia which is 'ordered and strong but also democratic and liberal'. He confirmed that he had raised the issue of human rights abuses in Chechnya, together with greater access for international observers. However, in an interview with the BBC's Robin Oakley a few days later, the prime minister again expressed sympathy for Putin's predicament. 'We recognize that the Russians do have a serious problem with terrorism . . . There are human rights abuses on either side.'

Tony Blair's St Petersburg mission meant that Russia had been engaged by a Western leader for the first time since Boris Yeltsin left office. Putin had shown some sensitivity, but not much movement, on the conflict in Chechnya. In the eyes of the Russian electorate, Putin appeared like a real leader, meeting and greeting one of the West's young leading lights. All in all it had been a good start. Even more significantly, when Putin came to choose his first major foreign visit abroad that April, he would choose London. It was a decision resonant with symbolism, with Putin consciously looking to the West, rather than the East, and Europe rather than the United States.

There was, however, the minor point of having to coast through the forthcoming presidential elections. When polling day arrived, Putin scored 53 per cent of the poll, with the Communist leader Gennady Zyuganov winning 29 per cent and Yabloko's liberal Grigory Yavlinsky gaining 6 per cent. Just under seven out of ten of

Russia's 108 million electorate had turned out to vote. Yavlinsky, an articulate fifty-year-old English-speaking liberal economist with strong Harvard connections, had never really endeared himself to the Russian electorate. Too associated in popular perceptions with the failed economic shock therapy of the early Yeltsin reformers, his Jewish background also worked against him in what remains a largely anti-Semitic society, especially in rural Russia. Yavlinsky's smooth media performances confirmed his status in many people's minds as the archetypal Russian liberal politician; a good speaker with an oversized ego who remained poor on delivering real change and improvement. In the 1996 presidential elections, he had come fourth behind the gravelly voiced nationalist General Alexander Lebed. It was Lebed who had brought the first Chechen war to a close that August, negotiating a ceasefire and Russian troop withdrawal, leaving Chechnya's final status to be decided by 2001. Although he came third this time, Yavlinsky's vote had actually fallen slightly since the previous presidential ballot. After the three front-runners, the other eight no-hope presidential candidates mopped up the remaining votes. They included Aman Tuleyev, the governor of Kemerovo region in south-west Siberia; Umar Dzhabrailov, Chechen general manager of Moscow's notorious Radisson Slavyanskaya hotel; and Yury Skuratov, the disgraced former prosecutor-general.

In theory, Putin's main presidential challenger in 2000 was the Communist Party and Gennady Zyuganov. But Zyuganov's Communists had already compromised themselves by doing a deal with Putin's followers in the Duma over the speakership and several important committee chairs. Zyuganov appeared terrified of winning the presidential race, and made it clear that he had absolutely no hope of doing so. His diminishing base of ageing party faithful in the country made it less likely with every passing year that the Russian Communist Party would ever regain power. Zyuganov never appeared confident of becoming president.

Gennady Andreyevich Zyuganov, a stocky fifty-five-year-old

former apparatchik, was born in the village of Mymrino, in a rural farming area in Russia's Black Earth region, 250 miles south of Moscow. Both his schoolteacher parents were card-carrying members of the Communist Party. Zyuganov went on to study mathematics at the Orel Pedagogical Institute in the regional capital, where he became involved in the local Komsomol Communist youth organization. After climbing the Orel Party structure, he ended up in Moscow working for the Soviet Communist Party's (CPSU) Central Committee, where he rose to become deputy head of the ideology department. At the first congress of the Russian Communist Party (KPRF) in June 1990, before the break-up of the USSR, he was elected secretary and member of the Politburo of the party's Central Committee. He was elected to the Duma in 1993, becoming leader of the party's faction in the parliament a year later. In 1995 he was awarded a doctorate in philosophy from Moscow State University. Zyuganov had been a second-rate apparatchik in the old Soviet system, and his prominence reflected the fact that very few of the old Communist Party elite remained loyal to the party after the collapse of the USSR. Diehards like Zyuganov had kept the faith even when the Communist Party was banned under President Yeltsin. Most other high-achievers abandoned the party far earlier, and went off to seek jobs in the private sector, working in government, or joined other parties.

Meanwhile, Zyuganov kept knocking out turgid books on the struggle between Westernizers and xenophobic Slavophiles, expressing overt sympathy for the latter. He controversially endorsed Russian Orthodoxy, and unconvincingly tried to suggest he favoured a mixed economy, suggesting he leaned towards 'social-democracy'. On the other hand, his faction in the Duma combined with other opposition elements during Yeltsin's presidency to frustrate economic reform and prevent the privatization of land. While moving away from centralized state planning, the party's policy emphasis was on protectionism, a culture of subsidies and high levels of social support. On foreign policy, Zyuganov had joined Russia's hawks in supporting the war in Chechnya to protect the country's territorial integrity. The Communist Party's attempts to impeach Yeltsin on the grounds that he was responsible for 'genocide against the Russian people' and the break-up of the USSR, had petered out in a welter of bribery and a loss of political nerve.

In reality, Zyuganov also veered towards the reactionary bigotry of the ageing 500,000 members of his party, by far the largest and best organized of all Russia's political parties. His political thinking is to be found in two books, *Beyond the Horizon* and *Russia and the World*. Zyuganov lamented the early passing of Stalin, and has claimed in speeches that Stalin 'only' killed about half a million people 'and most of those were party members'. Somehow Zyuganov thought that made the purges more acceptable. Stalin, he wrote, 'understood the urgent necessity of harmonizing new realities with a centuries-long Russian tradition'. If Stalin had only lived for a few more years, he would have 'restored Russia and saved it from the cosmopolitans'. Zyuganov was referring to the Jews. In a third book, *I Believe in Russia*, he stated that there was much to fear from Jewish influence, and had been since the nineteenth century. 'The ideology, culture and world outlook of the Western world became more and more influenced by the Jews scattered around the world. Jewish influence grew not by the day, but by the hour.' Zyuganov was later heavily criticized for failing to distance himself from inflammatory anti-Semitic remarks by one of the Communist Party's allies, former Soviet General Albert Makashov. Looking wider afield, China was the reform model Zyuganov admired, not the clumsy *perestroika* and *glasnost* introduced by Mikhail Gorbachev.

With such a background and programme, Zyuganov had only succeeded in uniting the rest of the country against the Communists. The entire Russian media backed Yeltsin's re-election to keep the Communists out of power, with the country's business tycoons, the oligarchs, jumping on the bandwagon. Zyuganov had lost against Yeltsin in the second round of the 1996 presidential elections after winning 40 per cent of the vote, a creditable enough score which the Communists were unlikely to repeat for demographic reasons. With Russia losing a million of its 148 million population every year through rising mortality and falling birth rates, the Communists were on a hiding to nothing if they relied on their traditional supporters. And so it proved in the 2000 presidential election. The media simply ignored Zyuganov. He and his party were a relic of the past, in spite of the fact that they had a core of incorrigible supporters in the country and the Duma. But Zyuganov's vote dipped by 10 per cent compared with 1996. Next time, inevitably, it would fall lower. The young, small traders, entrepreneurs and professional people just could no longer see what the Communist Party was for. It remained the party of old pensioners, the rural poor and the dispossessed. If Zyuganov's Communists remain Putin's main opponents, he can look forward to many more years in power.

The fact that Putin was elected on the first ballot, without the need for a second-round run-off against Zyuganov, was a triumph for his Kremlin campaign team. At one stage, as voting began in Russia's far east seven hours before polls opened in Moscow, it looked as if the Communist challenger might force a second ballot. Early returns had given Zyuganov 30 per cent, against about 45 per cent for Putin. But as the ballot count rolled across Russia from east to west, passing through Moscow and Putin's home city of St Petersburg, Putin moved into a comfortable majority. Moscow, one of the last areas in Russia's eleven time zones to announce its results, gave Putin his absolute majority. Just under half of all voters in the capital had supported the acting-president. In Chechnya, the Kremlin maintained the illusion of a normal vote, but most of those turning out to vote were the 90,000 Russian soldiers based there. The Communists considered the election a 'complete farce', Zyuganov said. 'There are no conditions for a normal honest election there.' He claimed the government had falsified the results and reduced the Communists' real vote. He supplied no evidence to support his increasingly wild allegations. Putin had meanwhile spent the hours running up to the election skiing and spending time in the banya. He looked confident when he voted in his local polling station, and appeared at his campaign headquarters around midnight. 'Tomorrow is Monday, a hard day, and I will have to go to work,' he said. As it became clearer that Putin would win, he told journalists that a first-round victory would give him a stronger moral mandate to rule the country. He warned Russians that they should hold their expectations in check. 'Well, perhaps no one should pin their hopes on a miracle,' he told reporters. 'In any case, I have no right to say that miracles will start to occur tomorrow. I believe that the situation is difficult in that the level of expectations is very high . . . Policies should be balanced and aimed at increasing living standards.'

Voting in Vladivostok, in Russia's far east, gave a flavour of the country's mood. Sunday 26 March was a cloudless, sunny day. About two-thirds of the voters turned out in Vladivostok and the surrounding Primorsky (Maritime) region. The city of Vladivostok lies 5,700 miles from Moscow on the Pacific coast, next to China's old Manchurian border. The home base of Russia's ageing Pacific fleet, it is also the largest port on the eastern coastline. Most of those voting expected Putin to win. 'I don't know why I voted for him,' one middle-aged woman said. 'He's young. He's quiet. He works effectively.' Alexander, another voter, said, 'Putin is the best of poor options . . . We don't know Putin. But there is no one else I can vote for.' Surveys showed local voters yearned for order and strong rule from the centre. 'His age gives him contrast,' said Igor Ilyushin, dean of the faculty of social technology at the University of the Far East. 'We've known the others for years, on television, in the media,' said Natalya, aged thirty. 'But we don't see action from them. Putin has been acting-president for a few months, but he's already proven he's worth our trust. He will change life for the better.'

Other voters in Vladivostok plumped for Zyuganov. 'What good did we see from Yeltsin?' said Elizaveta, a former nanny at a local kindergarten. 'Putin is Yeltsin's man,' said Yury, another

Communist supporter in his sixties. He went on, 'In the past, we lived several times better under Communism . . . We were receiving pensions and could afford to save money. Now our pensions are not enough to live on. They are not even enough for funerals. Let us vote for those who we lived under as human beings.' At the end of polling day, however, Putin's supporters outnumbered all the opposition.

In Russia's second city on the Neva, the mining institute where Vladimir Putin prepared his doctoral thesis was turned into one of dozens of 'Putin reception points', which had been established in St Petersburg and Moscow to show that the presidential candidate was listening to voters' concerns. Many voters came into the reception centres hoping for practical help. In St Petersburg, seventy-three-year-old Nikolai Ivanov wanted someone to sort out his pension. 'I'm only getting the average monthly pension of 650 roubles [$22] and I should be getting 800. I want the acting-president to do something about it. He's young, he's a lawyer, he's smart, and he's not compromised. We're proud of him around here.' Mr Ivanov admitted he didn't know much about Putin. 'But I see him on TV. He's a good sportsman. Old Yeltsin was sick. Putin will be better. I'll definitely be voting for him. We just want some stability.' In the town of Zhukovsky, a former Soviet aviation centre an hour's drive from Moscow, Victor Ivanovich gave other reasons for supporting Putin. 'He's like Stalin. He knows how to get the country into shape, and he will restore order. Putin is a strong man. Only he can help us,' said the fifty-five-year-old caretaker. Mikhail Nesterov, aged thirty-eight and a former aerodynamics academic, felt Putin's knowledge of a foreign language showed he was 'open to Western, liberal ideas'. Yelena Paltsova, an English teacher at the town's main secondary school, believed Putin's priorities would be tackling bureaucracy, capital flight and industrial development. In reality, as another voter from Zhukovsky noted, the electorate didn't have a clue what Putin stood for. Everyone enunciated their own priorities and hoped and believed Putin wanted the same. 'After Yeltsin, it's enough that he is young and energetic,' said Andrei, a building site foreman. 'I don't know what he plans to do with the country – we'll know that after the election. But he is the man we need.'

The Russian electorate were not the only ones in the dark about Putin's intentions. Keith Bush, director of Russian and Eurasian affairs at the Washington-based Centre for Strategic and International Studies, said: 'When it comes to reform, nobody knows what he's going to do. We'll have to wait until the swearing-in.' Putin, truly Russia's man for all seasons, won the presidential election in a haze of confusion and hope. He coasted to victory, winning over 60 per cent of the vote in his home city of St Petersburg, his best result in the country.

Not everyone was enamoured by Putin's campaign style. The Russian newspaper *Argumenty i fakty* called it the 'most boring election ever'. The *Moscow Times*, reflecting on the election outcome, felt that Russian citizens yearned for order, and so had invested their hope in a former intelligence officer. 'Grey is beautiful,' the newspaper declared. The *St Petersburg Times* said that the country had voted for 'style over substance'. It continued: 'Let's hope Russians like what Putin will now give them. Next time, though, it might be advisable to ask a few more questions first.' Konstanin Titov, the governor of the Samara region and a liberal presidential candidate, said it was not an election, but rather a 'dynastic transfer of power clearly cooked up by the oligarchs in accordance with the constitution and federal law'. Two of the presidential candidates, the former Communist MP Aleksei Podberezkin and the far-right Vladimir Zhirinovsky, had actually supported Vladimir Putin. The *Kukly* satirical puppet show on NTV had portrayed the eleven presidential 'challengers' as prostitutes vying for Putin's favours.

General Oleg Kalugin, former head of Soviet counter-intelligence who had denigrated Putin's KGB career, was even more dismissive of the election campaign. 'I don't believe in the Russia of Putin, criminalized and corrupt, with its lame justice and due process,' Kalugin wrote in an open letter to the acting-president. 'In this situation, I'll be bound to seek political asylum in the free world.' In his autobiography, Putin had denounced Kalugin as a 'traitor' and 'idler'. The ex-KGB general had revealed Cheka secrets, and compounded his sins by going to work in the US. Stripped of his awards by KGB hardliners in 1990, he had had them restored the following year. Kalugin suggested that Putin's recurrent use of the term 'traitor' showed a 'dulled awareness of the law', and a 'selective approach to the presumption of innocence'. The former KGB officer also alleged Putin had raised a toast to Stalin, had a plaque of Yury Andropov restored to the Lubyanka in Moscow and paid a friendly call on Vladimir Kryuchkov, the former head of the KGB who was a leader of the 1991 attempted hardline coup. None of this endeared Kalugin to the Kremlin. But overall, complaints about Putin's election campaign were pretty muted.

While voting took place across Russia, the vicious war continued in Chechnya unabated. On polling day, forty-year-old Colonel Yury Budanov of the 160th Russian tank division abducted, raped and strangled an eighteen-year-old Chechen girl after a raid on a house in the village of Tangi-Chu. Budanov later admitted killing Kheda Kungayeva, but pleaded insanity and was acquitted at a court hearing in Rostov-on-Don. After a huge outcry, the Russian Supreme Court ordered a retrial and he was found guilty of kidnapping, murder and abuse of power. He was stripped of his military rank, the Order of Courage he won in the breakaway republic, and sentenced to ten years in prison. In early March, John Sweeny of the British *Observer* reported details of an alleged massacre by Russian forces in the Chechen village of Katyr Yurt, west of Grozny. Sweeny found compelling evidence that up to 363 villagers and refugees had been killed by a Russian attack the month before in which military aircraft, helicopters, fuel-air bombs and Grad surface-to-air missiles levelled the village. Locals also alleged that a convoy of vehicles which had been offered safe passage under white flags was heavily bombed and rocketed, with grave loss of life. The use of fuel-air bombs was particularly terrifying. Dropped by parachute, the vacuum bomb releases a cloud of petrol vapour as it falls to the ground, which then ignites in the air causing a massive explosion. The 'killing mechanism' is a huge pressure wave, which ruptures the lungs and crushes the internal organs. Its use against civilians is banned by the Geneva Convention. Russia's Chechen 'anti-terrorist' operation was also destroying many innocent lives, and creating a legacy of bitterness, hatred and despair. The Russian military's heavy-handed and indiscriminate tactics acted as a recruiting sergeant for the more extreme Chechen separatists. It was a development which in turn led to ever more violent and reckless terror tactics from the increasingly radicalized Chechen rebels.

The day after the election, on Monday 27 March, Putin received a number of congratulatory calls: from Tony Blair, President Bill Clinton and China's President Jiang Jemin. Clinton and Putin spoke on the phone for sixteen minutes. Clinton said he emphasized to Putin the importance the world attached to strengthening the foundations of Russia's democracy, and deepening its integration into the international community. He also expressed his concerns about Chechnya, including the need to launch impartial and transparent investigations of reported human rights violations, and access to Chechnya for international organizations and the press. In an official statement released by the White House, Clinton declared the presidential vote 'an important milestone in the development of democratic Russia'. The statement continued: 'President-elect Putin has an opportunity to translate his electoral mandate into concrete steps to advance economic reform, to strengthen the rule of law, to intensify the fight against crime and corruption and to join with us in a broad common agenda of international security.' Clinton's call made it official, President Vladimir Putin was now a world leader. Tony Blair had also rung for a fifteen-minute congratulatory chat, but both Blair and Clinton had been beaten to it by the wily Jiang. China, it seemed, was determined to remind Russia's new president that Moscow could not afford to look exclusively westwards. It was not for nothing that Russia's vigilant imperial double-headed eagle, reinstated by Yeltsin, looks simultaneously east and west.

Putin always looks uncomfortable on big state occasions. His inauguration ceremony at the ornate nineteenth-century gilded Great Kremlin Palace was no exception. It was held on Sunday 7 May; everyone important was there. MPs, ambassadors, religious leaders, judges, dignitaries and friends packed the yellow and white palace. Swaying woodenly and looking tense, Putin awkwardly walked along a red carpet through an outer hall and into the sumptuous St Andrew's Hall, the former throne room of the Tsars, with its ten gilded pillars and bronze chandeliers, passing the hundreds of invited VIPs. He ascended a podium flanked by Boris Yeltsin and Kremlin guards dressed in nineteenth-century Tsarist uniforms, with Russia's giant double-headed golden eagle hovering in the background. Putin and the other politicians looked incongruous in their dark lounge suits, surrounded by the trappings of imperial Russia. Apart from Boris Yeltsin, Mikhail Gorbachev, the USSR's last president, stood in attendance. Just after midday, placing his right hand on a red leather-bound copy of the constitution, Putin promised to defend his country's independence and serve the people. For the next four years at least, he would be president, Russia's youngest leader since Stalin. The whole ceremony lasted half an hour. Outside the Great Palace and across the Moscow river, cannons fired a 30-gun presidential salute, while a troop of the Kremlin guard marched past in Cathedral Square carrying the presidential flag. As a military band struck up the national anthem, Russia's flag was raised over the Kremlin, its fluttering stripes of red, white and blue visible from Red Square.

Later that day, Putin would attend a service in the Kremlin's fifteenth-century, golden onion-domed Annunciation Cathedral with Lyudmila and the white-bearded head of the Russian Orthodox church, Patriach Alexei II. Barred from the cathedral as a penance for his sins, Ivan the Terrible had married his fourth wife in the porch just outside. Inside the dark and gloomy cathedral, the Putins were surrounded by ancient icons and frescos, portraying the Apocalypse and the Last Judgement, and proclaiming Moscow's status as the Third Rome. The well-worn floor, trod by the Tsars and their retainers through the centuries, was made of jasper. As part of his ceremonial duties, Putin would also lay a wreath at the Tomb of the Unknown Soldier lying outside the citadel's walls. In his eight-minute inauguration speech to the assembled throng in St Andrew's Hall, Putin said, 'We have proved that Russia is becoming a truly democratic modern state . . . The peaceful succession of power is the crucial element of the political stability which we have dreamed of, to which we have aspired and which we have sought.'

For the first time in Russia's history, one democratically elected president had handed over power to another. Before Putin's speech, a puffy-faced Yeltsin shakily told the gathering that Russia could be proud that the transfer of power was taking place without 'coups d'état, putsches or revolutions'. This was possible only because Russia was a 'free country' which had given its citizens liberty, he said. He reminded Putin of his words as he left his office on New Year's Eve: 'Take care of Russia.' The inauguration ceremony marked the passing of the *ancien régime*, and the start of the new. President Putin carried with him into the twenty-first century the hopes of his fellow citizens for a better, more prosperous Russia, where order reigned and the country's young had a future. No one knew whether their young president would succeed, but most fervently hoped and prayed that he would.

6

THE *KURSK* GOES DOWN

Journalist's question: 'What happened to the Kursk?'
President Putin: 'It sank.'

The *Kursk*, K-141, sank during a military exercise on Saturday 12 August 2000 in the Arctic Barents Sea, after two 'seismic events' were recorded measuring 1.5 and 3.5 on the Richter scale, at 11.28 a.m. and 11.30 a.m. local time. The *Kursk* was a state-of-the-art Project 949A Antei class (NATO designation 'OSCAR II') guided missile nuclear submarine, with a crew of 118. Described as the most effective multi-purpose submarine in the world, the 154-metre-long *Kursk* had been commissioned in 1994 at a cost of $1 billion. End-to-end, it was the size of two jumbo jets. The boat could dive to a depth of 600 metres and run at a maximum speed of 30 knots on the surface, 28 submerged. One of twelve Oscar II submarines built, it carried torpedoes and Granit cruise missiles. The *Kursk*'s primary mission was to operate against aircraft carriers and their battle groups close to Russian waters. The boat was the pride of Russia's Northern Fleet. The loss of the *Kursk* caused Putin's first major crisis, and one which shook his presidency and the whole country. The whole world looked on with sympathy and horror as the tragedy unfolded.

Vladimir Putin, then aged forty-seven, was not really trained or ready to run the country in March 2000. He had been plucked from obscurity, and had only held a political post (prime minister) for seven months before being elected president. It was no wonder he made a hash of the first week of the *Kursk* disaster, the loss of one of Russia's modern nuclear submarines and the entire crew. Putin's background had hardly prepared him for the rigours of political life. Like the rest of the military and security establishment, brought up in the old Soviet ways, his first reaction was apparent indifference. But he was genuinely shocked by the ensuing public and media outrage and learned some hard political lessons from the *Kursk* disaster. Afterwards he redoubled his efforts to bring the Russian media to heel, with profound consequences for Russia's still fledgling democracy.

On that fateful Saturday afternoon, Putin was in the Kremlin and about to head off for his annual holiday in the Black Sea resort of Sochi. He had been in power for just four months. After a meeting at 1 p.m. with Gennady Seleznyov, the Duma speaker, he sped out of the Kremlin's Spassky Tower gate in his armoured Zil limousine, heading towards Sheremetyevo airport. As he crossed Red Square, he had no idea the *Kursk* lay stricken and helpless at the bottom of the Barents Sea.

I do not intend to repeat here all the details of the *Kursk* disaster, what happened, how it happened, and how the Russian Navy tried to cover up the disaster and their own incompetence. But it is important here to record Putin's reaction to the disaster, how he responded, and the effect the tragedy had on the political direction of his presidency.

The Russian Navy eventually mounted a rescue operation eleven hours after the *Kursk* exploded. Admiral Vyacheslav Popov, the Northern Fleet's commander, had wasted much valuable time before he could face the inevitable truth: the *Kursk* had sunk. On his flagship cruiser, the *Pyotr Veliky* (Peter the Great), there can be no doubt that the explosions aboard the *Kursk* were picked up on the ship's sonar. Yet Popov, paralysed with typical Soviet fear and indecision, did nothing. He knew his head would be on the block if a disaster had occurred, and didn't want to break the bad news. Investigations showed that twenty-three submariners survived the initial explosions, and held on in the submarine's stern. After a fire, the last of the crew perished between 7 p.m. and 8 p.m. on Saturday 12 August, a fact confirmed by medical postmortems, the subsequent official inquiry, relatives' accounts of the state of their loved ones' bodies, and the monitoring of the sub's last hours by a nearby American submarine watching the military exercise (the USS *Memphis*). Subsequent stories that crew members survived in distress for several days lack even a scintilla of credibility.

At 7 a.m. on Sunday 13 August, Igor Sergeyev, the defence minister, telephoned Putin on vacation in Sochi. Sergeyev, then aged sixty-one, recalled the conversation with his president: 'I reported to the president from my work place that the submarine was not communicating [and] its location, although at that point it was still to be identified.' Putin's first reaction was to ask about the state of the nuclear reactors. The crew's fate seemed to be a secondary consideration. He constantly asked whether everything had been done and whether there was anything else that needed to be done. He also queried whether he needed to break off his family holiday on the Black Sea. Sergeyev reassuringly responded: 'To tell you the truth, I told the president: "Vladimir Vladimirovich, I personally believe that firm command has been organized and the successful deployment of the search means a shorter than expected time taken to find and identify the submarine . . . in my opinion, your presence there is not necessary now." I still believe that my advice was correct.'

Putin later regretted taking Sergeyev's counsel, but for the time being he remained by the beach. His onerous schedule included appointing the ambassadors to Chile and Jamaica, sending a seventieth birthday card to a famous actress and some jet-skiing. In the West, similar behaviour by a political leader would be unthinkable at a time of such grave crisis. This was Russia, however, and the old Soviet mentality was still very much in evidence. In future crises,

Putin would make sure he had his finger much more firmly on the country's pulse.

As the Russian Navy continued with its campaign of lies and obfuscation, the relatives of the *Kursk*'s crew faced a wall of disinformation and official indifference. For over eighteen months, the navy tried to maintain the fiction that the *Kursk* had sunk after a collision with a NATO submarine. Meanwhile, in the West, people couldn't understand why the Russians hadn't accepted international offers of help. Putin accepted assurances from the Russian Defence Ministry and navy that they were doing everything possible to save any survivors. The military were less than frank about the chances of success given Russia's rescue capabilities, and Putin was politically naive to take his commanders' word that all was under control.

As the hours ticked by, domestic and international pressure piled up on the president to act decisively. Then came a twenty-five-minute telephone call from President Bill Clinton on Wednesday 16 August. Clinton again offered US help, and urged Putin to take up the many offers of assistance he had received. Not only Russian domestic opinion but the whole world was concerned about the fate of those aboard the *Kursk*, and felt great compassion for their families. He knew that Putin would want to be seen to be doing everything he possibly could. The response of the West showed how much things had changed since the end of the Cold War, when NATO and the Warsaw Pact stood as adversaries. After Clinton's call, Putin felt he had no alternative but to accept Western help. To fail to do so would make him look callous, arrogant and, even worse, a politician in the old Soviet mould. He had to show the country, and the international community at large, that Russia had nothing to hide and was open to accept well-meaning offers of help. Putin was eager to dispel any image the West might have of him as a cold, calculating former KGB apparatchik.

The Russian military had other ideas, and a different mindset. For the Russian top brass, although NATO was not the direct military threat it had once been, it was still the enemy, and intent on stealing Russia's secrets at every possible opportunity. The Russian Navy may be working more closely with NATO these days, but they didn't trust it one bit. They firmly believed NATO countries would use any Western rescue operation as a chance to steal military secrets. The Northern Fleet, as part of Russia's strategic and tactical nuclear strike force, was historically secretive and the fleet's admirals were instinctively suspicious. After all, the *Kursk* was one of Russia's most modern nuclear submarines, and carried a lot of classified material on board, including secret weapon systems like the Granit cruise missile, capable of carrying nuclear warheads. The aims and perceptions of the political leadership as now personified by Putin were therefore very different from the aims and perceptions of his admirals. Yet as a former KGB officer, Putin instinctively had sympathy for the navy's desire to protect its secrets. However, Putin was starting to understand the political significance of the *Kursk* crisis. He could not afford to look ineffectual or indifferent. After all, he had been elected as a decisive 'man of action'. The navy, on the other hand, would still have preferred to try to save their men and fail than bring in the West to help.

After Clinton's crucial call, Putin overruled his conservative defence minister and ordered his admirals to accept Western assistance. The British, with their state-of-the-art mini rescue sub, the LR5, were already on their way to Russia. They were in the air even before the Russians finally accepted the offer of international help. But determined to maintain the *Kursk*'s military secrets, the Russians never let the LR5 into the water or anywhere near their sunken submarine. Foreign offers of help continued to come in; Sweden offered the use of its deep submergence rescue vehicle (DSRV), which could work at 400 metres, and the US checked the readiness of its two DSRVs, the *Avalon* and *Mystic*. Norway's *Seaway Eagle*, with a team of Anglo-Norwegian divers on board, also headed for the Barents Sea.

The Russian press, which had been critical of the president's handling of the crisis, stepped up its attack. *Komsomolskaya Pravda*, a popular tabloid, printed a headline in bold red type: 'The sailors on the *Kursk* fell silent yesterday. Why has the president been silent?' *Izvestiya*, the liberal daily newspaper, said: 'Together with the K-141 has sunk people's faith that the state can protect them from danger. It is the authorities themselves who have hit the bottom.' Meanwhile, showing a lack of urgency which typified the high command's whole approach to the crisis, Vice-Admiral Pobozhiy wrote to NATO in Brussels asking for a meeting to discuss organizational measures to save the *Kursk*'s crew. The admiral didn't appear to understand that it might be a little late to set up a joint Russia–NATO working party to save the submariners. In any event, as repeatedly made clear to the Russians, this was not a NATO rescue mission. Incredulous journalists were stunned by the admiral's smug bureaucratic complacency and the sheer stupidity of his proposal.

On Friday 18 August, the usually pro-Kremlin *Komsomolskaya Pravda*, having bribed a Northern Fleet officer 18,000 roubles ($600), finally published a full list of those aboard the *Kursk*. *Komsomolskaya Pravda* is controlled by the Interros group, owned by Vladimir Potanin, a former deputy prime minister and founder of the multi-billion-dollar Oneximbank. Power, politics and the press were inseparable in post-Soviet Russia. In one of the biggest scandals of the tragedy, the navy had steadfastly refused to publish a list of serving crew members, citing reasons of 'national security'. The bribe showed that anything in Russia is for sale. Relatives of crew members, thanks to *Komsomolskaya Pravda*, suddenly had confirmation that their loved ones were on the *Kursk*. In the afternoon, following allegations in the Duma (lower house of parliament) of American culpability, Defense Secretary William Cohen categorically stated no American sub was involved in the disaster. At the same time, the Russian Navy refuted the allegation that one of their ships' missiles had gone astray and hit the *Kursk*. Captain Igor Dygalo, Russian Navy press spokesman, also denied a story that a green and white distress buoy, of a type used by NATO, had been discovered in the Barents Sea. In late afternoon, Ilya Klebanov, the deputy prime minister, and Admiral Vladimir Kuroyedov flew to meet relatives in Vidyayevo, and had their first face-to-face meeting with the families of the *Kursk*'s crew.

Klebanov and Kuroyedov did not have an easy meeting. The Officers' Club in Vidyayevo was full that night. The gathered relatives were angry and frustrated, none more so than Nadezhda Tylik. Some families weren't present at the meeting, however. The navy had been doling out serious amounts of sedatives to the crew's relatives. Extra doctors and psychiatrists had been drafted in to the garrison town. Valaria, the wife of Andrei Milyutin (captain third rank), missed the meeting altogether because her dose knocked her out for a whole day. Half of Vidyayevo seemed doped-up, and some women were in a drugged daze for two or three days. Large or small, young or old, they were all given the same dose. At the meeting itself, Nadezhda was waiting for Klebanov to give an honest explanation of what had been going on, but became incensed when he started repeating the official version of the accident. The relatives thought the official account was a pack of lies. Some women fainted in the audience. Jumping up, Nadezhda shouted: 'Swines! What did I bring up my son for? You are sitting there getting fat but we haven't got anything. My husband was in the navy for twenty-five years. What for? And now my son is buried down there. I will never forgive you. Take off your epaulettes [addressing naval officers] and shoot yourselves now!' Captured on film by the local Murmansk television station, Klebanov looked shaken. A naval officer approached Nadezhda to calm her down, but she took no notice. The next instant a female medic approached from behind and injected Nadezhda in the arm, through her coat. Nadezhda Tylik immediately collapsed and was carried out of the room.

Strangely enough, no one in the room thought much of the injection incident itself. So many of the wives and mothers were on sedatives, they thought it was normal. Most just thought the medics were doing their job, and trying in their way to help a very distressed woman. Of course in the West, the incident was a massive public-relations disaster. The television camera had caught a very angry and upset mother upbraiding the Russian deputy prime minister, and the next minute she was 'silenced' by a forcibly injected sedative. On the front page of *The Times*, the headline was: 'How the mother of a *Kursk* sailor was silenced.' The newspaper said the 18 August incident was 'a stark reminder of the violent methods employed by the KGB against dissidents, particularly during the Brezhnev era'. While the newspaper was overstating its case somewhat, the impression was left in the West that Russia had not abandoned its former Soviet ways. Here was the proof. Klebanov's 'meet the people' event in Vidyayevo Officers' Club had it all and on camera: lies, incompetence, indifference to suffering and individual repression. At this point, Putin decided it was better to curtail his summer vacation and return to Moscow.

On Saturday 19 August, Putin finally slipped in to Moscow quietly at 4.40 a.m., arriving from Simferopol on the Black Sea. A week had passed since the sinking of the *Kursk*. In the United States, experts blamed the sinking on a torpedo explosion, supported by seismic reports from Canada, the UK, Germany, Norway and Alaska. The next day, Putin met Igor Spassky, general designer and head of the St Petersburg-based Rubin Design Bureau, responsible for designing the *Kursk*. Late in the day, Putin was at last trying to ensure he was fully briefed on the disaster. Between 5 and 5.30 a.m. on Monday 21 August, divers from the *Seaway Eagle* opened the outer escape hatch on the stern of the *Kursk*. Opening the inner escape hatch, they confirmed that the submarine was flooded and there could be no survivors. The Anglo-Norwegian divers had taken around six hours to achieve what the Russian effort had failed to do in seven days. The Russians were hampered by obsolete equipment, bad organization, bureaucratic delays and a blinkered attitude to Western offers of help. Having said that, given that the crew were all dead by the evening of the first day, it was unlikely any could have been rescued earlier. The real weakness of the submarine was in the design of the escape hatches and the poor escape training given to the crew.

On the morning of 21 August, Putin met his cabinet in the Kremlin. He did not make a statement on the *Kursk* but told the assembled press: 'The defence minister has delivered an account of various military-technical aspects of the operation in the Barents Sea. Now we are going to talk about the humanitarian aspects. The families of the sailors will get special help.' As the press were leaving, they heard their president tell his colleagues in a businesslike tone that the agenda included security issues in Central Asia and the tragedy in the Barents Sea. Putin made it sound as if the *Kursk* was just one of several 'military-technical' issues the cabinet was concerned with that day. The overwhelming impression was one of bureaucratic indifference. Putin and his ministerial colleagues misjudged the feeling in the country, and still had no real understanding of how deeply people in Russia and abroad had been touched by the *Kursk* disaster. Partly, it was a question of psychology and upbringing.

At 9 p.m. the Military Council of the Northern Fleet officially announced that all 118 crew members on board the *Kursk* were dead, and expressed its condolences to their relatives. National television channels began the evening news with solemn music or sounds of the sea and a slow roll-call of the names of all those lost on the submarine. Pictures of distraught relatives were shown, grieving for their loved ones. Vice-Admiral Motsak said: 'Our worst expectations are confirmed. All sections of the submarine are totally flooded and not a single member of the crew remains alive.' There was no statement from Putin, and no announcement of a day of mourning. As the country grieved, Russia felt leaderless.

Faced with a fresh barrage of criticism from the press, on Tuesday 22 August Putin declared the following Wednesday an official day of mourning and finally set off to meet the families of those lost on the *Kursk*. That evening he flew to Severomorsk, where he was met by Klebanov and members of the government's commission of inquiry. Klebanov had just had another bad day. Following a further meeting with the crew's relatives, he was almost half-strangled by an infuriated family member. Asked when the bodies from the *Kursk* would be recovered, he nonchalantly replied, 'In a few months . . . maybe a year. I don't know exactly.' According to Andrei Kolesnikov, a *Kommersant* journalist, the room erupted: 'A woman . . . shook him. "You swine, get out there and save them." The officers rushed to drag her away. It wasn't easy. She clung to Klebanov and shouted, "You're nothing but scum." '

Putin and the government were being pilloried by the press. Led by the independent television channel NTV, its stablemate, Moscow Echo radio, and the newspapers *Komsomolskaya Pravda*, *Novaya Gazeta* and *Vremya MN*, the media was having a field day criticizing Russia's leadership and unpicking contradictions in official accounts of the disaster. Nor was the criticism restricted to the Russian press. Western newspapers and TV coverage excoriated the president. *The New York Times* wrote in an editorial on 24 August: 'It is too soon to know if more active leadership on Mr Putin's part could have saved lives, but his performance has been disheartening for those who hoped to see a more democratic Russia shedding the habits of secrecy and indifference to human suffering that marred so many centuries of czarist and Soviet rule.'

Three days earlier, the London *Daily Telegraph*'s editorial attacked Putin's leadership, or lack of it: 'His remaining on holiday on the Black Sea until the end of last week looked both callous and irresponsible. His ambition to have the navy fly the flag of a reinvigorated great power around the world, proclaimed by posters reading 'Naval might is Russia's glory', appears absurdly vainglorious.' The *Telegraph* editorial of 21 August also lauded the role of the Russian media: 'In the style of a Soviet apparatchik, Mr Putin sought to stifle the press. That it has rightly rounded on him over the *Kursk* is the one compensating factor in a dismal tale of official hubris, lying and incompetence. One of the key components of a free society has been playing its role with a vengeance.'

The role of the Russian media and its relationship with the government was complex. The media had united full-square behind

Boris Yeltsin in his 1996 bid for re-election, running a blatant 'Red scare' campaign against Communist challenger Gennady Zyuganov. Previously, the media had been extremely critical of Yeltsin's 1994–96 war in Chechnya, and his opinion-poll ratings had fallen to single figures before the TV and press rallied to his side. Similarly, most of the media had backed Putin in his campaign to become president in 2000, indulging in wilful character assassination of Putin's main political opponents, former prime minister Yevgeny Primakov and Moscow mayor Yury Luzhkov. The second Chechen war (1999 onwards) was widely backed by the media, and was crucial in building support for Putin's presidential bid. By the time of the *Kursk* debacle, the Russian media had started to change its tune. Partly, this was because the oligarchs who were so influential under the rule of Yeltsin and his 'family' had found themselves suddenly sidelined.

The Media-Most conglomerate, owned by Vladimir Gusinsky, was the first to fall out, with his media holdings opposing Putin's presidential bid and backing Primakov. Primakov was also a former foreign minister and head of the SVR, the foreign intelligence successor to the KGB. Gusinsky's media companies were the most critical of Putin's handling of the *Kursk* disaster, including NTV television, Moscow Echo radio and the newspapers *Segodnya*, *Novaya Gazeta*, *Obshchaya Gazeta* and *Itogi* magazine. By the time of the *Kursk* disaster, Gusinsky had already been arrested on fraud charges and was in exile abroad. Boris Berezovsky, another oligarch, who owned ORT and TV6 television as well as the newspaper *Kommersant*, also found himself frozen out from the Kremlin and under investigation for fraud. The trio of moguls was completed with Vladimir Potanin, who controlled *Komsomolskaya Pravda* and *Izvestiya*. Although normally pro-government, Potanin could have easily feared his businesses were next in line for criminal investigation. All these oligarchs had made their fortunes in the early days of perestroika and post-Communism. The way they acquired their companies following privatization was a bone of contention, especially since the law on private property in those days was a grey area. Any investigation might potentially unravel their business empires, as Gusinsky was discovering to his cost.

There was another factor behind the media onslaught against Putin. Most of the Russian media always took it as their duty to support the 'party of power' during elections. They convinced themselves it was necessary for stability, to keep the Communists out or to ensure a smooth transfer of power. In any event, supporting the Kremlin's favourite was a way for the media bosses to call in favours later. Once the election was won, however, the media liked to assert its independence. The press, of course, had a vested interest in freedom of speech and freedom of expression, more so than any other part of Russian society. Putin's arrest of Gusinsky in June 2000 had threatened those freedoms. The media felt the president was reneging on the unspoken compact: we will support your re-election, and then you tolerate our freedom of expression the rest of the time. The *Kursk* disaster gave the Russian media the opportunity to 'bite back', to reassert the independence it had won in 1991, at the time of the attempted hardline coup against Gorbachev, and then subsequently with the collapse of the Soviet Union. Russian editors and journalists decided to remind the president that he had a free press. There were no holds barred, and the criticism was vitriolic. The message that he could not walk all over them or take them for granted was delivered to the president, combined with a warning not to take them on. Putin saw it differently, and was incandescent with rage. In his view, the press was challenging his authority as president, and hence the authority of the state. For a former KGB man, this was just too much. His retribution would come later.

The president's opinion-poll ratings had suffered a setback, reflecting public reaction to his handling of the crisis. The All-Russian Public Opinion Centre found that his approval rating had dropped 8 per cent in one week, from 73 to 65 per cent. Another poll, conducted by the Romir agency, showed that 28 per cent of Muscovites thought their opinion of Putin had deteriorated as a result of his mishandling of the disaster. Over three-quarters of those polled believed Russia should have sought international assistance sooner than it did, and one in five blamed the president for the submariners' deaths. Over a third of those asked thought the navy's high command was responsible for the loss of the *Kursk* and her crew. There was growing anecdotal evidence of a backlash against a president who previously could do no wrong. Mikhail Aleksandrovich, a former army diver on his way to Severomorsk, said of Putin's visit to see the submariners' families: 'The visit won't save anything. His reputation was ruined in the space of two days. So the government is suddenly running around trying to be active, but they should have done that in the beginning. It seems that it is a lot easier to bury a hundred men than open up a state secret.'

Irina Belozyorova, who lost her husband Nicolai Belozyorov (captain third rank) and lived in Vidyayevo with her ten-year-old son, Alexei, couldn't wait to tell the president what she thought of him. 'I'll just tell him how glad I am that I didn't vote for him. He's not a president. He's just a stooge,' she said with feeling. Although the naval community around Vidyayevo was understandably more bitter than the general public, it was surprising how widespread the feeling of anger and betrayal was throughout Russia. Attending a special memorial mass for the *Kursk*'s crew in Moscow's cathedral of Christ the Saviour, twenty-year-old Yevgeny Levlampiyev said of Putin: 'He got to power by exploiting the very strong nostalgia people have for the past, their national sense of humiliation, and the Chechen issue. I never thought he would betray the armed forces.' Levlampiyev had not voted for Putin because he mistrusted his commitment to free speech and democracy. According to another young Muscovite at the church service, sixteen-year-old Natasha Lemyagova: 'His mistake will cost him dearly. He should have gone to Murmansk on the first day.'

Politicians were also critical of Putin's response to the crisis. Alexander Rutskoi, former Soviet vice-president and governor of Kursk, referring to Putin's late arrival at the scene of the accident, said, 'If I was the president I would have arrived on the fastest plane.' Boris Nemtsov, the leader of the Union of Right Forces in the Duma and a former reformist deputy prime minister, called for a parliamentary inquiry. Nemtsov – young, articulate and fluent in English – said the inquiry should find out: 'First, the real cause of the catastrophe; and second, did our government and president do everything to save our sailors.' Nemtsov also criticized Putin personally. 'The behaviour of Putin was amoral,' he said. 'As supreme commander in chief he has no right to a holiday while his sailors face this drama. Nor is there a reasonable explanation of why he did not accept foreign help before so much time had been wasted.'

Gennady Zyuganov, the fifty-six-year-old former presidential candidate and leader of the Communist faction in the Duma, blamed the military and claimed it had not adequately informed the president. Not for the first time, Zyuganov let slip an opportunity to land a political blow against the Kremlin, and showed why he was destined to perpetual opposition. Some commentators suggested the Communists had become too cosy with Putin's administration, after making a deal to gain the Speaker's post in the parliament and carving up important committee places. Zyuganov had always given the impression that he was almost afraid of rocking the boat, and even more afraid of ending up as president. He had failed to beat Yeltsin, despite a healthy early lead, and never looked like beating Putin. History and demography, however, were even more potent reasons why the Communist bloc's ageing political support would ensure they remained unelectable in today's modern Russia.

As Putin arrived in Severomorsk on 22 August he faced a huge challenge to regain the political initiative and shore up his public support. With the press on the warpath, and negative opinion polls staring him in the face, he decided to launch a counter-attack. His strategy consisted first of all in travelling to meet the relatives of those lost on the *Kursk*, ten days after the submarine had first struck the bottom of the Barents Sea. He had to be seen offering his condolences to the families who had suffered the loss of their loved ones. Second, he would apologize for the fiasco and offer generous compensation to the bereaved. Third, he would go on the offensive to silence his critics. Following a short meeting with Klebanov and the government-appointed commission of inquiry at the headquarters of the Northern Fleet, Putin headed off to meet the crew's relatives in Vidyayevo, arriving around 8 p.m. The media had been kept out of Severomorsk and Vidyayevo, and Putin's visit was covered only by state-controlled RTR television. The president was dressed in a black suit and shirt, buttoned up to the neck, without a tie. One of the first people he met in Vidyayevo was Irina Lyachina, wife of the *Kursk*'s commander, Gennady Lyachin. The TV camera could not fail to pick up the damp, peeling walls of the officers' accommodation during his meeting with Irina and her daughter. Leaving the flat but still accompanied by Irina, Putin then did a brief walkabout, shaking hands and talking to the large crowd which had gathered. He went on to the submariners' Officers' Club, where around 600 angry and grief-stricken residents of Vidyayevo were waiting for him. Some 350 of the audience had lost their husbands, sons or brothers. Looking sombre, pale and drawn, Putin was given a hostile grilling for six hours as the tense conference continued into the early hours. He had certainly never experienced a meeting like the one he faced in Vidyayevo.

Talking to those present, it is apparent that many had turned from loyal presidential supporters to profoundly critical opponents. The anger, hatred even, was palpable. Not all of it was directed at Putin: sitting at his side were the senior navy men Kuroyedov and Popov, and people in the audience repeatedly called for the admirals to resign. The furious relatives bombarded Putin with questions like, 'Why have you murdered our lads?' or, 'Who are you going to punish for their deaths, and how?' Others asked, 'Do you believe our men are still alive?' One woman in the crowd fainted, while others became hysterical. The questions continued to flow: 'When would the bodies of the submariners be brought home?' 'When will we get them back, dead or alive?' Many simply could not come to terms with the fact that their loved ones were already dead. People shouted their questions, and strained to hear the president's replies. Putin was almost overwhelmed by the onslaught, but maintained a steely calm, listening intently to his hostile inquisitors. Irina Belozyorova, a *Kursk* widow, said, 'I even felt sorry for him. Everyone was shouting questions at once.' Putin tried to console them: 'The grief is immeasurable, there are not enough words for comfort. My heart hurts, but yours hurt even more.' Putin made a mistake by initially trying to patronize his audience: 'Just like you, I'm not an expert.' The audience, full of experienced submariners, baulked. Someone asked why international help hadn't been accepted sooner. Putin tried trotting out the official version: 'We accepted Western help as soon as it was offered on Wednesday the sixteenth of August . . .' Before he could finish, however, he was shouted down. Virtually everyone in the audience knew from media reports that foreign help had been offered on Monday 14 August. One woman in the audience shouted, 'They believed in the state, that the state would save them! You don't understand how they believed!' Another person bellowed: 'You could have saved just five! Bastards!'

Swiftly changing tack, Putin decided honesty was the best policy, adopting some of his famous bar-room language. During the second Chechen war, this had gone down a storm: 'We'll blast them out, even in the shit-house.' Putin's famous response to the Chechen rebels had become part of Russian folklore. A submariner's wife berated the president, asking him why Russia had to rely on Norway's deep-sea divers. Putin interjected: 'This country doesn't have a fig.' A little later, warming to his theme, the president told the assembled families: 'I'm willing to take responsibility for my hundred days in power. But when it comes to the last fifteen years, then I'm ready to sit on the bench with you and put the questions to them.' Putin glossed over the fact that he had been prime minister for seven months before becoming president, and before that had been head of the Federal Security Service (FSB), successor to the KGB. Although he had only been president for a hundred days, he had been near the centre of power since the mid-1990s. Putin undoubtedly impressed some with his straight-talking. He also tried to mollify others. So far, the relatives of the victims had only received 1,000 roubles ($37). He now offered the families compensation payments equivalent to ten years' salary. While some of the poorer members of the audience were faintly appreciative, many of those present were sceptical. One ex-submariner commented: 'The officers' wives understood straight away that they were being bought off and that the guilty parties would not be taken to court.' The hostile encounter had been such a bruising experience for the president that only a few seconds of the meeting were shown on RTR state television, minus any soundtrack. Although feelings on Putin's performance at the meeting were mixed, with some relatives thinking he handled himself well under pressure, others felt he still appeared too cold and self-assured.

Vladimir Chaikin had served as a sub-lieutenant on submarines for eleven years. He admitted he had voted for Putin as president, but felt his leader had badly miscalculated: 'He doesn't arrive when his presence is crucial, but he shows up when no one wants to see him.' Olga, widow of Captain-Lieutenant Dmitri Kolesnikov, said: 'Our president made a big mistake. He should have been out at sea supervising the rescue operation. And he should have come straight away to give moral support to us relatives and loved ones. That's what we were all expecting.' Olga Kolesnikova was disappointed and appalled by Putin's performance at the meeting: 'I was waiting for words of condolence and sympathy. What we got was talk about the compensation we'd be paid. It was disgusting, painful.' Some of the families couldn't face going to the meeting. Marina Stankevich, widow of the *Kursk*'s doctor, said: 'I didn't go because I just can't look at that man.' Other relatives were either too upset or too heavily sedated to attend. Lilia Shevtsova, of the Moscow Carnegie Centre, later summed it up. 'Putin,' Shevtsova said, 'couldn't understand that it was his time, his time to become a leader, and he missed this opportunity.'

Putin received a further setback at the meeting. The original plan was for the president to lay a wreath the next day at the site of the accident, surrounded by the crew's relatives. The event was meant to be the focal point of Wednesday's national day of mourning. The families, however, would have none of it. They didn't want to accept their loved ones were dead, and feared that once Putin's photo-opportunity was out of the way, they and their men would be forgotten. Faced with another public-relations disaster, Putin cancelled the ceremony and returned abruptly to Murmansk and then Moscow. It was the first time anybody could remember the Kremlin abandoning a ceremony because of public pressure. There is no doubt that Putin was shaken by the strength of feeling he encountered in Vidyayevo. It had been the most challenging public encounter of his career, and he had just about survived it. Before the meeting, he had not really understood the trauma and popular outrage which had gripped Russia following the sinking of the *Kursk*. But he felt it now, and was angry and alarmed that so much of the animus was directed personally at him. Stung, Putin promised the grieving families that he would raise the entire submarine and recover all the crew's bodies for proper burial.

Russia's Orthodox Church tried to come to his rescue. With Putin under withering attack, Patriarch Alexei, head of the Orthodox Church, said in a TV address that he knew how painful the tragedy had been for the president. The Church maintained a cosy relationship with the Kremlin, supporting it over the Chechen conflict and in return seeking government aid in restricting the spread of 'foreign' religions in Russia. The result had been some rather bizarre laws, banning the Salvation Army and the Baptists, for example, and even threatening the existence of other religions in Russia like Roman Catholicism. Only churches registered in Soviet days would be allowed to operate legally in the 'New Russia'. In religious terms, the Russian Orthodox Church was looking backwards to the days when the Soviet Union had given it a state monopoly. The corollary had been limited religious freedom, and a priesthood packed with KGB agents.

Returning to the Kremlin on Wednesday 23 August, Putin prepared at long last to broadcast to the nation. Appearing on RTR state television that evening, on the national day of mourning for the *Kursk*'s crew, with the Russian and presidential flags flying at half-mast atop the Kremlin, he offered a personal apology for the disaster: 'I feel a complete sense of responsibility and guilt for this tragedy.' Speaking slowly and carefully, the president showed little emotion. His KGB training often showed through at times like these, and he could indeed appear cold and calculating. He said anyone found culpable would be punished, but blame should only be apportioned when 'a full understanding has been gained about what happened and why'. Putin revealed that Defence Minister Sergeyev had offered to resign on Monday, after the Norwegians said the *Kursk* was flooded; and that Admirals Kuroyedov and Popov, commanders of the Russian Navy and Northern Fleet respectively, had offered to resign the following day. He also promised he would reform the armed forces, but rejected the idea that the navy's honour and the country's pride had sunk with the *Kursk*. 'Our country has survived worse than this,' he said. Having offered his apology to the nation, Putin pressed on with his three-pronged fight-back strategy which he had devised before visiting the *Kursk* families in Vidyayevo. His target now became the media, and the most remarkable part of his appearance on RTR was his vitriolic attack on the oligarchs who controlled Russia's vast multimedia enterprises. President Putin pointed out that the first to defend the *Kursk*'s submariners and their relatives over the last few days were the same people who 'had long promoted the destruction of the army, the fleet and the state'. He pointed the finger at 'some who had even given a million dollars' to the *Kursk*'s families, apparently referring to a campaign by Boris Berezovsky's *Kommersant* newspaper to raise voluntary donations for the crew's relatives. Warming to his theme, Putin acerbically added a veiled threat: 'They would have done better to sell their villas on the Mediterranean coast of France and in Spain. Only then could they explain why the property was registered under false names and behind legal firms. And we could probably ask the question: where did the money come from?'

The day before Putin's broadcast, the ORT and NTV television channels had carried news reports describing how the Kremlin had tried to limit media coverage of the president's fraught meeting with *Kursk* relatives in Vidyayevo. Boris Berezovsky, who controlled ORT television and three major daily newspapers, has a huge villa complex at Antibes on the Côte d'Azur. He had just resigned as a member of the Duma to launch a 'constructive opposition' to Putin. Vladimir Gusinsky, owner of NTV, a range of newspapers, magazines and a radio station, has an expensive villa in Sotogrande, southern Spain. As part of an extensive property portfolio, Berezovsky also has property in London, and Gusinsky property in London, Israel and New York. Putin knew exactly what he was talking about. As head of the FSB he had stayed at Gusinsky's Spanish villa as a personal guest of the tycoon. But now Putin was furious at the drubbing he had received at the hands of his erstwhile allies. He was determined to smash them and take control of their media outlets. By referring to the tycoons' allegedly dubious business histories and financial arrangements, which could be applied to virtually all Russia's new business elite (the so-called 'New Russians'), Putin was effectively declaring war on his oligarch critics. This was no bluff. He meant to destroy them, and destroy them he would. In the process he would tame Russia's independent media and force them to take a more deferential, pro-Kremlin line. That would also conveniently and felicitously ease his path to re-election in 2004.

On the same day as Putin's broadcast to the nation, Valentina Matviyenko, a deputy prime minister who later became governor of St Petersburg, announced compensation terms for the families of the *Kursk*'s victims. Each family was to receive a lump sum equivalent to ten years of an officer's salary, free housing in any Russian city, free college education for the victims' sixty-five children, and free counselling. This was an unprecedented package for those who had lost their loved ones in military service, both in terms of its generosity and the speed with which it was offered. In fact, in the context of an average wage of around $150 per month, the lump sum of $25,000 was a relative fortune in Russia. Most submariners on the *Kursk* had earned between $35–50 per month, with Captain Gennady Lyachin (the boat's commander) taking home $200. With a Moscow or St Petersburg flat thrown in, the *Kursk* families could consider themselves handsomely looked after. In fact the compensation terms were so generous they even caused a political backlash in Russia. Veronica Marchencko of the group Mothers' Rights and Valentina Melnikova of the Union of Soldiers' Committees bitterly complained that the relatives of those lost in Chechnya or elsewhere received a pittance from the state. Melnikova thought the government was attempting to 'buy the bereaved families' silence'. And with donations flooding in from across Russia and around the world, the *Kursk* families would eventually receive even more than the agreed state compensation package. Final pay-outs came to around $35,000 per family, not including the cost of brand-new flats or additional sums from charitable sources. Perhaps understandably, this led to a degree of bitterness and jealousy from those who had lost their husbands, brothers or sons in Chechnya or Afghanistan. It also fuelled a degree of cynicism about the government's motives in paying up so quickly and munificently.

Over the next two days, following his national address on RTR, Putin announced pay rises for the military and federal civil servants, and the creation of four new naval rescue centres. The armed forces, police, prison guards, custom officials and tax police were promised a rise of 20 per cent from December. From January 2001, all federal civil servants were also promised an additional 20 per cent. However, these seemingly generous rises would be offset by inflation and tax changes. Inflation was set to rise by 15 per cent in 2001, while military personnel would also have to pay tax for the first time. Putin's effort to improve the rescue resources of the navy, and boost the pay of the armed forces generally, was only a half-hearted stab at reform. A complete overhaul of the Russian military was urgently required, but Putin showed little sign of being ready or able to tackle such a massive task. His counter-attack had, however, enabled him to regain the political initiative. He had taken control of the agenda, and shown real leadership. The president had apologized to his people, provided compensation to the *Kursk* families, proposed some reforms and gone on the offensive against his critics. His attack on the oligarchs played well in a country where the leading business figures were often perceived as little better than thieves. The oligarchs were felt to have profited from tainted privatizations and their close connections to the Kremlin and Yeltsin's 'family'. An editor at *Kommersant* newspaper said of Putin: 'He is a cynic, but also a realist. It is too late to undo the system of private property in this country. But he will try to get the oligarchs to pay a little more tax. That's all, but it would be popular with everyone.'

On 19 September 2000, Putin took the decision to recover the submariners' bodies from the sunken *Kursk*. Two weeks before, he admitted the crew had probably died quickly after the submarine sank, and that there had been no signals from the distressed sub after it went down. A $5,800,000 contract for the recovery operation was signed with the Norwegian branch of the American firm, Halliburton. On 25 October, twelve bodies were retrieved from the vessel. Among the dead were Captain-Lieutenant Dmitri Kolesnikov, whose note to his superiors and his beloved Olga was still protected by a charred arm and clutched to his heart. He told her that he loved her, and not to despair. The note for his superiors gave a list of the twenty-three who survived the initial explosions. Kolesnikov's note threw the country into a frenzy of self-doubt and self-recrimination. At that stage, no one knew how long some of the crew survived, and whether they could have been saved. Kolesnikov was buried in his native St Petersburg, with full military honours. To his credit Putin kept his promise to raise the 18,000-ton *Kursk* and retrieve the bodies of those lost. The whole recovery and salvage operation was estimated to cost around $130 million. The sum allocated to the salvage operation alone was equivalent to almost twice the navy's budget for operating all its submarines for a year. There were those in the service who quietly criticized the recovery operation as a costly, politically-led face-saver for the president. Others felt that the operation was not only financial folly, but environmentally dangerous as well. If the reactors leaked during the course of the lifting operation, the result could be an underwater Chernobyl, with devastating consequences for the Arctic ecosystem and the rich fishing grounds of the Barents Sea. The Norwegians were understandably nervous. Apart from the *Kursk*, there were five nuclear submarines at the bottom of the ocean, two American and three Russian, buried at depths of up to 5,000 metres. As yet, no one had successfully raised one to the surface.

This time, things were different. The whole salvage operation was unprecedented in its transparency. The Russians launched a website, with hour-by-hour progress reports on the operation. Sergei Yastrzhembsky, one of Putin's closest aides and a master Kremlin spin-doctor, was put in charge of coordinating information about the *Kursk* lifting operation. The Halliburton consortium had been dropped after it declared it was not willing to compromise safety by trying to raise the *Kursk* by the end of 2001. It was replaced by two Dutch contractors, Mammoet and Smit International. Russian, British, Dutch and Norwegian divers were also employed. The lifting operation began on 7 October 2001, and was a spectacular technical success. The *Kursk* was raised from a depth of 108 metres, or 354 feet. The boat was taken back to dry dock in Roslyakovo on the Kola peninsula, and drained. The bodies of the remaining submariners were removed and buried in their home towns. Just three of the crew were unable to be identified. The 22 Granit cruise missiles were removed, together with a quantity of explosives. The nuclear reactors were made safe, while the *Kursk* itself was broken up at the Nerpa shipyard.

When Vladimir Ustinov, the prosecutor-general, produced a report in December 2001, pointing the finger of blame at the Russian Navy, retribution was swift. Putin was told that 'traditional negligence' caused the sinking. Within hours of the Kremlin meeting, Putin had demoted three senior admirals and sacked another eleven senior officers. In a press statement through the presidential press service, the president said the investigation into the *Kursk* accident had already provided enough evidence to 'draw a rather definite conclusion on the quality of preparations for and organization of military exercises and the organization of search-and-rescue operations'. Putin's purge of the navy not only showed the services who was boss, but that the old, anti-reformist and obstructionist ways in the military would not be tolerated by the Kremlin. He wanted military reform, and didn't need opposition from the old guard. The *Kursk* crisis gave him a chance to get rid of dead wood, and replace senior officers with men who owed their positions to him. Three days after the navy sackings, Putin attended the launch of Russia's latest nuclear submarine, the *Gepard* (Cheetah), in the Sevmash shipyard on the White Sea, the same shipyard that had launched the *Kursk* seven years earlier. Putin told his cabinet the day before that military spending would be next year's priority, as the government embarked on a 'serious and ambitious programme of military reform'. The multi-purpose *Gepard* is one of the quietest and fastest submarines in the world. At 110 metres long, 12,270 tonnes, it can dive to a depth of 600 metres and reach 35 knots submerged. Smaller than the *Kursk*, it can carry 24 nuclear-capable Granit cruise missiles. Admiral Kuroyedov, head of the navy, said it 'was symbolic for the lost boat to be replaced by a new submarine'. Russia, he said, was building a fleet which 'will be a tribute to the sailors who died on the *Kursk*.' Russia was trying to restore its lost pride. Putin's photo-opportunity with the *Gepard* had a clear message: look to the future, not the past. Russia is still a world power to be reckoned with.

In January 2002, the Russian authorities finally admitted that the *Kursk* sinking had not been caused by a collision with a foreign submarine. The following month, the prosecutor-general ordered a wide-ranging inquiry into senior naval officers' compliance with rules and regulations. Ilya Klebanov, the deputy prime minister, who had been part of the navy's cover-up, was sacked but kept his second post as minister for industry, science and technology.

Admiral Vladimir Kuroyedov, head of the Russian Navy, admitted for the first time that the *Kursk* may have sunk after a practice torpedo using unstable fuel exploded onboard. He confessed the navy had 'placed unfounded trust' in the weapon, which was propelled by highly volatile hydrogen peroxide. Kuroyedov said hydrogen peroxide, abandoned by the British Royal Navy after an explosion aboard the sub HMS *Sidon* in 1955, was 'highly unstable and its contact with certain metals may cause unpredictable consequences'. The Russians had continued using hydrogen peroxide because it was cheap, and they thought they could handle it safely. Now the suspect torpedoes were removed from all Russian submarines. When the Russian government issued its commission of inquiry's hundred-page report on 26 July 2002, Ustinov, the prosecutor-general, laid the blame squarely on an internal torpedo explosion. The report confirmed that the torpedo that exploded was a 'Fat' torpedo, a Type 65-76A, number 1336APV. The 65 referred to the diameter (65 cm), and 76 to the year in which this type of torpedo first entered service. The explosion had probably been caused by a mechanical breakdown in the old torpedo; a faulty component like an 'O' ring or sealant could have failed causing leakage and a chemical reaction, leading to an explosion. The fire in the first compartment then set off other torpedoes exactly two minutes fifteen seconds later, resulting in the second catastrophic explosion aboard the *Kursk*.

Putin soon put his ideas into action, moving against the oligarchs in a populist gesture designed to bolster his image as his own man. Embezzlement charges were once again levelled against Boris Berezovsky, whose media interests had played an important role in getting Putin elected president. Swiss authorities alleged Berezovsky had embezzled over $970 million from Aeroflot's revenue and ticket sales in the mid-1990s. He had previously faced such allegations during Yevgeny Primakov's premiership in late 1998, but these had not been pursued. Primakov was sacked before the case came to anything. But by the summer of 2000, the political environment had changed, and five of the country's leading oligarchs found themselves under investigation from government prosecutors and tax police. Vladimir Gusinsky and his Media-Most media empire also found himself under attack. He was arrested for embezzlement and immediately sent to Moscow's notorious Butyrskaya prison in June 2000. He was charged with embezzling $10 million of state funds during the takeover of a St Petersburg television company in 1997. The media mogul claimed his arrest was a heavy-handed attempt to intimidate him and silence his critical TV, radio and newspapers. Putin claimed not be involved in Gusinsky's arrest, but showed an intimate knowledge of Media-Most's affairs and the allegations against the oligarch when quizzed by journalists in Madrid, where he was on a state visit. According to Gusinsky, the Russian government offered to drop the charges and release him if he sold his controlling stake in his Media-Most empire.

Following an international outcry, Gusinsky was released, but not before he had (by his account) signed a promise under duress to sell off his media empire. By the winter, both Gusinsky (who had fled Russia once before under Yeltsin) and Berezovsky had left the country under threat of arrest. Insult was added to injury when Gusinsky, who holds joint Russian and Israeli nationality and is head of the Russian branch of the World Jewish Congress, had his house in Moscow's Chegasovo suburb seized by Russian prosecutors. It was the second time in six months that his house had been impounded by the prosecutor's office. The charge sheet against Gusinsky grew exponentially. The Russian prosecutor-general's office now accused him of 'deceit and abuse of trust' in securing more than $300 million in loans from gas monopoly Gazprom, for a group of companies that were insolvent. Gazprom, incidentally, was 38 per cent state-owned and heavily influenced by the Kremlin. The Russians tried to extradite Gusinsky from Spain in December 2000 and Greece in August 2003, but failed on both occasions.

European judges suspected the charges were more political than financial in their nature, a view also held by British judges when Gusinsky's old rival Boris Berezovsky also found himself being pursued by Russian prosecutors.

Putin's blistering attack on the oligarch-owned media continued. He had already installed Oleg Dobrodeyev, an NTV founder and government supporter, as head of Russia's second state channel, RTR. In January 2001, Berezovsky, now facing mounting legal pressure from Russian prosecutors, conceded defeat and offered to sell his 49 per cent stake in ORT television. The move failed to deter the Russian prosecutor's office, which prepared an international warrant for Berezovsky's arrest. The Russian authorities sought Berezovsky's extradition from the UK, but much to their chagrin, this was thrown out of court and the oligarch was granted political asylum in Britain in September 2003. Earlier, in April 2001, government supporters in Gazprom moved to take over NTV television. Gazprom owned 46 per cent of NTV's shares and boardroom changes ensured that the gas monopoly was dominated by Putin's supporters. A protest lock-in by NTV's journalists ended when most defected to TV6, a small television channel owned by Berezovsky. Even this escape was relatively short-lived, as TV6 was shut down by another state-controlled monopoly, the oil company Lukoil in January 2002. Lukoil closed down TV6 on a legal technicality, claiming its losses in 1998–2000 justified its liquidation. TV6 resisted the bankruptcy proceedings on the grounds that it was currently profitable. The move meant that all four major television channels with national coverage had fallen under government control. Seventeen months after President Putin had first brought his guns to bear against the oligarch-controlled media at the time of the *Kursk* disaster, Russia's major independent television channels had been extinguished.

Russia's political and intellectual elite knew that the takeover of NTV and the closure of TV6 had been politically inspired. Boris Nemtsov, leader of the Duma's right-wing Union of Right Forces (SPS) and a former deputy prime minister, said the decision to close

TV6 was 'dictated exclusively by political motive'. From exile in London, Berezovsky called the move 'pure politics'. Even the US State Department waded in with an unusually strongly worded statement. 'There's a strong appearance of political pressure in the judicial process against the independent media,' said Richard Boucher, a State Department spokesman. 'Press freedom and the rule of law can be best served by keeping TV6 on the air.' Ironically, Russia had changed the law on 1 January 2002, so that minority shareholders could no longer make an application for a company to be declared bankrupt. It was held not to apply in the TV6 case. Putin's victory over the media moguls was almost complete. In addition to taking over or closing NTV, ORT and TV6, Gusinsky lost control of his Sem Dnei publishing house. The newspaper *Segodnya* was closed on 16 April 2001. The next day the editor of *Itogi* and all the editorial staff were replaced by the new regime.

The final straw came on 22 June 2003, when the Russian authorities switched off TVS, the last remaining privately owned national television channel in the country. TVS had been the last refuge of journalists from NTV, and then TV6. The editor in chief at TVS was the respected former NTV anchorman, Yevgeny Kiselyov. Although TVS had financial troubles, its closure concerned Russian liberal politicians like Boris Nemtsov, and the US State Department. TVS was replaced with a sports channel. 'What we now have is a complete state monopoly of country-wide channels,' said the editor in chief of Moscow Echo radio station, Alexei Venediktov. 'It's like when all candidates are excluded from the election campaign, except only one.' It was the last TV station that had dared to criticize Russia's leaders. *Nezavisimaya Gazeta* wrote that Russia was now a 'one-channel country'. *Izvestiya* commented that national television would now consist of either 'entertainment channels or state channels', as in the Soviet era. To all intents and purposes, the opposition media had been closed down, with the exception of a handful of independent newspapers and the radio station Moscow Echo. Russia's president would never again face the barrage of criticism he had experienced at the time of the *Kursk* sinking. By the time of the December 2003 Duma elections and March 2004 presidential poll, Russia's media had been tamed by the Kremlin and turned into sycophantic cheerleaders for Vladimir Putin.

7

THE HOME FRONT

*Sasha was bitten by a stray rabid dog. Going to hospital he
was told he had two choices. He could wait and see if he
developed the fatal disease or pay $100 for immunization.
He paid up.*

Vladimir Putin's presidency has been about centralization and the
accretion of power. Putin wants to restore the top-down vertical
of power which existed under Tsarism and during much of the
Soviet period. He inherited a weak state from Boris Yeltsin, where
often Moscow's control didn't seem to extend beyond the city's ring
road. Chechnya, one of Russia's 89 'Subjects', had more or less
seceded before the Putin-led invasion of autumn 1999. Other parts
of the Russian Federation seemed as though they might too.
Vladivostok and the Primorsky or Maritime region in the far east
operated like the governor's personal fiefdom. Crime, corruption
and poverty were grinding down the people. Putin's remedy was to
strengthen the state, beginning at the centre. The media was cur-
tailed. He appointed seven federal super-governors to impose the
president's will in the regions. Laws were introduced so the president
could suspend incompetent or corrupt governors. He issued decrees
demanding that the regions of Bashkortostan, Ingushetia and Amur
bring their laws into line with federal legislation. Regional governors
and assembly speakers lost their right to sit in the Federation
Council, or upper house of parliament. Their places were taken by

two representatives nominated from each of the regional legislatures and executives. Instead, regional leaders attended the newly formed State Council, a toothless consultative body. The Federation Council had previously occasionally opposed former President Yeltsin. It would not dare defy President Putin. Alexander Rutskoi, the governor of Kursk who had rashly criticized the president over the *Kursk* submarine tragedy, was barred from standing for re-election. He had omitted the ownership of two cars and undervalued his Moscow flat on his property disclosure form.

Putin's seven federal super-governors or plenipotentiaries (*polnomochnii*) were appointed in May 2000 to oversee seven new federal divisions which mirrored Russia's military districts. Five of the heads of the federal districts were generals; two from the army, two from the security services, and one from the police or MVD. The two civilian representatives were Sergei Kiriyenko, the former reformist prime minister, who was sent to Nizhny Novgorod, and Leonid Drachevsky, former minister responsible for the Commonwealth of Independent States, who went to Novosibirsk. The role of the plenipotentiaries was ill-defined, but effectively their job was to monitor the regional administrations and be their master's voice in the provinces and the two 'federal' cities, Moscow and St Petersburg. Apart from the latter cities, the president's representatives were based in Khabarovsk in the far east, Rostov-on-Don in the south, Novosibirsk and Yekaterinburg in Siberia, and Nizhny Novgorod in central Russia. Under Yeltsin the more numerous presidential representatives had had little contact with the president and were dependent on regional heads for their offices, budgets and influence. The new plenipotentiaries sat on the influential Security Council, so had direct contact with the president and leading members of the administration. In beefing up the role of the presidential representatives and cutting their numbers, Putin's idea was to roll back the excessive autonomy which the regional leaders had acquired under Yeltsin, so imposing a degree of centralization on the far-flung Russian Federation.

Yeltsin had used increased autonomy as a bargaining counter to get controversial legislation through the Federation Council, and had encouraged the regions to take upon themselves as much power as they could handle. While this eased Yeltsin's short-term political problems, it had made the country progressively more ungovernable from the centre. Under Putin, the Kremlin made it clear that the threat to remove corrupt or underperforming governors was real and could apply to a number of regional leaders. Having been removed from the Federation Council, the regional leaders had forfeited their right to parliamentary immunity. Alexander Kotenkov, presidential representative to the federal legislature, cautioned that up to sixteen governors could be prosecuted. The none-too-subtle hint was that those who challenged the president's authority would find themselves in court and perhaps prison.

The president's super-governors mostly had military/security backgrounds, something that could intimidate the opposition. Each sat in an impressive building, designed to overawe the local bosses. The seven plenipotentiaries had a staff of 1,500 people, 70 per cent of whom had connections with the security services or the army. The president's man in St Petersburg was none other than General Victor Cherkesov, a former colleague in the Leningrad KGB with a tough reputation. Cherkesov chose his deputies from among his ex-KGB subordinates. In Khabarovsk, Putin's far-eastern representative was General Konstantin Pulikovsky, who told the *Obshchaya Gazeta* newspaper: 'I am available to everyone. But bear in mind: people who just once write a falsehood about me no longer exist as far as I'm concerned.' In an interview with *Izvestiya*, he went further, warning: '. . . if you disagree with me, you disagree with the President'. Messing with General Pulikovsky was not considered a good idea. To help re-establish a federal presence in the regions, Moscow ministries like the Procuracy, Ministry of Justice, the Audit Chamber, and the power ministries such as the Defence Ministry, Internal Affairs, Tax Police and FSB, began opening branches in the seven new districts.

Some of the weaker regional leaders were browbeaten by the new changes, and one or two were removed or replaced. Yevgeny Nazdratenko, the governor of the far-eastern Maritime Province, was removed in early February 2001, after being publicly reviled for alleged corruption and widespread energy shortages in his region. But in a classic move by Putin, instead of charging Nazdratenko with corruption, in February 2001 he appointed him to the lucrative job of head of the State Committee on Fisheries in Moscow. The committee was rumoured to regularly accept large bribes in return for generous fishing quotas. President Putin is usually cautious about moving against his opponents, and prefers to quietly neutralize them where possible. In fact, Yeltsin had been more aggressive in occasionally firing governors outright by decree, despite the dubious legality, including the democratically elected Yury Lodkin of Bryansk and Alexander Surat of Amur. Another example of Putin's guarded approach was the case of Governor Vladimir Yakovlev of St Petersburg. The Kremlin actively prepared Deputy Prime Minister Valentina Matvienko (responsible for social affairs) to challenge Yakovlev in his re-election battle in May 2000. Matvienko, whom I had the pleasure of meeting at Moscow's White House, is a 54-year-old former Soviet apparatchik and people's deputy of the USSR from Leningrad, and one-time ambassador to Malta and Greece. She is a very experienced operator who worked her way through Komsomol and the Communist Party's women's upper echelons, astutely becoming an ambassador abroad just as the USSR was imploding.

When it looked certain that Yakovlev would win against Putin's candidate in St Petersburg, Matvienko was withdrawn from the race. Allegations had meanwhile surfaced alleging corruption by Yakovlev and his closest associates. His wife reputedly ran companies with retail interests in St Petersburg and provided the city with its paving stones. A criminal case was initiated against Alexander Potekhin, the city's vice-governor, for illegal business activity, and his deputy was arrested and charged with embezzling public funds. Another vice-governor, Valery Malyshev, was suspended after being charged with bribery. Back in December 1999, Yakovlev himself had been charged with improperly using $2.7 million from city funds to finance hotel rooms and 'other services' for delegates to a Fatherland-All Russia party congress. Other allegations against Yakovlev focused on the misuse of the road-building budget and tens of millions of dollars purportedly embezzled from federal funds designated to refurbish St Petersburg. The Russian government had set aside $750 million to transform the city's buildings and infra-structure in time for the tercentenary celebrations. Plenipotentiary Cherkesov would spend years undermining Governor Yakovlev, before the latter withdrew in favour of the Kremlin's candidate in 2003. Yakovlev was then appointed a deputy prime minister, and the candidate he made way for was Valentina Matvienko. He was subse-quently appointed the president's representative for the Northern Caucasus, a dubious honour and equivalent to being UK minister responsible for Northern Ireland during the Troubles.

The Kremlin's strategy was not always successful, especially in the early days. Of the regional bosses whose seats were contested in the 2000 elections for governor, all but fifteen were re-elected. Some of the more important regional leaders remained sure of their hold on their fiefdoms, and either ignored the plenipotentiaries or used them to lobby Moscow for money and favours. Putin's super-governors relied on their closeness to the president for support, and had precious few real resources. According to the pro-Kremlin newspaper *Argumenti i fakty*, Mintimer Shaimiev, president of Tatarstan, treats Putin's representative like a waiter: 'First he listens attentively, then he orders his favourite dish.' Tatarstan, with a high proportion of ethnic tartars, had negotiated its own autonomy treaty with Moscow, giving it a significant say over its local economy and self-rule. Having visited Kazan, Tatarstan's capital in the late 1990s, it was clear to me that neither Shaimiev or his administration would be pushed around by Moscow. The Kremlin didn't need more political problems with another large Muslim population. In fact, for a while the 'Tartarstan model' was touted as the answer to the rift with Chechnya. However, Tartarstan, with its ethnically mixed marriages and location in the heart of Russia on the Volga river, is not comparable with Chechnya. In the Caucasus, ethnic divisions and hatreds now run deep.

Shortly after his inauguration in May, in a television interview, President Putin signalled his desire to overhaul federal relations, and he developed this theme in his July address to the Federal Assembly of the combined Duma and Federation Council. The problem as he saw it was not just relations between the regional leaders and Moscow, but the way the regions often violated the constitution and federal law. Constitutional court rulings which found regional laws unconstitutional were often ignored. A new law was passed giving the president the right to dissolve regional assemblies which persistently ignored court rulings. Vladimir Ustinov, President Putin's new prosecutor-general, declared that 70 per cent of regional legislative acts deviated from federal law, and gave regional leaders one month to bring them into line. He later reported that his initiative was largely successful, as the regions ensured most of their laws conformed to the constitution and federal legislation.

The Kremlin paid a price for all this cooperation from the regions. As a sop to the regional leaders, they were given the right to remove heads of local government, much as the president had the right to remove them. Regional bosses already had a good deal of influence over local self-government below the regional level (*mestnoye samoupravleniye*), including budgetary control and the appointment of personnel. Previously, only regional legislatures had the right to remove local heads of government. Putin's federal reforms, whilst they strengthened the centre, were a blow to the aspirations of local self-government, and paradoxically strengthened the grip of governors and regional executives over their own territories.

It took President Putin a year to make his mark on the government and get a reform process under way. Again, it showed Putin's natural caution and desire to prepare the groundwork. First of all, he brought more of his own people into government. When he initially became president, he had 'inherited' Mikhail Kasyanov, who became prime minister, and reappointed the 'power ministers' who served under Yeltsin. These men included Foreign Minister Igor Ivanov, Defence Minister Marshal Igor Sergeyev and Interior Minister Vladimir Rushailo. Almost a year later, in March 2001, he replaced Sergeyev with his friend, the English-speaking Sergei Ivanov, and brought in Lyubov Kudelina as the first woman deputy defence minister. Ivanov, Russia's first civilian defence minister, was a former lieutenant-general in the SVR foreign intelligence service and secretary of the Security Council. Boris Gryzlov, fifteen months before an electrical engineer from St Petersburg and leader of the Unity faction in the Duma, was appointed interior minister. The three new ministers reported directly to President Putin, bypassing the prime minister. Rushailo, a career policeman and organized crime expert, shifted over to become secretary of the Security Council.

The reshuffle was remarkable for those it left in place. Prime Minister Kasyanov, a member of the Yeltsin 'family', was left in situ, together with the career diplomat Igor Ivanov, who had served under Primakov when he was foreign minister and had been Moscow's ambassador to Spain. Igor Ivanov, now aged fifty-eight, favoured old-style Cold War rhetoric on occasions, and took a traditional Russian foreign ministry line. Alexander Voloshin, Yeltsin's chief of staff, remained as head of Putin's presidential administration.

There were now three distinct groups vying for influence in Putin's Kremlin, although membership of each was a bit of a movable feast. The first group were the puissant remnants of Yeltsin's 'family', and included Kasyanov, Voloshin and his deputy Vladislav Surkov, Vladimir Ustinov, the prosecutor-general who took over from the disgraced Yury Skuratov, and Mikhail Lesin, the press minister. Voloshin and Lesin were particularly close to Tatyana Dyachenko, Yeltsin's daughter. Oligarchs still part of the 'family' were Alexander Mamut of MDM-Bank and the Transneft oil company, and Roman Abramovich. Abramovich, who went on to buy Chelsea Football Club in England for over $232 million, was owner of Sibneft oil company and a business associate of the exiled Boris Berezovsky. On the fringes of this clan are people like the public opinion specialist Dr Alexander Oslon, president of the Public Opinion Foundation in Moscow. Around the time of his inauguration, Putin had wanted his St Petersburg friend and lawyer Dmitri Kozak brought in as prosecutor-general, but was over-ruled by Voloshin and a still-active Boris Yeltsin. Yeltsin reputedly called Putin at midnight and got him to rewrite the decree appointing Kozak, substituting Acting Prosecutor-General Vladimir Ustinov in his place. Rumours in Moscow suggested Voloshin was concerned that another more independent prosecutor-general might be too keen to launch investigations into oligarchs close to the 'family'. If the story published in *Obshchaya Gazeta* is true, it seems Putin felt it was too early to gainsay powerful 'family' interests.

Vladimir Putin had, however, eventually managed to get rid of another Yeltsin man, the allegedly corrupt transport minister, Nikolai Aksyonenko. Aksyonenko had family interests linked to his ministry. Mikhail Lesin, the press minister, who survived, still had commercial interests in television advertising. The perceived conflict of interest didn't seem to bother him. Kasyanov and the other 'family' members sought to keep control of the domestic economic agenda, which brought them into conflict with the second Kremlin group, the St Petersburg liberal economic reformers and technocrats. In March 2003 the infighting broke out in public, when Prime Minister Mikhail Kasyanov attacked German Gref, the trade and economic development minister, over economic growth and lambasted Alexei Kudrin, the finance minister, over tax reform. A few months later they also clashed over the reform of gas monopoly Gazprom, with Gref promoting change and Kasyanov opposing it.

The group of St Petersburg liberal economic reformers and technocrats were centred around German Gref, Putin's economic adviser Andrei Illarionov, Finance Minister Alexei Kudrin, Interior

Minister Boris Gryzlov and Ilya Klebanov, the deputy prime minister. Two notable St Petersburg lawyers in the administration were Dmitri Medvedev, thirty-eight, and Dmitri Kozak, forty-five. Both worked with Putin in Sobchak's term as mayor, and followed him to Moscow, where they worked in the Kremlin administration from 1999. Kozak was responsible for Putin's legal reform programme and bringing regional laws into line with federal legislation. One of Medvedev's key tasks was to reform Gazprom, in which he was only partially successful. When Voloshin resigned in late October 2003, Medvedev became chief of staff with Kozak as his deputy. Another St Petersburg lawyer was Sergei Mironov, who became Speaker of the Federation Council, or upper house of parliament. Like Medvedev, Kozak, Gref, Cherkesov and Putin, Mironov had also attended Leningrad University Law Faculty. Most of those in the second group knew President Putin from the days when he worked for St Petersburg mayor Anatoly Sobchak.

The third group of people were the Petersburg Chekists, who had come across Putin during his Leningrad KGB days, and were from security backgrounds. Most prominent was Putin's closest confidant and ex-SVR man Sergei Ivanov, but other leading figures were FSB head Nikolai Patrushev and north-west Russia plenipotentiary Victor Cherkesov. Other members were ex-KGB men Igor Sechin (head of the president's office) and Victor Ivanov, a former KGB general. They were primarily interested in dominating the so-called power ministries, and keeping the influence of the two other clans in check. It was the Petersburg Chekists who were particularly keen to reduce the power and reach of the business oligarchs who had previously been so close to the 'family', and which made the latter doubly nervous. The tycoons Boris Berezovsky and Vladimir Gusinsky lost influence and fell out with the Kremlin, and became targets of both the prosecutor-general's office and the Petersburg Chekists. But later on, other tycoons like Mikhail Khodorkovsky and Roman Abramovich would also discover they were no longer in favour, and start feeling the heat from the Kremlin.

Russia's business tycoons, christened the 'oligarchs' by *Izvestiya* in 1996 to reflect both their financial and political clout, had made billions during the golden era of Tsar Boris's rule. In those days it had seemed they could do no wrong. A number had benefited from Anatoly Chubais's 'voucher' privatization of the early 1990s, when state enterprises were sold off and vouchers issued to the population in lieu of cash or shares. Buying up the virtually worthless vouchers and gaining control of state enterprises made some tycoons their first millions. A bigger scandal was the 'loans for shares' scheme of 1995, when Russia's prime industrial assets were sold off to the oligarchs in exchange for loans to the government.

The idea was dreamt up by an oligarch, Vladimir Potanin, the head of Oneximbank. In a two-stage process, the oligarchs would lend money to the government and hold shares in government companies, bought at auction, as security. The oligarchs would only gain legal control of the companies after the election, when as planned, the government would be unable to repay the loans. The crown jewels of Russia's industry were sold to insiders in rigged auctions for a fraction of their real value. There was no real competition and foreign bids weren't allowed. Some of the bidders themselves managed the share auctions. The result was predictable. Potanin's Oneximbank bought 51 per cent of the Sidanko oil company for $130 million, in an auction that it managed itself. Less than two years later the company was valued by the market at $5 billion. Potanin also won control of Norilsk Nickel, which supplies a quarter of the world's nickel, for a sixth of the price that it would command on the market two years later. Oneximbank had also been placed in charge of the Norilsk Nickel company auction. Similarly, Boris Berezovsky bought 51 pent of the Sibneft oil company for $100 million; two years later it too was valued at $5 billion. Today it's worth an estimated $12.5 billion. His investment had appreciated by an astounding 2,400 per cent in just two years.

The pillage of Russia's industrial crown jewels continued. Mikhail Khodorkovsky paid $309 million for 78 per cent of Yukos oil; its value rose to over $6 billion in under two years. By 2003, it was worth $30 billion. Other companies sold off for a song included Sidanko, and a chunk of LUKoil. The government had generously provided the oligarchs with the funds necessary to purchase their equity stakes. Their 'pocket' banks received negative interest rate loans from the central bank, and received government funds which they kept on deposit at below market rates. They were also allowed exclusive access to the government's domestic bond (GKO) market, earning yields of over 100 per cent in dollar terms. In other words, the Yeltsin administration allowed the oligarchs' banks to profiteer at its expense, lend the government its own money, and buy its assets at knock-down prices in auctions they controlled. Later the companies would avoid and evade tax on a massive scale. In a sordid deal, the oligarchs in return promised to support President Boris Yeltsin's re-election in 1996, pumping up to $500 million into his campaign coffers (the legal maximum was under $3 million). Ironically, most of this money came indirectly from the government's own coffers, in the form of heavily discounted dollar bonds sold cheaply to the oligarchs which were then re-sold for enormous profit. Berezovsky and Gusinsky, two of the major beneficiaries of the state property sell-off, had complete backing from the Kremlin for their media empires. The two-stage nature of the 'loans for shares' scheme was designed to tie the oligarchs into supporting Yeltsin until after election day. Chubais, Yeltsin's campaign manager, ensured the oligarchs understood they would only get their hands on Russia's prime industrial assets if Yeltsin was re-elected. Chubais himself turned from gamekeeper to poacher. He subsequently became chief executive of UES, the massive Russian electricity monopoly, and joined the oligarchs at the trough.

Although the 'loans for shares' cost the Russian treasury billions of dollars, the irony was that winning backing from the oligarchs was unnecessary. Russia's business tycoons were terrified that a Communist presidency under Zyuganov would reverse all their previous dubious privatizations and instigate criminal investigations. It was a fact that four-fifths of Russia's privatizations had taken place without any law on privatization being passed. The privatizations were based on presidential decrees issued by President Yeltsin, and private deals struck with oligarchs. Even the 1993 Russian constitution, heavily slanted in favour of presidential executive power, gave Yeltsin no legal authority to sell off the state's industrial assets without Duma legislation. The whole privatization process was therefore of dubious legality. In those circumstances, failing to support Yeltsin's re-election would have been suicidal for the oligarchs. Chubais's argument that the privatization process had to be completed swiftly to make it irreversible does not bear close scrutiny. There were many ways in which the privatization of Russia's state assets, like the oil and nickel sectors, could have taken place without deliberately undervaluing them. Marshall Goldman, in his book *The Piratization of Russia*, points to the example of Poland to show how things might have been done differently. Instead, both the 'voucher' and 'loans for shares' privatizations were an unmitigated disaster which impoverished the country, deprived the treasury of precious funds, discouraged foreign investment, increased social inequality and undermined the rule of law.

It was no wonder that Putin was reported as saying around the time of his election that he wanted to 'liquidate the oligarchs as a class'. His words echoed Stalin's infamous plan to 'liquidate the kulaks', his extermination of the class of prosperous peasants and the enforced collectivization of the Soviet countryside. In private, Vladimir and Lyudmila Putin were known to be even more scathing about the oligarchs. They were regarded as total crooks who had robbed the country blind. When the Kremlin moved against the oligarchs, they knew they were acting in accordance with Vladimir Putin's views and wishes. The Kremlin may have had their 'favourite' oligarchs, like the St Petersburg banker Sergei Pugachev and Oleg Deripaska, but in Putin's opinion Russia's over-mighty business tycoons had brought precious little benefit to the country and were a positively malign influence.

Left: A Leningrader with his daily bread ration during the blockade.

Middle: Leningrad volunteers march out to the front from the Narva Gate, Stachek Prospect.

Bottom: Collecting water from the street in Leningrad during the 900-day siege.

Left: Young Vladimir was popular with women.

Middle left: Teenager Vladimir Putin throws his friend Vasily Shestakov while practising Judo in 1969.

Middle right: Vladimir showing off his judo skills.

Putin, now a KGB officer, with wife, Lyudmila, at the registration ceremony of their daughter, Masha, Leningrad, May 1985.

Above: Yeltsin says a final goodbye to the Kremlin, 7 May 2000.

Right: Putin on his way to his swearing-in ceremony in St Andrew's Hall in the Grand Kremlin Palace.

Below: Putin takes the Presidential Oath at his Kremlin Inauguration, May 2000.

Above: Putin and Tony Blair together in London, April 2000.

Left: Keeping his judo up, G8 Okinawa Summit, July 2000.

Below: Putin meets Bill Clinton, G8 Okinawa Summit, July 2000.

With President Bush at Crawford, Texas, November 2001.

Putin with traditional ally Kim Jong-Il of North Korea, Vladivostok, 23 August 2002.

The *Kursk* emerges from its watery tomb, Roslyakovo, October 2001.

Putin meets relatives of the *Kursk* victims in a walkabout in Vidyayevo, watched by Captain Gennady Lyachin's widow, Irina, August 2000.

Tony and Cherie Blair go for a walk in the woods at the Putins' dacha at Zavidovo, October 2002.

The Putins showing George and Laura Bush around the halls of Catherine Palace at Tsarkoye Selo, near St Petersburg, 22 November 2002.

Vladimir and Lyudmila with Queen Elizabeth and Prince Philip, Buckingham Palace, June 2003.

The Moscow theatre hostages are freed by Russian Spetsnaz (Special Forces), October 2002.

A Moscow siege survivor talks to relatives from a hospital window, October 2002.

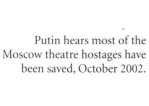

Putin hears most of the Moscow theatre hostages have been saved, October 2002.

So who were these oligarchs the Putins so despised? Vladimir Potanin, who thought up the 'loans for shares' scheme, was fairly unusual in the sense that he started in business well-connected. His father had been an official in the Soviet Ministry of Foreign Economic Relations, where Potanin had also worked. When the Berlin Wall fell, he used his ministry and Communist Party contacts to set up a trading company, and then two banks, MFK and Oneximbank, Russia's third and fourth largest banks. Potanin, worth over $3 billion, became a deputy prime minister under Yeltsin. Boris Berezovsky was a mathematician at a Moscow research institute, who formed the LogoVAZ car dealership to sell cars, and ended up worth $3 billion owning ORT television, the *Izvestiya* newspaper, and the Sibneft oil company. He also controlled Aeroflot and had shares in LUKoil. A close business partner was Roman Abramovich, who eventually bought his stake in Sibneft. Abramovich, an orphan who set up a co-operative making toys and then moved into oil trading in Omsk, became a Duma deputy then governor of Chukotka in Russia's far north along the way. Apart from his friend Berezovsky, who was also briefly a Duma deputy, Abramovich was also close to Tatyana Dyachenko, who provided him with access to Yeltsin. His other interests were Russian Aluminium (Rusal), the world's second largest producer, the Gaz car company, the Transneft oil company and a minority stake in Aeroflot.

A multi-billionaire, Abramovich is still just thirty-six, and recently reputedly put an offer on a $145 million house in London's exclusive Kensington Palace Gardens, owned by Formula 1 billion-aire Bernie Ecclestone. Abramovich started divesting himself of his assets in 2003, selling a 25 per cent stake in Rusal for $2 billion to his oligarch business partner, Oleg Deripaska. Two days later he sold Sibneft to his rival, Yukos. After his sell-offs, Abramovich was worth an estimated $8 billion. Deripaska, a former student at Moscow State University who built up his fortune in aluminium after becoming a broker on the stock exchange, called a truce with Abramovich in 2000 to corner about 90 per cent of Russia's aluminium market.

Over a hundred executives in the aluminium business were murdered in the 'aluminium wars' which marked the consolidation of the industry. Still only thirty-five, Deripaska himself has been on the receiving end of death threats and an assassination attempt with a grenade launcher. He recalled how he had to physically occupy one factory he owned, while he received murder threats on the telephone from the plant's former boss. He secured his political position by marrying Polina Yumashev, the daughter of Boris Yeltsin's son-in-law and former chief of staff. Described as the oligarch closest to President Putin (they go skiing together), Oleg Deripaska seems determined to invest in Russia and stay out of domestic politics. Deripaska and his partner Mikhail Chernoi were named in a $2.7 billion lawsuit alleging murder, fraud and corruption. Thrown out by a New York district judge in 2003, the case is being taken to appeal. Meanwhile, Deripaska was refused a visa to enter the US, because of his alleged criminal connections.

The links between the oligarchs, Yeltsin's 'family' and the Kremlin have been incestuous and closely intertwined. Big money and politics went together in Yeltsin's Russia. Without a political 'roof' at the highest level, the oligarchs would not have been in a position to exploit Russia's privatization process, and operate in the murky world of big business. Without political protection, the oligarchs could expect no favours and would find their business opportunities drying up.

Like his predecessor at the Kremlin Valentin Yumashev, Alexander Voloshin had had close business links with the oligarchs. Voloshin, both Yeltsin and Putin's chief of staff, had worked with Berezovsky to set up the AVVA (All-Russian Automobile Alliance) in 1993 to 1994, a pyramid scheme involving the sale of securities in the automobile industry. Berezovsky made $50 million on the operation, but more than 100,000 small Russian investors never saw their money back. Berezovsky's business association with both Yumashev and Voloshin gave him an entrée to the Kremlin's inner sanctums.

Berezovsky's great rival was Vladimir Gusinsky, another billionaire oligarch who trained as a stage director and after he couldn't find a job started working as a taxi driver and an illegal hard currency money changer. He built up a construction business working alongside Moscow mayor Yury Luzhkov, and branched out into banking and the Media-Most group, which included NTV, Moscow Echo radio, *Itogi* magazine and the *Segodnya* newspaper. According to Alexander Korzhakov, President Yeltsin's bodyguard, Berezovsky asked for Gusinsky's assassination. Berezovsky was himself the victim of an assassination attempt in 1994, when a car bomb decapitated his driver. Alexander Smolensky, another of Berezovsky's allies, started out printing Bibles and working in construction before running the SBS-Agro bank which lost tens of thousands of depositors' money in the August 1998 financial crash. He was subsequently investigated in connection with the Bank of New York $10 billion money-laundering scandal.

Mikhail Khodorkovsky, aged forty and a former Communist youth leader, went from working in cooperatives to owning Menatep Bank and Yukos oil. The richest man in Russia, and according to *Forbes* magazine the 26th richest person in the world – he's worth around $11 billion. His combined oil company, YukosSibneft, was valued at $45 billion, and was the world's fourth largest oil producer, after ExxonMobil, Shell and BP. After enduring early criticism for sharp business practice, including massive share dilution and ignoring the property rights of minority shareholders, Khodorkovsky's Yukos oil became one of the most transparent of Russia's companies. Yukos now follows international accounting standards and is trying to establish Western-style good governance principles. Khodorkovsky was one of the first Russian tycoons to understand he could become even richer if he adopted Western business standards, so attracting more foreign capital and boosting the market value of his companies in the process. The oligarch sees himself as a latter-day Rockefeller and philanthropist, donating millions to charity and sponsoring the Hermitage exhibition in London.

Another notable oligarch is Mikhail Fridman, the thirty-nine-year-old head of the Alfa group and owner of Russia's largest private bank, Alfa Bank. His other interests include the TNK (Tyumen) oil company and Vimpelcom, Russia's second biggest mobile phone company. According to *Forbes* magazine, he is the 68th wealthiest person in the world, with a personal fortune of around $4 billion. Fridman's oil company recently linked up with BP in a $6.8 billion investment, the largest foreign investment to date in Russia. The $16 billion joint venture will make the TNK-BP oil company Russia's third largest. Fridman's business partner is oligarch Pyotr Aven, president of Alfa Bank, who was trade minister in Yegor Gaidar's 1992 liberal economic reformist government.

What most of the dozen or so oligarchs had in common, apart from obscene amounts of money, was their relative youth. Seventeen Russian dollar billionaires are included in the 2003 *Forbes* list of the world's richest people. In the mid-1980s, none were worth more than a few thousand dollars. Most of the oligarchs were in their thirties, and had gone into business when the USSR was either about to implode or had already self-destructed. A number, like Berezovsky, Gusinsky, Fridman, Smolensky, Khodorkovsky and Abramovich came from Jewish families, which further incensed Russia's traditionally anti-Semitic nationalist and Communist cadres. Whether their Jewish backgrounds made them more determined to succeed in business as the USSR started collapsing is a moot point, and probably one more appropriately addressed by sociologists and psychologists. Certainly, all of them would have encountered a glass ceiling in the old Soviet state, which none too subtly discriminated against Jews. The business tycoons as a group became known as Russia's own 'robber barons', in the public consciousness stealing and stripping the country's prime industrial assets. That was a little unfair. At least in Gusinsky's case, one of the oligarch's created something new. NTV, Russia's best television channel, was the country's first independent national TV station. NTV was created out of nothing, and Gusinsky should be given credit for that if nothing else. His fellow oligarchs were generally less creative. Most made excessive banking profits or huge amounts of money through trading commodities or as *rentiers*, whilst starving Russia's enterprises of meaningful investment.

Berezovsky was a prime example of an oligarch who seemed to make a fortune without creating anything, leaving often impoverished businesses in his wake. Asset-stripping took place on a large scale. The idea that the oligarchs were Russia's equivalent of America's nineteenth- and early-twentieth-century robber barons is fanciful. While their US counterparts like Rockefeller, Carnegie, Ford and Morgan had built up oil, rail, steel, automobile and manufacturing empires from scratch, Russia's oligarchs were mainly interested in maximizing short-term profits and stripping existing state enterprises of any residual value. The law covering the oligarchs' early business activity was a grey area. The 'bankers' wars' of the 1990s left many business 'executives' dead, with disputes occasionally settled on Moscow's streets with rocket launchers. Professional contract killings were running at the rate of several hundred a year, most aimed at business rivals. In a country where the court system failed to arbitrate because it was so corrupt, businessmen were either given offers they couldn't refuse or ended up dead.

I remember visiting one business tycoon's company headquarters in Moscow in 1996. Vladimir Bryntsalov was a dollar billionaire, who stood for the presidency against Yeltsin for kicks that year and who had made his money selling black market honey in southern Russia, before cornering the pharmaceutical market. Entering his compound, the visitor was greeted by glum-looking gun-toting heavies in full combat gear. His guards were young, very fit and obviously ex-military. Bryntsalov himself had still to reach middle age; he was dark haired with a heavy-set face and bushy eyebrows. On his left hand he wore a gold watch, with a large diamond ring on his second finger. After entering the main building and passing yet more camouflaged security guards, Bryntsalov led me and his guests to a table set for twenty, groaning with lobster, caviar, champagne and other delicacies. The lobsters had been specially flown in from abroad. Pointing out the lavishly expensive dinner set, he informed me that the really good stuff was kept for his private use. In the corner of the room there was a portrait of our host, which had been painted to make him look strikingly similar to a younger version of Boris Yeltsin. On the table, he had his own brand of vodka, made in his own vodka factory, with a picture of his smiling face on the label. His wife, arriving later with her bodyguards in a chauffeur-driven Mercedes, told us all that she had only done a little shopping that afternoon, spending 'just $200'. It was one of those 'New Russian' moments, guaranteed to make you cringe. The sum was more than the average monthly wage, and our hostess's glib throwaway remark was meant to impress. Slim and petite with long dark hair and in her twenties, Bryntsalov's spouse was a typical Russian oligarch's 'trophy' wife. Bryntsalov, an outlandish extrovert with questionable taste, had smacked her exposed bottom on prime time TV.

Later, arriving at the count, I noticed a large stretch Mercedes turn up with a three-car escort. It wasn't the president, it was Bryntsalov. He polled extremely poorly in the elections, but one sensed that wasn't the point. Although Bryntsalov's boorish behaviour might seem a little extreme, it was not untypical among the 'New Russian' elite. President Boris Yeltsin complained bitterly that the police regularly held up the traffic for Vladimir Gusinsky's motorcade, while his wife and daughter were held back waiting for the great man to pass. Gusinsky's undoubted arrogance contributed to his ultimate downfall.

Following a number of raids and investigations, the oligarchs sought to make peace with President Putin. At the end of July 2000, about twenty businessmen met Putin at the Kremlin, and promised to pay their taxes and obey the law in return for a recognition that past privatizations would stand. The meeting was preceded by action against a number of them for corruption and embezzlement. Vladimir Gusinsky was arrested for embezzlement and Boris Berezovsky's affairs investigated. Other oligarchs under investigation for possible tax evasion or fraud included Vagit Alekperov, head of LUKoil; Vladimir Potanin, head of the Interros group; and Vladimir Kadannikov, a former deputy prime minister, head of the country's largest car maker, AvtoVAZ, and business partner of Berezovsky.

Mikhail Fridman, head of Alfa group, received a shock when police seized the group's 13 per cent stake in the Slavneft oil company, after following up a three-year-old criminal investigation. To the oligarchs it looked as though Putin was serious about his election pledges to crack down on the wayward business tycoons, and they went to him that July nervously seeking a truce. Putin told them they only had themselves to blame for the investigations into their business and tax affairs. But behind the scenes, the Kremlin did a subtle deal with the oligarchs. Putin had always said that he would not undo the privatizations of the past and re-nationalize Russia's prime industries. However, the Kremlin went further and promised to leave the oligarchs alone if they stayed out of politics and stuck to business. Instead of trying to deal with the president bilaterally, the oligarchs would increasingly organize themselves like a normal business lobby group, meeting as the Union of Industrialists and Entrepreneurs.

In the coming years, those oligarchs who dabbled in politics and gainsaid the Kremlin were ruthlessly crushed. Gusinsky and Berezovsky were made examples of, and when Khodorkovsky forgot the rules of the game, he was targeted as well. Back in December 2002, Khodorkovsky and a group of business leaders met Putin for talks. Khodorkovsky accused Russia's bureaucrats and tax collectors of corruption. Putin's reply was icily sharp: 'I put the ball back in your court.' One investor took it as a warning 'to shut up and sit down'. Some of Yukos's leading shareholders subsequently stood for the Communist Party in the forthcoming Duma elections. Khodorkovsky chanced his arm further, making the serious mistake (in the Kremlin's eyes) of generously funding opposition parties like the liberal Yabloko Party and Boris Nemtsov's Union of Right Forces, criticizing Russia's policy on Iraq and hinting at his own presidential ambitions post-2008. Under the constitution as it stands, President Putin must stand down after a maximum of two terms in office, ending in 2008.

Yukos was raided in the summer of 2003, and billionaire Platon Lebedev, a top Mentatep Group and Yukos executive, was incarcerated by the authorities. Lebedev, Khodorkovsky's right-hand man, was accused of a $280 million fraud during the privatization of the Apatit state fertilizer company in 1994. Charges were also levelled against two other Yukos employees for tax evasion and murder, for which company security chief Alexei Pichugin was arrested and detained. Police armed with machine guns raided the company's HQ, its internet provider and the office of Lebedev's lawyer. Khodorkovsky was called in for questioning, and finally arrested by armed FSB officers in Siberia in October 2003, and flown to Moscow. He had failed to appear as a witness in a criminal trial at short notice, and a warrant had been issued for his arrest. The prosecutor-general's office confirmed Khodorkovsky was being charged with large-scale theft, fraud and tax evasion, both personally and by his company, amounting to some $1 billion. He was jailed in a grim Moscow pre-trial detention centre called the Sailor's Rest (Matrosskaya Tishina), and held in a cell with five other prisoners.

Khodorkovsky's arrest sparked protests from the United States. Alexander (Sandy) Vershbow, America's man in Moscow, said the arrest could 'negatively affect' foreign investment in Russia, and that the law was apparently being 'used selectively'. As part of the investigation into Yukos, police raided a political consultancy working for the Yabloko Party, and took away confidential lists of activists, political databases and campaign plans. Yabloko's leader, Grigory Yavlinsky, called the raid 'illegal' and highly disruptive of the party's campaign in the run-up to the Duma elections on 7 December. Four of Khodorkovsky's Yukos colleagues were on Yabloko's list of parliamentary candidates. Around the same time the FSB visited the Moscow school attended by Mikhail Khodorkovsky's twelve-year-old daughter and demanded a list of her classmates. The FSB claimed it was part of an 'anti-terrorist exercise'. Earlier, police raided an orphanage funded by Yukos. Reports in the Russian press alleged two former senior KGB officials working in the Kremlin were overheard on their mobile phones discussing the need to put 'these upstart oligarchs' in their place. A large chunk of Khodorkovsky's shares were frozen by the prosecutor's office, the first time private assets had been seized by the state since 1991 and the fall of Communism. The pressure was being piled on Khodorkovsky, his family, his political supporters, his business associates and Yukos generally. When the Kremlin goes after you, you certainly feel it.

The assault launched against Yukos also showed that the Kremlin's right hand didn't know, care or understand what the left hand was doing. Although the Petersburg Chekists were obeying their master's voice in cracking down on the oligarchs, it was apparent that the impact of the Kremlin's actions had not been thought through. In the three weeks following Lebedev's arrest on 2 July, Yukos's share price dropped and the Russian stock market lost $20 billion, or 13 per cent of its value. Russia's Central Bank reserves fell by $900 million in a fortnight, indicating renewed capital flight. None of these figures were reported on Russia's tame state television media. Foreign investors and Russian oligarchs were getting nervous. Khodorkovsky's arrest that autumn saw Yukos's share price dive once again, and the RTS share index lost a tenth of its value in a single day. Share prices continued to plummet as Khodorkovsky's shares in Yukos were frozen. Putin's initial angry reaction was to urge 'an end to the hysteria' surrounding the arrest of Khodorkovsky. 'Everyone should be equal before the law, irrespective of how many millions of dollars a person has in his personal or corporate account,' the president said in a televised statement, with his cabinet looking on. Nevertheless, a few days later, Prime Minister Mikhail Kasyanov, expressed his 'deep concern' over the crisis, despite being previously warned by Putin to stay out of what he claimed was a legal matter. With Voloshin's resignation on Thursday 30 October, the 'family' clan were showing their displeasure and alarm at Putin and the Petersburg Chekists' new onslaught against the oligarchs, and the damage that it was doing to Russia's economy and the prospects for future investment.

In the meantime, President Putin assured a group of international investment bankers at a pre-arranged Kremlin meeting that he remained committed to market reform and private property rights. Oozing charm and shaking everyone by the hand, he stressed the arrest of Khodorkovsky and Lebedev was not an attack on Yukos as a corporate entity, and there was no intention to break up the company. The affair would not spill over to other companies, he said, pledging there was no intention to confiscate or renationalize assets, likening the crisis to the Enron case. According to one person present, the president said 'he was aware that other shareholders in Yukos would suffer in the medium term, but that in the long term they would benefit from the better rule of law'. As a sweetener, he promised that foreigners would soon be allowed to buy Gazprom's domestic shares, previously only available to Russian citizens, and welcomed tax breaks for investors in Russian debt and equity. But Putin made one slip, acknowledging his staff had been working closely with the prosecutor-general's office to ensure that only Khodorkovsky's personal shares were frozen. The next day, some of Yukos's shares were unfrozen, as the prosecutor's office admitted it had made a mistake over the ownership of some of the company's equity.

While the Berezovsky-owned *Kommersant* and *Nezavisimaya Gazeta* criticized the Kremlin's handling of the Yukos crisis, most of the press focused on the falling market and the negative effect on the economy. At the same time, with Khodorkovsky's arrest meeting popular approval, United Russia's opinion poll rating went up 4 per cent in a fortnight.

Putin's policy of reining in the overmighty oligarchs was conflicting with his desire to increase foreign direct investment and encourage economic growth. The problem was that the prosecutor-general's office and the security establishment do not really understand or care how modern markets work. Putin himself doesn't fully appreciate how heavy-handed action against Russia's business tycoons can play badly abroad, and frighten off the very investment he is so keen to attract. In this respect, his old-KGB career seems to have a greater influence on his mindset than his years working for Sobchak's liberal St Petersburg city administration. Of course, Putin may calculate that foreign investment will flow into Russia in any event, especially into the globally important energy sector. But being so blasé about the willingness of foreign investors to accept risk is a dangerous strategy, and may put off all but the most determined investors. As the impact of its moves dawned on the Kremlin (which nevertheless continued the assault), it was forced to issue a statement saying that President Putin did not initiate the attack on Yukos, and considered the action by the prosecutor-general's office harmful to the country's image and economy. Prime Minister Mikhail Kasyanov, always a friend of the oligarchs and the 'family's' man in the cabinet, said that protracted investigations into Yukos would hurt the investment climate. The prosecutor-general's office told him to mind his own business.

As the onslaught against Yukos and Khodorkovsky continued into the winter, it was obvious that it had received backing from the very top. It was inconceivable that the investigation would have been pursued if opposed by the president. Putin and his inner circle had decided it was essential to his political future to neutralize oppositionist oligarchs like Khodorkovsky. In a 'managed democracy' there was no room for powerful rogue elephants with ideas of their own. If that upset the market, then that was regrettable but unavoidable. Putin had to show the oligarchs who was boss.

Even 'family' member Roman Abramovich got nervous when he was investigated for tax evasion by Sergei Stephasin, the head of the national audit commission, and started selling his Russian assets. Abramovich had developed an almost saintly image as governor of Chukotka, the impoverished region in far eastern Russia, within the Arctic Circle. Chukotka forms part of the massive headland reaching towards the Bering Strait and Alaska, sold by Tsar Nicholas I to the United States in 1853. Rich in gold, gas and fish, the region is plagued by oil shortages and regular power cuts, potentially fatal at temperatures of minus 30 C and below. Abramovich brought hope to the isolated and forgotten communities of Chukotka, marooned in their icy wastes by the implosion of the USSR. Many inhabitants had been attracted there by generous wages, better housing, and longer holidays in the hotter parts of the Soviet Union. Now many of the settlements were facing near-starvation. A Duma deputy there from 1999, Abramovich was elected governor in December 2000, saying he felt great pity for local people. He poured millions of dollars of his fortune into the region, improving health services and buying books and computers for local schools. He deeply impressed local people by sending 3,700 children on extended holidays to the sunny Black Sea. For many, it was their first holiday in a warm climate.

It all seemed too good to be true, and in a way it was. Abramovich's companies were some of Russia's worst tax payers. The oligarch's oil and gas companies avoided taxes on a massive scale. After he became governor of Chukotka, Abramovich used his powers to grant large tax-breaks to his Sibneft oil company. A number of his companies became registered in Chukotka, where he used his powers to offer concessionary tax rates. According to Troika Dialog, Russia's largest investment bank, his company tax-breaks were worth $400 million, while Sibneft paid 'by far the lowest tax rate in the sector'. As the poor people of Chukotka huddle around their fires in the middle of winter, it's probably a comforting thought that Russian taxpayers contributed more than enough funds to enable Abramovich to buy Chelsea Football Club. For his part, the oligarch promised not to abandon the people he came to live among and represent. Whether he keeps his promise is an open question, particularly given his announcement from his London home that he will not be seeking re-election as Chukotka's governor.

Sergei Stepashin, the head of the audit commission, was clearly outraged that Abramovich was diverting so much Russian money to

London's fashionable Chelsea (Chelski), when the country so desperately needed more domestic investment. London was rapidly becoming known as 'Moscow on the Thames'. Stepashin, the former prime minister and Putin loyalist, was clearly acting with his president's consent when he launched the investigation against Abramovich. He described Abramovich's Sibneft as one of Russia's 'biggest tax cheats'. Like Putin, Stepashin was a Petersburger with a background in security and personally had no time for the oligarchs. His apparent willingness to take on the oligarchs had got him sacked as prime minister under Yeltsin. At the current rate of emigration among the business tycoons, there might soon be more Russian oligarchs living in London than Moscow. It looked as if the days of the obstreperous oligarch were coming to a close. Three years on, Putin and the Kremlin were moving away from the truce agreed with Russia's business tycoons in July 2000. Bashing the oligarchs was always going to be politically popular, especially in the run-up to elections.

Before the December 2003 Duma parliamentary race, a poll by Moscow Echo radio station showed 58 per cent of people in favour of confiscating all the wealth of the tycoons and reducing them to subsistence level. Another poll earlier in the year showed almost 90 per cent of Russians believed that all the large fortunes in the country had been accumulated dishonestly. Rather than renationalize the energy sector, the government started giving active consideration to 'differentiated taxation' of the oil companies' assets, which trade minister German Gref said could bring in an extra $1.5 billion in taxes per year. Putin's action against Khodorkovsky and Yukos increased his approval rating by 2 per cent in one month. By now, any oligarch who looked too rich and powerful, even if he stayed out of politics, could not be guaranteed a quiet life. Putin, supported by the Petersburg Chekists and the prosecutor-general's office, was slowly but surely attempting to put the squeeze on the oligarchs, if not quite 'liquidating' them as a class.

In 2001, Putin at last started introducing significant domestic reforms. These included a tax code chapter on the profit tax, new land and labour codes, three bills aimed at reducing bureaucratic interference in the economy, reforms introducing contributory and graduated pensions, electricity restructuring, an overhaul of bankruptcy laws, a law against money-laundering and a judicial reform package. As a lawyer, Putin was determined to make Russia's legal system more effective. Yeltsin's previous attempts at judicial reform had failed miserably. The Duma was induced to pass a package of laws which would raise the status, pay and accountability of judges; extend the number of courts and funding of the court system; introduce justices of the peace; extend trial by jury and limit pre-trial detention to a year (formerly 18 months). The Constitutional Court would be underpinned by effective sanctions to ensure that its decisions were obeyed. Plans to give defendants greater rights to challenge allegations against them and be given bail, and make courts rather than prosecutors responsible for issuing arrest warrants were initially stymied. Prosecutors objected to the reduction of their powers and making life easier for defendants. In the meantime, some one million prisoners are currently being kept in appalling conditions in Russia's antiquated jails awaiting overdue trials. TB, AIDS and other diseases are rife in the country's crumbling and shabby prisons. Human rights groups say many people inside could safely be given bail.

President Putin's legal reforms were crucial to restructure the old Soviet system of justice, which had served the state well but ignored individual rights. There had been many examples of Soviet judges simply being told what to do by their Communist Party bosses. Under the old system, prosecution led to a guilty verdict in more than 90 per cent of cases. Prosecutors controlled all stages of a case through investigation, search, arrest, prosecution and supervision. The outcome at court was almost a forgone conclusion. With the break-up of the Soviet Union, the judiciary became notorious for being bribed by the highest bidder. Businessmen preferred to solve their disputes privately, and often violently. Bankruptcy laws were invoked against financially viable rivals as a form of asset-stripping.

Prosecutors and police were often bribed to start bogus criminal investigations into business competitors. A gang of nine Moscow police officers from the criminal investigation department, led by a Lieutenant-General Vladimir Ganeyev, made millions of dollars in bribes to drop fabricated cases against wealthy individuals and companies. They would plant drugs, weapons and munitions on their victims, and later drop charges on payment of a bribe. The gang drove Mercedes cars, wore $30,000 watches and owned a $1 million tennis court. For years they operated undetected, mainly because their Moscow police colleagues were also 'earning' sums far beyond their nominal salaries of a few hundred dollars a month. The group were eventually arrested and tried in the summer of 2003. The word in Moscow was that they represented the tip of the iceberg, and in an election year were being made examples of by Interior Minister Boris Gryzlov, a Petersburger. It's not surprising that individuals and companies had no faith in the rule of law, let alone justice. Although Putin's reforms have a way to go, better salaries and training for the judiciary will make an important start in changing unacceptable practices in a previously poorly paid profession. Vladimir Putin's legal reforms may be one of his more lasting legacies.

For the first time in post-Communist Russia, President Putin's 2001 land reforms created a land market in urban areas and industrial zones, and for non-agricultural rural properties like dachas. However, this new market and land code covered only about 2 per cent of Russia's landmass. The purchase and sale of agricultural land, long opposed by the Communists in the Duma, was put off to the following year. The issue was so emotive, deputies had come to blows over the issue. The Duma finally approved the sale of farmland in June 2002, the first time agricultural land had been for sale since the Bolshevik Revolution. Under Communism, all land had been state owned, with all farms organized as collectives. Most had been inefficient and under-capitalized, a situation which deteriorated rapidly after the break-up of the USSR. More than half of Russia's farms are technically bankrupt.

Since 1991, some regions had allowed the partial sale of land, others had not. Under the new law, a billion acres (400 million hectares) of farmland across Russia could eventually be sold off, a land area half the size of Brazil. Many collective farm workers, supported by the Communist and Agrarian parties, feared they could lose their jobs, especially if the farms were sold to foreigners. To dilute Communist and nationalist opposition to the move, Putin promised that Russian farmland would not be sold to foreigners, although they could lease the land. In a further concession to opponents, he stressed that there would be no rush to sell off Russia's countryside. Before any land was sold, a proper land registry would be drawn up. With foreigners excluded from the purchase of Russia's poor and inefficient farms, predatory oligarchs waited in the wings to pick up the country's best real estate for a song. Nevertheless, introducing private land ownership in Russia was a major and historic step. Putin achieved in two years what Yeltsin had failed to manage in nine: the beginning of the privatization of land.

Tax reforms, implemented in January 2001, replaced progressive income tax with a 13 per cent flat rate. Social and profit taxes on enterprises were reduced, with VAT payments going into federal coffers and profit taxes and personal income tax revenues going to the regions. Since most regions get more in central transfers than they pay in taxes, they were not adversely affected by the tax changes. Corporate profit tax was cut from 35 to 24 per cent, and some import tariffs were reduced. Two years later, Putin abolished the corrupt and hated Tax Police, transferring their duties to a scaled-down department of the Interior Ministry. Entrepreneurs had been known to bribe the Tax Police to open criminal investigations against their competitors, while under-the-counter payments to reduce tax liabilities were ubiquitous.

Most of the 40,000 Tax Police were transferred to a new anti-drug agency, the State Committee for the Control of Narcotics and Psychotropic Substances. The head of the agency was Victor Cherkesov, Putin ally and former plenipotentiary for north-west

Russia. Despite fears that the tax reforms would reduce government revenue, the opposite has been the case. Lower taxation, better payment discipline and the move away from barter towards monetarization of the economy (i.e. using cash) provided an incentive for individuals and companies to pay rather than avoid their taxes. Federal tax revenues doubled as a share of GDP between 1998 and the first half of 2001. The economy benefited from the 1998 debt default and rouble devaluation, which boosted exports and strengthened domestic firms as cheaper Russian goods were substituted for expensive foreign imports. This favourable shift in Russia's terms of trade couldn't be ascribed to Putin's leadership, but he could take credit for the subsequent improvement in taxation revenues and his government's budgetary restraint.

The improved tax-take was combined with high raw material export prices, tight budgetary control and capped domestic expenditure, leading to a healthy budget surplus. Suddenly, from being an economic basket-case, Russia's economy looked remarkably robust. From a current account deficit of $6 billion in 1998, Russia moved into a $45 billion surplus in 2000. Such an economic inheritance provided Putin with a golden opportunity to create the conditions for solid economic growth and stability. From the hyperinflation of the early 1990s, and a rate of over 80 per cent at the end of 1998, inflation has now declined to around 14 per cent and falling, while annual economic growth rose to 9 per cent of GDP, one of the highest in the industrialized world. In 2003, although annual growth slipped a little, it was still running at an annual rate of 7 per cent, outpacing the UK, US, Canada, the rest of the European Union and Japan. Of the major economies, only China remained a serious competitor in terms of annual growth.

On cutting back on business bureaucracy, Putin intervened personally to push through the Duma a plan to reduce the number of activities which required a government licence from 500 to 102. It was seen as particularly important to relieve the bureaucratic stranglehold on business, which inhibited enterprise and wealth creation and provided endless opportunities for bribes and kickbacks. There were some 400,000 federal bureaucrats, and about one million more employed in the regions. Overall, there were 2000 licences covering a range of activities in the Russian Federation, mostly required at regional and local level. The licences required covered not only certain economic activities but the need to 'certify' goods or services sold. Setting up a business was a nightmare, as entrepreneurs spent weeks or months gathering the necessary licences and certifications, paying bribes along the way. One entrepreneur told how he had to visit twenty-four offices, pay $5,000 in 'fees', replace bulbs in thirty-five street lamps and resurface part of the street before being allowed to build a small extension to his café. Once established, businesses experienced a blizzard of inspections. One business survey found licences were checked an average of thirty-seven times a year, while certificates for goods and services were inspected an average of eighty-two times annually by the militia and forty times by other state bodies. Some thirty state bodies were involved, ranging from the notorious Tax Police (before abolition), through to licensing, fire, sanitation, trade, energy, building, labour, consumer rights, weights and measures, environmental protection, medical insurance fund and regional inspection authorities.

Putin's reforms simplified licensing procedures and placed limits on the number of state inspections. Although there was some scepticism that this would merely push corrupt activities further up the administrative food chain, subsequent business surveys showed a marked reduction in bureaucracy. According to the Moscow Centre for Economic and Financial Research (CEFIR) the number of inspections fell by a fifth between 2001 and 2002, and the number of companies forced to apply for licences or other certification halved. Less successful was the attempt to reform the customs service by introducing a new customs code in spring 2003, designed to reduce delays on customs clearance and the number of documents required by exporters and importers. With the average customs employee earning $5 a day, and collecting $1,000 a day in duties, the temptation to accept bribes is obvious. The new customs code still empowered officials to request additional documentation and interpret aspects of the code, which business saw as giving the custom authorities too much leverage to demand bribes in return for speedy clearance. The new code also failed to outlaw tolling, a scam whereby raw material exporters avoided duty by selling to their own offshore companies at deliberately depressed prices, only to sell-on later at inflated world prices. Abramovich and Deripaska's Russian Aluminum effectively lobbied the Duma to ensure that tolling continued unabated, costing the taxpayer dear. It is well known in Moscow political and business circles that Duma votes can be bought, at the right price.

Another reform initiative launched in summer 2001 was the plan to revamp housing and communal services. Russia's former state housing, rapidly becoming privatized, is on the verge of collapse. Huge housing estates require urgent investment in their fabric, services and local infrastructure. Parts of the older blocks are literally falling apart. Currently, most residents pay heavily subsidized service and fuel costs, underpinned by cross-subsidization in the energy market. Industry in effect subsidizes cheap domestic electricity and gas prices. The restructuring of the electricity monopoly UES, to provide a competitive market in energy, means that Russia's system of subsidized housing is under threat. A future break-up of Gazprom, the gas monopoly, would add to the pressures to free energy prices. In early 2001, Putin set a target for phasing out housing and utility subsidies for most people by the end of 2003, while providing a safety net of targeted assistance for the poorest citizens. However, it was quickly realized this would clash with the parliamentary Duma elections at the end of 2003 and the March 2004 presidential elections. The reforms were put off until at least 2004, with the government continuing to subsidize housing and utility costs for another ten to fifteen years.

The reason underlying the postponement was not difficult to fathom. President Putin's popularity stemmed from the fact that he was widely perceived to have made Russians generally better off, particularly by repeatedly raising pensions and ensuring federal wages were paid on time. Withdrawing housing subsidies, even with targeted assistance for the poorest, would massively hit Russia's citizens in their pockets. Many would suffer an immediate reduction in their living standards. For an elected politician, it is a tricky strategy. If implemented, it will be Vladimir Putin's most unpopular act to date. It is no wonder that President Putin gave the Housing and Municipal Subsidies (HMS) portfolio to one of his least favourite politicians. Step forward Deputy Prime Minister Vladimir Yakovlev, former governor of St Petersburg. Yakovlev was nicely placed to take the political flak for an unpopular reform, with probably the sack to follow.

None of these structural reforms happened on their own account. Putin repeatedly voiced the need for structural reforms, publicly calling for land reform, less bureaucratic interference in the economy, and the need to reduce the overall tax burden. Addressing the Federal Assembly of both chambers of parliament in April 2001, Putin stepped up his reformist rhetoric. He criticized almost every aspect of Russian society. Bribery and bureaucracy were crippling the economy, while the judicial system was riddled with abuse and corruption, he argued. 'Along with the shadow economy, we have shadow justice,' he said. One million Russians were in detention awaiting trial, while the public had lost faith in the courts. Customs, taxation, pensions, health and education all needed further reform. The country's fuel, energy and railway monopolies also required restructuring, he added. By putting his personal weight behind the domestic reform agenda, Putin sought to maintain the momentum of his attempt to transform Russian society. In domestic terms, he was at one with his liberal economic reformers, German Gref and Andrei Illarionov. A reformed Russia would be a modern, efficient country, both more prosperous and able to compete in global markets. That would be good for Russia's largely impoverished nation, and for the strength of the state.

There was another aspect to Putin's approach to the domestic reform agenda. Never one for overt confrontation unless he thinks it's unavoidable and politically essential, he prefers to co-opt or neutralize opponents. On the trickier reform subjects, he tried to build a consensus amongst the relevant stakeholders. Special commissions were formed to report back to the president on railway reform, electricity restructuring and pension reform. The commissions' reports heavily influenced the final shape of the government's reforms. In a sense, as he told Berezovsky's daily newspaper *Nezavisimaya Gazeta* before he was elected, he saw his role as no more than a man hired by the electorate on a four-year contract to fulfil certain functional and professional duties. Successfully implementing the necessary reforms was part of his contract with the electorate. His whole approach to the reform process was more technocratic than political; not in itself surprising, since throughout his career he had been more a civil servant than a politician.

In his state-of-the-nation address in the Marble Hall of the Kremlin on 18 April 2002, Putin pressed the case for domestic reform. He felt under pressure to deliver real improvements for Russia's citizens. Speaking to members of both houses of parliament, he claimed Russia was clogged with corruption and bureaucracy. Putin castigated his government for not being ambitious enough in pushing for economic growth. He argued that while life in Russia was improving, with unemployment down and incomes rising, 40 million Russians were still living in poverty. His audience heard him out in silence, stood for the national anthem, and shuffled out of the Kremlin. Putin had gone further the previous week, reprimanding his government for producing insufficiently high growth targets. The government's medium-term forecast was for an annual growth rate of 3 to 5 per cent. Putin said this was 'not helpful' and 'did not imply an active policy'. He argued that a 'cumbersome, clumsy and ineffective state apparatus' limited Russia's potential growth. At 5 per cent annual growth, he pointed out, Russia would take another eighteen years to reach Portugal's current

standard of living. His answer was a compact, open and less inter-
ventionist bureaucracy. His outburst brought to mind Gosplan and
the old central planning days, when targets reflected political diktat
rather than economic reality. Although Kasyanov's government had
predicted relatively modest growth, Putin's economic adviser Andrei
Illarionov demanded that GDP rise by 8 per cent annually. In the
southern city of Voronezh, people were already demonstrating
against the planned abolition of housing subsidies. For Putin, economic growth and material prosperity were essential to tackle the
situation whereby Russia remained in his words 'a rich country of
poor people'.

Putin supporters were placed in control of the massive gas
monopoly Gazprom and the Central Bank between 2001 and 2002.
The conservative and anti-reformist Victor Gerashchenko, head of
the Central Bank, was replaced by Sergei Ignatiev, a deputy finance
minister and a former deputy head of the bank. The Central Bank,
massively over-staffed, was riddled with corruption and a law unto
itself. The Fimaco affair (Fimaco was used as a vehicle by central
bank staff to re-invest billions of dollars of IMF loans and hard currency reserves in the speculative GKO market) and insider dealing in
GKO government treasury bills was the tip of a rather large iceberg.
Removing the tainted Gerashchenko was designed to clean up the
Central Bank's act and an attempt to reform its obscure and antiquated working practices. A modern, dynamic Russian economy
would need a more efficient and reformed Central Bank.
Introducing change at the bank remains an uphill struggle. Deputy
energy minister Alexei Miller, aged thirty-nine and an old friend
from Putin's days working for St Petersburg's city administration,
was appointed chief executive of the multi-billion dollar gas giant,
Gazprom. Miller had graduated from Leningrad's economic and
financial institute, and worked in St Petersburg's city administration
from 1991 to 1996, having an office next door to Vladimir Putin.
From there he had gone on to work as head of investment in St
Petersburg's port, then general director of the Baltic pipeline system

and finally for Putin in the energy ministry. Gazprom is the world's largest gas company, supplies Europe with a third of its gas, has more than a quarter of the world's gas reserves and accounts for nearly 8 per cent of Russia's GDP. With annual sales of over $19 billion and 300,000 employees, the company had been run as a private milch-cow for Gazprom's top executives and their families, reputedly making former prime minister Victor Chernomyrdin a dollar billionaire in the process.

Improper business relationships were alleged between Gazprom, Itera, a Florida-based gas company, and Stroytransgaz. Auditors investigated claims that Gazprom's assets and some gas distribution rights had been illicitly transferred to Itera. Gazprom had also signed a large contract with Stroytransgaz, whose shares happened to be owned by relatives of the national gas monopoly's management. Shareholders of the former included Vitaly and Andrei Chernomyrdin (sons of former Gazprom head and Prime Minister Victor Chernomyrdin), and Tatyana Dedikova (daughter of Gazprom boss Rem Vyakhirev). It looked like a classic case of asset-stripping. Replacing Vyakhirev with Miller was Putin's way to establish control over Gazprom and root out the worst excesses committed by the old-style corrupt Soviet management. As one Russian politician once said, what's good for Gazprom is good for Russia, and the reverse equally applies. Gazprom was too vital a company to be treated like a family concern. The Russian government's avowed long-term aim is to break up the company (38 per cent owned by the state), liberalize the gas market and privatize it in whole or part.

President Putin promised an extra 50 per cent spending on defence, and embarked upon reforms to streamline the military, including phasing out conscription. Boris Yeltsin's promise to end conscription by 2000 had been yet another empty pledge. The army's problems were exacerbated by the hundreds of thousands of troops returning from Eastern Europe, the Baltic States and other former Soviet republics. Many officers and their families had no homes to return to, creating an acute housing crisis. A number of officers, unable to feed and house their families, committed suicide. Russia's new president planned to reduce the number of men and women under arms to below 1.2 million, and introduce a system of contracts to supplement the ranks of conscripts with professional troops. The contract troops (*contrakniki*) gained a reputation for being particularly ruthless in Chechnya, and were accused of numerous human rights abuses. Some 365,000 defence ministry forces were to be axed, together with another 235,000 civilian and other personnel. The idea was to create more mobile and better equipped armed forces, and streamline expenditure. The military-industrial complex employed about 2 million people, and cost around an estimated $50 billion a year. In one year alone, 1992, domestic defence orders fell by 80 per cent. Arms sales, which had sustained the whole Soviet military-industrial complex, plummeted after the break-up of the USSR. Sales had fallen from $20 billion a year in 1988 to under $3 billion by 1993. The USSR had slipped from being one of the world's two top arms exporters (the other being the US) to sixth place under the Russian Federation, and found itself overtaken by countries like the UK and France. At the same time, the US had moved in to supply many of Russia's former arms customers, including the Eastern Europeans. Keen to join NATO, they saw the political benefits of buying American. Hundreds of thousands of Russians lost their jobs, and scores of one-industry cities lost their *raison d'être*. Nevertheless, the arms trade started picking up under Putin, reaching a post-Soviet peak of $6 billion by the end of his first year in office.

Turning the armed forces around would be a huge task. Russia's military might had been shown to be a chimera in Chechnya. With over a million men at arms, Moscow had been unable to crush a guerrilla army of a few thousand men. Worse still, the Chechens had managed to recapture Grozny in the first war in the mid-1990s, inflicting heavy losses on the Russian army in the process. Desertions were running at the rate of 50,000 a year, with about two thousand soldiers dying each year from accidents, suicide or murder. The going rate to buy a son out of the army was around $5,000. When a dispute broke out between Ivanov's predecessor as defence minister, Marshal Igor Sergeyev, and chief of army staff General Kvashnin, it was Putin who had to step in to streamline Russia's excessive expenditure on the country's strategic rocket forces. When Sergeyev was replaced by Putin's friend Ivanov in March 2001, reform of the armed forces was put on the political agenda in earnest. As always, however, the issue was one of resources. During Putin's first year as president, the army had resorted to force to prevent garrisons from having their electricity cut off because of unpaid bills. Armed troops from a base of the elite nuclear strategic missile forces of Ivanovo, north of Moscow, seized the local power station to reconnect their barracks. It was not an isolated incident. But by the second year of Putin's rule, at least the army started getting paid more-or-less on time.

As a gesture to the past, Putin reintroduced military training in schools, and had the Soviet anthem brought back, albeit with new words. Embarrassingly, Russia's athletes had been unable to sing Yeltsin's new wordless and unfamiliar anthem at the Sydney Olympic Games in September 2000. The Red Star was also restored as a symbol on the armed forces' flag. In autumn 2003, the Duma agreed that military training in schools would include how to strip an AK-47 automatic rifle, basic field dressings, parade drills and how to respond to biological, chemical or nuclear attack. President Putin told teachers such training was 'necessary and useful'. A special part of the state education was devoted to 'patriotic education', dealing with the history of Russia's military and political strength. The military training was part of Putin's desire to re-create Russia's 'Great Power' status, and restore pride in the state and military. He frankly admitted he put the strength of the state above democracy in his list of priorities. Addressing an old-style military parade in Red Square in his first year as president, some Soviet war veterans had to pinch themselves to remember it was almost ten years since the end of the

USSR. Commemorating the fifty-fifth anniversary of the end of the Second World War, Putin said: 'We defended our great Soviet motherland . . . and kept our independence. We are used to winning. It is in our blood. It is not just the way to win wars. In peacetime it will also help us. Hurrah!'

Nevertheless, the military remained chronically underfunded. Putin had upbraided his own Security Council following the *Kursk* disaster in August 2000. 'The current structure of the armed forces is hardly optimal,' he said on that occasion. 'How can it be considered optimal if training is not conducted in many units, pilots hardly ever fly and sailors hardly ever put to sea. The structure of the armed forces must precisely correspond to the threats Russia faces now and will face in the future,' he concluded. Progress was slow, and Putin found that effective implementation was a lot more difficult than policy pronouncements. In June 2001 he bitterly castigated his cabinet for requesting delays in bringing military pay into line with civil servants' salaries. Unusually, the Kremlin published Putin's frustrated outburst in full. 'We are speaking about the fate of millions of people – the military and their family members,' the exasperated president told his cabinet colleagues. 'The government must take measures . . . to ensure that the military's material conditions actually improve.' Most of the Russian armed forces are still waiting, although most no longer have wage arrears of six months or more.

Putin re-invigorated the KGB's successor agencies the FSB and the SVR. Boris Yeltsin had distrusted the KGB and had split it into various competing components. The fall of the Berlin Wall and the collapse of the USSR left it demoralized, poorly paid and lacking purpose. Putin had experienced it all first-hand. Between 1991 and 1993 some 300,000 KGB officers, almost half its entire number, left the agency. Many ended up working for private security firms, the oligarchs or the mafia. Putin started putting the security service together again, raising its prestige, power and morale. As we have seen, many of his appointments were either old KGB colleagues, friends from St Petersburg or both. The number of security service, police and military personnel in government received a substantial boost under Putin, rising to six times the number employed under Gorbachev. Signalling the final rehabilitation of the KGB, in May 2002 Russia marked the anniversary of Joseph Stalin's secret police by issuing a set of postage stamps bearing the portraits of six of his best secret agents. Ironically, five were executed by Stalin. No one seemed to notice that the fate of the agents wasn't much of a good advertisement for the KGB, service to the state, or Soviet-style leadership.

Putin's reform of the security structures had three phases. Phase one in May 2000 involved the creation of the seven federal administrative districts, headed by plenipotentiaries with mainly security backgrounds. As part of the reform, federal security and law enforcement agencies set up subdivisions within the seven districts, with the exception of the FSB. The second phase in March 2001 saw Putin's allies installed in the 'power ministries', including Sergei Ivanov as defence minister, Boris Gryzlov as interior minister and Vladimir Rushailo as head of the Security Council. Nikolai Patrushev was already head of the FSB. The third phase, in March 2003, established a new federal anti-drug agency under Victor Cherkesov. The FSB was strengthened by putting border guards and part of the communication agency (FAPSI) under its control. FAPSI, in charge of the government's coded communications and elec-tronic intelligence, was divided between the FSB and the Defence Ministry. Under Putin's leadership, the FSB started to resemble the old KGB, minus the foreign intelligence service. For a while Putin also put the FSB in charge of all 'anti-terrorist' actions in Chechnya, taking control away from the military. While command of opera-tions eventually reverted to the military, the move showed Putin's dissatisfaction with the army's handling of the conflict in the Caucasus, and his continuing faith in the security services.

At the same time, meanwhile, reviving memories of Stalin's cult of personality, two Moscow artists produced a best-selling cal-endar featuring the 'twelve moods of Putin'. Artists Dmitri Vrubel and Victoria Timofeyeva showed Putin in turns stern, smiling, athletically cross-legged in his judo outfit or in other reflective moods, with one portrait for every month of the year. The Kremlin was even concerned that the cult of personality could get out of hand, denting Putin's 'man of the people' image. Administration spin-doctors warned the bosses of two state-run national TV networks to stop 'bootlicking which verges on sabotage'. One example they cited was a programme aired on RTR in April 2002, which showed Putin on holiday at a ski resort. The Kremlin feared such sycophantic coverage, last seen in the days of Leonid Brezhnev, was in danger of turning off the public. However, little was done to discourage the apparently spontaneous hero-worship springing up across the country.

Putin had celebrated his first birthday as president quietly in a favourite traditional wooden-timbered Russian restaurant called Podvorie outside historic Pushkin, near St Petersburg. The building, with its jumbled timber construction and wooden tower, wouldn't have looked out of place in a Siberian village centuries before. The restaurant was closed to the public, and Putin ate sturgeon and drank vodka with his close friends, surrounded by stuffed bears and assorted dead wildlife. Two years later, celebrating his fiftieth birthday became almost a national event. His poll approval ratings hit 77 per cent, just below their peak at the time of the Russian forces' capture of Grozny in 1999. He had been the inspiration behind a spy thriller, the calendar, an opera featuring Monica Lewinsky, a pop song, a kebab house and a tomato. In the thriller, Putin was depicted as an all-action hero, who was wounded in a personal duel with the Chechen guerrilla leader Shamil Basayev. More practically, Putin's love of skiing gave the sport a massive boost, just as Yeltsin had made tennis trendy. Billboards in Moscow became plastered with adverts for new ski resorts and snow-wear, while sports shops did a roaring trade in brands worn by the president. Many Russians seemed to have a deep-seated psychological need to emulate their leader. Others felt they had to keep up with the latest fashion or fad. In the absence of a class system, the president became the arbiter of sophistication and good taste. Even ministers, MPs, businessmen, cosmonauts and other VIPs started taking up skiing, recognizing that it was the sport to be seen doing. For Russians, emulation remains the sincerest form of flattery.

Presents flooded in for the president's birthday, including a crystal crocodile from Moldova and a slow-growing Siberian pine tree from Tomsk. Schoolchildren sent the president obsequious birthday cards, while youth groups sent in hymns lauding the Russian leader and marched in his support. While it is normal to pay tributes on somebody's birthday in Russia, the public fawning associated with Putin's birthday reached new post-Soviet heights. A street was named in his honour in Ingushetia, and portraits of the president were to be found in thousands of government offices across the country. While the media gave prominence to the celebrations, Putin seemed faintly discomfited by the whole thing, and spent his birthday attending a Commonwealth of Independent States summit in Moldova, where he had a quiet celebratory drink with leaders of the former Soviet republics. Meanwhile, most bizarrely of all, sixty jewellers in the Ural Mountains spent six months preparing a replica of the Cap of Monomakh for his birthday. Named after Vladimir Monomakh, the Prince of Kiev whose son founded Moscow, the cap is a golden crown encrusted with jewels and lined with sable. The gift was insured for a staggering $10 million, and was symbolic because the real Cap of Monomakh, kept in the Kremlin, was used in coronation ceremonies to crown the Tsars. Weighing 2 pounds, the original cap was made by oriental craftsmen in the thirteenth and fourteenth centuries, and signified the succession of power from the Byzantine emperors to the Russian Tsars, and was used in the coronation of Peter the Great. The Kremlin, embarrassed that the gift was over-the-top and ingratiating, sheepishly denied that Putin tried the replica cap on for size.

Besides routinely appearing several times daily on the Russian evening news, Putin has sought to make himself available at press conferences, for the occasional webcast, and answering questions on TV and the internet. On 24 December 2001, Putin appeared on the ORT and RTR television networks, and fielded questions from the telephone and internet. A special website and free telephone hotline had been created for the question-and-answer session. Putin answered about forty-seven of the hundreds of thousands of questions asked, and the telelinks with members of the public gathered in ten city squares cost around $50,000 to set up. Although the whole event was live, everything had been pre-programmed and rehearsed twice. The questions came pre-prepared from Moscow, and the questioners were carefully vetted. Those with awkward questions had no chance of getting near a microphone or having their internet queries answered. Questions about corruption were barred, and even local politicians found themselves excluded. It seemed a hollow exercise in democracy, but one which suited the Kremlin well enough.

Politically, Putin reinforced his power in parliament when the pro- and former anti-Kremlin factions Unity and Fatherland-All Russia combined to form a single bloc in the Duma. Fatherland's regional bosses decided that opposing the president could be bad for their longevity and political health. Yury Luzhkov, mayor of Moscow, and former prime minister Yevgeny Primakov, decided to kiss hands with the Kremlin. The Russia Regions Party and the People's Deputy Party queued up to form a majority pro-Putin alliance in the Duma. The new party, the centrist Union of Unity and Fatherland (later known as United Russia) and its allies, came to exert control over both houses of parliament. United Russia became the new 'party of power', dependent upon the ruling elite rather than acting as a political power base. The danger was that United Russia, like the earlier incarnation of 'Our Home is Russia' under Yeltsin, could be discarded whenever convenient. United Russia was an entirely false construct, cobbled together with the sole purpose of supporting Putin and the Kremlin. It could be dismantled and reconstituted at any time. Even so, the opposition Communists found themselves a marginalized and spent force, together with other liberal and centre-right groupings.

In spring 2002 Putin consolidated his position by ensuring that the Communists were removed from the chairmanship of important Duma committees. Gennady Seleznyov, the erstwhile Communist speaker, was encouraged to defect from the Communist Party and establish his own loyalist left-wing social democratic party. Vladimir Zhirinovsky's ultra-right Liberal Democratic Party (LDPR) continued to talk tough but politically almost always supported the presidential administration. The LDPR seemed to be designed to attract the disaffected ultra-nationalist vote, and channel it in a way that sustained the Russian government. The Kremlin also connived at the creation of Putin ally Sergei Mironov's Party of Life. Mironov, a bearded middle-aged Petersburger, was Speaker of the emasculated Federation Council. Lyudmila Putina was mentioned as a possible member of the Party of Life, regarded as the home of animal lovers and environmentalists. The party's website says it is a moderate, socially orientated group, which is working to raise AIDS awareness.

The thinking behind the formation of these rival 'pro-Putin' parties was two-fold. First, they would give the electorate the appearance of political choice and variety, when there was in reality none. Second, if United Russia became a political liability (like Our Home is Russia) or started to be too independent a political force, it could be abandoned as the 'party of power'. The people who supported United Russia understood the score. Alina Kabayeva, a famous Russian gymnast, was one of many celebrities to publicly endorse United Russia. 'I support United Russia because it's Putin's party,' she said. 'If he stops supporting the party then I'll stop too. I attend party meetings and I am a member of the party's top council but right now my job is to win medals.' The Duma, which had caused Boris Yeltsin so much trouble in the past, had been tamed. President Putin now had no effective opposition in either parliament or the media.

In Putin's 180-page autobiography, *First Person*, the word democracy hardly features. He used it a number of times in the election campaign and in his inauguration speech, but it didn't appear to be at the core of his political philosophy. In an online webcast in March 2001, Putin again used the 'D' word. It seems to pop out whenever he needs to address a wider audience. Law and order and democracy are inseparable, he told his internet inquisitors. 'As long as I remain president I see no other alternative to democratic development and the market economy,' the president said. It is perhaps not the ringing endorsement of democratic values that many would like to see, but it is probably the most the West can expect from Vladimir Putin. He can see the necessity for democracy and a market economy in the modern world, but he is not an enthusiastic proselyte. Democracy can also take various forms, and the style of democracy practised in Russia still falls short of Western norms. The same, of course, can be said about Russia's still fledgling market economy.

Vladimir Putin believes in a 'managed democracy', one which does not threaten the state or the embodiment of the state, the president himself. The lesson that Putin learned from the *Kursk* crisis was that just as the media could make a president, it could also break a president. Following his drubbing from the Russian press, Putin resolved to consolidate the Kremlin's hold over the country's independent media. His campaign to muzzle the media was swift, brutal and ultimately victorious. Putin's own view, held since his KGB days, sees the state as more important than individual liberty. Putin, like most of his fellow countrymen, has no experience of the liberal humanism which heavily influenced Western concepts of democracy and individual freedom. Russia had not only been suppressed during the Communist era; it had missed out on the Renaissance and Reformation under the Tsars. Democracy and treatises like Thomas Paine's *The Rights of Man*, published in 1791, had simply passed Russia by. Entering the twenty-first century, Russia had still not caught up in philosophical terms with sixteenth-century Europe let alone eighteenth-century America. For some citizens, life in post-Communist Russia became 'nasty, brutish and short', a truly Hobbesian existence. A rapid transformation to democracy and a rule-based market economy was always wholly unrealistic in Russia's case. The failure to understand the country's unique past, even compared with east European states like Poland, the Czech Republic and Hungary, fatally undermined Western-inspired advice on economic reform.

Although the Russians botched their own privatization of large-scale state assets and squandered foreign aid, organizations like the IMF, World Bank and European Bank for Reconstruction and Development (EBRD) wasted billions of dollars throwing good money after bad. IMF loans to the Russian Federation alone totalled $20 billion after the break-up of the USSR. The US Congress's General Accounting Office estimated that Russia received international assistance of $66 billion up to 1998. Congress's accounting watchdog reported Western aid to Russia had lacked coordination and any overall strategy. James Leach, chairman of the Republican House Banking Committee, said the watchdog's study showed the aid money was 'worse than wasted'. President Yeltsin's tax breaks to his cronies amounted to over half the entire amount borrowed from overseas during his nine years in power. The National Sport Fund (NSF), for example, set up by Yeltsin's tennis coach and sports minister Shamil Tarpischev, was granted the right to import alcohol, cigarettes and luxury cars without paying any duty. It was a hugely lucrative concession. The idea was supposedly to divert funds to support Russian athletics. Instead, an estimated $3 to 4 billion per year disappeared, while an NSF official was murdered in a contract-style killing. This sum was the equivalent of the annual amount of IMF lending to Russia during the years 1992 to 1998. Other exemptions were granted to Gazprom, the Afghan War Veterans' Union and the Humanitarian Aid Commission.

In a meeting with social affairs minister Valentina Matvienko in the late 1990s, the deputy prime minister warned me that Western charities could exploit their charitable status by importing luxury cars and selling them on the Russian market. The reality was that certain Russian 'charities', hand-picked and often associated with Kremlin insiders, were abusing their duty-free status. If the government had collected the duties waived for the NSF and closed other 'charitable' tax loopholes, Russia wouldn't have needed to borrow any money whatsoever from abroad during the 1990s. As it was, IMF and other loans were squandered, diverted and stolen by Russian officials.

Banking and financial services remain one of Russia's weak spots, and Putin's reforms have so far failed to tackle it successfully. Russia has around 1,300 private banks, 90 per cent of which have under $10 million capital. Of the total, 482 have capital of less than 1 million euros. Many were set up as 'pocket' banks to service their parent companies and engaged in obscure financial practices. Examples of the healthier pocket banks are Gazprom's Gazprombank, LUKoil's Bank Petrocommerce, Yukos's Trust and Investment Bank and Rosbank of the Interros industrial group. A report by international rating agency Standard and Poor's condemned the 'significant concentration of business with single clients; the high risk practice of lending to affiliated members of financial-industrial groups or FIGs; weak implementation of regulatory policy; and lack of transparency with respect to bank owners'. Three-quarters of corporate loans were adjudged high risk. Only a minority provide a range of retail banking services like deposits and loans. Richard Hainsworth of Moscow's Renaissance Capital said: 'Russia has 1,300 banks and almost no banking system. There is little co-operation between the banks and they find it difficult to trust each other.' Almost a hundred bankers have been murdered over the last five years. America's FBI has reported that almost half of all Russia's banks are under the control of various mafia or organized crime groups, and implicated in illegal capital flight and money-laundering. Russia's Interior Ministry believes the mafia's grip on the economy is even worse. The ministry's figures suggest organized criminal groups control 85 per cent of Russia's banks, 60 per cent of state enterprises and 40 per cent of the country's private businesses. Up to half of the entire economy is controlled by the mafia.

Consolidation of the banking sector is well overdue, as is the introduction of international accounting standards, now postponed until at least 2004. Reform has historically been resisted by the banks, supported in the past by Moscow's conservative Central Bank. The reality is that many could not survive in an internationally competitive environment, and opening their books would publicize their financial weakness, threatening the whole banking system with collapse. A number of the banks only survived the 1998 crash after being protected by the Central Bank, and were in effect bankrupt. The Central Bank is finally becoming more liberal in its approach, encouraging greater transparency, supporting a deposit insurance scheme and new requirements on banking capital. Of the banks that do presently exist, the state Sberbank dominates the retail banking sector, with three-quarters of all household deposits and 20,000 branches. It is also the only bank currently offering a form of state deposit guarantee, a novelty in Russia. The next biggest bank has 280 branches. Fifteen of Russia's banks are in the top 1,000 in the world, in terms of their net worth. However, Sberbank's $2 billion worth of first-tier capital is far behind first-ranked Citigroup with $59 billion. The liberalization of Russia's banking system and the selling off of Sberbank has been a stumbling block for WTO membership.

Joining the World Trade Organization was a priority for Vladimir Putin, even though the Russians thought they might need a seven-year transition period to comply with the WTO's commitments. He was keen to show that Russia could be integrated into Western international organizations. Being accepted into the world's free trade club is a mark of respectability, and a sign that Russia has become a modern market economy. As usual with Russia, however, things weren't so straightforward. Hopes that Russia could join the

WTO by the end of 2003 came to naught. Plans to join the WTO were put back by at least a year. There was not only a problem with the banking and financial sectors (and later telecoms); a far more important stumbling block was Moscow's unwillingness to liberalize energy prices. From the WTO negotiators' point of view, the issue was plain enough. By having a dual-pricing system for energy costs (primarily oil, electricity and gas), Russia was cross-subsidizing its consumers and domestic industries and paying for it via its exports. Putin announced that he would resist demands for the liberalization of the Russian gas market and the ending of Gazprom's monopoly on exports. In turn, Pascal Lamy, the EU trade commissioner, insisted that gas pricing in the domestic market had to be sufficient to cover costs plus an additional margin to provide for capital and investment.

As the EU dug in its heels for Russia to adopt a market-orientated pricing system, Prime Minister Kasyanov said he wanted to see Russia enter the WTO on 'normal conditions'. The EU and WTO were naturally reluctant to see Russia subsidize domestic consumers while they, as customer states, paid higher prices for their gas and oil imports. At a meeting in the Urals between German Chancellor Gerhard Schroeder and businessmen from the two countries in October 2003, Putin rejected the notion that Russia should raise its gas and electricity prices to world levels. 'That is impossible,' he said. 'We would cause the whole Russian economy to collapse.' President Putin had a point. Russia's economy was dependent on low energy costs, while the country's finances rely on receiving high world prices for its exports. Every $1 increase in the world market price of a barrel of oil contributes $1.5 billion to federal coffers. But apart from the importance to GDP, exports, and tax receipts, cheap energy in Russia is a life and death issue. Millions of Russians depend on cheap gas and electricity for heating in the harsh winters.

Introducing the real 'economic cost' for energy would mean many could not afford to keep warm in the winter. In places like

Siberia, affordable heating is a question of survival. Cost of living there is four times higher than elsewhere in Russia, although workers earn a twelfth of the wages paid in Moscow. Transport costs are huge, winter fuel deliveries alone to the coldest regions cost the federal government $700 million in subsidies. Many people and businesses cannot pay their current utility bills. Some 40 million Russians live in cities where the average Russian temperature ranges from minus 15 C to minus 45 C. Of the world's coldest cities with a population over one million, the first nine are in the Russian Federation. Charging these people the 'full market cost' for their energy needs would be political suicide for President Putin, and would depopulate Russia's far eastern and northern territories at a stroke. With restrictions still in place on those entitled to residents' permits in cities like Moscow and St Petersburg, and housing and jobs in short supply elsewhere, it is questionable where else people could go. The break-up of UES, Russia's electricity monopoly, into a state-owned national grid and privately owned electricity companies, will present Russia with another challenge. Unless the WTO can give Russia special treatment, and/or allow the gradual phasing out of dual energy pricing, an early agreement on WTO entry seems unlikely.

Russia's ecological record under Putin has not been particularly impressive. Despite pledges by Prime Minister Mikhail Kasyanov to ratify the Kyoto protocol on reducing environmental emissions, the Kremlin stalled in a blatant attempt to extract the maximum financial pay-off. The terms of the treaty meant Russia could trade its relatively low emissions to other countries which polluted more. A Kremlin official remarked: 'This is not an environmental but an economic matter. Without a guarantee, we will not ratify.' He said a guarantee of $3 billion would be 'a starting point'. Russia, the official remarked with typical paranoia, had been 'cheated' too often in the past over issues like the WTO and sovereign debt, so this time it wanted water-tight assurances before proceeding. Two other factors holding Moscow back were the fact that the US administration of George W. Bush was happy to sink the whole treaty (which would fail without Russian ratification), and secondly that Kyoto might tie Russia's hands in the future. The impression remained, as is often the case in Russia, that money would be the determining factor if the rest of the West wished to see Kyoto ratified. Ratification could also be used as a bargaining counter to achieve WTO membership. Putin understood the pressure on Russia's environment, urging a radical review of environmental protection laws in June 2003, and telling his State Council that 15 per cent of the country's regions were on the brink of ecological disaster. Practical action, however, seemed limited. Generally, Putin's regime seemed as unconcerned with environmental degradation as its Soviet predecessors.

The West's G8 of leading industrial nations stepped in to offer Russia $20 billion to help decommission its unwanted weapons of mass destruction, including 30,000 nuclear weapons, and stocks of enriched uranium and plutonium. The offer was made at the Calgary G8 Canadian summit in June 2002 to Putin in person, with the United States pledging to come up with half the money. After September 11th, a US task force had reported that Russia's insecure nuclear weapons, materials and scientific knowledge were the 'most urgent unmet national security threat to the United States'. Some plutonium had been found stored in a shed, with just a padlock surrounded by barbed-wire. Other material had been dumped in the countryside. Poor Russian security was a danger both in terms of possible terrorist use and hazardous for the environment. Yury Vishnevsky, head of Russia's nuclear regulatory agency (Gosatomnadzor), admitted in 2002 that grammes of weapons-grade uranium and kilogrammes of uranium for nuclear fuel had simply disappeared. The fuel had gone missing over the previous decade, mainly from factories in the Siberian city of Novosibirsk and others outside Moscow.

One of the worst and most dangerous sites was in the Kola peninsula in Russia's far north, where some 100 Russian submarines, 300 nuclear reactors (about one-fifth of the world's total) and thousands of spent fuel rods had been left to rot in fjords and open ground. Britain had previously offered £80 million to clear up the nuclear mess, with funds also promised from the European Union. The UK spent £2 million supporting the work of Russia's first chemical weapon destruction facility at Shchuchye in Western Siberia, which had opened with US funding. Apart from the nuclear detritus from the Cold War, Russia suffered from serious oil spillages and pipeline leaks in Siberia, severe industrial pollution of Lake Baikal (the largest salt lake in the world), a threat to the waters off Sakhalin island from oil drilling, and the overfishing of sturgeon and decimation of its caviar trade. There are no signs yet that President Putin's administration prioritizes environmental and ecological issues.

One of Russia's other core economic weaknesses had been its inability to attract significant foreign investment. Foreign direct investment has rarely exceeded a puny $4 billion over the past decade, in absolute terms well below Hungary or the Czech Republic, and far behind the People's Republic of China. With a world corruption ranking just below Nigeria (86th out of 133 countries), and a record of mob wars, hyperinflation and debt default over the past decade, this is perhaps not surprising. Combine that with an opaque and corrupt legal system, unclear property rights, violations of minority shareholders' rights and technically tight exchange controls, and the picture looks even gloomier. However, the situation is changing under Putin, despite the assault launched against Yukos and the market jitters that that caused. The removal of the ailing and unpredictable Yeltsin has engendered a sense of political stability, although of a more domestically authoritarian nature. Where there was just chaos, there is now ordered chaos. Several of the oligarchs have come to understand that they will become wealthier than they already are if they play by the rules of the international market. This has led to companies like Yukos introducing international accountancy standards, and other firms like LUKoil floating on the London Stock Exchange. Mikhail Fridman, whose Alfa Group clashed with BP over ownership of a subsidiary of the Sidanco oil company (with BP alleging theft), found it was better to do a deal

with his rivals rather than fight them. Lord Browne, BP's chief executive, came to the same conclusion, while at the same time writing
off $200 million of its stake in Sidanco. Alfa Group had used Russia's
notorious bankruptcy laws to seize a valuable subsidiary and so
devalue BP's 10 per cent shareholding in Sidanco. Lord Browne's BP
had retaliated by successfully blocking a $500 million loan guaran-
tee to Fridman's TNK oil company.

The oligarchs came to the realization that raising capital and
loans abroad would massively raise the value of their domestic
investments and companies' market capitalization. The result in
Fridman's case was the TNK–BP joint venture, which also conveniently gives the tycoon the 'cover' of a foreign partner which may
provide protection from arbitrary Kremlin action. Khodorkovsky,
with his proposed part sell-off of YukosSibneft to US oil giants
ExxonMobil or Chevron Texaco, was thinking along the same lines.
Ironically, although the Russian government and the energy minister Igor Yusufov apparently supported a significant US purchase of
Yukos stock, the arrest of Khodorkovsky put the whole plan on hold.

The enlightened self-interest of the oligarchs is supported by
the Russian government's passage of the 'Code for Good Corporate
Governance'. The code is an attempt to wean Russian companies
away from the 'informal rules' which determine much of the country's business dealings. According to Vladimir Makarov, the deputy
head of the Interior Ministry's economic crime department, the
'shadow' or 'black' economy constitutes 45 per cent of Russia's GDP.
Much of the tax and service arrangements with local and federal
authorities thus lie beneath the counter, or are subject to informal
interpretation which has little to do with formal written rules.
Regional authorities have frequently waived or reduced tax liabilities
in return for 'off-budget' payments or goods and services in kind.
Non-tax benefits can include protection from competitors and cred-
itors, cheap energy or rents, or a relaxed attitude to inspections and
fines. Declared profits and wages are often a fiction. Tax reform has
undoubtedly eased the situation; in the past cumulative taxes rose to

more than 100 per cent of business revenue, making it impossible for companies to stay within the law.

The more stable political climate of the post-Yeltsin years was matched by a better economic environment. Apart from the favourable shift in the terms of trade, largely due to high world prices for raw materials, the Russian stock market led the world with a 77 per cent gain in 2001. By the autumn of 2003, the country's main RTS stock index had reached a record high, up by almost 75 per cent on the year, a ten-fold increase in five years. Oil and gas companies accounted for three-quarters of the value of the Russian stock exchange. The Russian market was now capitalized at over $200 billion, and was growing at the fastest rate on the globe. Around the same time, Russia was declared safe for low-risk investment. Moody's rating agency awarded the country its first investment grade in recognition of the government's 'prudence'. The Baa3 rating is the lowest investment grade, but was regarded as a triumph for Putin's stewardship of the economy. In the run-up to the Duma and presidential elections, the announcement could only enhance his domestic and international standing. Moody cited a relatively low risk of debt default and the 'strengthening of the government's commitment to prudent fiscal and debt management policies'. It was a far cry from the dark days of the $40 billion debt default and devaluation of just five years before. Institutional investors, especially in Japan, were previously barred from investing in Russia because of its low credit rating, but Moody's decision opened up the possibility of new loans and investment flooding into the country. *Izvestiya* reported that 'the most sacred dream of a whole generation of Russian politicians' had come true.

Foreign investors are again cautiously showing more interest in Russia, in spite of the spat with Yukos. Apart from the TNK–BP joint venture, Shell and ExxonMobil are investing billions of dollars in Sakhalin island and Siberia and Western bankers have invested in Gazprom's Blue Stream project to build a gas pipeline to Turkey. TotalFinaElf take oil from Western Siberia, which travels 2,500 miles to Saxony in Germany, from where it is distributed around Europe. Gas pipelines already link Siberia to western Europe and a further 1,800 mile pipeline is planned via the Baltic. More US and Western oil and gas firms, already committed to Caspian Sea developments, are inevitably interested in further investment opportunities. Russia's reserves of natural gas are the greatest in the world.

Citigroup, UBS, Deutsche Bank and Goldman Sachs, who had their hands badly burned in the 1998 crash, are back and recruiting staff in Moscow. With Russia already the world's second largest oil exporter after Saudi Arabia, and with the Iraq war again underlining the uncertainty of supplies from the Middle East, Moscow is well placed to become a major energy supplier to the West. Russia's oil production has jumped from 6 to 9 million barrels a day since 1998, making it an attractive alternative to the traditionally Arab-dominated OPEC. The United States in particular is keen to reduce its dependence on the Middle East for its oil needs. With an estimated 60 billion barrels in reserve, Russia has three times more crude oil than America and has the world's third largest oil reserves. Oil and gas products already account for half the value of all Russian exports, a third of its GDP and nearly half of government revenues. World prices for oil, hovering at around $28 per barrel in autumn 2003, had doubled in the previous five years. In 2004, they almost reached a record $45 a barrel.

Of the other major investments of recent years, General Motors has entered into a partnership with AvtoVAZ to produce the first Chevrolet Niva 4x4s in the southern city of Togliatti, Russia's answer to Detroit. Ford operates a car plant near St Petersburg. The retail giant Ikea has successfully opened stores in Moscow and St Petersburg, with an Ikea furniture factory in the latter city employing 250 people. In the second quarter of 2003, for the first time in post-Soviet history, capital inflows to Russia were greater than capital outflow. Nevertheless, these favourable figures were undoubtedly affected by the Yukos crisis. Despite a capital inflow of almost $5 billion in the first half of the year, the third quarter showed a net outflow of almost $8 billion, almost certainly reflecting business jitters caused by the Yukos arrests. Even so, Central Bank hard currency and gold reserves soared to a near-record $60 billion and the government had no trouble meeting its international debt repayments, and even paid off some debt. The rouble had remained remarkably stable, at around 30 to the dollar. During the Yeltsin years, capital flight amounted to $30 to 60 billion a year, much of it ending up in offshore accounts in Cyprus, Gibraltar, Switzerland, the Isle of Man and the Channel Islands. Moscow, the city booming, saw its citizens earning up to ten times Russia's national average wage. New buildings and shops sprang up all over the capital, with the rebuilt Cathedral of Christ the Saviour alone costing $700 million. Surprisingly, in recent years both the Leningrad and Moscow regions have been more successful in attracting new business investors than their respective hide-bound city administrations.

Giving his annual address to the Federal Assembly in May 2003, Putin called on Russia to double its GDP in ten years, and to make the rouble fully convertible. His speech was downbeat, complaining that while the country had been growing over the last three years, that growth was slowing as unemployment grew. Putin knew that Russia was still overwhelmingly dependent on its raw material exports, particularly oil and gas, to make ends meet. If the price of a barrel of oil fell below $18, the federal budget wouldn't add up. Without structural reform, if the price of oil fell to its 1998 price of just $10, the economy would collapse again. GDP was still below 1990 levels, and capital flight since 1994 had reached an enormous $191 billion, equivalent to about double the country's entire annual exports. Worse, for many Russians, their quality of life had barely improved. He pointed out 'a quarter of Russian citizens still have incomes lower than the subsistence minimum'. Putin knew that while things had got better since he came to power, there were still plenty of disgruntled poor people in the country. If he wanted a resounding victory in the coming Duma and presidential elections, he needed Russia's citizens to believe in material progress under his leadership. Thirty-five million Russians lived on less than $2 a day, and 70 million had barely benefited from post-Soviet reforms. The average wage was $138 (£83) a month, with pensioners subsisting on about half that. Over the previous decade, Russia had become one of the most unequal societies on earth, a galling paradox for a former Marxist state. For many citizens, there was a lot about Putin's Russia which still rankled and depressed.

The economy is still heavily dominated by the oligarchs, who control more than half Russia's industry and net profits. Small business growth has stagnated, as the oligarchs have continued to strengthen their stranglehold over the entire economy. Poverty and ill-health are ubiquitous in Russian society. Three-quarters of Russian families live on less than $100 (£60) a month, pensioners much less. In 1999, life expectancy had fallen to fifty-eight for men and seventy-one for women. One report indicated only about half of Russia's sixteen-year-old males would live to see sixty. Alcoholism is rampant, with annual per capita consumption running at 14.4 litres of pure alcohol, equivalent to 85 bottles of vodka. Tens of thousands of people die every year of drinking *samogon*, deadly home-brewed spirits, especially popular in rural areas where old social structures have disintegrated. In the villages where there is no work, the menfolk drink spirits all day. Four out of every ten Russians live in the country. Go to any Russian village, and you will see men sitting or lying on the ground completely paralytic. Gone are the guaranteed jobs for life, and the incomes that went with them. Russia's population has been falling precipitously since the end of Communism, due to a combination of heavy drinking, poor diet, pollution, low safety standards and a failing public health service. Projections are that Russia's population could shrink by one-third to 100 million by 2025, and is currently losing just under one million people a year. Falling life expectancy is matched by a rising death rate and calamitous birth rate. In the decade or so since the collapse of the USSR, the birth rate in Russia has halved. Pregnancy and child-rearing are ten times more dangerous for a Russian woman than a woman living in Germany.

President Putin has often stressed that the fight against population decline is one of his top priorities, saying the situation could endanger national security. In a desperate attempt to boost the birth rate, the government has reduced the number of grounds on which a woman can request a termination from thirteen to four, after twelve weeks of pregnancy. Whereas in the past abortion was the main form of contraception for Russian women, with abortion almost on demand, now women only have the option if they have been raped, are in jail, have a disabled husband or if a partner is deemed an unfit parent.

In Russia's far east and north, material poverty is compounded with energy poverty and frequent power cuts, making life miserable. The situation was so bad in the winter of 2001, with over half a million people in Siberia affected by poor heating, and 18,000 inhabitants with no heating at all, that Putin sacked his energy minister. Temperatures north of Vladivostok had fallen to minus 36 C. The far eastern governor, Yevgeny Nazdratenko, was finally forced to resign. The single largest cause of hospital admissions in the far east in 2003 was electrocution, as locals eschewed personal safety and dug up electric power cables and sold the scrap metal on the black market to the mafia. This has resulted in more power cuts and further misery. On top of all this, diseases such as TB, diphtheria and sexually-transmitted diseases and AIDS have increased exponentially. In 1997, Russia witnessed almost half a million cases of syphilis, compared with just 8,000 in the US (with double the population). There is a fear that HIV/AIDS could become a real epidemic, with cases of HIV increasing twenty-fold since 1998. A survey by British scientists predicts that one in twenty Russian adults will be infected with the HIV virus within five years, with the virus threatening to spread throughout Europe.

The spread of HIV in Russia is itself a symptom of poor health care and crime, especially prostitution. In 1998, Moscow police arrested 80,000 prostitutes. The number of organized crime groups in Russia has risen from 785 in the Gorbachev era to 8,000 today.

The original Russian gangs were based on the gulag, with leaders called a 'thief professing the code' (*vor v zakone*). They tended to deal in black market goods. With the implosion of the USSR, the traditional gangs were frequently muscled-out by more vicious groups from the Caucasus, who were often clan-based. Slavic and Chechen groups fought violent battles for control of parts of Moscow in the early 1990s. They engage in all the traditional organized crime activities, from prostitution to people trafficking, drug-running, casinos, clubs, money-laundering and protection rackets. Many own companies and control banks. Piracy and the counterfeit music market are big business for Russia's crime groups. Russia is second only to China in the world piracy stakes.

Presently 2,000 Russian organized crime groups operate in 58 countries across the globe. The term 'Russian mafia' is a generic term, because it's difficult to know where the mafia ends and legitimate business begins. Two of the biggest mafia gangs are the Dolgopruadnanskaya and the Solntsevskaya. The latter Moscow-based gang developed out of a group of 'sports clubs' in the eponymous suburb, has 5,000 members and is led by Sergei Mikhailov, known as Mikhas. Chechen and Georgian gangs are well-represented, the largest Chechen gang being known as the Obshina. In St Petersburg, the most feared gang is the Tambov mafia.

Most Russian businesses have a *krysha* or roof, which they pay for, usually a criminal gang but sometimes part of the security services, police or state apparatus. The krysha offers physical protection from other mafia gangs and business competitors, settles commercial or other disputes, promotes the interests of the business or organization and handles deals and pay-offs. Virtually every street market in Russia is controlled by the mafia and has a krysha. In one street market in St Petersburg, for example, a mafia group from the Caucasus engaged in a conflict with two local police district commanders for control of a share of the market's profits. For the market traders, the deal is simple. Pay your protection money or get beaten up or worse. The going rate for a contract killing is about $800, and there were 567 contract murders in the first five months of 1999, an increase on 1998. About 32,000 Russians are murdered during an average year, which is more than double the rate of the US. Other crime statistics make Russia one of the most criminalized countries, and Putin acknowledged that up to 7,000 murderers have not been brought to justice, partly because of 'feeble' law enforcement.

Putin called for more to be done to combat crime in Russia, particularly organized crime. He told senior police officers in February 2002: 'Murders, kidnappings, criminal attacks and robberies have turned into something of a fact of life.' Investigative judges in Russia earn an average of $130 a month, for which they have to risk life and limb trying well-trained killers. It is not surprising that no high profile contract killers have been brought to justice, although victims have often included prominent politicians and businessmen. One regional governor, Valentin Tsvetkov, was shot dead in front of his wife on Moscow's Novy Arbat, a main shopping thoroughfare, in autumn 2002. President Putin's motorcade uses the street every day on its way to the Kremlin. Such killings are distressingly common. Cracking down on crime remains essential to improve Russia's image, its business environment and the quality of life of its people. But with the government, officialdom, business, the police (some of whom have been accused of murder), parts of the security services and the judiciary riddled with corruption, Putin has a Herculean task ahead of him. The prosecutor-general's office issued a statement in April 2003 saying it wanted to question Prime Minister Kasyanov over his role in an alleged $6 million crab-fishing quota scam. When the prime minister is under suspicion of lining his own pockets, it gives an indication of the difficulties Putin faces in rooting out corruption in Russian society as a whole.

There were two measures passed in the Duma which strengthened Putin's control over the parliament and the media. The first law, passed in July 2001, limited the number of political parties and provided state funding for the remainder. Under the legislation, a political party needs to have at least 10,000 members, spread right across the country, to qualify for registration. Private donations are strictly limited, whilst a party must obtain more than 3 per cent of the popular vote to qualify for state funding. Putin argued that oligarchs would no longer be able to set up parties solely with the purpose of winning a seat and parliamentary immunity. Critics argued that the move reduced political pluralism, and ensured there would be fewer and more docile parties, making it easier for the Kremlin to control the Duma. More significant still were the changes in the law affecting media coverage during elections. In June 2003, the Duma passed a bill that gave authorities the right to shut down news media during a campaign if they violated election law. However, it soon became apparent that the way the law would be interpreted was highly selective. In theory, the law was designed to give equal coverage to all candidates and so prevent the 'black propaganda' or PR and *kompromat* that had been characteristic of previous elections. The media were banned from making judgements and recommendations on individual politicians, and senior officials were supposedly prevented from making political endorsements. In practice, newspapers were threatened for covering individual candidates and analysing their policies, supposedly because any article or broadcast should give equal coverage to all candidates. Of course the reality was that television and the press gave extensive coverage to the president, ministers, and favoured parties like United Russia. The latter was given extensive coverage on state TV, for example. Opposition parties simply did not appear.

President Putin himself was criticized when he was filmed with Valentina Matvienko just before the St Petersburg gubernatorial elections, and endorsed her as his favoured candidate. He did the same for the late Akhmed Kadyrov, just before he was elected president of Chechnya, and went as far as to attend a congress of United Russia. At the same time, two Chechen newspapers were fined for printing interviews with Kadyrov's opponents; a Communist newspaper in Tula was investigated for writing only about the Communist Party;

and the national magazine *Kommersant Vlast* was warned about writing an article about Yury Luzhkov. After two warnings, a newspaper could be closed down. In both Chechnya and St Petersburg, opponents complained about biased coverage, arbitrary arrest and harassment. The overall effect was to curtail free debate in the media about forthcoming elections, and to cow journalists and their proprietors. It gave a huge advantage to incumbents and government ministers (up to the president), who could argue they were just innocently going about their day-to-day business. Putin told French journalists before his visit to Paris in October 2000: 'The state has in its hands a cudgel that strikes only once. But on the head. We have not yet resorted to this cudgel. We have simply laid our hands on it, and this turned out to be enough to attract attention. But if we are angered, we won't hesitate to put it to use.' Putin may have been referring to his run-in with the oligarchs, especially Gusinsky and his media empire, but the general attitude was clear. If you mess with the Kremlin, it will come down on you hard. Russia's journalists were getting the message.

Vladimir Putin's belief in state supremacy means that anything which threatens the state or the president's personal position must be neutered – be it the media, the oligarchs, the military high command, Chechen rebels, regional governors, the Federation Council or the political opposition. As noted, Putin wanted to re-create what he calls the 'vertical of power', top-down government. Putin's ultimate goal, repeated many times in his election campaign, is to rule a re-invigorated Great Russia, respected at home and abroad. Democracy, it seems, is nothing more than a necessary add-on to appease the masses and the West. As Lilia Shevtsova of the Moscow Carnegie Centre said: 'This is an appointed monarchy. The successor was appointed and we, ordinary people, were also appointed to be his electorate.' Rather like choosing the colour of Ford's Model T, the Russian electorate was given the choice to elect any president in 2004, provided it was Vladimir Putin. An opinion poll conducted by the All-Russia Centre for Public Opinion Studies named Putin as

'Man of the Year' in 2001. The poll showed he had quickly recovered from his earlier setback in the *Kursk* crisis, when his approval ratings slipped eight points to the mid-60s. With his opinion poll ratings back at 76 per cent by January 2001, President Putin remained the bookies' racing favourite to be re-elected in March 2004. For the Russian people, at least Putin offered the hope of order, relative prosperity, economic reform and stability. His first term in office may not have fully delivered on all these areas, but his performance was undoubtedly a marked improvement on the sick and incompetent last years of Boris Yeltsin.

When Putin told the Federal Assembly in May 2003 that he would form the country's government 'based on the results of parliamentary elections', liberals in the Duma took heart. It appeared that Putin was offering to form a government which reflected the result at the ballot box, rather than create another government of technocrats. Putin told Radio Mayak the next month that two presidential terms should be sufficient and that the constitution should be cherished, and not amended to meet the tastes of those in power. Nevertheless, Putin's words should be weighed with care. Sergei Mironov, his ally and Speaker of the Federation Council, has also floated the idea that the four-year presidential term is too short. Mironov, a fifty-year-old fellow graduate of Leningrad University Law Faculty, a supporter of Sobchak's administration and early Putin follower, has known the president for a number of years. Perhaps, he has suggested, Russia should become a democracy along the lines of the French system, with a long-serving president standing almost aloof from politics and a government formed from the parliamentary majority. French presidents serve for seven years. Mironov has even proposed moving the capital to his home city, St Petersburg. In any event, as Putin's allies in the Duma achieved a two-thirds majority in December 2003, a change in the constitution which grants the relatively youthful Putin a third term beyond 2008 cannot be ruled out.

8

PUTIN IN THE WORLD

You cannot understand Russia with logic
You cannot measure Russia by the same yardstick
Russia has a special character
You can only believe in Russia

FYODOR IVANOVICH TYUTCHEV (1803–73),
CAREER DIPLOMAT AND POET

President Vladimir Putin came to power in March 2000 seeking to re-create Russia as a Great Power, after almost a decade of humiliating decline. Russia had still not come to terms with its identity crisis after the disintegration of the Soviet Union and the demise of Communism. Over twenty million Russians found themselves stranded in newly independent states, which had formed part of the old Soviet empire. Ignored as a serious player on the world stage, Russia was regarded as a hopeless and disturbing charity case. Less than two years after the economic crash of August 1998, the country looked weak and unreformed. Internationally, Russia's standing was lower still. Disagreement over war in Kosovo the summer before, NATO enlargement, Chechnya and America's proposed National Missile Defense (NMD) system had soured what was left of the special relationship between Russia and the West, and especially between Boris Yeltsin and Bill Clinton. Coming into office with precious little experience of international affairs (apart from a few months as prime minister), Putin's task of rebuilding Russia's global prestige seemed well-nigh impossible. The idea of 'Great Russia' appeared a pipe dream.

Putin's short time as prime minister had given him some limited experience of top-level diplomacy. US President Bill Clinton made a big impression on Vladimir (as he seems to make on everybody) when the two met in Auckland, New Zealand in September 1999. They were both attending the annual summit of the Asia-Pacific Economic Cooperation Forum. Patently awe-struck, Putin looked shy and dazzled when the two met, describing Clinton as a 'very charming person', and adding, 'I liked talking to him.' Putin was just another of Clinton's social conquests. President Clinton literally towered over the Russian leader, something Putin had experienced with his old boss, Boris Yeltsin. Sometimes the old Siberian bear had looked twice his protégé's size. The height thing was something Putin would have to get used to, but he would feel a little uncomfortable next to some of the world's taller leaders.

Putin described his first meeting with the American president in his autobiography, using the excited tones of a young administration intern: 'In that first meeting, he also paid special attention to me. When we were first in New Zealand – I don't recall whether it was at lunch or dinner – he made a point of coming up to me. We had been seated at different tables. We talked about something for a while, and then he said, "Well, shall we go?" Everyone lined up in a corridor – the leaders of other states, guests – and he and I walked down the corridor. We exited the hall to the sound of applause. I appreciated this sign of special regard. Maybe that's why he made such a good impression on me.'

Putin was not sufficiently experienced in diplomacy to know that Clinton was like that on all his first dates, especially if his partner was going to end up President of Russia one day. Yeltsin had already anointed Putin as his successor by this stage, a point not unnoticed by the US State Department and the White House. Some experienced diplomats rued the fact that they had not bothered to get to know Putin better earlier. Access to Putin was much easier when he was just a Kremlin apparatchik or minister. A few had met him when he was still deputy mayor of St Petersburg, but although regarded as a competent technocrat, he had not made an overwhelming impression. The fact was few people had viewed him as a future Russian leader, let alone a global player, so the opportunity was lost.

At the Auckland meeting, Putin thanked Clinton effusively for his continued support of Russia despite mounting US criticism, and expressed confidence about future relations between Moscow and Washington now that the war in Kosovo was over. When Clinton brought up the subject of Chechnya, the Russian premier said he understood the West's concerns but hoped the US shared his view that they were on the same side in a global war against terrorism. Pressed by Clinton to admit international monitors into Chechnya, Putin visibly stiffened, his mouth tightened and his eyes narrowed. He had listened to 'advice' from Russia's Western friends, and he was taking it, he replied. Drawing a map on a serviette, he promised that the Russian forces would stop at the Terek river, effectively occupying just a northern sliver of Chechnya. But, he warned, the US should understand that Russia was reacting to an invasion of its territory in Dagestan, an invasion initiated by the forces of international Islamic terrorism.

Afterwards, Putin held a meeting with the US's ambassador to Moscow, Jim Collins, where he alleged that Osama bin Laden had visited Chechnya several times that year, and was funding the separatist movement. He knew that bin Laden was fast becoming America's bogeyman. The Saudi renegade was already held responsible for the bombing of American embassies in East Africa in 1998, which led to Clinton's retaliatory cruise missile strikes on terrorist training camps in Afghanistan, and the bombing of alleged terrorist facilities in the Sudan. In spite of his calming words to Clinton in New Zealand, Putin went on to authorize the occupation of the whole of Chechnya and the bombardment of Grozny.

By the time Putin was acting-president, Bill Clinton was on the way out. He was serving his last year of his second and final term. There would be no Bill Clinton around in the future, and no rehash of the 'Bill and Boris' show. The United States was engrossed in the forthcoming November presidential election, and the only question was who would be the next US president, a Democrat (Al Gore, the vice-president) or a Republican (Texas Governor George W. Bush)? Putin, too, was wrapped up in his own election campaign until March 2000. The only international figure who had shown any interest in Russia was Tony Blair, who as described earlier made a fleeting visit to St Petersburg two weeks before election day.

With the lack of interest from America, Germany and France, and the latter two countries' strident condemnation of human rights abuses in Chechnya, the Kremlin thought an early visit to Britain a good idea. It would reward Blair for his interest and support (as seen from Moscow), and simultaneously allow Putin to make a politically symbolic gesture. Putin wanted to make the point that under his administration, Russia would look primarily, but not exclusively, westwards. In the old argument dating back to the nineteenth century between the Slavophiles and the Westernizers (*zapadniki*), Putin was unashamedly a Westernizer, if not a liberal democrat. Both he and his wife and children spoke foreign languages, especially German. Coming from St Petersburg, Peter the Great's 'Window on the West', Putin was the most European of Russia's leaders for generations. He didn't come from Siberia like Yeltsin, southern Russia like Gorbachev, the Ukraine like Khrushchev or Georgia like Stalin. As he wrote in his autobiography, as far as he was concerned, Russia was part of Western European culture. He went further, saying that in his view all Russians were culturally European 'Irrespective of where our people live – in the far east or in the south – we are Europeans.' But this is a debatable point. There is no real evidence the tartars of Kazan feel European, any more than the Chechens, Bashkiries or Chukcha nomadic people of Russia's frozen Arctic north.

Russia is vast, with its eleven time zones and over a hundred different ethnic groups. Growing up in St Petersburg it is easy to feel European; less so if you live in a hut wrapped in animal skins in the taiga, caring for reindeer as your ancestors have for hundreds of years. But in Putin's mind, Russia should be regarded as a European nation, and he wished to see his country integrated into the international community's trading, financial, political and military organizations. Addressing the Bundestag later in his presidency in September 2001 in flawless German, he portrayed Russia as a 'friendly European country' and a 'most dynamically developing part of the European continent'. At the outset of his presidency, the war in Kosovo had initially isolated and marginalized Russia, and relations with the West had not yet fully recovered. On his way to the United States in March 1999, Prime Minister Yevgeny Primakov had famously turned his plane around in the mid-Atlantic on being told of NATO's decision to bomb Serbia. Relations had been difficult ever since.

So, in his first foreign visit, Putin went to London to meet his new friend, Tony. He took Lyudmila with him. In his first few months as president, Lyudmila looked, in the words of one close observer, 'like a rabbit caught in the headlights of an oncoming car'. The rapidity of Putin's ascendancy to the presidency, and the sudden overpowering press interest in the first couple, was intimidating and threw her momentarily off balance. Her head, one can imagine, was swirling with a heady mix of emotions including elation, excitement, pride and sheer terror at the enormity of it all. To her credit, she subsequently regained her footing, giving speeches on her own to various groups and visiting the US to take part in charitable events with the American first lady, Laura Bush. Previously low-profile like most Russian business or political wives were expected to be (the unpopular exception being Raisa Gorbachev), Lyudmila developed a preference for elegant Escada suits. In London Lyudmila had her own schedule of meetings, including ones with Cherie Blair and Baroness Smith of Gilmorehill, a leading light of the Russo–British Chamber of Commerce and widow of the late Labour leader John Smith. Vladimir too would swiftly learn to take the rather dazed look off his face, and get down to the serious business of being a world leader.

When the Putins arrived in London in April 2000, Vladimir had not even yet been inaugurated as president. Technically, he was in breach of the constitution, which states that either the president or the prime minister had to be in the country at any one time. As both prime minister and president-elect, Putin should have by rights remained in Russia until he was inaugurated and a prime minister appointed. He explained his early return visit to the press by saying Tony Blair had demonstrated 'a willingness to cooperate with Russia'. Diplomats reported on how the pair had built up a good personal relationship during Blair's stopover in St Petersburg before Putin was elected. Behind the scenes, it was also said that it was crucial to make overtures to Putin during his early, formative career. The question 'Who is Mr Putin?', asked at the Davos business summit in January 2000 by Trudy Rubin of the *Philadelphia Inquirer*, still remained largely unanswered. The personal relationship would be important for Anglo–Russian relations, and make it 'much easier for them to pick up the phone and talk to each other'. Blair was positive about the visit too, telling the press beforehand that Putin 'has a very clear agenda of modernizing Russia. When he talks of a strong Russia, he means strength not in a threatening way but in a way that means the country economically and politically is capable of standing up for itself, which is a perfectly good aim to have.'

Apart from the diplomatic niceties, there were sound strategic reasons for Putin and Blair to improve relations between their two countries. Having advised both Downing Street and the Russian Embassy in London on the strategy behind the visit, I felt well placed to judge the diplomatic state of play at the time.

Margaret Thatcher once hailed Mikhail Gorbachev as a 'man she could do business with', so helping to open up the Soviet Union to the West, unfreeze the Cold War, and hastening *perestroika* and ultimately the collapse of the Berlin Wall and the Warsaw Pact. At the time, in the mid-1980s, Gorbachev was a new Soviet leader, on his first official visit to Britain and as yet ignored by the US. Following Mrs Thatcher's initiative, the US finally sat up and noticed they had a reformer and global partner in the Kremlin. The rest, as they say, is history.

As we saw, Britain had been one of the first Western countries to pursue a 'critical engagement' with the new man in the Kremlin. Robin Cook and George Robertson (as NATO Secretary General) had been swift to beat a path to Moscow, followed by Tony Blair's initiative as the first Western head of government to meet Putin in his native St Petersburg. In Britain's view, there were several important and strategic reasons behind the renewed interest in Anglo–Russian relations, and a desire to build bridges despite the bloody carnage in Chechnya. The first concerned the opportunities offered by regime change in Moscow. It had been apparent since at least December that Putin would succeed Boris Yeltsin as Russian president. Yeltsin had become increasingly difficult to do business with, as he was either unwell, under the influence, distracted by internal palace intrigues, or all three at the same time. Putin, on the other hand, was young (with only a year separating him and Blair), sober, vigorous, and had indicated he wanted to reform and modernize Russia.

Britain felt it had a chance to influence and encourage Putin's reformist tendencies. It was known that he had also been exposed to reformist influences; he had already spoken of the need to overhaul the tax system, and encourage Western investment in Russia by improving legislation in this field. It was a promise he would repeat when he met British business leaders from the Confederation of Business and Industry (CBI) during his London stay. However, it should not be forgotten that this was the man who had written the previous December: 'Western-style democracy and the free market must be adapted to Russian realities.' In other words, Putin was seeking reform while harking back to a 'Russia First' approach, so creating a uniquely Russian variant of democratic and economic models, and developing a more assertive and coherent foreign policy to express Russia's 'Great Power' aspirations. The 'Russia First' concept had emerged under Foreign Minister Yevgeny Primakov, following the end of Russia's 'honeymoon with the West' in the early 1990s. None of this, however, would prevent Britain or the West from striving for a closer relationship with Russia.

The need for better relations was a double-dependency. Putin realized Russia needed the West for investment, and to support its integration into global institutions and expand foreign trade. Equally, the West needed dialogue with Russia. It was still a major nuclear power, with 3,500 intercontinental warheads, thirteen nuclear missile submarines and 70 nuclear-bomber aircraft. The West desperately wanted the ratification of the START II Treaty cutting strategic nuclear weapons, which Yeltsin had repeatedly failed to deliver, and further cuts in warhead numbers. Putin successfully delivered the Duma's long-overdue ratification of START II before arriving in London, proving that his leadership could be a real asset to the West. Unlike the US Congress, the Duma had also ratified the nuclear Comprehensive Test Ban Treaty (CTBT). A START III looked on the cards, as Russia could ill-afford its ageing and potentially hazardous nuclear arsenal, especially with the development of the new and expensive Topol inter-continental ballistic missile (ICBM).

Russia's nuclear weapons were not only a potential threat to the world; they represented a grave environmental threat that Moscow needed help with. The United States was also hoping to see Russian agreement to amend the 1972 anti-ballistic missile treaty, so it could introduce its controversial missile defence system or shield, aimed at so-called 'rogue' states. In addition, Russia was important for its major trading links with Europe (the EU was Russia's largest trading partner); a source of energy; and as one of the five Permanent Members of the United Nations Security Council.

No one wanted to see an isolated and aggrieved Russia, and a new arms race, difficult as that would be given Russia's parlous finances (Putin's 50 per cent hike in defence spending still meant it was only a quarter of Britain's). There was also the delicate question of handling Russia's attitude to further NATO expansion (Lithuania wanted to join by 2002), and future potential crises in the Balkans and elsewhere. Putin's pledge to defend the rights of Russians vigorously in the former Soviet republics had made Moscow's neighbours nervous and even more keen to join NATO.

While calling for an end to the bloodshed in Chechnya, a political solution and an urgent inquiry into human rights abuses, the British also thought it was important to foster a long-term relationship with Putin. These views were shared in Downing Street and the Foreign Office, and by Tony Blair and Robin Cook, the foreign secretary. Cook felt there was no inconsistency between this approach and the 'ethical foreign policy' he had sought to promote from the beginning of his tenure in the Foreign Office in 1997. Others were not so convinced. Jonathan Powell, the former Foreign Office diplomat who became Tony Blair's chief of staff, reportedly thought Cook's ethical foreign policy was 'bollocks' and a hostage to fortune. Some British and US human rights organizations shared the same view of Cook's pledge, which they regarded as grossly hypocritical. Many of Britain's allies and trading partners were deeply undemocratic and had dubious human rights records – Saudi Arabia and Bahrain being just two examples. Cook's ethical foreign policy was finally fatally undermined by the sale of British Hawk military trainer jets to Indonesia, which then used them to repress domestic opponents.

Human Rights Watch and Amnesty International demanded that Blair tackle Putin over Chechnya; while the Council of Europe's parliamentary assembly withdrew Russia's voting rights as an act of protest. To make matters worse, UN Human Rights Commissioner Mary Robinson had been obstructed from visiting some Chechen refugee camps; and the US-based Human Rights Watch called on Blair to threaten to take Russia to the European Court of Human

Rights if the alleged massacres weren't properly investigated. Against this background, both Menzies Campbell for the British Liberal Democrats and Francis Maude for the Tories were extremely critical of Putin's visit, particularly his proposed meeting with the Queen. Feelings were running high, with Hugo Young, the *Guardian* newspaper's political columnist, describing Putin as 'the butcher of Chechnya'.

Blair and the British government were nevertheless determined to show the US and other Europeans that Putin was a man they 'could do business with', encouraging him along the path of economic and political reform. After all, Russia needed a friend in Europe, and an entrée to the Western club. A Downing Street official said the London visit was 'a potential turning point' in relations between Russia, Britain and the European Union. The big idea was that Britain would act as a bridge between Europe and the United States, a point agreed in advance between the Russians and the British. Before the talks in London, Alistair Campbell, the prime minister's spokesman, said: 'We believe it is in Britain and Europe's interest that we develop a strategic relationship with Russia. Russia is a great country with an important role in the world. This visit will help build this new relationship.' On Chechnya, Campbell stressed the UK's commitment to 'critical engagement'. He said Britain 'will express, as we did in St Petersburg, our concerns, but equally we believe the way to address those concerns is by negotiation, rather than by isolation'. It was a point repeated by Blair during Putin's visit. Putin and Russia wanted to be taken seriously on the international stage, and the London trip provided him with the ideal opportunity to grandstand diplomatically, boosting his image at home and abroad. Perhaps also, like after the Thatcher–Gorbachev summit, the Americans might even sit up and take notice.

When Vladimir and Lyudmila Putin arrived late on Sunday evening, 16 April, they were met at Heathrow airport by Russia's new ambassador to London, Grigory Karasin, a stocky and balding middle-aged senior diplomat and former deputy foreign minister.

Karasin's London posting indicated that the Russians were starting to take the London–Moscow relationship seriously again, after a period of decline. Putin showed he intended to be treated like a major world leader. Staying in a Kensington hotel next to the Russian Embassy in Kensington Palace Gardens, Putin gave his usual forty-five-minute early morning run a miss, leaving Karasin to jog around Kensington Gardens on his own. Putin travelled everywhere in a thirteen-car motorcade, accompanied by fifty journalists, fifty aides and a hundred security men, wearing trademark white macs. The motorcade included a Mercedes and two armoured Zil limousines specially flown in for the occasion. The lumbering black Zils were a throwback to Soviet times, the Politburo's car of choice, with leather interiors, bulletproof windows and 7.7 litre V8 engines. Costing about $120,000, they weighed two tons, had a top speed of 118 miles an hour and did about ten miles to the gallon. Although Stalin had had one, former president Boris Yeltsin preferred a Mercedes. Yeltsin admitted he couldn't stand the dated Zil models, which looked like American limos out of an old Hollywood movie.

The next day, Monday morning, Putin's entourage of two hundred people arrived at the grand National Liberal Club in Whitehall, next to the River Thames. Surrounded by busts and portraits of former Liberal leaders like Gladstone and Lloyd George, Putin addressed a seminar of the CBI. Business leaders from Russia's main UK investors were present, including top executives from Shell, BP Amoco, Unilever, Cadbury Schweppes and British American Tobacco. Putin made a pitch for the businessmen (they were mainly men) to have faith and invest in 'the new Russia'. In return, he promised to reform the business environment, cut red tape, overhaul the tax system, reduce taxes, fight corruption and respect private property rights. He told the CBI seminar that 'the most significant factor for us is the integration of Russia into the world economy'.

After the seminar, Putin's motorcade drove about 100 yards to Downing Street, past about sixty pro-Chechen protesters waving placards saying 'Stop the Genocide Now', and 'RasPUTIN'. Almost a third of a million people had been displaced by the conflict in the Caucasus. Four white vans in the presidential convey momentarily blocked Putin's view of the demonstrators as he swept past the wrought-iron gates into Downing Street. For many years the small street next to the Foreign Office had been publicly accessible, but had been closed off by Margaret Thatcher in a more security-conscious age. Tony Blair met his guest standing on a red carpet, leading into number 10 Downing Street, where the two had lunch together. Putin, in a nod to Cold War days, was followed into Downing Street by two Russian naval officers, carrying the president's 'nuclear briefcase' containing the launch codes for the country's strategic nuclear missiles. On the agenda for the talks were Russia's economy, Chechnya, the G8, the Balkans, crime, drugs, defence and Anglo–Russian relations in general. In more than three hours of talks, Putin also raised his concerns about the US plan for an anti-ballistic missile system, which he claimed could destabilize the world and start a new arms race. If this went ahead, the Russian president warned Blair, his country would be forced to 'react' and Russia would not feel itself bound by the START II nuclear missile reduction treaty if the deployment took place.

From Downing Street, the two leaders went into the ornate colonial-style Locarno room in the Foreign Office, stood on podiums in front of their respective national flags and answered questions from the press. Focusing on the 'big idea' behind the visit, Blair told the media Britain could act as a 'bridge of understanding' between Russia and Europe, and Russia and the US. Putin, seeking to defuse the row over abuses by the Russian military in Chechnya, announced a domestic inquiry into alleged human rights abuses in the breakaway republic. Human rights groups rejected the move as inadequate, and called for an international commission to investigate the claims. The press conference was notable for Putin's suppressed anger over Chechnya, the one subject where he seemed capable of losing his temper in public. He scolded European leaders for not supporting the military crackdown in Chechnya, claiming

Russia was engaged in a battle against 'Islamic terrorists' who posed a global threat to peace and security. 'For Russia it is completely unacceptable there should be a situation in which one of its republics is used as a launchpad for undermining Russian statehood and Russian sovereignty,' he said. European governments who couldn't support Russia for fear of alienating their Muslim populations were 'wrong'. 'Western Europe could pay very heavily for this,' he concluded. Pre-September 11th, Putin's arguments largely fell on stony ground. After the Twin Towers atrocity, the Russian president would find such sentiments would receive a much more sympathetic hearing.

Although Putin's outburst on Chechnya in London was tetchy, it paled into insignificance compared with his egregious performance at a press conference in Brussels in November 2002, when he was asked by a French journalist about the use of anti-personnel mines and the killing of Chechen civilians. On that occasion, he told the *Le Figaro* journalist that the Chechen rebels didn't care about anyone, and 'If you seriously want to become a radical Islamist and undergo circumcision, I invite you to come to Moscow.' He went on: 'We are a multi-confessional country, we also have a specialist on this matter and I will advise him to have the operation done in such a way that nothing would grow out of you ever again.' Putin's attempt to use bar-room slang was excruciatingly inappropriate. It was the first time he'd used such language outside Russia, and it went down badly. European Union officials expressed distaste for his remarks, seen as offensive to Muslims. His flare-up can be ascribed to his strongly-held views on Chechnya and the fact that he doesn't like his authority being challenged.

Back in April 2000 in London, Putin attended the new memorial to the Soviet Union's war dead outside the Imperial War Museum in south London, and laid a wreath. Waving to a crowd of 200-odd people, including many Russian diplomats, military personnel and their families based in Britain, Putin posed for photographs with a family of American tourists. At the end of his whistle-stop twenty-four-hour visit, he had a private thirty-minute meeting with the Queen at Windsor Castle, which according to Prince Philip, has the noisiest toilets in the country. The meeting was held at the request of the British government, and rounded off what both governments considered a very successful visit. 'Tony and Vladimir' would go on to develop a close personal relationship, only jeopardised later by the Iraqi war.

When Tony Blair flew to a rain-sodden Moscow to meet Putin in November 2000, it was already their fifth meeting in ten months. The style of the visit showed the type of personal relationship the two men had built up. This time, Blair travelled without Cherie and their new baby, Leo. On arriving on Monday evening, 20 November, Blair's entourage were told: 'We'll go for a beer. Dress casually.' With just their interpreters present, Putin and Blair were photographed having a jug of beer in a traditional German bierkeller on Lenin Prospect, just south of the Kremlin. Doubtless the setting reminded Vladimir Putin of those halcyon days in East Germany, when he used to enjoy a weekly 3-litre keg of beer in the small town of Radeberg. The meeting was immediately dubbed the 'bierkeller summit' by the press. The next day, Putin sought to maintain the atmosphere of bonhomie by cracking a joke before leading his guest off for lunch in the Kremlin. 'We have this joke in Russia,' he said, describing the previous night's drink in the bierkeller. 'When blokes get together on their own, they talk about women. When they get together with women, they talk shop, about their work.' Blair looked embarrassed; Alastair Campbell, his spokesman, fell about laughing. Apart from reinforcing the buddy-like atmosphere, the remark did reflect Putin's interest in women, and even his wife acknowledged that he 'noticed' beautiful women. Lyudmila, generously for a wife, thought he would be strange if he didn't.

Blair's Moscow stopover only lasted fifteen hours, but he did attempt to do some serious work. Before his lunch with Putin, Blair held discussions with Mikhail Kasyanov, the relatively new prime minister. The agenda for the Anglo–Russian talks covered economic reform, climate change, a range of foreign affairs issues and Moscow's plan to scale down its military. Putin was also keen to discuss the US's plans for a 'Son of Star Wars' national missile defence system, designed to knock rogue states' nuclear weapons out of the skies before they hit America. Once again, Blair was keen to strengthen his role as a European bridge between Russia and the United States. 'Our desire is to make sure we get a dialogue between the US and Russia,' he said before arriving in Moscow. But he declined to say whether Britain would help the United States set up the missile defence system by upgrading the Fylingdales listening station in Yorkshire. Downing Street had previously hinted it was willing to go along with US plans. The British Ministry of Defence supported America's National Missile Defense (NMD) scheme, the Foreign Office was less keen. Diplomats were worried that the threatened abrogation of the anti-ballistic missile treaty could make the world a more unstable and dangerous place. None of this affected American domestic political considerations. In the United States, both presidential candidates Al Gore and George W. Bush supported NMD. Blair and the British hoped the Americans would negotiate a change to the treaty rather than just unilaterally declare it dead. 'Whereas we have been understanding of the American desire to take action to defend itself against rogue nuclear states, we want to make sure that takes place within the context of the negotiated treaties,' Blair argued.

The heady love-in between Putin and Blair was at its peak in November 2000. Grigory Karasin, Russia's ambassador to London, told the press that the personal chemistry between the two leaders was so good that relations between Britain and Russia were now the 'best ever'. In his plane on the way to Moscow, Blair had told reporters: 'For him [Putin] to be a strong leader doesn't mean he is a threatening leader, but he does need to be a strong leader to sort his country out.' 'I do personally like him, yes,' the prime minister added. Later during the visit Blair described his host glowingly. 'He is someone who wants to do the right thing by himself and the world . . . he is highly intelligent, very capable, knows what he wants for Russia and is prepared to listen.' Putin returned the compliment, saying of Blair: 'He's very well informed and pleasant . . . I've come to the conclusion that our meetings tend to be very informal, frank and friendly.' Alastair Campbell's assessment was more measured. 'We have invested quite a lot in the relationship with Putin. He is somebody that the prime minister feels he can have very frank discussions with about what we see as the importance of the continuing reform programme in Russia.'

Even so, the Russian press couldn't make out what the Blair–Putin relationship was all about. 'Tony Blair arrived in Moscow. Why?' asked the newspaper *Izvestiya*. 'There's no burning need for a Russia–Britain summit right now. Most likely he's arrived just because of his deepening friendship with Vladimir Putin . . . an extremely strange European couple.' The *Moskovskiye Novosti* newspaper was also mystified. 'It's difficult to say what links the former head of the FSB with the liberal idealogue of the third way.' But for the time being, both Russia and Britain saw the advantage of an ever-closer relationship. Only a month before, Putin had finally risked visiting France for the first time, after months of strained relations over Russia's conduct in Chechnya. Hostility in Germany was even worse, while the Americans were still obsessed with their internal affairs and handing over power to a new administration. Sticking to his new friend Tony, Vladimir Putin remained on safe ground.

In Moscow, in June 2000, as part of his European 'farewell tour', Bill Clinton had tried to 'do business' with President Putin, but quickly sensed that the new Russian leader was waiting to see who won November's presidential election. With some resignation, Clinton came to the depressing conclusion that Putin felt he was a 'lame-duck' president, and it wasn't worth the effort making any significant deals which a new US president could later renounce. Clinton saw Putin was politically treading water. Putin appeared to be going through the motions of holding talks, but had no real intention of agreeing to anything of substance. Even on a personal level, Putin seemed to be waiting to develop a relationship with whoever got Clinton's job at the end of the year.

Clinton had come across Putin before, and not only in New Zealand the previous autumn. On a visit to St Petersburg in April 1996, Clinton had stayed in the famous nineteenth-century Hotel Grand Europe off Nevsky Prospect, arguably Russia's best hotel and the first in the country to be awarded five stars. The hotel, with its splendid Baroque façade designed by the Italian architect Carlo Rossi, had been one of the favourite haunts of Tchaikovsky, Anna Pavlova and Maxim Gorky. The most memorable part of the trip for Clinton was the suffocating security and poor itinerary. There were no walkabouts, and he didn't meet a single ordinary citizen, something that made him furious afterwards. As Strobe Talbot, US deputy secretary of state, recalls in his memoirs, the bureaucrat organizing Clinton's security was the young deputy mayor, Vladimir Putin.

Clinton also met Putin in Oslo in November 1999. Both were attending a memorial in Oslo city hall to mark the fifth anniversary of the death of Yitzhak Rabin. Putin's speech justifying Russia's intervention in Chechnya had not hit the right note. Once again, in a private meeting with Clinton, Putin had denied the Russians were about to occupy the whole of Chechnya. Clinton urged Putin to enter into talks with the Chechen rebels, rather than continue a pointless war of attrition. Putin countered by arguing that the Russians had no one reliable to negotiate with. He claimed that the Chechens not only wanted to break away from Russia, but were hell-bent on spreading radical Islam throughout the region. It seemed a political stalemate. Frustrated, Clinton told his advisers that at least he admired Putin's 'vigour'. 'I'll say this for that guy,' Clinton said. 'He's tough and he's strong and he's got a lot of energy and determination.' But there was none of the Bill-and-Boris warmth and rapport of the old days.

Clinton's visit to see the new Russian president in the summer of 2000, and say goodbye to the old one, was not an outstanding success. Given the political circumstances, it was difficult to see how it could have been. On his stop-offs in Portugal and Germany, Clinton faced growing European opposition to America's plans to develop a missile defence system. Moscow also adamantly opposed the scheme. It was Clinton's fifth and final presidential visit to Moscow, and his first meeting with Putin after his election. He had come to his first Moscow summit back in 1993, during a difficult year for Boris Yeltsin. Clinton and Putin began their summit with an almost three-hour dinner in the presidential quarters in the Kremlin on Saturday 3 June. Putin spoke some English during dinner, which he was learning so he could engage in small talk with his Western visitors (he would do the same with Tony Blair). Sometimes he would interject in English with 'okay' or 'excuse me', and seemed to be following Clinton's remarks before they were translated. Solicitously, he asked Clinton about his wife, Hillary, and daughter, Chelsea, and how the US election campaign was going. Clinton told his Russian interlocutor that he thought the election would be extremely close. Putin joked that now he was president, he was finding it hard to find judo sparring partners to keep him fit. To kill some time, the Russian leader took President Clinton on an evening tour of his Kremlin study, chapel, gym and massage room.

The Kremlin 'working dinner' consisted of traditional Russian cabbage soup, trout, spicy wild boar and goose with red berry sauce. The dinner was attended by the presidents and their two foreign policy advisers, Strobe Talbot, the US deputy secretary of state, and Sergei Prikhodko, Putin's deputy chief of staff. After dinner, the two leaders sat back and listened to jazz until midnight. Oleg Lundstrem, the band leader, brought along a saxophone just in case Clinton wanted to play his favourite instrument. On this occasion, Clinton resisted the temptation to join in. The formal part of the summit had discussed strategic nuclear arsenals, the planned US national missile defence system, economic reform and Chechnya. Six more hours of talks followed the next day, including more one-on-one discussions between the two presidents.

Although the summit was dominated by the US's proposed NMD system, designed to deal with threats from rogue states like North Korea, Iran and Iraq, the two presidents did manage to sign up to a couple of agreements. Clinton and Putin announced a deal to each scrap 34 tonnes of weapons-grade plutonium over the next twenty years, amounting to one-third of Russia's stockpile and one-half of America's. The disposal would cost almost $6 billion, with $4 billion being borne by the US, which had already spent more than $3 billion since 1994 helping Russia dismantle nuclear warheads. In what Clinton called a 'milestone in enhancing strategic stability', the US and Russia also agreed to establish the first ever early warning centre in Moscow, designed to reduce the chances of a nuclear war being triggered by accident. Initially running for ten years, the Moscow centre would be staffed by 16 US and 17 Russian military officers working twenty-four-hour shifts, seven days a week, using space-based satellites, infrared systems and early warning radar. The idea was to provide an exchange of information about the launch of ballistic missiles and space-launch vehicles, which might otherwise set off early warning system alerts in Russia and the US. Within a minute of a missile launch from either the US or Russia, information would be shared on the launch site, type of missile and the timing of impact. The elimination of 'uncertainties' around missile launches (such as test launches) would help prevent misunderstandings and eliminate the possibility of accidental retaliatory strikes.

Clinton also sought assurances from Putin that Russia would prevent technology and nuclear material transfers to rogue states like Iran. Putin had just signed a decree making it easier to arrange commercial nuclear technology exports, a measure which alarmed Washington given Moscow's role in building a $800 million nuclear power plant at Bushehr in Iran. More controversially, by the end of the year Putin had repudiated the 1995 Gore–Chernomyrdin agreement on Russian arms sales to Iran. A year on, Russia signed a military accord with Iran that envisaged the Kremlin selling an annual $300 million of jets, missiles and other weapons to Tehran. The Iranians were particularly interested in buying Russian anti-aircraft missile systems, high precision ground force weapons and anti-ship missiles. By jettisoning the Gore–Chernomyrdin agreement and signing the military accord, Putin was clearly signalling he was putting Russia's economic interests ahead of Washington's desire to contain Iran's regional and nuclear ambitions. Three years later, Iran announced the successful final testing of the Shabab-3 surface-to-surface ballistic missile, which with a range of 800 miles could hit Israel. Based on the North Korean Nodong-1 missile, it had been developed and improved with Russian technology.

NMD remained the stumbling block at the Moscow summit. Before Clinton had even arrived in Russia, Putin told American NBC television that the two countries could develop the proposed missile shield together. 'Such mechanisms are possible if we pool our efforts towards neutralizing the threats against the US, Russia, our allies, and Europe in general,' he said. 'We have such proposals and we intend to discuss them with President Clinton.' Kremlin officials said Putin would suggest a system of shooting down missiles with interceptors based on Russian soil. The missiles would be intercepted shortly after being launched, and before they reached a high trajectory. In the same interview, Putin said he saw the potential missile threat from countries like North Korea.

Although Bill Clinton was officially due to make a decision on NMD deployment by the coming autumn, Washington quickly poured cold water on Putin's proposal. A US official said Putin's offer reiterated a proposal made by Foreign Minister Igor Ivanov, and referred to theatre missile defence, rather than the US's idea of a national missile defence system. The US plan was for a $60 billion defence system, phased over four stages from an initial 20 missile interceptors in 2005 rising to 250 interceptors or 'kill vehicles' by 2011. The missiles would be housed in underground silos across Alaska and North Dakota, and guided by a global network of three command centres and five communications relay stations using 29 satellites and 15 space-based radar stations. The system would work by knocking out one missile with another in deep space, like hitting a bullet with a bullet.

The United States and Russia were still bound by the 1972 Anti-Ballistic Missile (ABM) Treaty, which banned the deployment of anti-ballistic missile defence systems. The ABM treaty sought to guarantee the balance of terror, or the doctrine of Mutually Assured Destruction (MAD), so making any pre-emptive missile attack or nuclear exchange suicidal. Each side in the Cold War could feel that its nuclear deterrent remained inviolable. The Russians, together with some Europeans and Scandinavians (particularly the Germans, French and Swedes) thought the American proposed nuclear defence shield would create uncertainty and instability, undermine nuclear non-proliferation, render the ABM treaty useless and foment a nuclear arms race. China had already warned it would escalate its own nuclear missile-building and modernization programme, with the result that India felt it might have to do the same to counter its Asian rival. If India upgraded its nuclear deterrent, Pakistan would not be far behind. The argument ran: How could the US expect other countries to abide by international non-proliferation treaties, when it had just torn up one of the foundations of international security and arms control? The Russians indicated that they would rethink their position on START II, which had just slashed Moscow's stockpile in half, if the US went ahead with NMD.

The day Clinton arrived in Moscow, Strategic Missile Force Commander Colonel-General Vladimir Yakovlev published an interview in the *Kommersant* daily newspaper. Yakovlev said that if Russia had to find the money to match America's defence shield, it would do so. He added that if the US went ahead with its plans, including the abrogation of the ABM treaty, Moscow would relocate its missiles and equip them with currently banned multiple warheads. The threat was none too subtle, and the type of bluster that Washington had encountered many times before. Nevertheless, it showed that Clinton had a problem if he thought the Russian bear would immediately roll over and let Uncle Sam tickle its tummy.

For his part, Clinton hoped the Russians would modify the ABM treaty to let the Americans press ahead with their nuclear shield. But he didn't rule out unilaterally abrogating the ABM treaty and going it alone. To a certain extent, Clinton was boxed in on the NMD issue. In a bipartisan vote the year before, Congress had mandated the president and the Pentagon to develop an heir to 'Star Wars'. The concept was popular in the United States, where citizens were becoming nervous about the missile threat from rogue states like North Korea, which US intelligence said would be capable of hitting America by 2005. Both presidential candidates supported the NMD shield. Al Gore had said he was ready to negotiate changes to the ABM treaty with Russia, but refused to rule out a unilateral breach if he thought it was 'necessary to US security'. Gore's Republican party rival, George W. Bush, sought to outflank the Democratic presidential hopeful by sounding even tougher. Governor Bush promised that he was prepared to tear up the ABM treaty and deploy a comprehensive defence system embracing space, ground and sea-based missiles. 'Our missile defence must be designed to protect all fifty states, and our friends and allies and forces deployed overseas,' Bush said. His defence shield would cost an estimated three times more than the Clinton–Gore version.

During the Kremlin talks, Clinton rejected Putin's offer of jointly developing a land-based missile defence in Russia, on the grounds that the system would take ten years to bring to fruition, five years longer than the US could afford to wait. The US–Russia summit saw both sides agreeing that stability in the twenty-first century faced a fresh and serious threat from rogue states and the proliferation of weapons of mass destruction, including ballistic missile technology. The leaders' joint statement on 'principles of strategic stability', issued on the Sunday, ran to a relatively brief seven hundred words. Even so, referring to NMD and scrapping the ABM treaty, Putin publicly warned his US counterpart: 'We're against having a cure which is worse than the disease.' Putin conceded that states like North Korea, Iran and Iraq posed a risk, appeared flexible on arms control but he refused to agree to an amendment of the ABM treaty. Clinton argued that the strategic environment had changed since the Cold War, and therefore the ABM treaty needed adapting. In the war of hearts and minds in Russia and Europe, Putin seemed to be winning over public opinion. On the other hand, Clinton and his administration knew the Russians were desperate to cut their nuclear arsenals for economic reasons. Measured in GDP terms, Russia's economy was fifty times smaller than that of the United States. Moscow had agreed to cut its strategic nuclear stockpile to 3,500 warheads under START II by 2007, and wanted to reduce the ceiling to around 1,500 warheads under START III. Clinton told Putin that the US would find it difficult to agree to go below 2,000 warheads unless the Russians accepted amendments to the ABM treaty and Washington's missile defence shield. For now, Putin didn't budge. With Clinton on the way out, time was on his side.

The two leaders held a press conference on Sunday 4 June, before Clinton addressed a session of the state Duma (the first US president to do so) the next day. Although there were lots of smiles and compliments, correspondents noticed a lack of any real warmth between the two men. Reuters reported that a confident Putin upstaged Clinton, who usually outshone his contemporaries. Speaking without notes after two days of talks and less than a month following his inauguration, Putin brimmed with confidence. 'I have to say that the Russian side cannot fail to express its satisfaction with the spirit, the quality and also the results of our negotiations,' Putin told reporters. It didn't matter who won the US presidential election, whether it was Al Gore or George W. Bush, relations between Russia and America would continue to improve, he added. Putin praised Clinton as a 'very pleasant and comfortable partner in negotiations'. Russia would continue with market reforms, he concluded. Clinton had responded in kind, saying the Russian president

was 'fully capable of building a prosperous, strong Russia while preserving freedom and the rule of law . . . and I'm encouraged by the
first two days of our really serious work.' Unlike Putin, Clinton read
from his notes. He criticized Russia's war in Chechnya, and annoyed
the Kremlin on the Sunday by taking part in a live phone-in with the
opposition radio station Moscow Echo.

In a private session with Clinton, Putin mocked reports of
'alleged, mythical atrocities by the Russian army'. Behind the scenes
Clinton showed he didn't much care for Putin. As the US president
made ready to leave the Kremlin, Putin asked for a private word
with his guest, not just in his capacity as president of the United
States, but as a 'human being'. Putin, speaking slowly, said that if
America went ahead with its missile defence shield, Russia would
take 'reciprocal action', threatening the very territory of the United
States. Clinton was incensed at this last-minute attempt to confront
him on NMD. He had been on the receiving end of heavy-handed
threats from Russia before. During the Kosovo conflict, in April
1999, Boris Yeltsin came close to threatening the US with nuclear
war. 'Don't push Russia into this war!' Yeltsin had said on that occasion, practically shouting down the phone at Clinton. 'You know
what Russia is! You know what it has at its disposal! Don't push
Russia into this!' Russia's threats, as usual, were hollow. If he wasn't
intimidated by Yeltsin's bluster, Clinton was less likely to be moved
by Putin's calculated sabre rattling.

Leaving the Kremlin after his irritating exchange with Putin,
Clinton confided to Strobe Talbot: 'I guess that guy thought I didn't get
it the first time . . . Either he's dense or thinks I am. Anyway, let's get
this thing over with so we can go see ol' Boris.' Strobe Talbot was not
impressed with Putin either, writing in his memoirs: 'He seemed to
have a knack for being in the right place at the right time with the right
protectors; he'd been promoted far beyond anything his experience or
apparent abilities would have prepared him for; he was tactically adroit
but, I suspected, strategically at sea.' Like other diplomats, Putin
reminded him of a policeman more than a politician. 'I still saw Putin

as essentially a suave cop who had lucked into a very big job that would require a lot more than luck to pull off,' Talbot concluded. Clinton and Talbot said their goodbyes and headed off to meet Boris Yeltsin one last time in his government dacha outside Moscow, before leaving the city. The next and final stop on Clinton's 'farewell tour' was Kiev in the Ukraine. It was undoubtedly the end of an era.

Clinton met Putin once more in an official capacity after the Moscow summit. The two men met up that July at the G8 meeting on the Japanese island of Okinawa. It was Putin's first major international summit, and by all accounts he favourably impressed his fellow leaders. This was partly because he wasn't Boris Yeltsin, and by comparison he came across as measured, intelligent, stable and well-briefed. He was also young and vigorous, and was pictured holding a young Japanese girl in a karate outfit, which of course reminded everyone of his athletic judo prowess. He didn't press Russian demands for relief of Soviet-era debt, and in his bilateral meeting with Clinton, spent little time going over familiar arguments against the US's missile defence plan. He told the other leaders he was unsure how to interpret North Korea's latest interest in using other countries' space launch capacity to conduct research in space. Putin had met the North Korean leader, Kim Jong-Il, the previous week. He was already trying to act as an intermediary between North Korea and its critics in the West. North Korea was another old Russian ally, and Moscow became increasingly involved in seeking to defuse the nuclear showdown between Pyongyang and the United States. Tony Blair was delighted by Putin's performance, saying the Russian president had 'made a very good start at the G8'. The prime minister's spokesman also said people felt that Putin had made 'a strong and favourable impression' at the Okinawa summit.

When George W. Bush beat Al Gore in America's presidential election in November 2000, some Russian politicians wryly suggested sending international election observers to oversee the Florida recounts. Florida's 'hanging' and 'pregnant' chads became a bit of a laughing-stock, as Florida's antiquated and technically inferior voting system led to a full-scale legal dispute over the outcome of the poll. Worse still, allegations persisted that some voters from ethnic minorities had been deliberately excluded from Florida's election register to benefit the Republicans.

In the event, as the US Supreme Court ruled Bush the winner (on a minority of the popular vote), Moscow found itself contemplating its future relationship with the new administration. Whatever Putin had told Clinton in Moscow, the Democrats and Al Gore were a known quantity, with an established and generally supportive policy. Clinton had consistently shown interest in Russia's economic and political development, and tried to keep Moscow onboard over issues like the Balkans, albeit with mixed success. The Republicans, on the other hand, had made a campaign issue of the fact that in their view, the Democrats had focused too much on personalities in Russia, rather than policies. To a certain extent they were right. President Clinton had given Boris Yeltsin almost uncritical support at home, through his unconstitutional dissolution of parliament and bombardment of the Moscow White House in 1993, to his re-election in 1996. Clinton had turned up at a pre-election Moscow summit with the sole aim of endorsing Yeltsin as Russia's leader. Hitching his star so closely to a mercurial and unpredictable character like Yeltsin was always going to be risky, even if Washington thought he was better than the likely Communist alternative.

Bush's new team soon made it pretty clear they were intent on 'down-grading' relations with Russia. Condoleezza Rice, the national security adviser, was a Russian-speaking Soviet expert and former Cold War warrior who had served under George Bush senior. During the Clinton era she returned to Stanford where she became the university's youngest provost, and the first woman and non-white person to hold the post. Rice was supported by Donald Rumsfeld, who was further out on the Republican right and a former defence secretary under Gerald Ford. Back in 1975 he had been the youngest ever US defence secretary; under George W. Bush, he was the oldest. Dick Cheney, vice-president and defence secretary under George Bush senior during the first Gulf War, completed the hardline triumvirate. The trio generally thought Russia was politically, economically and militarily washed up. In their view, it wasn't worth the effort of developing a close relationship with Russia, and the country had exacerbated its position by squandering billions of dollars of financial aid.

Leaning heavily on the hardline triumvirate, George W. Bush freely admitted to Britain's man in Washington at the time, Sir Christopher Meyer, that he didn't have a clue about foreign policy. Colin Powell, secretary of state and former chairman of the joint chiefs of staff during the Gulf War's Operation Desert Storm in 1991, was more moderate and inclined towards engagement, but struggled to win influence in the White House. Prominent US think-tanks supported a hardline stance towards Russia, reporting that the country had effectively become a kleptocracy over the previous decade, a view shared by the influential Washington-based Center for Strategic and International Studies. The CSIS's 2000 study on 'Russian Organized Crime and Corruption' made exceedingly grim reading, portraying a picture of endemic corruption, organized crime and graft in high places. One chapter heading was entitled 'The Russian Federation as a Criminal-Syndicalist State'.

US–Russian relations were further strained by a spy scandal which broke in 2001 only two months after George W. Bush came to power. Fifty Russian diplomats were expelled from Washington DC after being accused of spying. The mass expulsions were the US's response to the arrest earlier that year of Robert Hanssen, a senior FBI counter-intelligence agent who had been caught red-handed selling secrets to the Russians. Hanssen had been working for the Russians for twenty-two years, which somewhat undermined KGB defector Vasily Mitrokhin's confident assurances to British secret services that the Russians had failed in recent times to penetrate Western intelligence agencies. In a classic 'tit-for-tat' retaliation,

Moscow expelled four US diplomats for 'activities incompatible with their status', the usual diplomatic euphemism for spying. Hanssen had passed the Russians 6,000 pages of documents and twenty-seven computer disks, and told them the Americans had dug a surveillance tunnel under their Washington Embassy. In return, the fifty-six-year-old FBI agent had received illicit payments amounting to about $600,000. Hanssen tried to turn the tables on his employers, accusing the FBI of 'criminal negligence' in making it so easy for him to spy for the former Soviet Union, and its successor state, Russia. What the Hanssen case did indicate was how some of the old Cold War rivalries persisted. The 'spying game' continued unabated, as both sides' nuclear submarines unceasingly played-out games of hide and seek in the Barents Sea and elsewhere. The whole *Kursk* disaster had displayed Russia's suspicion of Western espionage, and exposed the military's perhaps justifiable paranoia. Russia had reason to be suspicious of the West. Both sides knew that each was up to all their old tricks.

While the spy scandal further soured relations with the new administration in Washington, Moscow fretted as the Bush team showed no sign of wanting to meet Russia's new president. The Kremlin kept pressing for a meeting, with no result. The message from Bush's people was that Moscow no longer counted, so a Bush–Putin summit was not on the cards. Worse, the Bush administration described Russia as a problem and potential adversary, and loudly denounced Clinton's Russian policies as an abject failure. Condoleezza Rice, the national security adviser, was one of those who had been quoted referring to Russia as 'problematic' and a possible enemy. At the same time, Donald Rumsfeld, the hawkish defence secretary, had flatly refused to meet his Russian counterpart Sergei Ivanov, despite the fact that both men had attended the same Munich security conference earlier in the year. Publicly snubbed, Putin busied himself by meeting everyone but the most powerful man in the world. In the first four months of his presidency, showing that Russia had an alternative set of friends, Putin visited China,

North Korea and Cuba. This diplomatic display fooled no one, least of all Putin himself. He knew that the importance of Russia's relationship with the United States surpassed all others. Politically, strategically, economically and militarily, relations with America were crucial to Russia's place in the world, and perhaps to its very survival as a sovereign state. A hostile United States could undermine Russia's economy or let it sink, isolate Moscow internationally, encourage separatism (*in extremis*) and diminish its influence with its neighbours. No other country, in Europe or Asia, could come close to matching the power and authority of the United States. Against this background, a nervous Igor Ivanov, Russia's veteran foreign minister, confided to Colin Powell, the secretary of state, that he would be sacked unless Washington agreed to a meeting between the two leaders soon.

The impasse was finally broken by a bilateral summit in Ljubljana, Slovenia, in June 2001. The meeting between the two presidents was slotted into President Bush's first visit to Europe since his election, part of a five-nation tour and one of his relatively rare visits to the continent. Before meeting Putin, Bush's tour had not gone particularly well. Although he had received a warm welcome in Poland, the preceding acrimonious EU–US summit in Gothenburg had laid bare divisions over America's missile defence shield and refusal to ratify the Kyoto Protocol on limiting greenhouse gas emissions. European Union leaders pointedly issued a statement calling for action to tackle nuclear proliferation, and a 'global and multilateral approach' to missile defence, including an international conference on the issue. President Bush reiterated Washington's commitment to NATO expansion and the new democracies of Eastern Europe, while promising 'partnership' and 'consultation' with Russia and Europe. 'All of Europe's democracies, from the Baltic to the Black Sea and all that lie between, should have the same chance for security and freedom – and the same chance to join the institutions of Europe – as Europe's old democracies,' he said. Poland, Hungary and the Czech Republic had already

joined NATO in 1999, and the Baltic States were queuing up to join
the Atlantic Alliance. As far as Russia was concerned, Bush stated he
would tell Putin his country was part of Europe and 'therefore does
not need a buffer zone of insecure states separating it from Europe.
NATO, even as it grows, is no enemy of Russia.' But Bush also made
it plain that whatever the Europeans or Russians thought, the
Republicans were determined to break with Bill Clinton's cosy foreign policy and impose their own brand of 'new realism'. The world's
only superpower would get its way with cooperation or without it,
and Washington's will would prevail regardless.

This 'get tough' approach with Europe played well in the States
but didn't seem to augur well for the Bush–Putin summit.
Beforehand, Putin had joined the 'Shanghai Five' to relaunch a new
regional and security body called the 'Shanghai Cooperation
Forum.' The forum comprised the original five members of China,
Russia, Kazakhstan, Kyrgyzstan and Tajikistan, with the addition of
Uzbekistan. Although mainly concerned with Islamic separatism,
extremism and terrorism in Central Asia, the group condemned the
US's missile defence plan and backed the 1972 ABM treaty. Putin's
Shanghai sojourn appeared to be another Russian attempt to use the
'Chinese card' to rein in the United States. While Russian diplomats
generally distrust China, traditionally Moscow has found it useful to
implicitly threaten Washington with an eastern strategic alliance.
China was Russia's largest arms market, and the two countries were
rapidly developing closer trade and energy links. Beijing, opposed to
the US missile defence shield, found it attractive to strengthen
Moscow's negotiating hand. The Chinese were also worried the
defence shield might be extended to Taiwan, which they still viewed
as a breakaway province. In reality, neither China nor Russia is interested in a full-blown alliance which would alienate and confront
the United States. There is simply too much at stake for both countries to 'take on' Washington.

The EU Gothenburg summit had left a question mark over
future relations between America's traditional European allies and

the new Republican administration in Washington. Unlike Clinton, Bush had not wooed and won over Europe's leaders, or pushed the right buttons. Now all the talk in Europe was about America's 'unilateralist' tendencies and the imposition of the *Pax Americana*. Yet George Bush was determined to come home with a clear foreign policy success if at all possible. If he could win Russia's acquiescence to US plans for a missile defence shield, this would undoubtedly make Bush's European tour a resounding triumph. The rancour at Gothenburg would be swiftly forgotten. For his own reasons, Putin was willing to play ball, up to a point. Putin also needed to make the summit a success and start the new US–Russian relationship off on the right footing. An acrimonious summit would be a disaster for the Russians, confirming their weakness and marginalizing Moscow for years to come. So both men had a vested interest in the Slovenian summit's success.

At Ljubljana on Saturday 16 June 2001, George Bush astonished his staff and the world's press by veering from studied disinterest in Putin and all things Russian to wholehearted emotional engagement. The dramatic U-turn in Republican policy towards Russia was mind-boggling. Suddenly, Russia counted again, and all the talk was of 'partnership' between 'allies', albeit in Colin Powell's phrase with a small 'a'. The hundred-minute meeting at a sixteenth-century renaissance-era castle in Ljubljana, Slovenia's capital, ended in something approaching a love-fest. The two men emerged into the sunlight beaming like new lovers. Vladimir Putin, the old courtier, had worked his charms on the US President. Bush told the assembled press that the two men had had a very good meeting. 'I looked the man in the eye,' said President Bush. 'I was able to get a sense of his soul. I found him to be very straightforward and trustworthy.' He had invited Putin to his Texas ranch later that year, and in return been invited to Moscow. 'I wouldn't have invited him to my ranch if I didn't trust him.' George Bush heaped praise on the Russian leader, gushingly describing him as 'an honest and straightforward man who loves his country. He loves his family. We share a lot of values.' Some of the international press pilloried Bush for his instant judgement on Putin, which seemed to rely more on extra-sensory perception than cool reflection. The *Washington Post* wrote that Bush's 'easy trust in the former KGB man makes Mr Bush look naïve'. Chechnya, Russia's crackdown against the independent media, and the country's past profligacy were all forgotten.

Nevertheless, Condi Rice, not for the first time, raced to keep up with her boss's pronouncements. 'No one has ever said that it's not a good thing for the president of Russia and the president of the United States to have a good, warm relationship,' she elucidated. 'This president has been very clear that he wants a good relationship with President Putin.' The rest of the administration shuffled into line. Rice noted how well the two leaders had got along. 'Both men connected. They have a sense of humour. It was not a very scripted meeting,' she said. Rice summed up the summit as 'quite remarkable'. The mood of chumminess at Ljubljana continued as Bush told the press Putin had the best interests of his people at heart. He had told his Russian counterpart he had named one of his daughters after his mother, in the interests of good family relations. Putin told Bush he had done the same. 'Mr President,' Bush had told Putin, 'you are a diplomat too.' It was time to get beyond the old Cold War mentality of mistrust and forge a new relationship built on mutual respect, Bush said. 'Russia is not the enemy of the United States,' Bush added. 'After our meeting today I'm convinced it can be our strong partner and friend, more than people could imagine.' Bush also promised to help Russia join the World Trade Organization, saying the US would work with Moscow 'toward that end'. Putin looked extremely happy with the outcome of the talks, saying the frankness of the meeting had exceeded his expectations, and he nodded enthusiastically in agreement with many of Bush's comments. Putin said he was 'counting on a pragmatic relationship between Russia and the US'. Responding to Bush's warm words, he continued: 'When a president of a great power says he wants to see Russia as a partner, and maybe even as an ally, this is worth so much to us.'

Along with the bonhomie and mutual back-slapping, the Americans were delighted with what they saw as a crucial Russian concession. Although Putin insisted on the validity and value of the 1972 ABM treaty, which banned missile defence, the Russians said they were willing to discuss a deal. For the US, it meant the Russians were willing to discuss either the amendment or scrapping of the ABM treaty, so allowing them to proceed with their missile defence shield. Bush and his team quickly understood this was a key concession which they could parade at home as a foreign policy triumph. Both countries' foreign and defence ministers would meet to discuss an agreement. Over the next few weeks four US ministers would arrive in Moscow for talks. The commerce and treasury secretaries would discuss the potential for future US trade and investment, while the defence secretary and secretary of state would hold talks on the proposed new global security agreement, including missile defence. Colin Powell said that he and his Russian counterpart, Igor Ivanov, would be in charge of the negotiations, and that expert joint committees would be set up to discuss the 'new security framework'. Putin delighted the Americans by saying both countries bore a 'responsibility for building a new architecture of world security'. This tied in with Bush's argument that the ABM treaty was past its sell-by date, and that after more than a decade since the end of the Cold War it was, in his words, 'time to move beyond mutually assured destruction and towards mutually earned respect'.

Putin, not for the last time, played a weak hand well. He had wooed and wowed the US president, and made concessions without giving significant ground. Putin had won time over the ABM treaty, which he knew Bush's new Republican administration was determined to scrap with or without Russian consent. Negotiations on the ABM treaty could win Russia some concessions on missile defence or elsewhere, and ally it with Washington's own sceptical allies in Europe. Always the pragmatist, Putin rarely railed against the inevitable. Most important of all, Ljubljana made Vladimir Putin and Russia a real player on the world stage. The fear that the new US administration would simply ignore Russia, treating it like some impoverished Third World basket-case, had receded. Bizarrely, Bush could be accused of falling into the very trap he had berated the Clinton administration for. Once again, US policy towards Russia looked primarily focused on the leader. Bush had personalized the US–Russian relationship as much as Clinton ever had with his old buddy the bear-hugging Boris Yeltsin. Putin and the establishment in Moscow were mightily relieved with the outcome. As a bonus, it looked as if Bush genuinely liked Russia's most famous ex-KGB colonel. It was an unlikely partnership, and it reflected well on Putin that he had carried it off against the odds.

Putin had made a good start on building a close relationship with George Bush and the United States, but what transformed everything was Tuesday 11 September 2001. The terrorist suicide attacks on the Twin Towers and the Pentagon shocked the world and jolted the Bush administration out of its cocooned insularity. A president who couldn't remember the name of the president of Pakistan (among others) had a crash course in global diplomacy. Vladimir Putin was the first world leader to ring Bush on September 11th to express his personal condolences and offer his country's unconditional moral support. It was a masterful stroke of diplomacy, taken on Putin's own initiative. Most of Moscow's political and military elite favoured taking a more neutral stance, in order to see how Russia might exploit America's discomfiture. The US's status as the world's sole hyperpower still rankled in Russia, with even Yeltsin some years before accusing Washington of insti-gating a 'cold peace' and trying to impose its will through a unipolar world order. Old suspicions and rivalries died hard. To his credit, Putin ignored his advisers and embraced the United States in its time of need. Public opinion in Russia backed their president's stance, with an outpouring of sympathy and affection for the suf-fering of the American people. Mounds of flowers were placed outside the US Embassy in Moscow. Now, people thought, the Americans were suffering at the hands of terrorists just like the

Russians had before them. The once invincible superpower looked human and vulnerable. A hundred Russian nationals had also died in the attack on New York's World Trade Center, bringing the full horror of the loss home to Russia's citizens. In the UK, the Queen's Guards outside Buckingham Palace played the US national anthem in solidarity and sympathy with the American people. Of course, Putin's motives weren't entirely altruistic and compassionate, to put it kindly. September 11th provided a remarkable opportunity to advance Russia's interests, and Putin seized the chance with both hands.

Russia had been arguing for years that it was fighting Islamic extremists in Chechnya. Russian diplomats had tried, so far unsuccessfully, to make parallels with Britain's fight against terrorism in Northern Ireland. September 11th gave Putin the opportunity to show solidarity with the United States. Now Moscow could plausibly argue that the West was confronting a threat Russia had known about for years: international terrorism rooted in Islamic extremism, which sought to extend its reach across the globe. In Russia, security officials referred to it as 'the threat to the south'. Putin had time and again said the Chechen rebels sought not only to seize Chechnya, but to spread their form of Islamic fundamentalism throughout the Russian Federation and Central Asia. Russia, it was said in Moscow, was acting as the bulwark of Western civilization, protecting the rest of the civilized world against terrorism and Islamic extremism. Osama bin Laden, the evil mastermind behind the US atrocities, had known links to Chechnya. Backed by the CIA, Pakistani intelligence (ISI) and British SAS special forces, the Saudi-born Osama bin Laden was one of the many foreign mujahideen who had fought against the Soviet occupation of Afghanistan from 1979 onwards. Like so many other Western-inspired insurgencies, the West's support for the anti-Soviet mujahideen would come back to haunt it. Chechen separatists had also fought and trained in Afghanistan alongside the Taliban, and were later to be discovered fighting against US-led forces before the fall of Kabul. Suddenly, Russia became a key ally in the emerging war against global terrorism.

It was a myth that Putin 'allowed' the United States to use bases in Central Asia as launchpads against the Taliban and al-Qaeda in Afghanistan. The point was that Putin was again ahead of the game. Within days of September 11th, several Central Asian countries, formerly part of the Soviet Union, were openly inviting US forces into their countries. Putin simply recognized the inevitable and acquiesced in the face of America's use of military bases in Russia's 'backyard'. Some of Putin's advisers were again slower to adjust to the new realities. Following a NATO meeting on 13 September, Defence Minister Sergei Ivanov told the press: 'I don't see any basis for even the hypothetical possibility of NATO military operations on the territory of Central Asian nations that belong to the Commonwealth of Independent States (CIS).' He then announced a meeting of the twelve CIS defence ministers to discuss the crisis, comprising all the defence ministers of the former Soviet Union, excluding the Baltic States (who were not CIS members). On Wednesday 19 September, the *New York Times* reported a meeting between President Bush, Colin Powell and Igor Ivanov, the Russian foreign minister. Ivanov expressed concerns about the use of military force in Central Asia, but pledged to provide intelligence and cooperate in other ways. Russia's long occupation of Afghanistan throughout the 1980s had provided the country's security agencies with invaluable local intelligence (they had run the Afghan intelligence service), and Moscow knew more about the location of Osama bin Laden's al-Qaeda bases than Washington. The Russians could identify 55 bases in Afghanistan used by al-Qaeda (meaning 'the base') and their allies, and backed the Northern Alliance, the ruling Taliban's implacable opponents.

Even so, Sergei Ivanov and General Anatoly Kvashnin, the armed forces chief of staff, made it clear that they too opposed the US using Central Asia as a launchpad for an attack on Afghanistan. America, in their view, could not be permitted to base military forces within Russia's traditional 'sphere of influence'. However, events were moving too swiftly for Moscow's military elite to contain. On 19 September, the same day as the Ivanov-Bush-Powell meeting, the *Kansas City Star* reported the US Defence Department as saying that US planes were already being deployed to the former Soviet republics of Uzbekistan and Tajikistan. Dozens of fighters, bombers, tankers and spy planes were dispatched to the Persian Gulf, the Indian Ocean and Central Asia. No matter what Moscow said, US forces were on their way and would be based in Central Asia, adjacent to the Afghan border. President Islam Karimov of Uzbekistan in particular was no Moscow puppet, and the authoritarian ruler had repeatedly displayed his independence in the past. Russia did not have the strength or authority to stop the Uzbeks inviting the Americans in, which Karimov no doubt thought would be useful to counter his own Islamic terrorists and Moscow's overweening regional ambitions. Eliminating the Taliban would also open up the possibilities of trade, pipelines and transport to the south and the Indian Ocean. When the Americans did invade Afghanistan, they would find themselves fighting some Uzbek fundamentalists of the Islamic Movement of Uzbekistan (IMU), trained and partly funded by the Taliban. Three thousand IMU sympathizers were imprisoned inside Uzbekistan, and there were more active abroad. Human rights groups regularly accused the Uzbek authorities of ignoring democratic and human rights, and engaging in brutal torture. Tajikistan and Kyrgyzstan, bedeviled by Islamic fundamentalists operating out of Afghanistan, would also welcome a US military presence in their countries. After a security council meeting in Sochi on the Black Sea on 22 September, and following consultations with Central Asia's leaders, Putin turned necessity into a virtue and endorsed the region's de facto military cooperation with the United States. Putin the pragmatist saw little diplomatic or strategic gain in spitting in the wind.

In a telephone conversation held on 28 September, Putin and Blair discussed the necessity of joint action against terrorism, and how the two countries could cooperate over Afghanistan. The Russian president promised to provide air corridors for humanitarian operations, share intelligence and continue supplying weapons to Moscow's allies fighting the Taliban in northern Afghanistan. But Putin also sought to calm Muslims at home by pointing out that terrorism should not be equated with Islam. One in seven of Russia's population is Muslim, and Putin was wary of alienating the country's overwhelmingly moderate Islamic community. Nevertheless, he threw his support behind the US-led anti-terrorist coalition, and urged the predominantly Muslim nations of Central Asia to follow suit. Landlocked Uzbekistan, for example, is 80 per cent Muslim. Both Uzbekistan and Tajikistan feared a possible flood of refugees from neighbouring Afghanistan if the security situation deteriorated. Broadcasting on Russian television, Putin said: 'Our countries are multi-ethnic and multi-religious, and it's not simply counterproductive but harmful to mix terrorism and Islam. Terrorists covering themselves up with Islamic slogans have nothing in common with this world religion.' Meanwhile, less than a week after September 11th, Chechen Islamic separatists launched a new major ground offensive against Chechnya's second city, Gudermes. NATO invoked Article 5 for the first time in its history, declaring the September 11th terrorist atrocities an attack on all nineteen member states. Somewhat embarrassingly for the Atlantic Alliance, Washington ignored the gesture. The Bush administration was out for revenge, and didn't want to be tied up in endless NATO committees debating the best form of response. Washington and the Pentagon had on occasion felt hamstrung during the Kosovo war, and wasn't prepared to repeat the experience in such a dire national emergency. Washington wanted retribution, and it wanted it now.

As the momentum for swift military action gathered pace, Putin upped the stakes. Arriving for the eighth EU–Russia summit in Brussels at the beginning of October 2001, the fight against international terrorism naturally topped the agenda. Putin was accompanied by thirty ministers and officials. Putin also used the visit to hold talks with Lord Robertson, British NATO secretary-general. During the Brussels summit Putin voiced his strongest support so far for the US-led anti-terrorist coalition. He said the fight against terrorism would only be effective 'if we unite the efforts of the entire international community'. He stated that Russia was ready to work closely with the West by 'profoundly' changing its relations with NATO and the EU's embryonic military structures. Comparing international terrorism to a bacteria, which 'adapts to the organism bearing it', Putin went on to criticize Saudi Arabia, whose nationals had largely perpetrated the terrorist attacks on the Twin Towers. He vociferously condemned the Saudis for refusing to let America strike at Afghanistan from military bases on its territory.

On Chechnya, Putin's message seemed to be getting through. A few days before the EU summit, German Chancellor Gerhard Schroeder, previously one of Putin's fiercest critics on Chechnya, said the Chechen conflict might have to be re-evaluated in the light of what happened in the United States. The previous week Lord Robertson had met Sergei Ivanov, and emphasized that Russia had a right to defend its territorial integrity. In Brussels, Putin told reporters: 'For us there are obvious links between international terrorism and those who have taken up arms to resolve whatever problems there might be in the northern Caucasus, above all in Chechnya.' He added that the 1999 apartment bombings in Moscow and elsewhere bore 'the same signature as the suicide plane attacks on New York and Washington'.

Putin had apparently come to Brussels armed with a 'shopping list' of demands, most of which were met to some degree or other. First, he wanted Russia to be involved in the work of the EU's political and security committee, which was responsible for overseeing the European Security and Defence Policy (ESDP). The EU's military structure was rapidly evolving, with a 60,000 strong Rapid Reaction Force due to be in place by early 2003, and Russia wanted to keep an eye on developments. The summit agreed that Russia's EU ambassador would be consulted on a monthly basis. Second,

Putin was keen to move ahead with Russia's application to join the World Trade Organization. The EU obliged by agreeing to accelerate preparatory work on this. Finally, and more trickily, Putin wanted an enhanced relationship with NATO. President Bush had made it clear in Warsaw that Russia would have no veto over further NATO enlargement, but Putin was still unhappy about the three former Soviet Baltic states joining the Atlantic Alliance. He repeated Moscow's line that NATO had no need to enlarge because it no longer faced a hostile Soviet Union. NATO would be on Russia's very borders, and within 93 miles of its second city, St Petersburg. 'As for NATO expansion,' President Putin told his European partners, 'one can take another, entirely new, look at this – if NATO takes on a different shade and is becoming a political organization.' He added: 'Of course we would reconsider our position with regard to such expansion if we were to feel involved in such processes.' Russia wanted NATO to move away from being a solely military alliance towards becoming a political organization, and one where Moscow had a real say. Vladimir Putin had laid his cards on the table, and waited for NATO to deliver.

Putin expected great benefits from his whole-hearted support of the US-led coalition against terrorism, as the Brussels summit indicated. In America's sights were the Afghan Taliban, the Islamic fundamentalists who were giving shelter to Osama bin Laden and his al-Qaeda terrorists. At least they were first on the list. Some senior administration officials, led by the hawkish Paul D. Wolfowitz, deputy secretary of defence, and I. Lewis Libby, chief of staff to Vice-President Dick Cheney, had pressed almost from the outset for attacks not only against al-Qaeda in Afghanistan, but also for a broad-based military campaign against other terrorist bases in Iraq and the Lebanon's Bekaa valley. The conservatives' avowed aim was to topple the Iraqi dictator irrespective of his role in the US atrocities, and a week after the Twin Towers a number of them circulated a letter calling upon President Bush to 'make a determined effort to remove Saddam Hussein from power'. Although they would temporarily settle for Afghanistan, a hardcore of conservative senior administration officials kept Iraq on their future hit-list.

By the time Putin showed up in Washington and at George Bush's Crawford ranch in Texas, the Taliban had been routed by the US-led coalition and Kabul had just fallen. Before arriving in the US capital, Putin told American reporters in Moscow that Russia–US cooperation was 'on a scale . . . that never existed and which was difficult to imagine' before September 11th. Apart from giving his wholehearted support for the US inspired 'war on terrorism', Putin had underlined the new style of relationship with Washington by closing Russia's Cold War bases in Cuba and Vietnam. Sandy Vershbow, US ambassador in Moscow, admitted Russia's support in the war against terrorism was not just moral: 'Except for the UK, the US has had a broader package of support from Russia than any other ally.' Joseph Biden, Democratic chairman of the Senate foreign relations committee, went further. 'It appears, on the face of it, that no Russian leader since Peter the Great has looked as far west as Putin seems to have,' he said. 'The proof of the pudding will be in the eating, but thus far it seems as though there is a genuine attempt to establish a genuine relationship with Europe and the United States that has not existed before.' James Baker, former secretary of state to George W. Bush's father, even suggested that Russia could join NATO. Back home in Moscow, many of the political and military-security elite were looking askance at Putin's stance, and wondered whether all his tactical concessions in the face of US hegemony would pay off. 'Within two or three months, he has to demonstrate that he has got some positive results,' said Andrei Ryabov, of the Carnegie Moscow Centre. Without some signs that Putin's tactical retreat was working, he might find himself in serious trouble at home. As he left for Washington, Putin called for Russia to have a decision-making role in NATO. Russia's 1990s strategy of building up the Organization for Security and Cooperation in Europe (OSCE) as Europe's primary security body had failed to make any headway. The OSCE had remained a largely toothless talking shop, hence Putin's renewed interest in having a greater say in NATO. Kosovo had proven once and for all that the only security organization that counted in Europe was the Atlantic Alliance. Yet, for the first time in a decade, Russia was able to come to a US summit with the opportunity to negotiate for concessions, rather than beg for them. September 11th (and Putin's handling of it) meant that Russia was no longer a supplicant at the master's table. Russia's strong economy and commodity prices meant that Moscow had no need to beg for loans or international aid. Fortuitously, Putin was for once in a strong position vis-à-vis the United States, but he still needed results.

After meeting for a couple of hours in the White House on Tuesday 13 November, President Bush rewarded Putin's loyal support by announcing a unilateral two-thirds cut in the US's nuclear arsenal over the next ten years. For this, their fourth summit, the two leaders were pictured sitting in the Oval Office, shaking hands in front of the fireplace under the White House's sparkling chandeliers. The US would cut the number of deployed strategic nuclear warheads to between 1,700 and 2,200 over the next decade, a reduction that Bush said would be 'full [sic] consistent with American security'. Washington made the calculation that in the modern world, around 2,000 strategic nuclear warheads were more than enough to deter and finish off any possible opponent. Additionally, the Bush administration hoped the nuclear weapon cuts would encourage the Russians to accept the US's missile defence shield and discard the ABM treaty. Putin, who was aware the announcement would be made before arriving in Washington, sat with a poker face. The Russian president welcomed the move, and said Moscow would reply in kind. In a later speech at the Russian Embassy in Washington, Putin proposed a two-thirds reduction in Moscow's strategic nuclear arsenal. He described the talks as 'constructive, interesting and useful', adding in technospeak: 'We evaluate the preliminary results as extremely positive.' But he also made it clear he wanted an agreement in writing, something the Americans said wasn't necessary. 'For the Russian part, [we] are prepared to present all our agreements in a treaty form, including the issue of verification and control.' The Russians were worried that America's unilateral nuclear arms cuts might be unverifiable, and lack the legal force of a treaty. President Bush once again turned on his Texan charm. 'I looked the man in the eye and shook his hand, and if we need to write it down on a piece of paper, I'll be glad to do that.' Bush was keen to underline the summit's significance. 'This is a new day in the long history of Russian–American relations, a day of progress and a day of hope,' he said. 'We are transferring our relationship from one of hostility and suspicion to one based on cooperation and trust.' Endearingly, when he discussed Russia and Putin with his aides in private, Bush called Putin 'Pootie-Poot.'

Bush and Putin also agreed to make preventing weapons of mass destruction reaching terrorists a priority, and announced cooperation on limiting the spread of biological, nuclear and chemical weapons. There was no movement over Bush's request for Russia to abandon the ABM treaty, although after September 11th, the planned missile defence shield had ceased being a controversial issue in the US. Crucially for Putin, Bush said new cooperation and consultation agreements were needed between NATO and Russia. However, the high point of this summit was supposed to be taking Putin to Bush's home ranch in Crawford, Texas. Following their relatively short talks in the White House, Putin was whisked off to rural Crawford. Only a few foreign leaders have had the privilege of visiting Bush's Texan home – Tony Blair, President Jiang Zemin of China and Crown Prince Abdullah of Saudi Arabia being three (France's President Chirac is unlikely to be invited).

On his home turf, President Bush's homey charm and charisma were at full force. It was Putin's turn to be suitably impressed, with him and his entourage treated to a barbecue and country music. In the end, the two days in Crawford were more about bonding than anything else. Bush drove Putin around in his pick-up truck, while the small population of nearby Crawford was overwhelmed by the accompanying media circus. On the ranch,

Putin ate traditional Texan rancher fare including huge T-bone beef steaks, and danced the 'country-eyed joe' with Condi Rice, who taught him the steps. Quite how Condoleezza Rice, herself from Birmingham, Alabama, knew the dance is a mystery. Pictures of Putin dancing the traditional Texan country dance with the US national security adviser must be priceless. Agreement on missile defence and scrapping or amending the ABM treaty eluded the leaders, as did any consensus on sanctions against Iraq and Russia's nuclear and other supplies to Iran. Putin hammered away on NATO, telling an audience at Houston's Rice University that all NATO leaders 'should recognize that if there is an ally that can make a full contribution in countering [these threats], that ally is Russia'. The Crawford summit was essentially about atmospherics and building a personal relationship between the two men. 'The relationship began in a very strong fashion in Ljubljana and it's become even more so since then,' said White House spokesman Ari Fleischer.

Unlike Tony Blair, who usually met Putin with just one foreign policy adviser and interpreter on each side, Bush tended to have several advisers at every encounter. Sergei Prikhodko was Putin's adviser; from June 2000 Sir David Manning (later ambassador to the US) was Tony Blair's. But Bush, who can master his briefs despite the widespread belief to the contrary, at least did without the 'idiot' prompt cards used by Ronald Reagan and, surprisingly, former Vice-President Al Gore. Interestingly, Putin later developed a real one-on-one relationship with Chancellor Gerhard Schroeder, where to the despair of their advisers, they frequently talk alone in German.

Despite the warmth of Crawford, it was actually the British who succeeded in pressing Russia's case for a closer relationship with NATO. Tony Blair wrote to Lord Robertson, NATO's secretary-general and Britain's former defence secretary, and the other NATO leaders. Blair and his advisers believed the existing five-year-old NATO–Russia Joint Council, which met monthly, had proved an ineffective 'talking shop' that had achieved little. The Russians felt the same. The British prime minister suggested replacing it with a

'Russia North Atlantic Council', giving Moscow a bigger and more meaningful say in the military organization. The new body would discuss security cooperation in the fight against terrorism, counter- ing proliferation of weapons of mass destruction, peacekeeping operations and combating new threats. However, Russia wouldn't be part of NATO's military structure or have a veto over NATO's oper- ations.

At a twenty-four-hour summit in the UK on 21–22 December 2001, Tony Blair promised Putin that Britain would press for greater Russian involvement in NATO and support future membership of the WTO. The talks at Chequers, the prime minister's Buckingham- shire country residence, was set against the background of Bush's decision the week before to withdraw from the 1972 ABM anti- ballistic treaty. Both wives were present, allowing for a group photo opportunity in the grounds of the splendid sixteenth-century red- brick residence. Blair was convinced Russia should be rewarded for its support in the war against terror, a position strongly endorsed by France. Putin, it was known, needed to show his domestic audience something in return for his wholehearted backing of the US-led anti-terror coalition. Earlier divisions within the Bush adminis- tration over Blair's NATO proposals had threatened to scupper the whole idea. Donald Rumsfeld and the Pentagon were known to be unhappy with the plan for a new NATO–Russia council. Rumsfeld, concerned that Russia might gain a veto over NATO decision- making, lobbied hard against Blair's idea. He clashed with Colin Powell, US secretary of state, who backed the proposal.

Some of NATO's east European members (and potential mem- bers) were not keen on giving Russia an enhanced role within NATO. Many, like the Baltic States, were joining the alliance to escape Russian influence or the possibility of future clashes. The US administration played for time as the State Department and the Pentagon slugged it out, with Powell for once coming out on top. Back at Chequers, the British and Russians agreed to set up a joint working group to pool intelligence on terrorism. Senior officials from the Foreign Office, the Ministry of Defence and MI6 would join their Russian counterparts to coordinate the hunt for Osama bin Laden and al-Qaeda. The joint working group would formalize the increased cooperation on terrorism since September 11th. A senior British source said: 'The cooperation there has been on terrorism has been very close, particularly in terms of intelligence. Our intelligence people sit down with theirs and go through some very detailed stuff. There is a sense of mutual trust. The intelligence people are really struck by the way the Russians have engaged with them.' Whether this cooperation would continue if the coalition against terrorism fell apart, was a different matter. It did, however, bring some useful results in the war against terror. A raid in January 2003 on a flat in Wood Green, north London, discovered traces and production facilities for the poison ricin, which led back to al-Qaeda and Chechen guerrilla training camps in Georgia's Pankisi Gorge on Chechnya's border. A joint intelligence 'sting' in August 2003 involving British, US and Russian secret services trapped an alleged illicit British arms dealer in New York, who was reportedly willing to supply terrorists. Hekmat Lakhani, a Briton of Indian origin, was charged in New York with attempting to sell an $85,000 Russian-made Igla shoulder-held surface-to-air missile to an undercover FBI agent, posing as an Islamic militant.

In any event, at Chequers, Blair delighted his guest by likening the 1999 apartment bombings with the September 11th attacks on the US. After the first round of talks, he said: 'People sometimes forget there were hundreds killed in Moscow before September 11th.' Putin looked surprised and grateful for his host's comments. Blair went on to say that Anglo–Russian relations were the warmest they had been for 'many years'. Responding, Putin said he had no wish to 'over-dramatize' the US decision to withdraw from the ABM treaty, which he naturally condemned. The British also pledged £12 million to help destroy stocks of Russian nuclear weapons. At a joint press conference at RAF Holton near Chequers, Blair again pleased Putin by enthusiastically supporting growing links between

Russia, the EU and NATO, while endorsing the Russian leader's claims that economic reforms were starting to turn his country around.

Following a meeting of NATO and Russian foreign ministers in the Icelandic capital Reykjavik on 13 May 2002, the Atlantic Alliance finally endorsed Blair's original proposal for a NATO–Russia council of twenty equal members. The new council met in Rome on 28 May 2002, where Putin gave a thoughtful speech and offered Russia's services as an intermediary in the stand-off between India and Pakistan. Incidentally, on a visit to India (an old ally and important arms importer) that December, a Russian microbiologist used vodka as a disinfectant to clean up the cutlery and plates used by Putin and Lyudmila at their hotel. Vodka maintains its place in Russian hearts as a miracle cure for all ills, even in the president's entourage. Apparently, the president's favourite dishes were tandoori preparations like chicken and prawns. The New Delhi visit followed a trip to China, and Putin's largely unsuccessful attempt to forge a strategic 'triangle' between the three powers to counterbalance US dominance. It was always an unlikely outcome, given the enduring hostility between India and China. Meanwhile, back in Rome, NATO confirmed its new working arrangements. As Blair had suggested, the new NATO–Russia council would discuss, decide and act on a range of issues from fighting terrorism, crisis management and peacekeeping, to combating the spread of nuclear, biological and chemical weapons. At around the same time and as part of a package deal, Washington and Moscow agreed deep cuts in their respective strategic nuclear arsenals. During a visit to Moscow and St Petersburg beginning on 24 May, President Bush and President Putin formally signed the treaty the Russians had craved for. The 'Treaty of Moscow', as it was called, was signed by both leaders inside Peter the Great's 300-year-old Kremlin Hall of St Andrew, surrounded by gilded pillars, ermine drapes and pictures of crucified saints. The treaty reduced each country's strategic stockpile by two-thirds, to between 1,700 and

2,200 warheads by 2012. A new bilateral commission would continue the US–Russia dialogue on nuclear disarmament. The treaty didn't cover the thousands of tactical nuclear weapons held by each side. Even so, it eased some worries about the US's nuclear intentions, coming a few months after the Pentagon's Nuclear Posture review, which named seven countries as potential threats. The seven countries listed by the US defence department were Russia, China, Iraq, Iran, Syria, Libya and North Korea. Donald Rumsfeld had to reassure Russia it was not in danger of becoming a nuclear target.

The two leaders in Moscow once again clashed over Russian nuclear and other exports to Iran, which President Bush had included (together with Iraq and North Korea) in his 'axis of evil' state-of-the-union address earlier in the year. Putin argued there was no risk of Russian technology being used for military purposes by Iran, and in any case, the civilian nuclear power station Moscow was building at Bushehr was no different to the one the US had offered to build for North Korea. If the US had questions about Iran, Russia had questions about missile programmes in Taiwan and other countries. The spat about Iran was the nadir of an otherwise harmonious summit. The two countries pledged to develop deeper economic cooperation, including an 'energy dialogue', and improve trade relations. President Bush promised to ask the US Congress to repeal the 1974 Jackson–Vanik amendment, which linked trade deals to Soviet emigration policy, especially Jewish emigration to Israel.

On a lighter note, President Bush had been caught on camera chewing a sweet, then having second thoughts and spitting it out as Putin was talking during their morning meeting at the May Moscow summit. The US president then completed a scheduled thirty-minute tour of the Kremlin and its churches and cathedrals in just seven, quite an achievement. After dinner at Putin's presidential dacha in Zavidovo, ninety miles north of Moscow, the presidents and their wives, Lyudmila and Laura, moved on to St Petersburg. In Putin's hometown, the trip began with a visit to the Piskarevsky memorial cemetery, where hundreds of thousands of Russians killed in the siege of Leningrad lie buried. The leaders moved on to the Hermitage Museum in the Tsars' old Winter Palace, and President Bush was allotted thirty minutes to browse around one of the largest and finest art collections in the world. After stopping off at Putin's old university, the 'George and Vlad show' answered questions from students, with Bush diplomatically praising his host's economic reforms and condemning the export tariffs still in place on Russian goods. President Bush got a little carried away, promising the students 'the most sophisticated seminar in international relations' they had ever heard. Some of the White House press corps in the audience started choking, valiantly trying to suppress a belly laugh.

In the evening, the presidents and their spouses attended a performance of the *Nutcracker* by the excellent Kirov Ballet at the city's Marinsky Theatre, and travelled up the Neva river to see the midnight sun. President Bush always seemed slightly taken aback by Russia's beauty, as if before he came he thought it was all concrete apartment blocks, tinny Lada cars and grim 1960s Peoples' Palaces. This was Bush's fifth meeting with Putin in a year, and if nothing else, he was learning a lot about Russia and the Russians.

So Putin got his Treaty of Moscow and a closer relationship with NATO. But all this was at a price. He had to back down on scrapping the ABM treaty (which he still labelled 'a mistake') and accept the US would press ahead with its missile defence shield regardless. The Pentagon started work on constructing the national missile defence system in Alaska before the ink on the Treaty of Moscow was dry. NATO enlargement was gathering pace, despite Moscow's long-standing opposition. The nineteen members would be joined in May 2004 by the three Baltic States, Slovakia, Slovenia, Bulgaria and Romania, taking Atlantic Alliance membership up to twenty-six. Russia had no veto over NATO action, and the issues it could jointly decide with the Alliance were strictly circumscribed, and didn't cover military operations. At an annual spend of $59 billion, Russia's 2000 defence budget was one-fifth the size of

America's, and represented one-eighth of NATO's combined military expenditure. In security terms, Russia was in danger of slipping further behind the Atlantic Alliance.

A sting in the tail of the Treaty of Moscow, criticized by arms control specialists, meant that not all nuclear weapons taken out of commission would be destroyed. The US could keep a majority of the 4,000 decommissioned nuclear warheads in storage, ready to be used a later date. This hardly suited Russia, which wanted to dismantle much of its obsolescent and costly nuclear arsenal. Moscow's response to all this, including the abandonment of the ABM treaty and America's missile defence deployment, came in August 2002. Russia announced plans to overhaul 144 'Satan' intercontinental ballistic missiles, which were to be scrapped by 2007 under the START II arms reduction treaty signed between Yeltsin and George Bush senior. Based in deep silos beyond the Ural Mountains, each Satan missile weighs 200 tonnes and can carry 10 warheads. The commander in chief of Russia's strategic nuclear forces, Colonel-General Nikolai Solovstov, said the missiles would be refurbished and kept fully operational until 2014, seven years longer than originally intended.

As part of the West's reward for Putin's support during the 'war on terror', Russia had been promised backing for its WTO membership bid, but talks became bogged down. Putin's firm commitment to the international war against terror came with the inevitable corollary of a US military presence in Central Asia. The Americans would soon also be sending troops to train the Georgian army in the Caucasus in 'anti-terrorist' operations. In fact, following the launch of the international war against terrorism, US global influence and reach had increased dramatically. US military forces were operating from Eastern Europe, across the Mediterranean, throughout the Middle East and Horn of Africa, across Central Asia and in Pakistan and Afghanistan. Western and specifically American influence and military might had not been so ubiquitous since the Second World War.

Meanwhile, Russia's influence in its very backyard was under assault, although the war against the Taliban meant that Moscow's troops based in Tajikistan were later supported by a new Russian military base in Kyrgyzstan (next to a US base). Much to the horror of the Afghans, Russian troops once again appeared in Afghanistan as part of the occupying coalition forces. Some Russian commentators and politicians saw the practical benefits of American involvement in the war against terror. Mikhail Margelov, chairman of the Federation Council's international affairs committee, saw the war in a positive light. 'In Afghanistan, the Americans are doing our job for us,' he said. 'I hate to say this, but fortunately for us the Americans got involved. In Georgia, before last week it was only our question. Now it is an American question. We share the responsibility.' Margelov added: 'We opened the first front against international terrorism in 1999 in Dagestan. Now the Americans have opened the second front. September 11th showed that we have a common enemy. Either we fight that together, or we will be killed.' The belief that Russia was fighting Islamic fundamentalism, and that the West had only belatedly woken up to the global threat of Islamic extremism, was a widely held view in the Russian Federation. While Putin had won some diplomatic victories after September 11th, these should not be overstated. What was important was that Russia and President Putin were firmly established on the world stage as a key player. Russia was undeniably a useful ally and partner for the West. That was not the case before September 11th.

The crisis over Iraq changed everything. Those who said Putin had fixed on developing a pro-Western, 'Westerncentric' or 'Eurocentric' foreign policy were left with egg on their faces. While it is certainly true that Putin has pursued what had been described as a 'multi-vectored' foreign policy, Iraq reminded everyone who had forgotten or never knew that Russia's foreign policy is about putting the strategic interests of Russia First. Before Iraq, Putin undoubtedly believed he could have it all, appearing European in

Europe, a transatlantic ally with the US, simultaneously an Asian and Eurasian power in Asia and the Far East, and a leader of the former Soviet republics in the Commonwealth of Independent States. While courting Europe and the US, he also signed cooperation agreements with North Korea and China (establishing a new 'strategic partnership' with the latter), and boosted Russian participation in APEC (Asia-Pacific Economic Cooperation), the Shanghai Cooperation Organization (SCO) the ASEAN Regional Forum (ARF), and the G8. At the same time, he resisted Japanese efforts to negotiate the return of the Pacific Kuril Islands (seized after the Second World War), and studiously avoided proceeding with ambitious but risky plans to unite with Belarus, under its unstable and dictatorial President Alexander Lukashenko. There is a joke in Russia about Lukashenko where the Belarusian leader says: 'I'm tired of being president. The coronation will be on Wednesday.' After the defeat of the Taliban in Afghanistan, Russia still maintained garrisons in Tajikistan, Kyrgyzstan and Georgia, quietly supporting separatist movements in the latter country and keeping Tbilisi firmly under Moscow's sway. Georgia's 'rose revolution', and the removal of weak and tainted president Eduard Shevardnadze in late 2003, was an unpleasant shock for the Kremlin. Control of essential energy supplies and strategic pipelines nevertheless ensured Russia exerted strong influence in Central Asia and will retain an iron grip on the Ukraine and Georgia for the foreseeable future.

Iraq shocked Putin because it proved Russia could not sustain its international balancing act. In choosing to oppose the United States over invading Iraq, Putin at once alienated a crucial partner, and one in which he had invested much effort. Putin's reaction to the Iraq crisis went through several phases. First, Russia tried to block US action through the United Nations, working in cooperation with France and Germany. As France and Russia were two of the five permanent members of the United Nations Security Council, this alliance was guaranteed to spell trouble for the US, especially since it only took one of the five to veto UN action. Second, when this failed, Putin and Russia displayed their usual impotent rage and distress at being by-passed. Third, when the dust settled, the Russians came to their senses, tried to make the best of a bad job, and sought to kiss and make up. Sadly, all this was highly predictable. Although Putin had made much of the fact that he was a new type of Russian leader, he acted just as Boris Yeltsin had before him over the NATO attack on Kosovo in 1999. Yeltsin had ranted and raved, and threatened to stop the West taking action against Serbian President Slobodan Milosevic and the massacres and 'ethnic cleansing' in Kosovo. The result was that the US by-passed the UN (where Russia threatened their veto) and bombed Serbia into submission. Putin witnessed all that at the time from close hand, yet went down the same path. Why did he do it and risk a major rift with the United States, which he knew was more important to Moscow than any other country? The possible gain from confrontation looked zero; the potential political and economic fallout appeared enormous.

One of the main explanations for Putin and Russia's behaviour was rooted in economics. Russia's economic stake in Saddam Hussein's regime was huge, and war threatened to lose Moscow billions of dollars. Iraq was a traditional Russian ally, and the friendship had given the USSR leverage and influence in the Middle East. Soviet-era debt owed by Iraq amounted to $8 billion, and Russian diplomats have said several times over the years that Moscow wanted its money back. Although Moscow was no fan of the Baghdad dictator, if Saddam was overthrown, would a new regime honour the debt? LUKoil, the massive Russian oil company, had signed a $20 billion contract in 1997 to drill in the Iraqi West Qurna oil field. Zarubezhneft, another Russian company, had been granted a concession to develop the bin Umar oilfield, which could be worth $90 billion. The company won the contract after it had been taken away from TotalFinaElf, because France backed UN sanctions. UN sanctions meant that all the contracts were frozen for the time being.

Even so, the stakes remained high, since Iraq's oil reserves were second only to Saudi Arabia's. Russia and Iraq had also signed a $40 billion trade and development agreement, and according to the International Energy Agency, the total value of Saddam's foreign contracts could have reached around $1 trillion dollars. Much of Iraq's industry had been built by Russia, and was still serviced by Russian engineers and technicians. Scores of Russian companies had valuable export contracts with Baghdad, which included agricultural machinery and over 2,000 taxis to be provided by the cash-strapped Gaz automobile company. Russia remained by far the main beneficiary of the UN's humanitarian oil-for-food scheme. Some of the most important industries in the Russian Federation lobbied the Kremlin hard to protect their interests in Iraq. A US-led invasion would put all these interests at stake, and the US was giving no guarantees for the future, something which increasingly rankled in Moscow. A Russian official told the press he believed the US government had made a deal with the Iraqi opposition that all oil contracts granted by Saddam would be declared null and void. 'The concern of my government,' the official said, 'is that the concessions agreed between Baghdad and the numerous enterprises will be reneged on, and that US companies will enter to take the greatest share of those existing contracts . . . Yes, if you could say it that way – an oil grab by Washington.'

Known links between the Bush family and the US oil industry, and between leading administration figures and some of America's largest oil companies, did little to assuage Russian concerns. The 2001 National Energy Policy Report, known as the 'Cheney Report' after its author Vice-President Dick Cheney, had prioritized easing US access to Persian Gulf oil supplies. America needed 20 million barrels of crude oil daily to keep running, and Iraq could meet half the US's requirements. The free flow of Iraqi oil would break Saudi Arabia's hold on the OPEC cartel and boost the US economy by supplying relatively cheap crude oil. Saudi Arabia was in any case becoming an unreliable Middle East ally. It was no secret that Dick

Cheney was one of America's leading oilmen, and had been boss of Halliburton, the oil industry service group. Halliburton subsequently won over $7 billion worth of Iraqi reconstruction contracts. The Kremlin was also upset that the promised rewards for backing the war against terror had largely failed to materialize. Moscow's expectations were perhaps exaggerated, but a Russian UN official felt there was an air of 'broken promises' following Putin's support for America after 9/11. US–Russian trade restrictions and the Jackson–Vanek amendment remained in place; WTO negotiations had stalled; and other benefits of the new transatlantic partnership were thin on the ground. A senior Bush administration official told the *Washington Post* the Russians had been making the point strongly that 'this can't be an all-give-and-no-get relationship ... They do have a point that the growing relationship has got to be reciprocal.' Part of the problem was Russian psychology. In business or private life, one favour deserved another. Traditional Russian horse-trading demanded an immediate pay-off or quid pro quo. Russian politicians have the same mentality. There is no sense of agreeing a deal for the sake of goodwill, to be banked for later use. The Russians had given concessions, and they expected an immediate return. There was no sense that what they had done was for the long-term good of US–Russian relations; Russian people tend not to think long term, perhaps influenced by their relatively short life-expectancy and the tendency for everything in the country to go belly-up at a moment's notice. The Russian establishment's sense of disappointment after September 11th boded ill for possible cooperation over the Iraq crisis.

There was also an element of self-delusion in Putin's opposition to the approaching war with Iraq. Putin believed his alliance with France and Germany would stop the United States in its tracks. Hiding behind France, Putin could point to the growing international opposition to the war. As a lawyer, he convinced himself that the US simply would not or could not ignore international law. When the US, Britain and other members of the Washington-led coalition simply by-passed the UN, he couldn't believe it. Watching his frequent appearances on Russian television at the time, you could see Putin was genuinely both peeved and very angry. Of course, the run-in with the US played well at home, where nine out of ten Russian people were against the war. In Russia, like most of Europe, the well of sympathy for the US after September 11th had dissipated and turned to anger. In Spain – like the UK, one of America's staunchest allies – nearly 90 per cent of people opposed the war.

Russian tactics over Iraq thus followed a pattern. Together with France and Germany, Russia demanded more time for the weapons' inspectors to find the alleged weapons of mass destruction. In a tense meeting with Tony Blair at his Zavidovo dacha in October 2002, Putin expressed scepticism about 10 Downing Street's Iraqi dossier on weapons of mass destruction, and questioned their very existence. Putin scathingly told the press the UK dossier 'could be seen as a propagandistic step' to sway public opinion. While he said he would back more UN resolutions if necessary, Putin also remarked at the joint press conference: 'Russia does not have in its possession any trustworthy data that supports the existence of nuclear weapons or any weapons of mass destruction in Iraq and we have not received any such information from our partners as yet. This fact has also been supported by the information sent by the CIA to the US Congress.'

Russia showed few signs of backing the British–US position in the United Nations, with Putin telling journalists the world must 'unquestionably ensure' UN weapons inspectors returned to Iraq to deal with Saddam Hussein's weapons programme. Putin and Blair had now met a dozen times in thirty months. The presidential dacha at Zavidovo and the surrounding trees were coated with the first of Russia's winter snows, a fitting backdrop to a frosty bilateral summit.

Yevgeny Primakov, former prime minister, spymaster and Middle East expert, was once more sent to Iraq to broker a deal. He had done so before in 1990–91 and 1998. A February 2003 joint

Putin–Chirac communiqué said war should be a 'last resort'. A second UN resolution, authorizing the use of force, became a critical struggle between the powers in the UN Security Council. While Tony Blair saw it as essential to win over support in the UK, the US was more relaxed about using the 'UN route', and merely humoured their foremost ally. In March, Igor Ivanov, the Russian foreign minister, said his country would veto a proposed new US–British resolution at the UN Security Council in New York, which contained an ultimatum to Iraq to disarm by 17 March. Sandy Vershbow, the US's ambassador to Moscow, warned that economic and diplomatic relations with the US could be damaged if Russia vetoed a UN resolution authorizing war with Iraq. In an interview with *Izvestiya*, Vershbow cautioned Russia to 'carefully weigh all the consequences' before voting in the UN Security Council. 'It makes a big difference whether Russia decides to use its veto or abstain,' he said. Implicitly threatened were US–Russian cooperation in space, energy and security.

Earlier, returning from a weekend in Sochi, Putin held a crisis meeting with his closest advisers at his country retreat of Novo-Ogareyevo. Present were Mikhail Kasyanov, the prime minister, Alexander Voloshin, his chief of staff, Vladimir Rushailo, the Security Council secretary, Sergei Ivanov, the defence minister, Boris Gryzlov, the interior minister, Nicolai Patrushev, the head of the FSB and Igor Ivanov, the foreign minister. As Russia failed to halt military action against Iraq, Putin ratcheted-up the rhetoric. Moscow called for a meeting of the UN Security Council to examine the legality of the US-led war on Iraq. At a meeting at the Kremlin on Thursday 20 March 2003, the day the coalition invaded Iraq, Putin issued a statement reported by the Interfax news agency saying the US-led military operation was being carried out 'in defiance of international public opinion and in defiance of the principles and standards of international law and the UN Charter'. Putin seemed to be falling back on his legal training at Leningrad University, but his statement did convey a sense of his outrage. The president's statement noted that the military operation against Iraq could not be justified and 'there was no need for it whatsoever'. It continued: 'If we allow international law to be replaced by fist-law, in which the one who is strong is always right, has a right to do anything and is not restricted by anything in the choice of means to achieve his aims, then one of the basic principles of international law, the inviolability of state sovereignty, will be put in question.' The reality was that state sovereignty had already been violated in Kosovo, and Tony Blair, in a speech in Chicago in 1999, had outlined how in his opinion humanitarian intervention could in some circumstances justifiably supercede issues of national sovereignty. Looking at the humanitarian catastrophe in Chechnya, it was not an argument the Russians particularly wanted to hear. On the same day as the Interfax statement, ITAR-TASS reported that President Putin 'insists that military operations [against Iraq] must be stopped without delay'. By the beginning of April 2003, US forces had thundered into downtown Baghdad.

Allegations that both Russia and the Ukraine had sold weapons to Iraq further worsened relations with the United States, a situation not helped by a US bomb attack close to the country's Baghdad embassy, and an incident a few days later when a convoy of Russian diplomats and journalists came under fire. Four or five people were injured, one seriously. Vladimir Titorenko, the Russian ambassador, escaped with minor scratches when a bullet hit his windscreen. As Russian-made night-vision goggles were found in Iraq, there were also reports that Russian military advisers had been helping Baghdad on US tactics. Complaining about US behaviour, Russia lodged a formal protest over U2 reconnaissance 'spy' flights along the Georgian–Russian border. Condoleezza Rice was dispatched to Moscow to calm things down and mend fences, following a Saturday telephone call between George Bush and Vladimir Putin. The phone call was the first conversation between the two presidents since the outbreak of hostilities in Iraq.

Condi Rice arrived in Moscow on Monday 7 April 2003 determined to soothe the Russians' ruffled feathers, and to tell them her boss was committed to a long-term partnership, despite present difficulties. A senior US diplomat in Moscow said the US–Russian relationship had suffered 'serious difficulties', and that Rice's trip was to 'keep the relationship on track'. The Russians were eager to listen, and Rice was given presidential-level meetings far beyond her status as national security adviser. She met Vladimir Rushailo, Igor Ivanov, Sergei Ivanov and Alexander Voloshin. President Putin 'dropped in' to join his colleagues and Ms Rice for a significant forty-five-minute meeting, a fact the Kremlin attempted to cover up on the grounds that the president should not have 'demeaned' himself by holding a session with a second-tier US official. In effect Condoleezza Rice was holding court with Russia's inner cabinet, including the president himself. It showed that the Russians were keen to repair the relationship, and anxious about their interests in Iraq. She later met with Alexander Voloshin for two hours, on the basis that he was seen as the main architect of Putin's turn towards the West after 9/11. Voloshin had also recently been in Washington DC, trying to secure Russia's post-conflict place in Iraq.

Before meeting Rice, Putin had already started rowing back on his prewar Iraqi rhetoric. The previous week he had pledged to expedite ratification of the Treaty of Moscow arms control pact, and said a US defeat in Iraq wouldn't be in Russia's interest. In their recent phone conversation, both Putin and Bush stressed their desire to keep open an 'intensive political dialogue on Iraq'. Rice told Putin and his colleagues that the US wanted to instal an interim Iraqi administration as soon as possible, and that her country wanted to work with both the UN and Russia on rebuilding Iraq. Such cooperation, she told her Russian interlocutors, would be 'an important element of helping to keep the bilateral relations moving forward'. Rice added that they needed to work to find a practical solution to the many issues 'relating both to the humanitarian aspects and to the broader reconstruction of the country'. Expressing an interest in taking a role in the reconstruction of Iraq, Putin and his ministers listened to these words with rapt attention. They were praying that despite their opposition to the war, when it came to the commercial spoils, Russia would somehow manage to get its share. Condoleezza Rice later disclosed the US's post-Iraq strategy to the press: 'We should forgive Russia, ignore Germany and punish France.'

Putin gathered the other 'anti-war' leaders together in St Petersburg on Friday 11 April. The 'Summit of the Losers' (as it was dubbed by one Russian newspaper) was a pretty sad affair, underlined by the fact that UN Secretary-General Kofi Annan refused to join Chirac, Schroeder and Putin in the Russian leader's home town. Annan had reportedly pulled out at the last moment, having second thoughts about being associated with the three UN malcontents. At their press conference, Putin and his two guests looked shifty and somewhat embarrassed to be together at all. They all knew the game was up, and each was looking to the future and how they could repair relations with the United States. Having failed to block the war, the three leaders now tried to stake a claim in the peace. President Jacques Chirac summed up the concerns of all three that the UN should play a central role in the reconstruction of Iraq, and pleaded for a 'multi-polar . . . well balanced world'. Putin warned of the perils of undermining sovereign nations and diplomacy in the 'export of capitalist, democratic revolution'.

Russia abandoned its opposition to a UN resolution lifting sanctions on Iraq when it received apparent US guarantees that its Soviet-era debt and huge oil contracts would be honoured. But not before giving Tony Blair an almighty snub and raspberry at a 'fence-building' summit in Moscow at the end of April 2003. Blair had gone to Moscow to build bridges after the repeated clashes over the war. The last time the two had met was the previous autumn, when the leaders and their wives had walked together in the woods, dressed in casual clothes and chatting. That summit had been difficult; Blair had sought Putin's support in the UN and been rebuffed. In public relations terms, the meeting on Tuesday 28 April was far worse. Again the summit was at the president's dacha, and again Blair and Putin went for a stroll in the woods. But this time Putin sought to humiliate the British prime minister by publicly dressing him down at a sixty-three-minute press conference, in front of the world's media. Blair spent twice as long travelling than actually meeting the Russian president. Putin let rip with all his pent-up frustration and annoyance. Standing next to a grim-faced Tony Blair, he mocked the US–British military coalition's failure to find any biological or nuclear weapons, saying oil sanctions should not be lifted until they were discovered. (The US and Britain were hoping for sanctions to be swiftly removed to help finance Iraq's reconstruction.)

Putin reminded Blair he had gone to war to eliminate the danger posed by weapons of mass destruction. He went on: 'Where is Saddam? Where are those arsenals of weapons of mass destruction, if indeed they ever existed? Perhaps Saddam is still hiding somewhere in a bunker underground, sitting on cases of weapons of mass destruction and is preparing to blow the whole thing up and bring down the lives of thousands of Iraqi people.' The Russian journalists present laughed, Tony Blair didn't. Putin went on to say that only the UN Security Council could lift the sanctions, since they put them there in the first place. The UN's oil-for-food programme could be renewed instead. The day before, Blair had said that a failure to form a new strategic alliance could result in two rival camps, reviving the tensions and divisions of the Cold War. Putin ripped into Blair on that score too, saying: 'If the decision-making process in such a framework is democratic then that is something we could agree with, but if decisions are being made by just one member of the international community and all the others are required to support them that is something we could not find acceptable.' By July, when Putin delivered his annual press conference briefing to hundreds of foreign and domestic journalists at the Kremlin, he triumphantly declared Russian intelligence was '100 per cent accurate in predicting the course of events in Iraq'.

Responding to Putin's outburst at the summit, Blair argued it was possible to create a two-way process where the US would listen to concerns on the Middle East peace process, global poverty and development, while other countries helped the US with its war on terror and weapons of mass destruction. He interrupted his interpreter at one point to say the bickering had to stop. He said, 'The kind of stand-off we've had in the last few months, in the end, is in no one's interests. That is why we need to find a way through. To make that partnership real.' On one occasion, the press conference became heated as Blair told Putin that there was no way that British and US soldiers who had 'fought and died' in the Gulf could 'simply hand Iraq to the sole charge of the UN while the coalition forces are there on the ground stabilizing the situation'. Getting UN agreement was important, as was getting a vital roll for the UN, but Britain was not getting into the 'rigmarole' it had last time over the second UN resolution. It was a bad day for Britain, as on the same day in Brussels, France, Germany, Belgium and Luxembourg agreed to a 'multinational force HQ for non-NATO operations'. Blair made it clear he would not support the initiative if it meant undermining NATO or duplicating its activities. The feeling in official circles was that the move by the European 'anti-war axis' was timed to embarrass the British.

Behind the scenes, there was a different story to the latest Moscow summit. Putin made it plain that his anger was directed against the Americans, who had so far refused to give the Russians any guarantees over their Soviet-era debts or contracts. The whole public spat was for the benefit of the press, and to show the US that Putin was seriously upset about being cold-shouldered. Tony Blair, who was shaken by Putin's tirade, was annoyed by his advisers' failure to warn him just how angry the Russian president was over Iraq. He felt he had been set-up by the Russians, who had especially invited him over to insult him. This was an old Russian tactic, and Blair had experienced a similar episode himself when he visited Damascus in November 2001, and was forced to listen to Syrian President Bashar al-Assad rant on about Palestine and Israeli terrorism at a joint press conference. Watching Putin closely over the past few months, it was obvious he was getting increasingly wound-up over Iraq, and was incensed when his tactics to block the invasion failed. Many in Russia's political and military elite thought Russia had not received enough in return for its post-September 11 coop-eration, a point which Putin himself seemed to be questioning. With the Duma elections in December, and the presidential elections fol-lowing in March 2004, President Putin had to watch public opinion, and his back. Not only that, but Putin realized that all Russia's inter-ests in Iraq could be imperiled by his rather risky strategy of confronting Washington. Putin felt rather humiliated and ignored, and he made Blair suffer the consequences. Ironically, it was the 'tantrum summit' which laid the groundwork for the compromise resolution lifting Iraqi sanctions and starting reconstruction work. Tony Blair proposed that if Russia agreed to the Anglo–US demand to lift sanctions on Iraq, the UN would be given an as yet unspecified 'vital role' in the reconstruction of Iraq and its new government. Additionally, Iraq's $8 billion-odd of Soviet-era debt would be examined by the Paris Club, comprising the central bankers of the leading industrialized countries.

Tony Blair was genuinely concerned about the possibility of a rift with the US on one side, and Germany, Russia and France on the other. Britain, an EU member but the US's closest ally, would be stranded in mid-Atlantic. When he spoke about developing a 'two-way process' with the United States, he believed it passionately. Politically, there was never any chance that the British would fail to support the US in Iraq. The whole of Britain's post-war foreign policy has been rooted in the Atlantic Alliance, and more particu-larly its close alliance with the United States. For many years, that was based on the British belief that US military might was necessary to defeat the Soviet Union, if the Cold War turned hot. The UK never had any illusions that the Europeans could be trusted to defend themselves properly, a view which has hardly changed. More latterly, the much-vaunted 'special relationship' has been predicated on another basis. Since the collapse of the USSR there is only one global superpower or hyperpower, and that country is the United States. If Britain wants any influence over the United States, and on its global policy impacting on security issues, trade, investment, development, AIDS, the environment, climate change and other vital issues, then it must remain America's staunchest ally. Cultural, historic and economic links strengthen Britain's ties to the US, divided as they are by a common language. Britain has only bucked this trend twice in the last fifty years, over Suez and Vietnam. Britain's attempt in 1956 to go it alone over Suez with the French and Israelis lasted a matter of days and ended in ignominy, the collapse of sterling and the resignation of the British Prime Minister, Anthony Eden. In the case of Vietnam, the British Labour Prime Minister of the time, Harold Wilson, kept out because of the strength of his party's left wing and the Trade Union movement. Wilson would never have succeeded in taking the country to war over Vietnam in the sixties against his own party and public opinion, something Tony Blair managed with much heartache. I remember interviewing Harold Wilson for my doctoral thesis on the Korean War, and he chuckled as he described how US President Lyndon Johnson begged him to send just a platoon of Scottish Highlanders to Vietnam, wearing their kilts and playing bagpipes. Wilson refused. Of course the 'special relationship' is often derided today, and Clinton resisted using the term, although Bush seems happy to oblige his British hosts by repeating the phrase at every opportunity. Whatever remains of the 'special relationship', Tony Blair evidently sincerely believes his mantra that Britain is stronger with the US when it is strong in the European Union, and vice versa. Blair vigorously refutes the argument that he has to choose between closeness to the US and being at the heart of the European Union.

At the end of May 2003, Russia had dropped its opposition to the UN resolution lifting Iraqi sanctions, having won the guarantees it sought. *Izvestiya* wrote: 'Russia "sold" its vote in exchange for the respect of contracts and debt.' The newspaper confirmed the key US concession was to offer to reschedule Iraq's $8 billion owed to

Moscow through the Paris Club. Some US hardliners like Paul Wolfowitz, the deputy defence secretary, had called for the $8 billion of debt to be written off, without Moscow getting a cent. Nevertheless, *Kommersant* accused the Russian government of abandoning its principles and the demand that UN inspectors return to Iraq to ensure that it was free of weapons of mass destruction. Igor Ivanov, the foreign minister, speaking in Paris, claimed the new resolution would create a favourable environment for Russia to take part in the postwar rebuilding of Iraq. He also said that Moscow would insist on existing contracts being honoured.

That June, Putin told Sir David Frost and the BBC that President Bush had said that Russian companies had 'the right to take part in the development of Iraq'. Bush had assured Putin that the US-led coalition had 'no aims of forcing Russian companies out of Iraq. What is more,' he said, 'they were prepared to provide conditions for joint work. And I have no reason to disbelieve this.' Putin's confidence that Russia would get a slice of the reconstruction pie may be misplaced. The US House of Representatives caused a stir by passing a controversial bill which stipulated that none of the $81 billion Iraqi war and reconstruction budget should go to companies from the anti-war countries of France, Germany, Russia or Syria. The policy was reaffirmed by Paul Wolfowitz in early December 2003, in a policy document that made it clear that reconstruction contracts would be limited to countries from 'the United States, Iraq, coalition partners and force-contributing nations'. The contracts were being restricted, Wolfowitz's paper said, in order to protect America's 'essential security interests'. Howls of protest immediately went up from France and Germany, but as Condi Rice had said, they were to be respectively punished and ignored. Russia belatedly joined the chorus of disapproval, with little effect.

Putin was determined to get relations with the US back on an even keel. This was not only in Russia's long-term interests, it was also in Putin's short-term interests too. St Petersburg's long-planned tercentenary celebrations were coming up at the end of May 2003, and Putin had invited forty government leaders and heads of state, plus their spouses. The city had been founded by the towering seven-foot Tsar Peter the Great on 27 May 1703, and carved out of the surrounding swamps. The Russian government had spent $1.5 billion on sprucing up the city, restoring old buildings and surrounding palaces, and Putin had also planned a series of ambitious political summits. Konstantinovsky Palace, in the St Petersburg suburb of Strelna and destroyed by the Nazis, was entirely rebuilt in eighteen months, a restoration job that would normally take decades. The palace was restored at a cost of over $300 million, and used by Putin to receive his international guests. There would be a Commonwealth of International States summit on Friday 30 May, a meeting of the Shanghai Cooperation Council and an EU–Russia summit on Saturday 31 May. Putin would hold a whole series of bilateral meetings with world leaders, including George Bush and Tony Blair. Chirac and Schroeder were also coming, although the French president would leave thirty minutes before Bush's arrival in St Petersburg, supposedly to join the G8 summit starting at Evian in France. The whole event was a massive photo opportunity for Putin in an election year (the Duma elections were that December), and an opportunity to showcase St Petersburg in all its glory. The Russian authorities spent over $30 million dollars spraying the clouds with chemicals from fighter jets to provide perfect, bright sunny weather. Arriving on 26 May, I found the city unnaturally hot, with dazzling, brilliant sunlight. I blinked and shielded my eyes, thinking to myself this must surely be July or August. Not everything went to plan for Putin and St Petersburg. The government and Valentina Matvienko accused the governor (and Putin's old enemy) Vladimir Yakovlev of misusing tens of millions of dollars meant for the tercentenary makeover. The Russian government could affect the sun, but couldn't control the wind. At one event on the Neva embankment, Putin was almost inaudible as the wind roared behind him, and his VIPs huddled beneath blankets, while others froze. At an open-air gala performance at Peter the Great's

Peterhof summer palace on the Saturday, Pavarotti entertained world leaders while vicious mosquitoes feasted on their bodies. Peter the Great had got rid of the swamps, but the hardy mosquitoes remained. The five million citizens of St Petersburg remained generally unimpressed with the celebrations. The massive security operation to protect the visiting world leaders had resulted in the authorities warning people to 'stay off the streets and stay at home'. Millions of Petersburgers took no part in the celebrations (most watched them on TV), and many headed off to their dachas for the week, if they could get away.

Events for the city's inhabitants were haphazard and badly organized. No one knew when any of the street parades were due to take place, and an official city tercentenary website offered no information. A laser show on the Neva, attended by hundreds of thousands of people on Tuesday 27 May, turned into a damp squib. Most of the week's planned events were solely for the benefit of foreign and Russian VIPs, including a range of concerts at the Marinsky and other city theatres. Hundreds of commuters and locals were stranded for several days as one railway station was closed down without notice or explanation, and the international airport was also completely shut for three days. It transpired that the railway line ran past the international airport, and the authorities were taking no chances as VIPs flew in and out of the city. Presumably the fear was that a rocket launcher could fire a missile from a passing train. With Chechen terrorists a constant threat, the security risks weren't imaginary. Nevertheless, the whole security operation seemed to hark back to Soviet days, treating local inhabitants with scant respect and lacking any transparency. Thousands of extra police were drafted into St Petersburg for the week, many from Siberia. One cyclist, finding himself on the receiving end of a string of expletives from a Siberian policeman, calmly told the officer, 'Our police officers don't swear like that in St Petersburg,' and cycled on watched by the dumbfounded cop. It wasn't all miserable. One undoubted popular success of the celebrations was the Hermitage Museum's decision to stay open for twenty-four hours. Another was the completion of the restoration of the famous Amber room in Catherine the Great's Palace at nearby Pushkin, visited by Jacques Chirac and Gerhard Schroeder (and partly funded by Germany's Ruhrgas).

The St Petersburg celebrations all looked much better on television, and at the end of the day that's what counted for Putin. On television, Russia's 'Venice of the North' undoubtedly looked spectacular. Putin himself, as intended, seemed to be everywhere, meeting everyone who counted. Now all the talk was of reconciliation and making up. At a meeting at the newly refurbished Konstantinovsky Palace on Sunday 1 June, both the US President and Putin said that despite their differences over Iraq, they remained 'friends'. It was almost like old times. 'I do like him a lot,' Putin said, explaining why he called Bush 'my friend, not only personally but also [as] my counterpart in a friendly nation'. Bush said he had also felt closer to Putin, '. . . this experience will make our relationship stronger not weaker. As we go forward, we will show the world that friends can disagree, move beyond disagreement and work in a very constructive and important way to maintain the peace.'

Mischievously, the Russians sat Tony Blair next to Jacques Chirac at the Marinsky Theatre on the Friday evening, while Putin sat next to Gerhard Schroeder. Keen to avoid both the opera and Chirac, Bush arrived the following evening. The political results from the various summits were less important than the overall atmosphere. Heads of state and government leaders adopted the 'St Petersburg Appeal' and called on nations to show solidarity in the face of 'international terrorism, organized crime and the drugs business, acute social problems, environmental pollution and epidemics'. The Shanghai Cooperation Organization issued a worthy statement on future cooperation, and the EU–Russia summit issued a joint statement. A joint declaration called for stronger political representation for Russia, the creation of 'common spaces' (including a common economic space) and the prospect of visa-free travel for Russian citizens visiting the EU. Putin made a big deal about visa-free travel, but in reality there was a lot of resistance within the EU, especially from the Scandinavian states led by Finland. Although the EU had agreed a special multiple-transit travel document to help Russian citizens travel to and from Kaliningrad on the Baltic, which would otherwise be cut off as the EU enlarged, universal visa-free travel was a different matter. Many EU states shuddered to think about a possible influx of illegal economic migrants, making people trafficking easier and unwittingly helping the spread of Russian organized crime. Kaliningrad itself, cut off from Russia by Lithuania, suffers from endemic corruption, high levels of organized crime, widespread poverty and the greatest incidence of AIDS in the former Soviet Union. Russia will have to wait some little time yet before the EU agrees to Putin's demand for visa-free travel for Russian citizens, with the summit only agreeing to look at the question 'as a long-term perspective'. Russia's relationship with the EU was puzzling. The EU is Russia's main trading partner, accounting for almost 40 per cent of the country's exports, a figure which would rise to over 50 per cent as the EU expanded. But apart from energy cooperation and sometimes acrimonious discussions over trade and latterly Kaliningrad, the Russians had not made much of the relationship. The Partnership and Cooperation Agreement signed between Moscow and Brussels in June 1994 was under-utilized. Partly, the diplomatic void was not helped by the fact that Russian diplomats never seemed to get to grips with the roles of the different European institutions, ranging from the EU's Council, Commission, Parliament and Court of Justice and quite separate continental institutions like the Council of Europe and the European Court of Human Rights. It was clear that the Russian missions supposedly following these European institutions had no real idea how they operated or inter-related. The Russians preferred simpler bilateral relations, which could produce immediate political and economic results. Hence Putin's emphasis on his personal relationships with Jacques Chirac and Gerhard Schroeder. Broader EU–Russian relations had thus fallen into a diplomatic stupor, and were not at the top of Moscow's list of priorities.

Putin rounded off his *rapprochement* with the Anglo–US war coalition by a long-planned state visit to the United Kingdom in the summer of 2003. As Grigory Karasin, Russia's ambassador pointed out, it was the first state visit since Tsar Nicholas I visited Britain in 1844. A few days before the visit, Putin told the BBC's Sir David Frost that he hadn't been attacking Blair when he chided him in Moscow about finding Saddam's weapons of mass destruction. 'No, it was just part of our debate,' he responded. 'My relations with the Prime Minister are very open and friendly.' He also admitted that Blair had laid the foundations for lifting sanctions against Iraq: 'But we actually agree on the main parameters for a possible future resolution on Iraq . . . the positions that we agreed upon during the Prime Minister's visit to Moscow were made the basis of the Security Council resolution on Iraq, which returned a significant amount of these problems to the UN platform.' On the third day of Putin's state visit, Thursday 26 June, Tony Blair and his Russian guest raced through a joint press conference. Again, all was sweetness and light. Chechnya didn't get a mention. Blair said the differences the two countries had over Iraq 'are a matter of history and record, but the international community came back together in the United Nations'. Putin strenuously denied he had ridiculed Blair in Moscow in April: 'I am very sorry you have construed our dialogue in Moscow like that. I said nothing funny,' he said sharply. 'Russia also thought that Iraq might possess weapons of mass destruction.' The pair still expressed their mutual appreciation, as if they needed to reaffirm it. Blair described Putin as 'a partner and a friend', saying the Russian president's leadership offered 'tremendous hope' for the whole world. He added the last three years 'have shown a real development in the relationship between Britain and Russia, and I like to think those relations are today probably stronger than they have been for many, many years'. Putin responded that the talks had been held in a 'constructive and open manner' and the 'strategic character of our partnership' had been reiterated. He thanked the Queen for her hospitality, and the 'warm feelings' he and his wife had seen everywhere they had been. 'Warm feelings are a tradition for our relations between our countries and our contacts at all levels. Here we see the manifestation of the mutual liking and respect for each other,' Putin concluded.

The rest of the visit, as traditional on these occasions, was heavy with pomp and ceremony. Lyudmila caused a bit of a furore at one point by wearing a hat wider than the Queen's, a breach of protocol which scandalized the monarch's ageing courtiers. The Russian first family had been met at Heathrow airport by Prince Charles, and been given the red carpet treatment. Vladimir and Lyudmila Putin were then officially greeted at Horse Guards Parade in Whitehall by the Queen, Prince Philip and Tony Blair. With Putin standing next to the Queen on a raised dais, an artillery salute sounded from Green Park and the band of the Grenadier Guards struck up the Russian national anthem. After inspecting the troops with Prince Philip, Vladimir and Lyudmila were driven in an open carriage along the short ride to Buckingham Palace, where the couple would be staying for the next three days. Putin later laid a wreath at the Tomb of the Unknown Warrior at Westminster Abbey, and visited St Paul's Cathedral, the Tower of London, the Royal Observatory at Greenwich, and opened a Russia–UK energy conference at Lancaster House. Accompanied by Prince Philip, Putin attended a ceremony in the gardens of Buckingham Palace to mark the return of the Colour (flag) of the Russian Lifeguards Grenadier Regiment, a symbolic recognition that Russian Communism had gone for good.

Putin impressed his English hosts by opening his speech at a banquet at Buckingham Palace in faultless English: 'We would like to express to Her Majesty and the people of the United Kingdom our sincere condolences for the loss of the British soldiers in Iraq. It's clear for everyone that, in spite of our differences that existed before today, we need to act jointly.' He then continued in Russian. In her address, the Queen said a long-term partnership between Russia and Britain was of 'profound importance' to both countries. She said: 'My message to you, Mr President, is therefore one of admiration, respect and support.' Putin also captivated his audience when he made a speech without notes at London's Guildhall House on Wednesday 25 June, and wisecracked that he hoped the beaver hats he saw were imported from Russia. True to form, and abiding by the habit of a lifetime, Putin was late for a meeting with the Queen when he was held up in traffic. *Komsomolskaya Pravda* pointed out the last time this happened was in 1874, when Tsar Alexander II was on his way to Britain and his yacht ran aground on a sandbank.

Putin also made a flying visit to Edinburgh, which British officials said he had asked to visit because of the contribution of eighteenth-century Scottish architects to his native St Petersburg. Putin gave another version when he addressed an audience in the grand hall of the Scottish capital's Signet library. Among those listening was Jack McConnell, first minister of the devolved Scottish parliament. 'I was bound to come here because the man with whom I have a very warm personal relationship, the prime minister, Mr Blair, originates from here,' Putin told his invited audience. 'I asked him yesterday whether he can play the bagpipes. He said no, but he still recommended that I visit Scotland.' There were a few small-scale protests about the war in Chechnya, and as Putin's motorcade drove through the gates of Holyroodhouse Palace, a lone protestor threw himself in front of the president's car shouting about the conflict, before he was wrestled to the ground by police. Vladimir and Lyudmila's trip included a visit to Edinburgh Castle, and a display of traditional Scottish music and dancing. Unlike at Crawford in Texas, Putin didn't join in.

Putin never looked comfortable in all the formal clothes he had to wear on the state visit, including dinner jackets, tails and morning suits, which somehow looked ill-fitting. His white bow-tie was adjudged too large, he mistakenly wore a cummerbund with the wrong suit and his dinner jacket was too long. He admitted when he came home they were not his kind of clothes. In truth, he never looks at ease on formal occasions. A survey commissioned by the

Russian state news agency *RIA-Novosti* in late May confirmed that both countries still had a lot to learn about each other. Nearly four out of ten Russians had nothing to say when asked for the first thing that came into their mind about the UK, and when prompted 16 per cent mentioned the weather, which in Russia is thought to be wet and foggy. When asked about Russia, Britons mentioned snow and fur hats, Communism and deprivation, although surprisingly, 50 per cent knew Putin was the president of Russia. The most well known Briton in Russia was Margaret Thatcher.

The Putins returned to Russia after what was generally regarded as a successful state visit to the UK. Yet in spite of all the warm words he left behind him in London, after Iraq, Putin would never again be seen as the West's blue-eyed boy who could do no wrong. He had squandered a lot of goodwill in squaring up to Washington, something he might later come to regret.

9

THE MOSCOW THEATRE SIEGE

'This was our 9/11.' Comment on the Dubrovka theatre hostage crisis.

At 9 p.m. on Wednesday 23 October 2002, forty-one heavily armed Chechen terrorists seized over 900 hostages at the Dubrovka theatre in south-east Moscow, just outside the city centre. The Chechens not only had AK-47 Kalashnikov assault rifles and a variety of pistols and 140 grenades, but carried with them large amounts of explosives, some of which was strapped to the waists of the eighteen women hostage-takers. They carried two 99-pound bombs with them into the theatre. The seizure of the Dubrovka theatre during a performance of the popular musical *Nord-Ost* heralded the worst crisis of Putin's thirty-month presidency, worse even than the *Kursk* disaster. Early broadcasts of the president, shown without sound, pictured a drawn and anxious figure conferring with his Kremlin advisers. The second Chechen war, which had helped bring him to power, had come to Moscow with a vengeance. The president's claim in April 2000, one of several, that the war in Chechnya was over and won, looked hollow. Putin had promised to 'wipe out' the 'Chechen bandits' and bring peace to the troubled breakaway republic. Now it looked as if he couldn't manage to guarantee peace in his own capital, as terrorists struck less than three miles from the Kremlin itself.

For the audience in the Dubrovka, an old Soviet Palace of Culture, the Chechen seizure of the theatre was at once unbelievable and terrifying. The musical was a romantic love story set in the Second World War, involving a dashing Soviet pilot and the beautiful daughter of an Arctic Fleet commander. When Chechen terrorists burst on to the stage five minutes into the second act and shot into the air, many believed it was just part of the show. As the cast of forty adults and twenty children were thrown off the stage, and the twenty-five musicians ordered out of the orchestra pit at gunpoint, the awful truth began to dawn on the audience: this was for real. Movsar Barayev, also known as Suleimonov, the cool and supremely confident twenty-four-year-old leader of the group, announced from the stage that those with mobile phones should ring their loved ones for the last time and say goodbye; they were all going to die.

Some women tried to hide in the toilets. On the second floor Olga Treyman, a pregnant eighteen-year-old, was in the women's toilets when a cleaning lady came in and said a gang of thieves had got into the theatre. They spent two hours hiding in the locked lavatory, until a masked Chechen gunman broke down the door with the butt of his Kalashnikov rifle, and ordered the two women to join the rest of the hostages. Olga recalled: 'He took us to a balcony where they were separating the men from the women. There were lots of children, many were crying, others were in shock.' The columns supporting the dress circle were wired with explosives. If they blew up, the whole floor would have collapsed, killing hundreds of people. Three women actors managed to get away after making their escape from a window in their locked dressing room. Masha Shostova was understudy to the lead role in *Nord-Ost*, and described her escape. 'When the first shots rang out I was walking from the dressing room to the stage. I turned to stone. Then I heard two more shots.' An intercom announced: 'Security, quick to the stage, an armed man is there.' She returned to the dressing room, and remained there with the two others for an hour. After they heard armed men running around and shooting at a nearby steel bolted door which separated their annex from the main building, they decided to make a run for it. 'I switched off the light and went out through the open window,' Masha said. 'Ten seconds later after we got out somebody forced the door in and came into the dressing room. When I was down I saw the light go on in the room, but, thank God, we were safe.' They escaped using curtains and scarves as a makeshift rope ladder. Not everyone, of course, was so lucky. Olga Romanova, twenty-six, lived opposite the theatre and saw the news of the theatre siege on the television. She was somewhat drunk at the time, and walking past the police and growing military cordon, walked into the theatre and starting haranguing the Chechens and telling the hostages they should simply ignore their captors and leave. Some of the hostages pleaded with the Chechens that it was just the drink talking, and they should throw her out. Several Chechens marched Olga through the auditorium doors and shot her dead within earshot of the horrified captives.

The Chechens had burst into the theatre after springing from three mini-vans with darkened windscreens parked just outside. They had planned the attack meticulously, gathering in nearby apartments over a three-week period, arriving from Chechnya in small groups. Each terrorist had lost a relative or close friend in Chechnya. Some of the gang had taken construction jobs on a site next to the theatre, using the opportunity to gather intelligence. A Moscow flat was used as a safe house to store weapons and ammunition. The Dubrovka had been chosen because not being in the immediate centre, passing traffic was less subject to regular spot checks and there were fewer police around. The layout of the 1,000-seat theatre meant that it would be easy for one group to control access to the main auditorium. Once the group had seized the theatre, it wasn't so large that it would be difficult to seal off from the inside. Spraying the glass entrance doors with machine gun fire and setting off an explosion, Barayev's group had easily overpowered the theatre's unarmed security men. The terrorists later announced they were Chechens, and that nothing would happen to the theatre-goers if the war in

Chechnya was stopped. The men wore balaclavas and camouflaged combat gear, the women black burqa-like robes with Koranic script on green headbands proclaiming them mujahideen. Each of the women had five kilos of explosives strapped to their waist and carried pistols. When the Chechens took over the theatre they dispersed among the audience and placed two larger bombs at different points in the auditorium. It transpired that at least fifteen of the Chechen women were widows of guerrillas who had been killed by the Russians, and most were in their twenties.

The horrific attack emphasized the radicalization and desperation of the Chechen separatist movement. The use of potential women suicide bombers, and the expressed willingness of the whole group to die if the Russians failed to meet their demands, represented an escalation of the Chechen conflict. In the past, it was overwhelmingly the men who did the fighting in Chechnya, and guerrilla leaders had taken evident pride in extracting themselves from almost hopeless situations, living to fight another day. That had been the case in Budyonnovsk, when Shamil Basayev extracted himself from a savage hospital siege (which he initiated) in 1995, and had also happened at another incident at Kislyar in 1996, where 2,000 hostages had been seized. The latter raid was led by Salman Raduyev, a Chechen commander who was later captured and died in a Russian prison aged thirty-five. The difference with the Moscow theatre operation was that Movsar Barayev's men and women were not only prepared to die; they relished the prospect of becoming Islamic martyrs. But there is also a good chance that Barayev himself may have miscalculated the mood in the Kremlin, thinking that the Russians would not countenance a massacre in their capital city and would therefore be forced to negotiate. In the Budyonnovsk incident, the Chechens fought off an attack from the Russian military and released 1,500 hostages after being given safe passage and the promise of a ceasefire in Chechyna from Russian prime minister Victor Chernomyrdin. One hundred and fifty people had been killed. Barayev also claimed to be taking orders from Shamil

Basayev, the radical Chechen leader who had led the Budyonnovsk raid. The latter had subsequently lost a leg to a Russian mine, after fighting his way out of Grozny. If Barayev thought the Dubrovka siege would be a replay of Budyonnovsk, he would be bitterly disappointed. At no time did Putin's government even consider a Chechen ceasefire, much less withdrawal. For Vladimir Putin, who built his reputation as a tough leader on the Chechen issue, any significant concession to Barayev or his ilk would be anathema. Fifteen hours after the siege began, Putin issued his first statement on the Dubrovka hostage crisis. Interfax news agency quoted the president as saying that the seizure of hundreds of hostages was planned abroad and led by 'the same criminals' acting against Russian forces in Chechnya. 'The first information which has come from the representatives of the terrorists who have . . . seized hostages in Moscow has come from abroad. This confirms once again that the terrorist act was planned abroad,' Interfax reported he told security ministers. 'There is no doubt that these are the same criminals who for many years have terrorized Chechnya and who are now calling for a halt to military activity.' RIA news agency added that Putin told his ministers that the main task facing the security forces was to secure the safe release of the hostages. Putin cancelled a planned visit to Germany and Portugal, postponing a summit with Chancellor Gerhard Schroeder.

The suspicion of foreign influence on the Dubrovka hostage-takers had some validity. Russian security services picked up a number of calls to the United Arab Emirates from the Chechen terrorists' mobile phones. Links between al-Qaeda and the Chechen separatist movement were well known, although these mainly appeared to consist of financial support and the interchange of personnel. One of Osama bin Laden's lieutenants, Ayman al-Zawahiri (an Egyptian doctor), was arrested in Dagestan in December 1996, and handed over to the FSB after trying to enter Chechnya secretly. He had come to Chechnya in search of a new base after he and bin Laden were expelled from the Sudan. Zawahiri used a false name,

Amin Abdulah Aman, was tried and found guilty of entering Russia without a visa, and released in May 1997. The FSB security agency hadn't realized whom they had caught. A Hamburg court also heard in October 2002 how Mohammed Atta, the leader of the September 11 hijackers, had planned to travel to Chechnya to fight alongside the Chechen rebels. As noted previously, Chechen fighters also trained and fought alongside al-Qaeda and the Taliban in Afghanistan. In October 2002, Georgian special forces detained fifteen al-Qaeda operatives in the Pankisi gorge on the Chechen border, and handed them over to the American authorities. The men, including a senior operative with close links to Osama bin Laden, are now believed to be incarcerated in the US military prison at Guantanamo Bay, Cuba.

Movsar Barayev himself came from one of Chechnya's most notorious guerrilla clans, which until recently had been led by his uncle, Arbi Barayev. Arbi and his 300 men were heavily into lucrative kidnapping, regularly demanding up to $1 million a time. He had been behind the kidnapping of the telecom workers, three Britons and one New Zealander, in 1998, and reportedly beheaded them when he was offered more money for them dead than alive. He was seeking a $10 million ransom from British Telecom and Surrey-based Granger Telecom, the men's employers. Al-Qaeda reportedly offered $20 million more if Arbi Barayev executed them, which he did. Arbi had also been behind the abduction and physical abuse of the two Britons, Jon James and Camilla Carr, a year before. When Russian commandos killed Arbi in July 2002, Movsar took over control of the family business, Arbi's so-called 'Islamic Regiment'. The Russians had previously announced the death of his nephew Movsar, but in that they were mistaken. Movsar's involvement in his uncle's kidnappings is unknown, but given the clannish nature of Chechen society, it is likely he played a role. Whereas the clan had been run as a money-making operation between 1996–99, dealing in hostages, guns and drugs, by the second Chechen war everything had become more complicated. Arabs like the Saudi Khattab

radicalized the Chechen separatist movement, which in the first
Chechen war had been more nationalist than Islamic. Most
Chechens followed a moderate form of Sunni Islam, called Sufism
or Muslim mysticism, and led largely secular lives. The Arabs, with
links to al-Qaeda, followed the more extreme form of Wahabi fun-
damentalism, which sought a theocratic pan-Islamic state in the
Caucasus, run under *sharia* law (like the Taliban in Afghanistan).
The Wahabis thought the Sunni tradition too liberal and positively
heretical. Young Movsar and his clan came under the influence of
Wahabis like Khattab, and other Islamic fundamentalists.

As Chechen losses mounted in the bloody second war from
1999 onwards, the fight for independence became not only a
national goal, but a religious and personal struggle. Jihad combined
the belief in liberation and extreme Islamism with the Chechen clan
tradition of the blood feud. The violent death of a relative
demanded blood in recompense. Revenge killing was almost commonplace in the breakaway republic. In Chechnya, Russians were at
once both the oppressors and victims. Apart from ties to the guerrilla commander Shamil Basayev, Barayev's brutal group was linked
to two failed Chechen politicians, former Vice-President Zelimkhan
Yandarbayev and Movladi Udugov, former information minister.
Udugov was an opportunist who embraced the Islamic cause and
received funding from Saudi Arabia. Yandarbayev was implicated in
the Dubrovka theatre seige, and later assassinated by two Russian
SVR intelligence agents in Qatar. The two SVR men deny involvement, but were convicted and jailed in Qatar for Yandarbayev's
murder in a bomb attack in February 2004.

Movsar Barayev was also a sworn enemy of Chechnya's relatively moderate elected president, Aslan Maskhadov. Ahmed Zakayev,
Maskhadov's European spokesman and former deputy prime minister, distanced his leader's rebel government from the Moscow theatre
siege. 'We said from the beginning, these are not our methods,' said
Zakayev, a former guerrilla commander. He added: 'We cannot come
down to the level of our opponents, targeting innocent people.'

Maskhadov may have known about the operation through the Chechen guerrilla commanders' grapevine, but didn't seem to be responsible for initiating it. Despite a court case demanding his extradition, much to the fury of the Kremlin, Zakayev was later granted political asylum in the UK. Russia had issued arrest warrants through Interpol for Zakayev, Maskhadov, and all his cabinet.

It was the young women Chechen suicide bombers in the Dubrovka theatre who particularly shocked many. They were not only young, but several appeared strikingly attractive and well-educated. What on earth could have driven these young women to such a desperate act? The only television pictures from inside the theatre were taken by NTV, at the terrorists' request, on the second night of the siege. The camera crew filmed an unmasked Barayev, with stubble beard and slight moustache, confidently sitting next to one of his masked men with a Kalashnikov on his lap. 'Our dream is to become *shkhidi*, martyrs of Allah,' Barayev told his Russian audience. 'The ball is in Putin's court now. It's up to him if he wants to have the lives of all these people on his conscience. We are more than determined to die here. Allah has already fulfilled our dreams just by allowing us to come to Moscow and mount this operation successfully. The war in Chechnya must stop. If Putin doesn't act we will go all the way.' The gang leader spoke clearly, without menace but with dull, expressionless eyes. He appeared so calm, he could have been on drugs. The camera also showed three veiled women dressed in black, showing only their eyes, toting guns and holding detonators, with explosives taped around their waists. I remember that one of the women particularly stood out. She was tall and slim, with beautiful dark eyes and an olive complexion.

In New York, Aset Chadayeva, a thiry-one-year-old former paediatric nurse, recognized her former friend and neighbour on the evening news. Aset broke down in tears as she realized her eyes weren't deceiving her – the girl on the news was her friend Kaira. The last Aset had heard of her, two years ago, Kaira was a twenty-two-year-old student at Grozny University. Although Chechen fighters had started to wear Islamic green headbands in the first Chechen war of 1994–96, the influence of the Arab fundamentalists only came into its own during the second war beginning in 1999. A few Chechen women fought in the first war; most stayed at home to look after the family, and care for their menfolk when they returned from the fighting. When Chechnya was part of the Soviet Union, only elderly women wore headscarves, and many Chechen women worked in hospitals, schools and on farms, and some went to university. Women had joined the professional classes, becoming lawyers, doctors, teachers and could work in civil administration. Kaira's family were well-to-do, and her disabled father ran a successful restaurant. The family lived in a large house, and although the family were devout Muslims, all the women studied and worked. Kaira liked expensive European-style clothes and had a penchant for mini-skirts, Western music and dancing. She was a happy and attractive-looking girl, tall and elegant like a model. After the start of the second Chechen war, Kaira met a man, fell in love and married. Like many young Chechen men, her husband soon joined the guerrillas. The young married couple both believed it was the right thing to do. In their minds the choice was either to fight, or wait for one of the interminable round-ups, detention and probable death. It was 2000, and her husband was killed in battle six months later.

The Russian army learned Kaira's husband's identity, and one night rounded up her sixteen-year-old brother Magomet as a reprisal. Raiding the family home one night, the army took Kaira's brother away. The family never saw him alive again. Much later they discovered his badly mutilated body, apparently dumped after being summarily executed. Kaira blamed herself for marrying a fighter, but blamed the Russians more. Next, Kaira's twenty-four-year-old cousin was killed in action, and the family home was destroyed by a Russian artillery barrage. Human rights groups alleged some bodies of those routinely seized were blown up, in an apparent attempt at concealment. The Russian army was accused of employing 'death squads' in the notorious *zachisti*, or 'cleansing operations'.

Conditions in terrorist 'filtration camps' were dire, with persistent allegations of torture and male and female rape. Some women were allegedly raped by troops in front of their fathers, brothers and husbands. Now Chechen women were covering their heads and wearing black as a sign of mourning, and to guard against Russian soldiers raping them.

Chechen women became increasingly active, and desperate. Two years before the Dubrovka siege, twenty-two-year-old Khava Barayeva, a relative of the Moscow terrorists' leader, drove a truck loaded with explosives into a Russian army base. The base was in her home village of Alkhan-Khala, six miles south of Grozny. Seventeen Russian soldiers died with Khava as the lorry exploded. One of Arbi Barayev's widows, Zura, was among the Dubrovka suicide bombers. Zura knew the Saudi extremist Khattab very well, and they had met a number of times. Khattab's influence had helped radicalize Barayev's clan, and of course Khattab was himself heavily influenced by Osama bin Laden. As noted earlier, he had close links to the al-Qaeda leader. Five of the Dubrovka women suicide bombers filmed a video before the attack, which was broadcast by the Al-Jazeera television station in Qatar on Thursday 24 October, the second day of the siege. Al-Jazeera, which is hugely popular in the Middle East, was often used as a channel for al-Qaeda propaganda. Among the five women was Zura, dressed in black with only her eyes showing. The TV broadcast showed them in front of banners in Arabic referring to Moscow and saying 'God is Great'. They proclaimed their willingness to die. Each of the women had about three kilogrammes of explosive strapped to their waists. 'Even if we are killed, thousands of brothers and sisters will come after us ready to sacrifice themselves,' said one of the women. It looked and sounded like a fanatical al-Qaeda-type operation.

Hostages who survived their theatre ordeal said the Chechen women were the most aggressive and cruel among the terrorist gang. 'The women kept threatening us, saying they would blow us all up,' said Modest Silin, a thirty-four-year-old dentist. 'They behaved like prison guards. They wouldn't let us stand up or talk. At times the auditorium was so quiet one could have heard a fly.' The women seemed determined to be martyrs. 'We have come here to die. To kill even one non-Muslim is enough to end up in heaven,' Silin said the women used to say. Kaira's friend Aset said the terrorists 'came together out of a common desire for vengeance against Russians more than a fundamentalist ideology. If anything, the Islamic trappings were for show.' A desire for vengeance and retribution, mixed with some confused and extreme religious fervour, made for a heady and dangerous concoction.

The terrorists released some hostages early, near the beginning of the siege. Some thirty people from the Caucasus (almost entirely Muslims) were freed. Inside the main hall, conditions worsened as the orchestra pit was used as a large public latrine. The only food was biscuits and chocolates, plus water and fruit juice from the theatre café (the terrorists wouldn't accept any food from outside). Most tried not to drink too much, so they wouldn't have to use the awful orchestra pit too often. The lights in the auditorium were kept on around the clock, to forestall an attack from outside. No one got any sleep; there was no hot food, hot drinks, washing facilities or toilet paper. People were naturally terrified. Their captors encouraged them to ring relatives and radio stations to beg the Russian authorities not to storm the theatre and to negotiate a peaceful solution with the terrorists. One woman hostage, broadcasting on Russian radio, pleaded that the hostages should not become a second *Kursk*. NTV established contact with Tatiana Solnishtina, who begged police not to storm the building, for fear the Chechens would detonate the explosives and kill them all. The terrorists had threatened to execute a hundred captives for every Chechen killed in any police raid. The hostage-takers started negotiating with the Russians on their mobile phones (which weren't always switched on) and refused the offer of a walkie-talkie for easier communication. On the Russian side, the FSB security service was in charge of the negotiations. Gradually, the Chechens accepted some visits from doctors, the

Red Cross, some media, and one or two members of the Duma including the popular singer Josef Kobzon. Politicians, like Moscow Mayor Yury Luzhkov and the former Chechen Speaker of the Russian parliament, Ruslan Khasbulatov, turned up at police and military lines outside the theatre offering themselves as mediators or hostages. Mark Franchetti of the *Sunday Times* risked his life to carry out an exclusive twenty-minute interview with Movsar Barayev inside the theatre, the only Western journalist to do so. Barayev told Franchetti the women suicide bombers worked in shifts. 'Those on duty have their finger on the detonator at all times. One push of the button and they will explode. The auditorium is mined, all wired up with heavy explosives. Just let the Russians try to break in and the whole place will explode.' He told the British journalist: 'Our aim is not to stay alive. It is to force the Russian troops out of Chechnya. We are not terrorists. If we were, we would have demanded millions of dollars and a plane to escape.' Another Chechen told Franchetti: 'We cherish death more than you do life.' Requests to free all the women and children were refused. One of Barayev's lieutenant's declined the request saying women and children died in Chechnya every day. Among the hostages were seventy-five foreigners, including eighteen from Western countries such as Britain (3), the US (4), Germany (2), Canada, Austria, Australia, Switzerland and the Netherlands. Western diplomats based in Moscow started arriving at the theatre to try to arrange for their nationals to be released.

Richard Low, a twenty-year-old British student studying Russian at Lady Margaret Hall, Oxford, had brought his visiting parents to the Dubrovka that night. When Barayev told the audience to make last calls to their loved ones, he rang his twenty-four-year-old sister, Louise, in London on his mobile. When he told her they were being held hostage, she didn't believe him. 'Richard passed me the phone,' said his mother. 'I told Louise that it was true and the line went dead. Later we found Louise was in such a state of shock when she understood what was happening that she dropped the phone.' Louise managed to tell the British Foreign Office in London that her father had a heart condition that needed daily medical treatment. By mid-morning on Thursday, about twelve hours into the siege, the Russians passed the Chechens a message about Peter Low, Richard's father, who was in his sixties. An armed Chechen entered the auditorium and asked for the 'English', and Mr Low was marched away. On leaving the main hall, he first saw a group of masked gunmen, and thought that his time was up. He and his family thought he was led away to be shot, but in fact he was released into the care of the Red Cross and Mark Franchetti, the *Sunday Times* correspondent, who had helped secure his release. Peter Low was relieved he wasn't going to be shot after all, but was sick with worry about his son and wife. Luckily, all three came out of the siege alive, perhaps helped by the Lows' proximity to a theatre exit. The same day, President Bush called Putin and labelled the hostage standoff an act of 'terrorism', telling the president that the US stood in solidarity with him and the Russian people. Later, the US promised to look at adding the Chechen separatists to their list of terrorists, a pledge they subsequently implemented.

On Friday, the Chechens decided to pile on the pressure by releasing some hostages, and promising to free all the foreign captives. Seven hostages were released at 6.30 in the morning, and six hours later, eight children were freed. But Barayev had no intention of freeing the foreign hostages; he thought they were his best card. The Chechens offered to release fifty hostages if the head of the pro-Chechen administration, Ahmed Kadyrov, joined them in the theatre. It would have been suicide for him to agree, and it is doubtful the demand was ever put to him. Outside the besieged theatre there had already been a demonstration, mainly of exhausted relatives with placards calling for mercy from the terrorists, restraint from the Russian government and peace in Chechnya. Some of the younger onlookers were more belligerent. 'We shouldn't stop the war just because of this,' said Slava, a twenty-year-old who had come to watch unfolding events out of curiosity. 'It's just a principle – we shouldn't stop the war.' In central Moscow, a teenager called Pasha expressed a generally-held view: 'We should kick out the terrorists,' he said. 'Out of the theatre and out of Chechnya. If we give in they'll think they've scared us, and then things will really start.' Even so, according to Russian polling agency VtsIOM, the number of Russians supporting military action in Chechnya itself had fallen from 70 per cent at the beginning of 2000, to a level of 34 per cent by the time of the Moscow siege. Whilst enthusiasm for the war in Chechnya was waning, public opinion was fully behind a hardline approach to the siege. The same poll showed 67 per cent agreed with the statement that 'Chechens only understand the language of force'. Over seven out of ten Russians saw Chechens primarily as 'bandits, kidnappers and murderers'. If anything, the theatre siege would harden stereotypical attitudes towards Chechnya and the independence movement.

In the Kremlin, Putin was holding continuous meetings on the hostage crisis. He stressed that he was 'open for any kinds of contact' on the condition that the rebels lay down their arms, a principle he had demanded the previous September. This was not the *Kursk*, there would be no attempt to duck the seriousness of the issue or bury the government's collective head in the sand. At 7 p.m. on Friday evening, Putin, in only his second statement, said the priority was to save hostages' lives. Nikolai Patrushev, head of the FSB, said the terrorists' lives would be guaranteed in exchange for the release of all the hostages. The Kremlin's negotiating position was simple: there would be no troop withdrawal or end to Moscow's presence in Chechnya. Needless to say, this hardline approach did not play well with the increasingly nervous and trigger-happy Chechen gang in the Dubrovka. In response to Putin's offer, they threatened to start killing the hostages at 6 a.m. on Saturday 26 October.

When Anna Politkovskaya came out of the theatre at midnight on Friday, she brought with her a demand from Barayev that Putin should appoint a senior political negotiator. Politkovskaya was a courageous journalist who had exposed Russian army abuses in Chechnya, and who had been threatened as a consequence. Earlier in the siege a gunman exclaimed: 'Why hasn't Putin called us? Who does he think he is? Is he that important, is he that big that he cannot find time to deal with this situation? What else does he have to do which is more important than us?' Putin had a direct line to his people outside the theatre, but had no intention of personally negotiating with the Chechens. The Kremlin went through the motions of appointing General Victor Kazantsev, a former Russian commander and Putin's representative in Chechnya, as their negotiator. But it was a sham to calm down the terrorists, Kazantsev wasn't even in Moscow and had no intention of coming to negotiate. Nevertheless, a meeting was agreed between him and the terrorists for 10 a.m. on Saturday morning. On Friday night the Russians told Western diplomats to prepare for a pre-dawn raid on the theatre. The Russians said the talks were going nowhere. An FSB agent was by chance in the audience, and the Russians spread rumours within the theatre that a raid would take place at 3.30 a.m. Around that time there had been a commotion inside the theatre, and a man and woman were shot at by jumpy Chechens, an incident perhaps triggered by the FSB man or a nervous child. When nothing else happened, the terrorists relaxed again. They hoped meaningful talks would begin the next morning. They had even been told that Putin was making an announcement in the morning saying he would consider stopping the war in Chechnya. Barayev and his men retired to a separate room to watch a video of their seizure of the theatre, leaving the women suicide bombers scattered throughout the auditorium. They had moved into position early on Friday night, fearing an attack. Now most of the Chechens thought they were on the verge of a historic victory; and they would all be Islamic heroes.

In fact, the Russians had been painstakingly preparing an assault. FAPSI, the secret service eavesdropping agency, had set up listening devices in the walls and floors of the auditorium, and now had a detailed picture of where all the bombers and terrorists were. Every voice and movement had been monitored around the clock and relayed to an emergency headquarters 200 yards away. Putin personally gave the order for the attack, and a mystery gas was pumped into the theatre through air vents. Alfa and Vympel, *Spetsnaz* (special forces) units, Russia's equivalent of the SAS and US Navy Seals, emerged through drains and executed slumped women suicide bombers where they sat. Each woman, whether conscious or not, was killed with a single bullet to the temple. One former *Spetsnaz* commando I met, who served in Afghanistan in the 1980s, has the number of his confirmed 'kills' tattooed on one of his fingers (17). Killing, rather than taking prisoners, is their specialty. The Moscow *Spetsnaz* units had been busy practising storming a similar Moscow theatre. The gas appeared to be a form of fentanyl, an opiate-based compound like an anesthetic, developed to be used as an aerosol spray and reputedly a hundred times stronger than morphine. Medics later used naloxone as an antidote, a drug administered to revive people from heroin overdoses. The gas itself had no smell, but the hostages and their captors could see it. Someone shouted 'Gas! Gas!', there was confusion with shots and explosions. Some people covered their faces, some collapsed immediately. Without orders, the female suicide bombers were momentarily confused and leaderless. Before they could decide to detonate their explosives, they were either overcome by the gas or shot dead. The *Spetsnaz* had entered the building less than three minutes after the gas had been released. Barayev and the other Chechen gunmen were quickly disposed of, with the group's leader shot holding a bottle of Armenian brandy. Some of the hostages fled into the open air, and were led out by the Russian commandos. Before the commandos struck, Richard Low's mother Sidica was at the end of her tether. 'I wanted the Russians to storm. I wanted something, anything, to happen. We were deprived of food and sleep, we were losing all sense of time and people were getting killed. I could see no way out.' Being near an exit, the Lows were among the first to be evacuated from the theatre. 'We owe our lives to the Russians. That's the bottom line,' her son said. After fifty-seven hours of terror, the siege was finally brought to an end. When Putin heard the news, he held his head in both hands in relief, a picture which was shown around the world.

Militarily speaking, it was a brilliant attack. Only one Russian soldier was killed, whilst all forty-one terrorists were killed on the spot. However, what then ensued was a medical disaster. Only forty ambulances were on standby when Putin gave the order to launch the attack. By the time the operation was over, just eighty ambulances had turned up, a fraction of the number required for the hundreds of people suffering from the effects of the gas. Special forces and rescue workers brought out many hostages, but the ambulances couldn't drive up to the theatre entrance, so people just piled up outside, with hostages in various stages of distress. Many were unconscious or semi-conscious. There were no doctors standing by, no mobile intensive care units, and the troops hadn't been trained in basic resuscitation or first aid. A lot of the victims were carried with their heads thrown back, with their tongues blocking their air ways. Others suffocated or chocked to death on their own vomit. There were no stretchers, and a number of victims were placed on buses, sitting upright, with no doctors on board. Many died on their way to hospital. Only four people died in hospital, and two from gunshot wounds. Yet the total death toll was 129 hostages and 41 terrorists. It is unknown how many died from respiratory and heart failure as a direct result of the use of the gas. Victims' relatives were treated poorly, and they found it difficult to find out which hospital their loved ones were in, whether they were alive or dead, and if dead, how they had died. Sometimes, they were only shown part of their relative's bodies, the rest hidden by a sheet. Arguments still persist to this day over how many died, how they perished and the level of compensation offered by the state. Eventually, each family who lost a loved one received $9,500, each survivor $2,700. Initially, the Russian authorities covered up the scale of the losses by saying only about twenty hostages had died. The West insisted on knowing details of the mystery knock-out gas used, but apparent medical concerns were tainted with the thought that they were keen to find out more about Russia's 'secret gas'. In the UK, it was revealed that the Home Office was investigating the purchase of knock-out gas, similar to the gas used in Moscow. Traditionally, operations like the Moscow siege had been carried out using stun grenades and CS gas. I had certainly thought along those lines, thinking back to the London Iranian Embassy siege in 1980, but it was my Russian-born wife, Svetlana, who correctly predicted the Russians would use a form of knock-out gas (perhaps being a Red Army colonel's daughter helped). It is certainly true that the gas used had to be almost instantaneously debilitating, to prevent the suicide bombers setting off their charges.

Overall, Putin heralded the operation to free the Dubrovka theatre hostages a great success, and in that he was generally supported by Western leaders. President Bush firmly blamed the deaths of the hostages on the terrorists. French Prime Minister Jean-Pierre Raffarin said the human toll was very heavy, 'but France is relieved because the worst was ultimately avoided'. Tony Blair said there were 'no easy, risk-free, safe solutions' in such a situation. 'I hope people will understand the enormity of the dilemma facing President Putin as he weighed what to do, in both trying to end the siege with minimum loss of life and recognizing the dangers of doing anything that conceded to this latest outrage of terrorism from Chechnya,' he told parliament. He concluded: 'A deadly mixture of religious and political fanaticism is being pursued by those who have no compunction about taking human lives, no matter how innocent, and care little about losing their own,' he concluded. Britain had sent over five anti-terrorist experts as a gesture of support. Launching the attack was an appalling decision for any leader to have to make. After the storming of the theatre 793 hostages survived, 129 did not. In this sort of hostage situation, as the security experts say, the losses were broadly 'acceptable'; no comfort at all to those who lost their loved ones. It was a Pyrrhic victory. Not acceptable, though, were the appalling medical support and rescue preparations, which inevitably cost many needless deaths. Leading Russian doctors, remaining anonymous to protect themselves, confidentially told Duma deputies that up to half the hostages who died did so because of too little medical care at the scene.

Monday 28 October was declared a day of mourning in Russia, flags at the Kremlin flew at half mast, and black ribbons were attached to official buildings. The city hadn't seen anything like it since the *Kursk* disaster over two years before. As Moscow police cracked down on the thousands of Chechens living in the city, Movsar Barayev's mother went into hiding. As Berezovsky predicted in the London *Times*, Putin pledged to root out Chechen militants and show them no mercy. He called on the military to draw up new plans to combat terrorism and for Russians to unite against a common enemy. *Nord-Ost* briefly re-opened at the Dubrovka in 2003 with government support, but folded in May after just three months as audiences stayed away. The memories of the terrifying siege remained too painful for Muscovites.

Politically, the Moscow theatre siege hardened Putin's resolve not to do a U-turn over Chechnya. Instead he proceeded with his own plan for an amnesty for guerrillas, elections, a new constitution and partial autonomy for Chechnya. To date, none of this has led to any reduction in terrorist violence or eradicated conflict in the blighted republic. Several thousand Chechen guerrillas continue to face over 60,000 Russian troops in Chechnya, with over 4,500 Russian troops dying in the republic since 1999. Boris Berzovsky was also right in his *Times* article in October 2002, when he argued that Putin would go after the terrorists. Another by-product was the removal of Boris Jordan as head of NTV. The channel, taken over and run by Gazprom on behalf of the Kremlin, was seen as too critical of the government's handling of the Moscow theatre siege. Its twenty-four-hour coverage of the siege was attacked by Putin himself, who made scathing remarks about the reportage of the crisis. NTV had included interviews with angry relatives of the 129 hostages who died, which was picked up by foreign and domestic journalists. Despite all this, Putin came out of the Moscow theatre siege with his domestic and international reputation enhanced. He had ended a potentially horrific hostage situation with a modicum of success. 'We had never faced a situation of such complexity before, yet no one had any doubt for even a second that the operation was necessary,' Putin said in early November, speaking to surviving members of the cast of *Nord-Ost*. 'We have come out of this situation at the price of terrible tragedy, heavy losses,' he said in televised remarks. 'The consequences could have been far worse' but for the hostages' 'courage, reserve and self-control'.

Putin's reputation for being tough and decisive was reinforced, something which was very important for the image of a Russian leader at home. After the Dubrovka theatre siege, Putin's line that you couldn't negotiate with the Chechens because there was no one reasonable to negotiate with, looked more plausible. The Russian people were in no mood to go soft on the Chechens after the Dubrovka siege. Whether this stance is sustainable in the long term is another matter. Will the Russians tire of Chechnya and think of just giving it up? With Putin firmly in the saddle in the Kremlin, any chance of Chechen independence looks as unlikely as a bear riding a motorbike across Red Square.

Epilogue

We hoped for the best, but it turned out as it always does.

VICTOR CHERNOMYRDIN,
FORMER RUSSIAN PRIME MINISTER

The Duma elections on Sunday 7 December 2003 predictably strengthened Putin's position in the lower house of parliament. For the first time in the post-Soviet era, the Kremlin's supporters would have the ability to control two-thirds of the Duma, giving the president the option of changing the constitution. Putin will be able to stand for a third term if he wishes, although he continues to deny any desire to serve beyond 2008 and his mid-fifties. He had stayed awake all the previous night, but it wasn't election worries that had made him sleepless. His favourite pet Labrador had given birth to eight puppies.

A total of eighteen political parties and five blocs had been registered to fight the elections, and United Russia was expected to do well. Half of the 450 deputies were elected directly from single-mandate constituencies, and half were elected proportionally from party lists. In fact, United Russia, whose only manifesto commitment and ideology was to support the president, scored almost 40 per cent of the vote and won 222 seats on a 56 per cent turnout. The Communists (KPRF), who became associated with the oligarchs and big business, saw their vote halve to 13 per cent. Foolishly, in electoral terms, they had let rich businessmen, including a number of executives from Khodorkovsky's Yukos oil company, buy places on their party candidate lists. A quarter of the Communist Party's elected deputies were now dollar millionaires. The businessmen gained immunity from prosecution, and the Communist Party allegedly received cash in return. Eleven of the top eighteen people on their list weren't even party members, and five were linked to Yukos.

The Union of Right Forces (SPS) and Yabloko, the two liberal centre and centre-right parties who supported democracy and the free market, failed to reach the 5 per cent hurdle, and so didn't win any national list seats. They were left with just five single-constituency seats between them. They were trumped by a resurgent Liberal Democratic Party (LDPR) under the far-right nationalist clown Vladimir Zhirinovsky, and the new Kremlin creation, the nationalist Rodina or Motherland Party. Rodina had been established to split the Communist vote. It opposed the neo-liberal economics of the SPS and Yabloko, but was a strange mixture of social democracy and nationalism. The party's co-leader was the progressive economist and former communist Sergei Glaziev, who was allied with Rodina's other leading figure, Dmitri Rogozin, an authoritarian former general. Kremlin spin-doctors rightly saw Rodina as an attractive alternative for disillusioned Communist supporters. Yabloko and the SPS had the problem of competing for a diminishing stock of votes in the centre. SPS was damned by association with its leader Anatoly Chubais, the architect of Russia's botched and widely reviled privatizations of the 1990s, head of the electricity monopoly UES, and one of the most hated figures in the country. Both parties were tainted by receiving funding from Mikhail Khodorkovsky (safely locked up in prison) and divided by ideological and personality clashes. Although both were seen as pro-Western and liberal, Yabloko was social democratic and left of centre by inclination, SPS was centre-right and closer to the oligarchs, and supported the privatization of the remaining state oil pipelines. In St Petersburg, Irina Khakamada, an SPS leader, symbolically lost her seat to Gennady Seleznyov, the former Communist Duma Speaker who had set up a pro-Kremlin party (Russia's Rebirth). The seat, in a liberal stronghold in St Petersburg, had previously been held by the leading democrat Galina Starovoitova, who was assassinated in November 1998.

The upshot was that the LDPR and Rodina scored 12 and 9 per cent respectively. Zhirinovsky's band, which was allegedly packed with criminal elements, and had in the past supported the Kremlin despite its nationalist and xenophobic anti-establishment rhetoric, saw its number of seats almost triple compared to 1999. The LDPR had thirty-eight seats to Rodina's thirty-seven. Both populist nationalist parties could be expected to support Putin in the Duma. Out of the 450 deputies elected, Putin and the Kremlin could count on at least 316 votes from United Russia, the LDPR, Rodina and other nationalists (representing 70 per cent of the entire Duma). Further votes could be bought; the Presidential Administration reputedly has a whole department responsible for swaying deputies' voting intentions. The Duma's post-election make-up gave Putin unprecedented personal power, even though the parliamentary institution itself was not particularly influential. The president and the Kremlin continue to take all the important decisions. With his opinion poll approval rating reaching 80 per cent, Putin was a racing certainty to be re-elected in March 2004.

Normally, the elimination of the Communists as a credible political force, and its replacement by a pro-government centrist grouping would be welcomed in the West. Yet the Organization for Security and Cooperation in Europe's (OSCE) international election observer team, monitoring the Duma elections in Russia, issued a stinging indictment of the parliamentary poll. The OSCE monitoring group called the elections a step backwards in Russia's transition towards democracy. The OSCE concluded: 'The main impression of the overall electoral process is of regression in the democratization process in Russia.' What was surprising were not the allegations of unfairness, but the apparent lack of understanding that all Russia's post-Soviet elections had been similarly unfair. In fact, they had been far worse. The OSCE claimed the result was 'fundamentally distorted' in favour of United Russia because of the abuse of 'administrative resources' and preferential coverage in the state media. But there was nothing new in that. The use of government administrative resources favouring pro-Kremlin candidates and biased media coverage had been a characteristic of all Russia's post-Soviet elections, especially the presidential election of 1996 and the Duma elections of 1995 and 1999. These elections had also been monitored by the OSCE. As shown in this book, the 1999 Duma elections were far more vicious and the use of TV media in undermining the opposition (especially Primakov and Luzhkov) was far more pronounced than in 2003.

Having officially observed three Duma elections and one presidential election in Russia, and having followed politics there for over twelve years, I was surprised by the OSCE's report on the 2003 Duma elections. Throughout the 1990s, the OSCE had more or less looked the other way as the Kremlin attempted to use all the power of the state to tip elections in their favour. In the 1996 presidential election, Western leaders and international organizations had turned a blind eye as the Russian independent media (as it then was) colluded with the Kremlin to savage the Communist Party as the 'red menace', repeating endless programmes on the Soviet gulag to press the point home that there should be 'no return to the past'. Because those elections were about beating the Communists, the lesser of two evils seemed to dictate that the West prop up the ailing Yeltsin. The Kremlin's disgraceful manipulation of the media and allegedly huge illegal campaign spending was ignored. In the 1999 Duma elections, the political atmosphere, levels of manipulation, and what the Russians call 'black PR' were far worse than four years later. Yet the OSCE report on that election was barely critical, and certainly didn't talk about the backward step of Russian democracy.

The development of Russian democracy, such as it is, has been an historical process. If the West doesn't like how it has developed over the last decade, it is a bit late to start crying 'foul' now, however factually correct. Jonathan Steele was absolutely right when he wrote in the UK's *Guardian* on 10 December 2003: 'Low turn-outs, a lack of debate, unfair use of the state-controlled media, heavy intervention by oligarchs in the funding process, and "virtual parties" which have no members or branches and offer voters empty slogans rather than detailed programmes – these have been characteristic of Russian politics for almost a generation.' Steele was among those contemporary journalists who identified Yeltsin's 1993 violation of the constitution and suspension of parliament (reducing MPs' powers in the process) as the start of a slippery slope. Russia has been sliding down that slippery slope ever since. By recent historical standards, the 2003 Duma elections were a restrained and dignified affair.

What had changed by late 2003 was the political relationship between Russia and the West. Although broadly harmonious, the days of blindly backing the Kremlin against the 'red menace' were over. Although there had never been any chance of Russia's democratic credentials being seriously questioned under Yeltsin or Putin in his early years, times had moved on. In the West there was an air of disappointment that Putin's Russia had failed to make sufficient democratic progress. Putin was no longer the West's posterboy. He had opposed the US-led coalition on Iraq. With the overthrow of President Eduard Shevardnadze in Georgia in November 2003, Russia accused Washington of fomenting the 'rose revolution' in its own interests. The weak and malleable Shevardnaze (from Moscow's point of view) was replaced by the 36-year-old US-leaning Mikhail Saakashvili. Great power rivalry seems to be stirring once more in Russia's backyard.

Putin himself is no longer immune from US criticism. The White House was quick to back up the OSCE's severely critical report on the 2003 Duma elections: 'It was the OSCE that monitored the elections, and they expressed concerns about the fairness of the election campaign,' said White House spokesman Scott McClellan.

'We share those concerns.' Meanwhile, in Uzbekistan, the US ambassador attacked his British colleague for condemning the human rights abuses of Washington's new Central Asian ally, which has boiled domestic opponents alive.

David Hoffman, in his book *The Oligarchs*, recounts how Anatoly Chubais and Boris Nemtsov (another SPS leader), visiting London in 1997, asked Prime Minister Tony Blair a question: 'What do you think is better, Communism or bandit capitalism?' According to Chubais, Tony Blair thought for a minute and said, 'Bandit capitalism is better'. Chubais added, 'Absolutely right.' With Roman Abramovich desperate to unravel the $11 billion merger of Yukos and Sibneft (with Yukos facing a $7 billion back-tax bill and rising), it appears the age of 'bandit capitalism' in Russia may give way to a form of 'statist capitalism'. Abramovich's response to the Yukos crisis can be seen partly as a commercial act to detach his Sibneft company from Khordorkovsky's politically vulnerable oil giant, but also represents new political realities. After failing to win control of the joint YukosSibneft company himself, the well-connected Abramovich is aware that a number of the security establishment are hostile to the idea of selling off the combined Yukos conglomerate to foreign interests. ExxonMobile and ChevronTexaco, Yukos's suitors, could not fail to be put off by the political uncertainty surrounding Yukos and its executives. With the Duma elections giving nationalist-populist parties such a strong showing, selling off a chunk of Russia's prime industrial assets would not have played well in an election year. And as ever in Russia, those close to the Kremlin were also hoping to make a financial killing from Yukos' distress and dismemberment. As Yukos's assets were frozen, the government threatened the forced fire sale of Yuganskneftegaz, the company's flagship production subsidiary. In today's Russia, oligarchs like Abramovich (unlike his colleague Khordorkovsky) are increasingly careful not to rock the Kremlin's boat. Commercial and state interests are becoming inseparable, as the days of the independent oligarch come to a close.

An otherwise predictable presidential poll in March 2004 became noteworthy for its combination of tragedy and farce. In early February almost forty people died and 100 were injured in a bomb blast at a Moscow metro station, blamed on Chechen terrorists. None of Russia's main political leaders contested the 14 March presidential elections. Of President Putin's six opponents, only Rodina's Sergei Glaziev and the SPS's Irina Khakamada had a national party political profile. Neither was backed by their respective parties. Communist leader Gennady Zyuganov and the LDPR's Vladimir Zhirinovsky declined to stand against Putin. The Communist presidential nominee wasn't even a party member. Their man, Nikolai Kharitonov, was leader of the left-wing Agrarian Party and a former KGB colonel. The misnamed Liberal Democrats fielded the former boxer and Zhirinovsky's bodyguard, Oleg Malyshkin. Sergei Mironov, Federation Speaker, representing the ill-defined Party of Life, said he wanted Putin to be elected president. Last on the list of presidential candidates was the former Duma Speaker and Security Council secretary Ivan Rybkin, who was funded by Boris Berezovsky. Rybkin bizarrely went missing during the campaign, surfacing later in Kiev and London, complaining he had been drugged and kidnapped. Most commentators, including his wife, seemed to think the whole thing was a publicity stunt. Rybkin withdrew nine days before the presidential poll, saying he feared for his personal safety.

While Sergei Galziev and Khakamada bitterly complained they were denied equal media coverage, Putin went about his presidential duties as normal, refusing to take part in a debate with the other candidates. In Nizhny Novgorod, the electricity was cut off at a venue where presidential candidate Glaziev was just about to hold a press conference. In his familiar style, President Putin largely avoided any overt political campaigning. He was, however, given saturation coverage in the media, especially on the now wholly state-controlled television channels. At one event the cameras rolled for several minutes, idly filming an audience waiting for the president to address them. The Kremlin's main concern was that apathy might mean that less than 50 per cent of the electorate bothered to turn out and vote, making the poll invalid. Everyone seemed to expect Putin to win handsomely, and his 80 per cent approval rating was far above his next closest challenger. The former communist and liberal economist Sergei Glaziev struggled to reach 5 per cent in the opinion polls. The fact remained that Putin was genuinely popular.

Speaking at Moscow State University in February, Putin made one of his few 'campaign speeches', promising faster reforms if elected to a second four-year term as president. 'A new period has arrived, a period in which we can create conditions for a fundamental improvement in the quality of lives,' he said. Putin vaguely promised that he would work to establish a society with Western-style social institutions. By the end of the month, in an attempt to stir-up interest in the election and stamp his mark on the government, Putin sacked his entire cabinet, including long-serving premier Mikhail Kasyanov. Out went the last remnants of the Yeltsin 'family', including Foreign Minister Igor Ivanov, and in came a mixture of technocrats and Putin loyalists. In early March Putin appointed 53-year-old Mikhail Fradkov as his new prime minister. Fradkov was previously Russia's ambassador to the European Union, head of the tax police and a trade minister. He was the archetypal Soviet bureaucrat, who would obey orders to the letter but not take any initiatives without authority from above. Prime Minister Fradkov did nevertheless pledge to push ahead with economic reform and restructure the civil service.

Just days before the poll, Alexei Kudrin and German Gref were confirmed in their old roles as finance minister and economic development minister respectively. The liberally-orientated Alexander Zhukov was named first deputy prime minister. These appointments were generally welcomed as indicating Putin's continued commitment to reforming Russia's economy. In economic terms at least, the liberal reformers in Putin's government seemed in the ascendant, which was exactly the message the Kremlin sought to portray in the run-up to the elections on 14 March. Sergei Ivanov, Putin's friend and confidant, was also reappointed Defence Minister. By brushing aside the last vestiges of the Yeltsin regime, Putin was showing he was now entirely his own man, and master of all he surveyed. As a final gesture, Putin announced he was cutting the number of cabinet posts from thirty to seventeen, showing he was determined to 'make war' on Russia's bloated and corrupt bureaucracy. He had become Russia's 'good Tsar', removing his unworthy advisers and ministers, and slashing Moscow's bureaucracy. However, as a reminder of the darker side of Russian corruption, it was discovered that the natural resources minister, Vitaly Artyukhov, had awarded at least forty-five oil exploration licences in his last three days in office. His successor vowed to rescind the questionable licences.

Not everything had gone to plan in the election campaign. Apart from the appalling metro terrorist attack, the military once again let Putin down. Watching naval exercises in the Barents Sea in February, one submarine's missile had failed to launch and another had been forced to self-destruct as it veered off course, State TV covered the president's visit, but failed to report the malfunctions. After the election, the Northern Fleet's *Peter the Great* cruiser was ordered back to port as the Navy's Commander Admiral Kuroyedov said it was too dangerous to keep at sea and 'could go sky high at any minute.'

Come presidential polling day, the authorities did everything they could to boost the turnout. Free or reduced-price goods and groceries were offered to voters at numerous polling stations across Russia. Voting pensioners were offered free haircuts and the young complementary cinema tickets. One over-zealous hospital director in Kharbarovsk, in Russia's far east, refused to accept patients unless they had absent-voter forms. Provincial and local bosses were told to ensure the turnout was high, and a nationwide poster-campaign encouraged people to vote, implicitly for President Putin of course. A common refrain was that there was no realistic alternative to voting for Putin. Valery, a 40-year-old taxi driver, said he would vote for Putin: 'The [terrorist] explosions continue, and human life is not worth a kopek, but everyone else is a nobody.' Yury, a 55-year-old engineer summed up the mood: 'We have a joke here. In America, you find out who wins the elections two months after they've finished. In Russia, we know two months beforehand.' Colin Powell, US Secretary of State, displayed his despair at the state of Russian politics, telling US Fox News: 'Russians have to understand that to have full democracy of the kind that the international community will recognize, you've got to let candidates have all access to the media that the president has. It's not entirely clear to me why they go out of their way to keep opposition candidates from fully participating in the electoral process. It's not good but I don't think it signals the total demise of democracy of Russia.'

In the event the turnout was almost 65 per cent of Russia's 109 million voters. Vladimir Putin coasted to victory with 71 per cent of the popular vote. His nearest challenger was communist-backed Nikolai Kharitonov with 14 per cent. The other candidates received less than 5 per cent of the vote. The OSCE criticism this time around was more muted. Its observers said the election was 'well-administered' but 'lacked elements of a genuine democratic contest'. President Putin brushed aside Colin Powell's criticisms as 'dictated by the domestic political balance' and influenced by the forthcoming US elections. He none too subtly alluded to America's own problems with its democratic and voting procedures. Speaking from his campaign headquarters in the Kremlin, Putin promised that the 'democratic accomplishments of our people will be unconditionally defended and guaranteed'. Russia would strengthen its multi-party system and would 'strengthen civic society and do everything to ensure freedom of mass media'. The economic and social stability which was achieved in his first term was not a goal in itself. It merely provided the necessary background in order to ensure that the well-being of the Russian people could be improved, he added.

A poll published a month after the election showed that

Vladimir Putin had done especially well with women voters, who admired his relative youthfulness, fitness and the fact that he didn't drink (unlike many of their menfolk). Amongst all voters, Putin's strongest points were seen as his youth (mentioned by 33 per cent), dynamism, health and professionalism (all mentioned by 30 per cent). But, as usual with politics, 'It's the economy, stupid', which smoothed Putin's path to re-election. Wages and pensions were more or less paid on time, and the macro-economic indicators were all looking up. The rouble was stable; inflation had come down from three figures in the 90s to about 12 per cent; interest rates had fallen from 150 per cent in 1998 to around 14 per cent. GDP rose by 8 per cent in the first quarter of 2004, and investment by 13 per cent. Real income grew by almost 14 per cent. High oil and gas prices underpinned the Russian economy, and allowed the government to cut debt and foreign borrowing. Hard currency reserves had improved, and capital flight the previous year had dramatically declined.

So going into his second term aged just fifty-one, President Putin seemed to have steered Russia through a rough patch and into calmer waters. Up to a point. Many problems remain to be tackled, ranging from reform of the military and state bureaucracy, through to endemic corruption, economic reform and the reduction of Russia's dependency on its exports of natural resources. Chechnya remains a running sore, a point underlined by the assassination of Moscow's man in Grozny, President Akhmed Kadyrov in May 2004, and the blowing-up of two Russian planes and ninety people by Chechen hijackers in August the same year. Amid horrific scenes of carnage, hundreds of children were killed in September 2004 when Chechen terrorists seized a school in Beslan, North Ossetia, close to the recalcitrant republic. Russia is now not only one of the most corrupt nations on earth, but also one of the most unequal, with the remaining oligarchs still controlling the lion's share of the Russian economy.

Many Russia watchers will be concerned by disturbing signs of growing authoritarianism, a fact not unnoticed by the country's own growing middle class. Elections in Chechnya are blatantly rigged in favour of Moscow's puppets. Russian state propaganda on television is sometimes disturbingly crude. Blanket and sycophantic coverage of President Putin is the norm on daily news programmes. 'Svoboda Slova' (meaning 'free speech' in English) one of NTY's most popular programmes and the only live political debate on Russian TV, was taken off the air in July 2004. Russian TV was being increasingly 'sanitized'. Paul Klebnikov, the 41-year-old widely admired journalist and author of *Godfather to the Kremlin,* returned from the US to his roots to edit the Russian version of the *Forbes* magazine. After publishing a list of Russia's wealthiest people, including the revelation that Moscow Mayor Yury Luzhkov's wife was a billionaire, Klebnikov was shot dead on a Moscow street outside his office on Friday 9 July the same year. Klebnikov had had a long-standing legal dispute with Boris Berezovsky, although the oligarch was the first to say that the *Forbes* journalist may have ruffled many other feathers amongst Russia's new super-rich elite. Many wealthy people in Russia, Berezovsky pointed out, do not like being investigated or having their wealth revealed. Even so, Klebnikov's death seemed an ominous sign that Russia is still partly a 'bandit state'. Other journalists too, have been murdered or 'disappeared' in recent times.

Apart from what the Yukos crisis says about private property rights in Russia, the arrest of Khodorkovsky and the action against his oil company has started to have some detrimental effects on the Russian economy. Capital flight, which largely dried-up in 2003, is once more on the rise as Russia's business elite takes fright. In March 2004, Finance Minister Alexei Kudrin had forecast post-Soviet Russia would record its first ever net capital influx of around $3–4 billion. Khodorkovsky's incarceration and Yukos changed all that. Capital outflow overall was just $2.3 billion in 2003, but after the Yukos affair escalated, it threatened to more than quadruple to between $8–12 billion the following year. Nervous Russians bought a record $1.7 billion in hard currency in June 2004, as the Yukos crisis and a lack of confidence in the unreformed banking sector deepened. The Kremlin, however, can take heart as foreign oil majors continue to show interest in exploiting Russia's massive untapped reserves. US oil and gas giant ConocoPhillips is the latest company to show a keen interest in investing in Russia, despite the Yukos *imbroglio*. Russia, the Western energy companies may well observe, is no more corrupt or potentially unstable than Nigeria, Venezuela, or parts of the Middle East.

President Putin may face yet another problem if he seeks re-election for a third term in 2008, and his supporters in the Duma amend the constitution to allow him to stand. His personal popularity, always his strong point, shows signs of being on the slide. In a poll organized by the Public Opinion Foundation on 3 and 4 July 2004, only 49 per cent of respondents said they would vote for Putin again. Vladimir Putin, previously so popular with his people, looks like losing some of his appeal. One of the main reasons for the dramatic fall in his support is his backing for a Duma bill replacing benefits for socially vulnerable people with cash payments. The benefits that will be lost range from free medicine to free trips on public transport. The cash payments promised in return are inadequate (starting from as little as $15), and people know it, despite a welter of TV propaganda telling them the reforms will be good for them. President Putin and his liberal economic advisers are trying to wean the public, especially the poor, off their dependence on state subsidies, but the outcome is likely to be massive hardship and further unpopularity for the government. The question then becomes, what, hypothetically, would an unpopular president and the Kremlin resort to, to ensure re-election? Russia's 'managed democracy' would be in danger of becoming no democracy at all. We shall have to see if President Putin and his advisers again change tack or pull some new rabbit out of the hat to avert defeat in 2008.

Vladimir Putin is not a unique individual. As he said himself, he is a typical product of Soviet patriotic education. He is also a typical product of his generation of middle-ranking and well-educated

KGB officers. Putin and his contemporaries are not as blinkered in their world view as the veterans of the Brezhnev era, but at the end of the day they are still KGB men to the core: intelligent, loyal, disciplined and patriotic. These were the qualities which Yeltsin's 'family' saw in him in those early days, and which marked him out for high office. Under President Putin, Russia will remain a power to be reckoned with, but one where Western-style democracy, and a free media, is still some way off.

Source Notes

I: INTERVIEWS, MEETINGS AND DISCUSSIONS

President François Mitterrand, President Mikhail Gorbachev, President
Lennart Meri, PM Victor Chernomyrdin, PM Yevgeny Primakov, PM
Sergei Stepashin, PM Michel Rocard, the late PM Sir Harold Wilson,
Deputy PM Valentina Matvienko, Deputy PM Ilya Klebanov, Deputy PM
Alexander Shokin, Speaker Gennady Seleznyov, Speaker Ivan Rybkin,
Speaker Yegor Stroyev, Mayor Yury Luzhkov, Governor Vladimir Yakovlev,
Sergei Shoigu, Gennady Zyuganov MP, Grigory Yavlinsky MP, the late
Anatoly Sobchak, Dr Alexander Shishlov MP, Vladimir Lukin MP, Kara-kys
Arakchaa MP, the late Col Professor Nikolai Chernikov, Ambassador
Grigory Karasin, Ambassador Alexander Trofimov, Ambassador Yury
Fokine, Stanislav Zhebrovsky MP, Vladimir Zhirinovsky MP, Alzam
Saifullin MP, Dr Vladimir Taracheov MP, Dr Vyacheslav Nikonov MP,
Nicolai Bindiukov MP, Valery Borchev MP, Pavel Bunich MP, Namdak
Zhambalov MP, Tamara Zlotnikov MP, Professor Victor Kukushin,
Professor Vladimir Lisichkin, Dr Vladimir Kostiushev, Dr Alexander
Oslon, Igor Artemyev, Ivan Korastelev, Vitaly Volkov, Vladimir Brintsalov,
Svyatoslav Fyodorov, Sergei Filatov, Nicolai Ryabov, Ambassador Sir David
Manning, Ambassador Sir Brian Fall, Ambassador Sir Andrew Wood,
Ambassador Sir Roderic Lyne, Ambassador Alexander Vershbow,
Ambassador Richard Samuel, Martin Nicholson, Eric Penton-Voak, Kate
Horner, Duncan Allan, Janet Gunn, Nigel Gould-Davies, Dr Jonathan Aves,
Consul-General Ulrich Schöning, Consul-General Barbara Hay, Thomas
M Leary, Vice-Minister Chen Ziyang, Field Marshal Lord Vincent, General
Sir Rupert Smith, Dr John Hamre, Dr Bill Schneider, Hon David Oliver,
Robin Beard, Geoff Hoon MP, George Robertson MP, Robin Cook MP,
Joyce Quin MP, Doug Henderson MP, Jonathan Steele, Robert Cooper, Dr

Gunter Burghardt, Hans van den Broek, Ismat Kitani, Lt-Col Jean-Marie
Leclerq, Helene Carrere D'Encausse MEP, Dr Andrei Zakharov, Konstantin
Eggert, Lou Naumovski, Peter Kurlansky, Yelena Tsvetkova, Jean-Pierre
Reymondet-Commoy, Alexander Batachan, Tim Kennedy, Tiberius Braun,
Pavel Smirnov, Vasily Ponomarev, Max Gounelle, Dr Elena Nemirovskaya,
Professor Vyacheslav Seregin, Professor Nikita Tchaldymov, Robert Posnor,
Natalia Votintseva, P Stobdan, Irina Adinayeva, Anarbek Matisakov, Bakyt
Baketaev, Jerry Wieclaw, Ambassador Fatih Teshabaev, John and Helen
Hambly, Dr Adam Daniel Rotfeld, Dr Natalie Goldring, Lotte Lecht,
Speaker Usup Mukambayev, Deputy Minister Erkinbek Mamyrov, Mirgul
Smanalieva, Omurzak Mamausupov, Dr Leila Muzaparova, Karabek
Uzabaev, Ambassador Rosa Otunbayeva, Olena Skomorochtchenko,
Ambassasdor Rusudan Lordkipanidze, Professor Nicolai Hovhannisyan,
Ruslan Tchimaev, Boris Pankin, Deputy PM Noukhaev, Anarbek
Matisakov, Valentin Yakushik, Mostafa Zahrani, Vladimir Mityayev, Valeria
Milyutina, Natalia Tylik, Ludmila Milyutina and Sergei Chernyshev.

2: CHAPTER SOURCES

1 The 900 Days

Vladimir Putin, *First Person*, London, 2000; Oleg Blotsky, *Vladimir Putin:
Life Story* (book 1, in Russian), Moscow 2002; Harrison Salisbury, *The 900
Days: The Siege of Leningrad*, London, 1969; Leningrad Blockade Museum;
Cynthia Simmons & Nina Perlina, *Writing the Siege of Leningrad*,
Pittsburgh 2002; private information

2 Vladimir Junior

RTR Russian TV, 7 October 2002; Harrison Salisbury, *The 900 Days*;
Vladimir Putin, *First Person*; www.news.bbc.co.uk; Oleg Blotsky, *Vladimir
Putin: Life Story* (book 1); Oleg Blotsky, *Vladimir Putin: Road to Power*
(book 2, in Russian), Moscow 2002; private information

3 The Spy Who Loved Me

Izvestiya, 4 March 2003; Oleg Blotsky (books 1 and 2); *First Person*; Mikhail
Chepelov, *Izvestiya*, 4 March 2003; www.news.bbc.co.uk; Mark Franchetti,
'Agent reveals young Putin's spy disaster', *Sunday Times*, 19 March 2000;
RTR, 7 Oct 2002; Yevgenia Borisova, '$488M Kremlin face-lift overrides pen-
sions', *St Petersburg Times*, 22 June 1999; author's interview with Anatoly
Sobchak, December 1999; Peter Truscott, *Kursk: Russia's Lost Pride*, London

2002; Centre for Strategic and International Studies (CSIS) Task Force report 'Russian Organized Crime and Corruption: Putin's Challenge' Washington DC, 2000; Yevgenia Albats and Michael Hirsh, 'End of an Era', *Newsweek*, 135(2), 10 January 2000; private info; *Agence France Presse*, 'Mabetex admits opening Yeltsin credit card accounts', 8 December 1999; Peter Truscott, *Kursk*

4 On the Way Up

Vladimir Putin, *First Person*; Oleg Blotsky (books 1 and 2); Ian Traynor, 'The spy who would be king', *Guardian*, 25 March 2000; Paul Klebnikov, 'Godfather to the Kremlin', New York, 2000; Boris Yeltsin, *Midnight Diaries*, London, 2000; Otto Luchterhandt, 'Putin's "strong state" ', *Internationale Politik*, 27 January 2003; A.A. Murkin, 'Who is Mr Putin and who came with him?' Moscow, 2001 (in Russian); private info; CSIS Task Force Report, 'Russian Organized Crime and Corruption'; David E Hoffman, *The Oligarchs: Wealth and Power in the New Russia*, Oxford, 2002; Nationwide VCIOM surveys, 1998–2000; Lilia Shevtsova, *Putin's Russia*, Washington DC, 2003; Peter Truscott, *Russia First: Breaking with the West*, London, 1997; www.news.bbc.co.uk; Mark Franchetti, 'Russian returns after 13 years of Chechen slavery', *Sunday Times*, 31 March 2002; BBC World Service, 5 March 1999; Interfax, 8 March 1999; Paul Klebnikov, 'Godfather of the Kremlin', BBC news; Mark Franchetti, 'Poisoned letter kills Chechen warlord', *Sunday Times*, 19 May 2002; Ian Traynor, 'Russia claims to have killed Arab warlord in Chechnya', *Guardian*, 26 April 2002; Sharon LaFraniere, 'How Jihad made its way to Chechnya', *Washington Post*, 26 April 2003; Andrew Jack, 'Rebels claim withdrawal from Dagestan', *Financial Times*, 24 August 1999; Jonathan Steele, 'The Ryazan Incident', *Guardian*, 24 March 2000; John Sweeny, 'Explosive picture puts secret police in frame for Moscow atrocities', *Observer*, 12 March 2000; Jonathan Steele and Ian Traynor, 'Former ally links Putin to Moscow blasts', *Guardian*, 6 March 2002; Nick Paton Walsh, 'A spy out in the cold', *Guardian*, 27 May 2002; Christopher Andrew and Vasili Mitrokhin, 'The Mitrokhin Archive', London, 1999; *Guardian*, 6 March 2002; ITAR-TASS, 27 June 2003; Lilia Shevtsova, *Putin's Russia*, Washington DC, 2003; Yury Luzhkov meeting with the author; Peter Truscott, *Kursk*.

5 President Putin Gets Elected

Vladimir Putin, *First Person*; 'Putin thanks Russian troops', 1 January 2000, news.bbc.co.uk; interview with Acting-President Vladimir Putin, *Kommersant Daily*, Natalia Gevorkian and Andrei Kolesnikov, 10 March 2000; Hoffman, *The Oligarchs*; Ian Traynor, *Guardian*, 'Weary Russia turns to Putin', 16 March 2000; Vladimir Putin, 'Russia at the turn of the millennium',

29 December 1999, kindly supplied by the British Foreign Office; CNN.com; BBC news; *Guardian*, 6 March 2002; *Komsomolskaya Pravda*, 11 February 2000; Peter Truscott, *Kursk: Russia's Lost Pride*, London, 2003; private info; BBC news; Lilia Shevtsova, 'Putin's Russia'; World Service; news.bbc.co.uk; 'Russia First'; Ian Traynor, 'Mystery death of Kremlin critic', *Guardian*, 10 March 2000; Andrew Jack, 'Book on Putin ruled to be poll propaganda', *Financial Times*, 14 March 2000; Andrew Jack, 'Putin's young Rasputins'; *Financial Times*, 25–26 March 2000; author's interview with Dr Alexander Oslon, Moscow, 2003; Johnson's Russia List, 14 February 2000; Giles Whittell 'Putin lines up old KGB pals to run Kremlin', *Times*, 14 February 2000; Agence France Presse, 10 March 2000; www.russiatoday.com; news.bbc.co.uk; Radio Free Europe/Radio Liberty Newsline, 26 November 2001, rferl.org; Ian Traynor and Michael White, 'Blair courts outrage with Putin visit', *Guardian*, 11 March 2000; Brian Groom and John Thornhill, 'Blair's personal visit to Putin condemned', *Financial Times*, 7 March 2000; *Nezavisimaya Gazeta*, 11 March 2000; *Times*, 11 March 2000; private info; John Thornhill, 'Blair praises Putin as "impressive" ', *Financial Times*, 13 March 2000; 'Blair's Russian retreat', *Guardian*, 15 March 2000; Amelia Gentleman 'Putin's art – being all things to everyman', *Guardian*, 23 March 2000; Ian Traynor, 'Weary Russia turns to Putin', *Guardian*, 16 March 2000; Ian Traynor and Julian Borger, 'Putin keeps West in dark on foreign policy', *Guardian*, 28 March 2000; Ian Traynor, 'Rivals give up hope as Putin rolls to victory', *Guardian*, 21 March 2000; *Moscow Times*, 29 March 2000; *St Petersburg Times*, 27 March 2000; Ian Traynor, 'KGB veteran says Putin's rule is return to Soviet era', *Guardian*, 24 March 2000; John Sweeny, 'Revealed: Russia's worst war crime in Chechnya,' *Observer*, 5 March 2000; Ian Traynor, 'Historic milestone for Russia as Putin sworn in', *Guardian*, 8 May 2000; Andrew Jack, 'Putin sworn in as Russian President', *Financial Times*, 8 May 2000; Roy Medvedev, 'Vladimir Putin: Acting President', Moscow 2002 (in Russian); Alexander Rahr, 'Vladimir Putin: A German in the Kremlin', Munich 2000 (in Russian); Robert Service, *Russia: Experiment with a People*, London, 2002; en.putin.ru; president.kremlin.ru; www.putin2000.ru; www.fsb.ru.

6 The *Kursk* Goes Down

Peter Truscott, *Kursk: Russia's Lost Pride*, London, 2003 (paperback edition)

7 The Home Front

Archie Brown and Lilia Shevtsova (eds), *Gorbachev, Yeltsin and Putin: Political leadership in Russia's transition*, Washington DC, 2001; *Izvestiya*, 5 June 2000; Matthew Hyde, 'Putin's federal reforms and their implications for presidential power in Russia', Essex papers in politics and government, No. 154, Department of Government, University of Essex, December 2000; Arkady Ostrovsky, 'Putin oversees big rise in influence of security apparatus', *Financial Times*, 1–2 November 2003; CSIS Task Force Report: Russian organized crime and corruption; private info; Nick Paton Walsh, 'City scandal: St Petersburg renovation money disappears', *Guardian*, 25 February 2003; author's meeting with Valentina Matvienko; Vladimir Kovalyev, 'Another Vice Governor faces probe', *St Petersburg Times*, 30 November 2001; RFE/RL Russian Political Weekly, 'Igor Sergeevich Ivanov: A portrait of a survivor', 1 October 2001, 1(23); Shevtsova, 'Putin's Russia', *Obshchaya gazeta*, 25–31 May 2000; Valeria Korchagina, 'Cabinet assessment set to yield major overhaul', *St Petersburg Times*, 18 March 2003; Martin Nicholson, op. cit.; BBC monitoring, TVS, Moscow, 16 May 2003; Amelia Gentleman, 'Putin shakes up his "inherited" cabinet', *Guardian*, 29 March 2001; BBC news, Europe; Martin Nicholson, 'Putin's Russia: slowing the pendulum without stopping the clock', *International Affairs* 77(3), 2001, 867–884; BBC news; Andrew Jack, 'A smooth talking hardman', *Financial Times*, 1–2 November 2003; Michael Binyon, Caroline McGregor and Simon Saradzhyan, 'Marshal law in the wild east', *Times*, 1 November 2003; Paul Klebanov, 'Godfather of the Kremlin', New York, 2000; Russia First; FT.com; Simon Piriani, 'Putin's new war: Yeltsin's fire sale of Russian assets created a breed of power-hungry billionaires – but now state bureaucrats are challenging their supremacy', *Guardian*, 8 August 2003; David Hoffman, *The Oligarchs*; Robert Service, *Russia: Experiment with a People*, London, 2002; Marshall I. Goldman, *The Piratization of Russia: Russian reform goes awry*, London, 2003; CSIS Task Force report, op. cit.; Simon Bell, 'Siberia's hell factories fuel energy empire', *Sunday Times*, 5 October 2003; Robert Winnet, 'Chelsea boss eyes Bernie's £85 million home', *Sunday Times*, 23 November 2003; Jonathan Thatcher, 'An entrepreneur who prefers to start from scratch', *St Petersburg Times*, 8 July 2003; Amanda Hall, 'Russian learns language of the West', *Sunday Times*, 29 September 2002; Arkady Ostrovsky, 'The oligarch who wants to be accepted', *Financial Times*, 21 July 2000; Vladimir Potanin, 'Why I became a Russian oligarch', *Financial Times*, 29 June 2000; Paul Klebnikov, 'Godfather of the Kremlin'; BBC news; Andrew Jack, 'Russian liberal party warns raid may harm poll chances', *Financial Times*, 25–26 October,2003; Marshall Goldman, 'Russia will pay for the fortunes of its oligarchs', *Financial Times*, 26 July 2003; Andrew Jack and Arkady Ostrovsky, 'Khodorkovsky arrest halts talks with Yukos', *Financial Times*, 27 October 2003; Mark Franchetti, 'Kremlin hardliners lock up Russia's richest man', *Sunday Times*, 26 October 2003; Nick

Paton Walsh, 'Russian oil baron jailed on tax charge' and 'Turning point shows his authoritarian hand', *Guardian*, 27 October 2003; Nick Paton Walsh, 'Russian billionaire seized in dawn raid', *Observer*, 26 October 2003; BBC news; Simon Saradzhyan and Valeria Korchagina, 'Khodorkovsky caught by shifting politics', *St Petersburg Times*, 8 July 2003; Arkady Ostrovsky and Stefan Wagsyl, 'If they can break Yukos, they can break anyone', *Financial Times*, 30 July 2003; Chrystia Freeland, 'A falling star: the Khodorkovsky interview', *Financial Times* magazine, 1 November 2003; Arkady Ostrovsky, 'Kremlin says Yukos investigation harming economy', *Financial Times*, 30 July 2003; Arkady Ostrovsky and Tom Warner, 'Lebedev to remain in custody', *Financial Times*, 23 July 2003; Arkady Ostrovsky and Carola Hoyos, 'Investor concerns remain despite rebound inequity and bond markets', *Financial Times*, 28 October 2003; Arkady Ostrovsky and Andrew Jack, 'Affair signals assertion of power by former KGB elite', *Financial Times*, 28 October; Andrew Jack, 'The would-be Rockefeller of Russian business', *Financial Times*, 28 October 2003; Arkady Ostrovsky, 'Putin turns on the charm to ease bankers' worries', *Financial Times*, 31 October 2003; Andrew Jack and Arkady Ostrovsky, 'Putin warms to tough stance', *Financial Times*, 1–2 November 2003; Mark Franchetti, 'Kremlin's shadow falls over Britain as tycoon cull goes on', *Sunday Times*, 2 November 2003; Insight, 'Chelsea boss made millions from tax breaks', *Sunday Times*, 14 September 2003; John Lloyd, 'A miracle worker', *Financial Times*, 6–7 January 2001; Arkady Ostrovsky, 'Oligarchs seek peace deal with Putin', *Financial Times*, 24 July 2000; BBC news; Andrew Jack, 'Moscow to put squeeze on oil company taxes', *Financial Times*, 30 September 2003; William Tompson, op. cit.; BBC World Service; BBC Monitoring Service, 'Two Moscow police officers charged in crackdown on corruption', 2 July 2003; BBC Monitoring Service; 'Russian police corruption mere electoral window dressing', *Observer*, 3 July 2003; Ekho Moskvy radio, Moscow, 3 July 2003; BBC Monitoring Service, 'Cautious optimism advised as cracks appear in Russia's monolithic elite', 2 July 2003; *Vremya MN*, Moscow, 27 June 2003; Yulia Latynina, 'Putting the cuffs on PR and the electoral image', *St Petersburg Times*, 8 July 2003; BBC news and business; Daniel Treisman, 'Russia Renewed?', *Foreign Affairs*, November/December 2002; OECD Economic Surveys, 2001–2002, Russian Federation, Vol 2002/5 February, Paris, 2002; FT.com; BBC Monitoring Service; Valeria Korchagina, 'Growth surpasses expectations', *St Petersburg Times*, 22 April 2003; Andrew Jack, 'A new dawn brightens Moscow's skyline', *Financial Times*, 9 October 2003; Alex Nicholson, 'Tax Police will not be sorely missed', *St Petersburg Times*, 14 March 2003; CSIS Task Force report; Daniel Treisman, 'Russia Renewed?', *Foreign Affairs*, Vol 81 No 6, November/December 2002; OECD Economic Surveys, op. cit.; Martin Nicholson, op. cit.; Lyuba Pronina, 'Customs code passed by Duma', *St Petersburg Times*, 22 April 2003; BBC Business news; Lyuba Pronina, 'New customs code aiming to open world's longest frontier', *St Petersburg Times*, 1 April 2003; William Tompson, 'Putin's challenge: The politics of structural reform in Russia', *Europe-Asia Studies*, 54(6), 2002, 935–957; BBC news; *Nezavisimaya gazeta*, 26 December 2000; Andrew Jack, 'Putin under pressure as economy slows', *Financial Times*, 17 April 2002; Robert Cottrell and Andrew Jack, 'Putin warns on prospects for growth', *Financial Times*, 19 April 2002; Andrew Jack, 'Kremlin insider takes helm at Gazprom', *Financial Times*, 31 May 2001; Andrew Jack, 'Gazprom auditors to probe links with Itera', *Financial Times*, 15 March 2001; Andrew Jack, 'Link between Gazprom and Itera found', *Financial Times*, 14 March 2001; Amelia Gentleman, 'Putin puts old crony in to shake up huge gas firm racked by scandal', *Guardian*, 31 May 2001; Robert Cottrell, 'Putin forces out Central Bank head,' *Financial Times*, 16–17 March 2002; Alena Lederman, 'Unwritten rules: How Russia really works', CER pamphlet, 2001; *Russia First*; Robert Cottrell, 'Russia reforms defence as arms exports rise', *Financial Times*, 23 January 2001; Ian Traynor, 'Plug pulled on Russia's debtor army', *Guardian*, 15 September 2000; *Kursk*, BBC news; Nick Paton Walsh, 'Military drill for Russian pupils', *Guardian*, 14 October 2003; Andrei Zolotov, 'President Reshuffles Security Agencies', *St Petersburg Times*, 14 March 2003; Nikolai Petrov, 'Putin's refoms, round 3: Security Agencies', *St Petersburg Times*; 14 March 2003; Andrew Jack and Charles Glover, 'Putin changes course on Chechnya', *Financial Times*, 23 January 2001; Arkady Ostrovsky, 'Putin oversees big rise in influence of security apparatus', *Financial Times*, 1–2 November 2003; Russian Mirror, Yury Filippov, RIA Novosti political analyst, 'As Vladimir Putin turns 50 polls show support amongst Russians reaches 77%', No. 23, October 2002; Nationwide VCIOM surveys, 1999–2000; RussianObserver.com; Andrei Yegorov, 'President Putin retains high level of trust amongst Russians', 29 March 2002; *St Petersburg Times*, Steve Gutterman, Associated Press, 'Putin again centre of attention', 8 October 2002; Andrew Jack, 'The Empire strikes back: Putin cult reaches new levels', *Financial Times*, 12–13 October 2002; 'Behind the scenes of Putin's telephone chat', RFE/RL Russian Political Weekly, www.rferl.org/rpw/2001/12/33-311201.html; Mark Franchetti, 'Big ballerina dances to aid of Putin party', *Sunday Times*, 19 October 2003; Lilia Shevtsova, 'Putin's Russia'; Nabi Abdullaev, 'Party of Life coming out of the shadows', *St Petersburg Times*, 8 April 2003; *Russia*

First; Stephen Fiddler, 'Western aid to Russia "lacking overall strategy"', *Financial Times*, 3 November 2000; Augusto Lopez-Claros and Mikhail M. Zadornov, 'Economic Reforms: Steady as she goes', Centre for Strategic and International Studies, Massachusetts Institute of Technology, *The Washington Quarterly*, Winter 2002; Igor Semenenko, 'Leading banks make top 1,000', *St Petersburg Times*, 8 July 2003; Arkady Ostrovsky, 'Russia's banking system remains its weakest link', *Financial Times*, 20 August 2003; John Thornhill, 'Banking in a climate of mistrust', *Financial Times*, 9 October 2003; BBC news; Victoria Lavrentieva, 'S&P Report: Lending by banks in Russia too risky', *St Petersburg Times*, 3 June 2003; Angelina Davydora, 'City's bankers on reform pace', *St Petersburg Times*, 3 June 2003; Fiona Hill, 'A land too cold for a free market in energy', *Financial Times*, 17 October 2003; Andrew Jack and Arkady Ostrovsky, 'Russia rules out WTO membership this year', *Financial Times*, 21 May 2003; Andrew Jack and Tobias Buck, 'Russia toughens stance on energy prices', *Financial Times*, 17 October 2003; Andrew Jack, 'Russia says it is keen to join world trade body', *Financial Times*, 31 March–1 April 2001; *Kursk*; British Embassy in the Russian Federation Press Release, 'UK completes first chemical weapon destruction project in Russia', 28 March 2003; Larry Elliot, 'West gives Russia $20 billion to make nuclear sites safe', *Guardian*, 28 June 2002; Andrew Jack, 'Russian nuclear rubbish tip challenges clean-up experts', *Financial Times*, 19 November 2002; Nick Paton Walsh, 'Kremlin threatens to stop Shell drilling', *Guardian*, 22 October 2003; Andrew Jack, 'Russia admits missing uranium', *Financial Times*, 16–17 November 2002; Peter Koenig, 'BP: from hate to love in Russia', *Sunday Times*, 5 October 2003; Arkady Ostrovsky, 'Russian oligarchs dig up the dirt to present a clean image to the West', *Financial Times*, 24 October 2003; BBC news; Alena Lebeneva, 'Unwritten rules: How Russia really works', Centre for European Reform, May 2001; William Tompson, op. cit.; Andrew Jack, 'Moscow supports US investment in Yukos', *Financial Times*, 8 October 2003; Andrew Jack, 'Yukos to list if sell-off falls through', *Financial Times*, 13 October 2003; Peter Baker, 'Russian oil companies complete merger', Washingtonpost.com, 4 October 2003; BBC Monitoring Service, Ekho Moskvy radio, 24 September 2003; 'Russian oligarchs wheeling and dealing: Most businesses are for sale at the right price right now', *Financial Post*, Canada, 6 October 2003; Stefan Wagstyl, 'Rusal chief wins aluminium war', *Financial Times*, 3 October 2003; Arkady Ostrovsky and Andrew Jack, 'Russia enjoys record level of inward investment', *Financial Times*, 22 June 2003; Charles Clover, 'Gazprom borrows E250m for Blue Stream pipeline', *Financial Times*, 1 March 2001; Nick Paton Walsh, 'Kremlin threatens to stop Shell drilling', *Guardian*, 22 October 2003; Oliver Morgan, 'Black cloud over BP oil deal', *Observer*, 19 October 2003; Conal Walsh, 'Russia's risky revolution', *Observer*, 26 October 2003; BBC news; Andrew Jack, 'Moscow calls for pipeline partners', *Financial Times*, 11–12 October 2003; Reuters, '£8.6 bln left Russia during Q3', *Moscow Times*, 10 November 2003; Nick Paton Walsh, 'Governor shot dead in Moscow rush hour', *Guardian*, 19 October 2002; Ian Traynor, 'For Siberia, a return to waste-land', *Guardian*, 12 June 2002; Ian Traynor, 'Russia dying of drink and despair', *Guardian*, 30 June 2000; 'Vodka and smoking lay Russians low', Reuters, *Guardian*, 25 October 2000; Ian Traynor, 'Plea for vote on nuclear dumping', *Guardian*, 25 October 2000; Arkady Ostrovsky, 'Russian professionals find hard times all too close to home', *Financial Times*, 21 August 2003; Nick Paton Walsh, 'Low-birth Russia curbs abortions', *Guardian*, 24 September 2003; Yevgenia Borisov, 'Prosecutor interested in Kasyanov', *St Petersburg Times*, 8 April 2003; Nick Paton Walsh, 'Russian AIDS plague to hit Europe', *Observer*, 2 June 2002; *Kursk*; *Russia First*; Amelia Gentleman, 'It's minus 60, there's no heating and no electricity. Welcome to Vladivostok', *Guardian*, 16 February 2001; Nick Paton Walsh, 'Russia's child alcoholics get their own clinic', *Observer*, 26 October 2003; Alex Nicholson, 'Piracy peddlers feel the pinch', *St Petersburg Times*, 22 July 2003; NTV; Martin Woolf, 'Putin's clampdown could put prosperity at risk', *Financial Times*, 5 November 2003; *Kommersant*, 27 October 2000; BBC news; 'EU media warning', *St Petersburg Times*, 8 July 2003; Andrew Jack, 'Critics fear muzzle on Russian media as poll law starts to bite', *Financial Times*, 8 October 2003; Andrew Jack, 'Kremlin candidates set to win regional polls', *Financial Times*, 6 October 2003; 'Putin rules out possible third term', RFE/RL Newsline, www.rferl.org/newsline/2003/06/1-Rus/rus-060603.asp; Sergei Mikhailovich Mironov: 'A friend in deed', RFE/RL Newsline, www.rferl.org/rpw/2001/12/32-181201.html; www.rian.ru

8 Putin in the World

Vladimir Putin, *First Person*; Strobe Talbot, *The Russia Hand: A Memoir of Presidential Diplomacy*, New York, 2002; 'Russia First'; Bobo Lo, 'Vladimir Putin and the evolution of Russian Foreign Policy', Royal Institute of International Affairs, London, 2003; Andrew Jack, 'Envoy's mission signals foreign policy shift', *Financial Times*, 27 February 2003; Ewen MacAskill and Graham Diggines, 'Russian evades human rights issue', *Guardian*, 18 April 2000; Andrew Parker, David Buchan, Andrew Jack, 'Putin announces investigation into Chechnya "abuse"', *Financial Times*, 18 April 2000; Ewen MacAskill, 'Defiant Putin flies in', *Guardian*, 17 April 2000; Ian Traynor and

Ewen MacAskill, 'Putin visit to London claimed as No 10 coup', *Guardian* 11 April 2000; Brian Groom, 'Putin set to meet with Blair in London', *Financial Times*, 11 April 2000; Andrew Jack, 'Envoy's mission signals foreign policy shift', *Financial Times*, 27 February 2003; Quentin Peel, 'Russia's invitation to reform', *Financial Times*, 17 April 2000; Richard Beeston and Alice Lagnado, 'Opposition grows to Putin audience with the Queen', *The Times*, 12 April 2000; Richard Beeston, 'Wife's debut on the world stage', *The Times*, 12 April 2000; Peter Truscott, 'In bed with Putin', *Guardian*, 11 April 2000; Menzies Campbell, 'Stay at home, Mr Putin', *Guardian*, 12 April 2000; Hugo Young, 'A welcome for Putin, the butcher of Chechnya', *Guardian*, 18 April 2000; *Guardian* editorial, 'To London without love: Blair should get tougher with Putin', 17 April 2000; Amelia Gentleman, 'Putin to visit "poodle" at No 10', *Observer*, 16 April 2000; Andrew Jack and David Buchan, 'Blair under fire as Putin arrives in the UK', *Financial Times*, 17 April 2000; BBC news; Ian Black, 'Russia walks out on its European critics', *Guardian*, 7 April 2000; International staff, 'Council of Europe threat to Russia', *Financial Times*, 7 April 2000; private info; Ian Traynor, 'Odd couple laugh at doubters', *Guardian*, 22 November 2000; BBC news; Andrew Parker, 'Blair seeks to assist US–Russia dialogue', *Financial Times*, 21 November 2000; author's meeting with Ambassador Grigory Karasin; www.russiatoday.com; CNN.com; John Thornhill and Stephen Fidler, 'Russia gets real', *Financial Times*, 3–4 June 2000; Stephen Fidler, 'US missile defence programme "may renew arms race"', *Financial Times*, 2 June 2000; Jonathan Steele, 'Empty Encounters', *Guardian*, 2 June 2000; Tony Paterson, Ian Black and Ian Traynor, 'Clinton faces European flak for "son of star wars"', *Guardian*, 3 June 2000; Amelia Gentleman, 'Putin and Clinton jazz it up at Kremlin', *Observer*, 4 June 2000; Stephen Fidler, 'US, Russia in accord on disposal of plutonium', *Financial Times*, 5 June 2000; Leader, 'No new arms race', *Observer*, 4 June 2000; Ian Traynor, 'Clinton lauds peace milestone', *Guardian*, 5 June 2000; Leader, 'Papering cracks in Moscow', *Financial Times*, 5 June 2000; Peter Preston, 'Americans really do want this dotty missile shield', *Guardian*, 5 June 2000; Ian Traynor, 'US and Russia clash over missile shield', *Guardian*, 5 June 2000; Stephen Fidler and John Thornhill, 'US offers Moscow nuclear arms deal', *Financial Times*, 5 June 2000; Ed Vulliamy, 'Star Wars falls to earth', *Observer*, 9 July 2000; www.russianobservercom; www.strana.ru.; Stephen Fidler and Brian Groom, 'Summit gives leaders an insight into Putin', *Financial Times*, 24 July 2000; Parisa Hafesi, 'Iran's new missile within range of Israel', *St Petersburg Times*, 8 July 2003; Ian Traynor, 'Bush embraces new ally', *Observer*, 17 June 2001; Matthew Campbell, 'Bush finds a friend in Putin after Euro rows', *Sunday Times*, 17 June 2001; 'Mr Putin's Soul', www.washingtonpost.com, 19 June 2001; Ian Traynor, 'Leaders melt in mutual charm war', *Guardian*, 18 June 2001; news.bbc.co.uk; cnn.com; John Kampfner, *Blair's Wars*, London, 2003; Christopher Andrew and Vasily Mitrokhin, 'The Mitrokhin archive', London, 1999; CSIS Task Force report, 'Russian organized crime and corruption'; Stephen Fidler, 'Bush backs expansion of NATO in eastern Europe', *Financial Times*, 16–17 June 2001; Robert Cottrell, 'Putin looks for working relationship with Bush White House', *Financial Times*, 16–17 June 2001; Frances Williams, 'Russia seeks missile shield dialogue', *Financial Times*, 2 February 2001; Richard McGregor, 'Shanghai Forum unites against US missile plan', *Financial Times*, 16–17 June 2001; Bobo Lo, 'Vladimir Putin and the evolution of Russian foreign policy', London, 2003; Stephen Fidler, 'Pragmatic Putin sees advantages of US engagement', *Financial Times*, 18 June 2001; russianobserver.com; dailynews.yahoo.com; Reuters; Associated Press; Steve Kraske, 'US deploys forces to Persian Gulf, Indian Ocean, Central Asia', *Kansas City Star*, 19 September 2001; Patrick E. Tyler and Eliane Sciolino, 'Bush advisers split on scope of retaliation', *The New York Times*, 19 September 2001; Judy Dempsey, 'Canny Putin secures shopping list from obliging EU and NATO', *Financial Times*, 4 October 2001; Ian Black, 'Russia hints at rethink on NATO', *Guardian*, 4 October 2001; Andrew Jack, 'Poker-faced Putin raises the stakes at Texas table', *Financial Times*, 12 November 2001; Stephen Fidler and Andrew Jack, 'High hopes', *Financial Times*, 13 November 2001; Stephen Fidler, 'Bush to slash US nuclear arsenal', *Financial Times*, 14 November 2001; Matthew Engel and Ewen MacAskill, 'Bush plans big nuclear warheads cut', *Guardian*, 14 November 2001; Matthew Engel, 'Bush tells Putin he will slash warheads', *Guardian*, 14 November 2001; Stephen Fidler, 'Missile pact eludes Bush and Putin', *Financial Times*, 15 November 2001; Joan Smith, 'Russia needs a regime change', *Tribune*, 1 November 2002; Anton La Guardia, 'MI6 and Russians join forces to fight al-Qa'eda', *Daily Telegraph*, 21 December 2001; Brian Groom, 'Blair and Putin to step up moves against terror', *Financial Times*, 21 December 2001; Gerard Baker and Robert Cottrell, 'Treaty marks "new era" for old foes', *Financial Times*, 25–26 May 2002; Nick Paton Walsh, 'Bush grins again after summit hiccup', *Observer*, 26 May 2002; Ian Black, 'Russia hints at rethink at NATO', *Guardian*, 4 October 2001; Alexander Nicoll, 'Blair seeks closer NATO ties with Kremlin', *Financial Times*, 17–18 November 2001; Michael White, 'PM recalls Moscow bombings as he agrees to pool terrorism data with ally Putin', *Guardian*, 22 December 2001; Rosemary Bennett and David Buchan, 'Blair pledge on greater

Russian role with NATO', *Financial Times*, 22–23 December 2001; Simon Tisdall, 'Bush cabinet at odds over NATO pact with Russia', *Guardian*, 10 December 2001; Ian Traynor, 'Russia and NATO reach historic deal', *Guardian*, 15 May 2002; Stephen Fidler, 'Bush gives up some ground on weapons agreement', *Financial Times*, 14 May 2002; Andrew Jack, 'Putin: a pragmatic push for closer ties with the US', *Financial Times*, 20 February 2002; Rory McCarthy, 'Déjà vu in Kabul as Russian forces return', 28 November 2001; Ian Traynor and Julian Borger, 'Bush wins the final battle for Star Wars', *Guardian*, 16 May 2002; Richard Norton-Taylor, 'Bush-Putin missile deal raises questions for Britain', *Guardian*, 16 May 2002; Jonathan Steele, 'New era as alliance arrives on Soviet turf', *Guardian*, 22 November 2002; Richard Wolffe, 'Prospect of new Russian ties dominates Bush trip', *Financial Times*, 22 May 2002; Richard Wolffe and Andrew Jack, 'Russia and US agree to cut nuclear warheads', *Financial Times*, 14 May 2002; Nick Paton Walsh, 'Moscow extends the life of 144 cold war ballistic missiles', *Guardian*, 20 August 2002; 'Russia First'; Oliver Burkeman, 'Bush tells foes to beware nuclear response', *Guardian*, 14 March 2002; www.1n.mid.ru.; Quentin Peel, 'Putin plays a weak hand well', *Financial Times*, 18 March 2002; Mark Huband and David Stern, 'Ricin poison trail "traced to camps in Georgia"', *Financial Times*, 17 January 2003; Richard Norton-Taylor, Nick Hopkins and Jon Henley, 'Toxin suspect trained at al-Qaida camp', *Guardian*, 10 January 2001; Ian Traynor, 'Get circumcised, angry Putin tells reporter', *Guardian*, 13 November 2002; FT.com; www.observer.co.uk; strana.ru; www.guardian.co.uk; ITAR-TASS; Interfax news agency; washingtonpost.com; Johnson's Russia List, www.cdi.org; www.timesonline.co.uk; Ministry of Foreign Affairs of the Russian Federation, www.1n.mid.ru; Ian Traynor, 'Russia offers arms to Iran', *Guardian*, 28 November 2000; Gillian Tett, 'Putin turns blind eye to island dispute with Japan', *Financial Times*, 4 September 2000; Andrew Jack and John Thornhill, 'Russia's Afghan agenda prompts coalition concern', *Financial Times*, 30 November 2001; David Ibison and Andrew Jack, 'Little progress by Putin and Mori on resolving Kurile Islands dispute', *Financial Times*, 26 March 2001; Charles Glover, Guy Dinmore and Stephen Fidler, 'Russia, Iran in $300 million arms sale plan', *Financial Times*, 13 March 2001; Ian Traynor, 'Will it be third time lucky for canny Putin?', *Guardian*, 15 May 2002; Edna Fernandes, 'India and Russia to join forces on terrorism', *Financial Times*, 5 December 2002; James Blitz and Carola Hoyos, 'Putin softens line over Iraq', *Financial Times*, 12–13 October 2002; *Financial Times*, 5 December 2002; Robert Cottrell and Charles Clover 'Putin, Jiang sign treaty on co-operation', *Financial Times*, 17 July 2001; Andrew Jack,

'Envoy's mission signals foreign policy shift', *Financial Times*, 27 February 2003; Leader, 'Vodka and smiles: But how useful was Blair's Russian visit?', *Guardian*, 12 October 2002; 'Ivanov: Russia will use UN veto', *St Petersburg Times*, 11 March 2003; 'Russia "sells" vote for Iraqi oil', *St Petersburg Times*, 27 May 2003; Michael White, 'Putin demands proof over Iraqi weapons', *Guardian*, 12 October 2002; Simon Saradzhyan, 'Ukrainians deny US arms-deal allegations', *St Petersburg Times*, 1 April 2003; Nick Paton Walsh, 'Kremlin asks: where's your proof on Iraq?', *Guardian*, 11 October 2002; Michael White and Nick Paton Walsh, 'Support us on Iraq, Putin urged', *Guardian*, 11 October 2002; Andrei Zolotov Jr, 'Rice visit aims at mending fences', *St Petersburg Times*, 8 April 2003; private info; Jeanne Whalen, 'US and Russia start to mend relationship strained by Iraq', *Wall Street Journal*, 8 April 2003; Thom Shanker and Eric Schmitt, 'Pentagon plans expanded military presence', *St Petersburg Times*, 22 April 2003; Patrick Wintour, 'The message from Moscow: We are not with you and we don't believe you', *Guardian*, 30 April 2003; Patrick Hennessy, 'Mocked and snubbed: Blair more isolated than ever over war', *London Evening Standard*, 30 April 2003; Paul Eastham, 'From Russia with scorn', *Daily Mail*, 30 April 2003; James Kynge and Andrew Jack, 'China, Russia seek to halt North Korea nuclear drive', *Financial Times*, 3 December 2002; RFE/RL Newsline, www.rferl.org; Council of the European Union, Council Report to the European Council on Implementation of the Common Strategy of the European Union on Russia, Brussels, 14 June 2000; Richard Balmforth and Mike Peacock, Reuters, 'Leaders put split in past', 27 June 2003; Alex Kwaitkowski, 'Putin's English skills pass toughest test of all', Associated Press, 27 June 2003; RTR Russia TV; *Komsomolskaya Pravda*; *Gazeta*; *Izvestiya*, *Novaya Gazeta*; *Rossiyskaya Gazeta*; *Le Temps*; *Moskovsky Komsomolets*; Claire Bigg, 'EU announces pans for city anniversary', *St Petersburg Times*, 14 March 2003; RIA-Novosti FOM poll on Russia and Britain, 24–25 May 2003; Ian Traynor, Edward Pilkington, 'Russians begin long trek to EU', *Guardian*, 26 May 2001; Simon Saradzhyan and Natalia Yefimova, 'Putin shows off hometown to world', *St Petersburg Times*, 2 June 2003; Ian Traynor, 'EU and Russia clash over Baltic enclave', 30 May 2002; www.therussianissues.com; www.300spb.ru; www.europa.ru.int; www.defense.gov; www.fco.gov.uk; www.mod.gov.uk; www.moscow.usembassy.gov; www.number-10.gov.uk; www.rian.ru; www.rusemblon.org; www.whitehouse.gov; www.state.gov

9 The Moscow Theatre Siege

There was extensive media coverage of the siege, especially between 24 October to 24 November 2003. See for example: *Guardian*, *Daily Telegraph*,

The Times, Financial Times, Independent, Sunday Times, Sunday Telegraph, Observer. See also NTV, *St Petersburg Times*, *Moscow Times*, Reuters, news.bbc.co.uk, CCN.com, FT.com, www.guardian.co.uk, www.timesonline.co.uk, www.sptimesrussia.com, www.moscowtimescom, ITAR-TASS (ITAR-TASS.com), www.russianobserver.com; www.russiatoday.com, dailynews.yahoo.com, www.interfax.news.com, www.gazeta.ru; private information

Epilogue

Catherine Belton and Lyuba Pronina, 'New Duma loyal to President, lacks Liberals', *St Petersburg Times*, 9 December 2003; www.sptimesrussia.com; Jonathan Steele, 'Russia's election was a disaster for democracy. Things can only get better', *Guardian*, 10 December 2003; Tom Gill, 'Putin party gives communists a thrashing', *Tribune*, 12 December 2003; Nick Paton Walsh, 'Observers condemn Russian elections', *Guardian*, 9 December 2003; Andrew Jack and Arkady Ostrovsky, 'Putin holds political cards after opponents trounced', *Financial Times*, 9 December 2003; OSCE, 'Russian Federation State Duma Elections, 7 December 2003: Statement of Preliminary Findings and Conclusions'; www.osce.org; www.news.bbc.org; itar-tass.com; FT.com; Nick Paton Walsh, 'Putin's press law overruled', *Guardian*, 31 October 2003; Andrew Jack and Arkady Ostrovsky, 'Putin set to win parliamentary majority in Russian elections', *Financial Times*, 8 December 2003; Nick Paton Walsh and Jonathan Steele, 'Russian election leaves little to the voters', *Guardian*, 8 December 2003; Nick Paton Walsh, 'Communists crushed in Putin's iron grip', *Guardian*, 9 December 2003; Arkady Ostrovsky and Andrew Jack, 'Duma polls more dirty tricks than politics', *Financial Times*, 6–7 December 2003; CNN.com; Nick Paton Walsh, 'Putin heading for decisive victory in Russian poll', *Guardian*, 8 December 2003; Arkady Ostrovsky, 'Raid adds to pressure on Yukos as deal unravels', *Financial Times*, 11 December 2003; Arkady Ostrovsky, Andrew Jack and Carola Hoyos, 'Russia's biggest merger collapses', *Financial Times*, 10 December 2003; Chrystia Freeland, Carola Hoyos and Arkady Ostrovsky, 'Yukos "in no hurry" to relinquish Sibneft', *Financial Times*, 12 December 2003; personal first-hand observations on the 1995, 1999 and 2003 Duma elections (plus the 1996 presidential election); www.timesonline.co.uk; OSCE Election Observation Mission report on the 2004 Russian presidential election, Interim Report 6–16 February 2004; OSCE International Observation Mission, Election of the President of the Russian Federation, 14 March 2004, Statement of Preliminary Findings and Conclusions, 15 March 2004; Andrew Jack, 'Voters' backing for Kremlin spurs Putin to begin campaigning', *Financial Times*, 19 December 2003; Arkady

Ostrovsky, 'Putin warns oligarchs of hard line', *Financial Times*, 24 December 2003; Arkady Ostrovsky, 'Anti-Putin parties fail to nominate candidate', *Financial Times*, 22 December 2003; Arkady Ostovsky, 'Overarching Putin puts everyone in election shade', *Financial Times*, 2 January 2004; Nick Paton Walsh, 'Putin angry at history book slur', *Guardian*, 14 January 2004; Jonathan Steele and Nick Paton Walsh, 'Putin opponent crises foul over media onslaught' *Guardian*, 20 February 2004; Stephen Kotkin 'What is to be done?', *FT Magazine*, 6 March 2004; Nick Paton Walsh, 'A triumph of hope over experience: why Russia's poor still believe in the Putin fairytale', *Guardian*, 8 March 2004; Stefan Wagstyl, 'Russia's provincial bosses learn how to suffer in silence' *Financial Times*, 10 March 2004; Arkady Ostrovsky, 'Yeltsin generation prepares to meet its doom', *Financial Times*, 12 March 2004; Carola Hoyos and James Politi, 'Abramovich in talks over Sibneft stake', *Financial Times*, 12 March 2004; Jeremy Page, 'Creature comforts aid Putin's image', *The Times*, 13 March 2004; Nick Paton Walsh, 'Bloodless victory to Georgia's president', *Guardian*, 29 March 2004; Nick Paton Walsh, 'Putin's reshuffle gets tough', *Guardian*, 10 March 2004; Nick Paton Walsh, 'Cheap groceries used to lure weary Russians to polls', *Guardian*, 11 March 2004; Andrew Jack, 'Russian premier outlines reforms', *Financial Times*, 3 March 2004; Nick Paton Walsh, 'Putin accused over cost of election campaign', *Guardian*, 13 March 2004; Michael Sheridan, 'Giants of the East vie for Russia's oil', *Sunday Times*, 14 March 2004; Arkady Ostrovsky, 'Oil exploration licences issued as Russian minister leaves office come under scrutiny', *Financial Times*, 13–14 March 2004; Nick Paton Walsh, 'Putin beats apathy to win another term', *Guardian*, 15 March 2004; Mikhail Khodorkovsky, 'The crisis of liberalism: What is to be done?', *St Petersburg Times*, 6 April 2004; Valeria Korchagina, 'Kudrin insistent on tax, mulls amnesty', *St Petersburg Times*, 20 April 2004, Irina Titova, 'President Putin wins admiration from women', *St Petersburg Times*, 30 April 2004; Nick Paton Walsh, 'How strongman of Grozny turned into a rebel target', *Guardian*, 10 May 2004; Jonathan Steele and Nick Paton Walsh, 'Putin faces long battle to tame Chechnya', *Guardian*, 10 May 2004; Vladimir Kovalev, 'Former LDPR Deputy Said behind Starovoitova slaying', *St Petersburg Times*, 9 July 2004; Caroline McGregor, 'Friday's "Svoboda Slova" expected to be last', *St Petersburg Times*, 9 July 2004; Oksana Yablokova, 'Survey: Putin's popularity drops below 50 per cent', *St Petersburg Times*, 13 July 2004; Carola Hoyos, 'Moscow clouds oil scene', *Financial Times*, 23 July 2004; 'Seven candidates on ballot for Chechnya's elections', *St Petersburg Times*, 27 July 2004; Reuters, 'Conoco aims to become a "major" Russian player', *St Petersburg Times*, 3 August 2004, Beslan: NTV; Channel 1 (Russia); RTR Television, CNN and BBC.

Index

POCKET
BOOKS

KURSK

The Gripping True Story of Russia's Worst Submarine Disaster

Peter Truscott

'Reads like a cross between a thriller and
a litany of cover-ups' – IRISH TIMES

Peter Truscott's account of the worst peacetime
disaster experienced by the Russian Navy not only
vividly re-creates the terrifying final hours of the 188
submariners as they waited in vain for salvation at the
bottom of the Barents Sea; it also throws sharp light on
the nature of the 'democracy' this billion-dollar vessel
was designed to protect. His masterly analysis, now
fully updated, assesses and dismisses a number of wild
claims that have been made and provides a gripping
illustration not just of human courage, but of human
failing at the highest levels of government.

'[The *Kursk*'s] story, harrowingly detailed here, stands
as a testament to the bravery and loyalty of men
to a nation that failed them' – THE TIMES

PRICE £6.99
ISBN 0-7434-4941-X

KHRUSHCHEV
The Man and his Era

William Taubman

A magisterial, definitive and compelling assessment of
one of the giants of twentieth-century history:
former Soviet leader Nikita Khrushchev.

'Outstanding, superbly gripping and surely
definitive . . . Fascinating'
– Simon Sebag Montefiore,
DAILY TELEGRAPH

'[A] monumental biography, one that is likely
to be definitive for years to come'
– Leon Aron, NEW YORK TIMES

'Masterly . . . Taubman has painted a
remarkable portrait of a politician'
– Richard Overy, SUNDAY TELEGRAPH

'A monumental book . . . A masterpiece, magnificently
researched and well written, bringing out
the true dimensions of his subject'
– Simon Heffer, SPECTATOR

PRICE £14.99
ISBN 0-7432-3166-X

BLAIR

Anthony Seldon

'The best account so far of the high politics of
the Blair era' – Nick Cohen, NEW STATESMAN

'Superbly well-informed and exhaustively
researched' – Peter Oborne, THE TABLET

Rejecting the constraints of formal biography,
Anthony Seldon has produced a profile of the
Prime Minister that rewrites the bibliography
of Blair studies. Gripping and revelatory,
it is a major book about the man
who has shaped modern Britain.

'Pulls together almost everything
we know about Blair . . . This book will become
the automatic reference point for studies of
a political period that promised so much'
– John Kampfner, OBSERVER

PRICE £20.00
ISBN 0-7432-3211-9

FREE PRESS

GENERALISSIMO
Chiang Kai-Shek and
the China He Lost

Jonathan Fenby

'A man swept up in extraordinary historical
turmoil . . . Masterly . . . A fascinating portrait'
– OBSERVER

'Highly readable . . . It is an epic tale and
Fenby tells it with panache'
– SUNDAY TIMES

Between the fall of the Manchu Empire in 1911 and
the Communist victory in 1949, Chiang Kai-Shek,
the Generalissimo of China, stood at the centre of
a uniquely turbulent period in the modern history
of the world's most populous nation. Focusing
on Chiang's life up to and including his defeat by
Mao, *Generalissimo* is an extraordinarily rich
and gripping biography that also represents a
riveting history of pre-Communist China.

'Excellent . . . History, somehow, just isn't
as colourful any more' – DAILY TELEGRAPH

PRICE £25.00
ISBN 0-7432-314-9

**SIMON &
SCHUSTER**

This book and other **Simon & Schuster** titles are available from your bookshop or can be ordered direct from the publisher.

0-7434-4941-**X**	**Kursk**	**Peter Truscott**	£6.99
0-7432-3166-**X**	**Khrushchev**	**William Taubman**	£14.99
0-7432-3211-9	**Blair**	**Anthony Seldon**	£20.00
0-7432-3144-9	**Generalissimo**	**Jonathan Fenby**	£25.00

Please send cheque or postal order for the value of the book, free postage and packing within the UK; OVERSEAS including Republic of Ireland £2 per book.

OR: Please debit this amount from my VISA/ACCESS/MASTERCARD:

CARD NO:. . . . .

EXPIRY DATE:. . . . .

AMOUNT: £. . . . .

NAME: . . . .

ADDRESS:. . . . .

. . . .

SIGNATURE: . . . .

Please send cheque or postal order for the value of the book,
free postage and packing within the UK, to
SIMON & SCHUSTER CASH SALES
PO Box 29, Douglas Isle of Man, IM99 1BQ
Tel: 01624 677237, Fax: 01624 670923
Email: bookshop@enterprise.net
www.bookpost.co.uk

Please allow 14 days for delivery. Prices and availability
subject to change without notice.